Cuba: The Economic and Social Revolution

CHAPEL HILL

THE UNIVERSITY OF NORTH CAROLINA PRESS

CUBA

THE

ECONOMIC

AND SOCIAL

REVOLUTION

By Dudley Seers
Andrés Bianchi
Richard Jolly
Max Nolff

Edited by Dudley Seers

Editor's Preface

For most people, Cuba at this time is the focus of crises, a bone of contention between the United States and the Soviet Union, a little country that seemed for a few terrible days as if it might be the cause of a thermonuclear war.

In all the speculation about its role in global politics, we tend to overlook two points about Cuba. The first is that this government of a somewhat backward, tropical country, traditionally dependent on sugar exports, is attempting to achieve a very rapid rate of social change and economic growth. Second, the former plantation economy of Cuba is now using techniques of highly centralized planning; it is in fact the only major exporter of primary products to have taken this path.

The problems of social and economic backwardness which the Cuban government is attempting to solve are common to the whole of Latin America (as indeed they are to Africa and Asia as well), though their severity varies widely both between countries and within them. These problems can be grouped under three main headings: unemployment (including underemployment), poverty (so acute that it means malnutrition if not hunger), and ignorance (of how to read a book, not to mention modern techniques). The economic causes of these evils are not hard to find. The most important are backward agriculture, inadequate and inefficient industries, and excessive dependence on exports of a few primary commodities. Economic weaknesses of this magnitude are both the effect and the cause of archaic social structures, showing very unequal distributions of property and income; of educational systems that leave some children completely untaught and offer the great majority little hope of reaching secondary or technical schools; of administrations that are inefficient and in varying degrees corrupt; and of political institutions that give the bulk of the population no effective influence on the formation of public policy.

There is now a widespread realization of the severity of these problems, and the Alliance for Progress represents one approach to their solution; the program of the Cuban government is another. This government is engaged in an ambitious attempt to eliminate within a few years unemployment, poverty, and illiteracy. Whatever one's political views, the experience of Cuba in this attempt can hardly be ignored. It provides particularly interesting material for professional economists and students of socialist regimes. There are useful lessons to be drawn from this experience, from mistakes made and setbacks encountered, as well as from successes achieved.

How big a transformation of the Cuban economic structure is being attempted? What problems arise in this effort? How successfully are they being solved? These questions are of fundamental importance. Already the social and institutional changes that have occurred are big enough to cause lasting repercussions and to influence the course of Latin America in ways as yet unpredictable. This is a preliminary attempt to describe and appraise its results.

The story of how this book came to be written starts with a passing visit I made to Havana in February, 1962. After a few days I began to realize how very interesting the Cuban attempt to accelerate development was. At that time I was given every facility and was shown many of the available statistics and preliminary drafts of plans. This material was made available to me through the help of Regino Boti, the Minister of Economics and head of the planning office secretariat, who had worked in ECLA (the United Nations Economic Commission for Latin America) when I was there, and Juan Noyola, a senior official in the planning office and another former ECLA staff member.[1] I suggested that a more extended return visit might prove practicable and that it would be worthwhile in view of the almost total ignorance about Cuba in the outside world. Noyola agreed, and he told me that Boti did too.

When I returned to Yale, where I was working in 1962, I began to search for some source of finance that would make it possible to do a more complete job on the economic changes in Cuba and on its future prospects than I could do myself in the time available. The financial and administrative aspects of this project were not free of problems, but eventually I was promised a grant from the Cabot Foundation of Boston. Mr. Louis Cabot assured me personally that there were no strings attached: I would have a completely free hand.

On the basis of this grant, I set out to form a team of economists. I was looking for people with a number of special characteristics: previous professional experience in underdeveloped areas, especially Latin America; a working knowledge of Spanish; and a desire to find out what was happening rather than to obtain material for propaganda of one sort or another. For obvious reasons, neither Americans nor Cubans were suitable, and in fact, though not by intention, it turned out that the group consisted of Chilean and English economists:

Andrés Bianchi—from Chile, a former student and teacher of law in the University of Chile, who later studied economics in the Graduate School of Yale University, where he became an assistant instructor in the Department of Economics for 1962-63; currently teaching at the Centro Interamericano de Enseñanza de Estadística in Santiago.

Richard Jolly—from England, a graduate of economics from Cambridge University, who worked in community development and adult education in Kenya and afterwards studied economics at Yale University, where he was Associate Chubb Fellow in

1960-61; currently working on the economics of educational expansion in Africa.

Max Nolff—from Chile, an economist with extensive experience in Chilean industry and the author of numerous articles on Latin American economics, who was a founder and former editor of *Panorama Económico,* the well-known Chilean economics journal; currently on the staff of the United Nations Economic Commission for Latin America, working for the Venezuelan government as a consultant on industrial planning.

The plan was to spend from four to six weeks each in Cuba in August and September of 1962, with each member working on some aspect of the Cuban economy. After sending a letter and a cable to Boti, telling him I was going ahead as arranged, I made a preliminary visit to Havana at the end of July to make sure that the authorities were still willing to give us the cooperation needed. I submitted an outline of our program, showing that our primary object was to compare the present position in various fields with the situation before the Revolution and that we also hoped to assess recent trends and prospects. On this visit, I never managed to see Boti, but one of his aides, Manuel Hevia, gave me a verbal message that the Minister agreed in principle to provide the help we needed. I went on to visit my family in Jamaica, informed other members of the group that the trip was on, and then returned to Cuba.

I did eventually see Boti on August 8. He told me that the verbal message of agreement in principle had been given me without his knowledge and that, on the contrary, he felt the visit was inopportune. Everyone was very busy; in any case, the United States was suffering from lack of information about Cuba, and he did not intend to make it easier for them. He could not see that more information about Cuba in the outside world would be of any use—people had already made their minds up either to support or oppose the Cuban Revolution. Moreover, Cuba had found that it could not rely on the objectivity of foreigners. Far from being willing to help Max Nolff obtain a visa (one of the requests I made), he said it was a mistake that any of us had been allowed to enter the country. He refused point-blank to give us letters of introduction or arrange itineraries, though he did say that there was nothing to stop us from going around and finding out what we could by personal inspection.[2]

One can only conjecture the reasons for this complete change of attitude, compared with February (if not July). Perhaps Boti had some misgivings, which, as will be seen, would not be entirely without foundation, about the professional quality of the economic plan. His own position did not seem particularly strong while we were there. Our American source of finance (about which I made no secret) may have bothered him. Be that as it may, the outcome was that we did not have much access to the statistics of Junta Central de Planificación (Central Planning Board), or JUCEPLAN. Consequently we had to spend a good deal of time developing supplementary sources of information in the capital, and visiting local offices in the provinces.

In some respects, this setback was by no means as bad as we at first feared. For one thing, we centainly did not see merely what the authorities wanted us to see. We traveled, together with two members of my family, almost the length of the island, individually or together, taking trains, planes, taxis, and buses, and arrived unannounced, often without any contact or introduction, at intervening towns. Between us we visited many schools, farms, and factories in various provinces. After conversations with hundreds of people, from casual passersby to administrators, we were better able to gauge what the economic and social changes really amounted to. Using public transportation, buying meals for ourselves, and making telephone calls, in various towns, we could also get a much clearer impression of the problems of the consumer, and of the efficiency of basic services, than does the routine official visitor who has everything organized for him. Last, after seeing how data are collected at the local level, we were in a much better position to assess the reliability of national statistics.

Indeed, we might well have used Cuban statistics with excessive confidence, if we had not had this experience. For example, in the case of agriculture, we cannot now put much confidence in production totals, except for some traditional crops, and the same is true of national income series (if only because they depend in large part on agricultural statistics).[3] Other examples will be given below.

Our task was by no means an easy one. To start with, there is practically no information to be drawn on in the outside world. Most of the books and articles recently published on Cuba are superficial propaganda exercises, from one viewpoint or another, rather than serious attempts to analyze what has happened. Anyone living outside Cuba who wants to know, say, what has been done about university education, or what new industries are being established, will find it impossible to get the information he needs. Even in Cuba there is no statistical bulletin or annual.

One source of information is the reports of speeches of Cuban leaders. These reports are of course relevant material, especially on qualitative questions such as the attitude of the government (and we use them as such), but they are not easy to interpret. Politicians anywhere may be misreported, or they may say something different from what they really mean, especially in long, extemporaneous orations. Sometimes their statements appear ambiguous or internally inconsistent. They may exaggerate either positive points or negative, in order to encourage people or to shock them into activity.

Despite the negative attitude of Boti, we were not by any means deprived of official data. (It is worth mentioning that he made no attempt, as far as I know, to create difficulties for us.) Some material we needed was published in the Cuban press or was available in conference reports, and we got an increasing degree of cooperation from various official quarters—notably the Ministries of Industry (after a letter to Comandante Guevara) and Education, but also those of Labor, Finance, and the Navy, as well as INRA (the National Institute for Agrarian Reform, which is now effectively the Ministry of Agriculture) and a number of planning officials. While the information we got was often of poor quality and sometimes inconsistent, we found no reason to suspect that it was doctored for our benefit. It is reasonable to suppose that some of the material sent overseas may be less than completely objective, but officials of ministries dealing with local matters are preoccupied with the problems of the moment; they have no time for two sets of books. We were able to check some of our conclusions by asking the same questions in different provinces or from each other's experience. Certain patterns in past development began to emerge, and the general outline of future plans became clearer. In view of the quality of statistics, it is doubtful whether we would actually have been very much better off if we had seen every figure in the official files.

Because of this lack of data, we could not carry out a comprehensive analysis, showing, for example, changes in the output of various sectors and relating them to trends in trade, investment, or consumption; nor could we discuss the role of education in its full economic context. Not only was our information incomplete but we could not always clear up factual inconsistencies or obtain supplementary information. The exact status of some statistics, especially targets, was not easy to assess. Our problem was to some extent like that of a historian who has an incomplete set of official documents and yet is unable to ask questions about the gaps. There was the additional danger that by the time of publication, the situation would be very different from what it was when we wrote (at the end of 1962).

We debated whether under the circumstances we would be able to write anything at all valuable.[4] What really decided the issue was that information is so badly needed on what is one of the most important political developments in this century. Few people are able to visit Cuba (United States citizens are normally not allowed to do so, and others may find it too expensive or politically inadvisable or they may have difficulties with visas[5]). It is doubtful whether in the future a visit like ours will be possible at all.

We concluded therefore that we should try to write an account of some aspects of Cuban experience from a professional point of view. The incompleteness of the data and the impossibility of a comprehensive analysis must however be emphasized. The conclusions are inevitably tentative in many places and should be so judged by the reader. Because information is incomplete and because a revolutionary situation precludes a strictly economic analysis, the margin for personal judgment is considerable.

Any group writing about a subject as sensitive as Cuba does so knowing well that they will be criticized, and that the grounds will not only be professional. The Cuban Revolution, precisely because of its significance, arouses deep political emotions. The combination of strong feelings and lack of information creates an atmosphere in which fantasy flourishes, and those who do not write for one side or another, but who try to assess honestly what they have seen, are suspected and resented by both.

One cannot but be reminded of the course of controversy over the Soviet Union. In the early years of the Bolshevik regime, the most extraordinary stories were circulating (based either on rumors in refugee circles or on the reports of uncritical admirers). Since Sputnik I, at least, the cost of self-delusion in the West has become widely recognized, just as Communist circles now have good reason to wish that they had not allowed themselves to be bemused by Stalinist propaganda.

We are most grateful to our American sources of finance and our Cuban sources of information—they both implicitly showed a belief in the possibility and the usefulness of honest research, even on such a controversial question as the Cuban economy. I would like also to acknowledge the assistance of Mr. George Cumper, of the University of the West Indies, who worked with the group for a week in Havana, and my daughter Pauline and my son Philip, who each spent some time helping us. I must acknowledge the facilities made available by the Yale University Economic Growth Center; Miss Joyce Blakeslee is due special thanks for patiently typing my almost illegible manuscripts. We are all indebted to numerous people who helped us both in Cuba and in the United States, but since many are best left unmentioned, none will be listed here.

The book begins with a general account of the economic and social background. The other chapters deal with the fields of agriculture, education, and industry. In each, there is some reference to the tendencies before the Revolution and the problems encountered by the government when it took office; this is followed by an analytical description of what has happened since the Revolution, and there is finally some assessment of future prospects.

I should like to make it clear that, while we have exchanged drafts and comments, each author has been free to accept or reject advice, and he alone bears responsibility for what he has written. There are therefore repetition at some points and differences in interpretation at others and perhaps factual inconsistency. Such things are inevitable when a number of people—

each with his own approach to economic problems and to statistical material, and each using his own sources of information—write separate essays on different aspects of the same subject.

PUBLISHER'S NOTE

In the interest of early publication, not all of the information is provided in certain footnote citations of documents in Spanish. The publisher feels that topicality of the statistical information provided by this book justifies these infrequent omissions.

Contents

Tables

Cuba: The Economic and Social Revolution

CHAPTER I

The Economic and
Social Background

i

At the risk of seeming trite, I should begin by stressing the fact that Cuba was *not*, on the eve of the Revolution, by
any means a developed country. Economically, socially, and
politically, it was in numerous ways different from the countries
of North America and Western Europe, even the small ones.

In the first place, it relied heavily on exports of a single
product, sugar. A sugar economy has certain well-known characteristics. Plantations are the predominant form of agricultural
organization, and sugar mills account for the majority of industry.

To say that sugar output provided a fifth of Cuba's national
product is in a way an understatement, because a great deal of
the rest of the product was bought out of sugar incomes or out of
taxes on imports financed by sugar exports or out of incomes
created by those incomes and taxes, and so on. If exports of
sugar rose, the national income rose, and investment became

profitable, sustaining the rise; when sugar markets fell, many forces combined to pull the whole economy downwards.

This was true of seasonal fluctuations, trade cycles, and long-term trends alike. Each year, the pulse of economic life quickened early in the New Year when the sugar harvest commenced and then fell off in the second half of the year, after the sugar mills closed. When sugar exports declined in a world recession (as they did in 1920-21, the early 1930's, and after the Korean boom), the domestic economy contracted too: among "built in" features, de-stabilizers predominated. And the slow growth of sugar exports in recent decades was associated, as will be shown, with the slow growth of the Cuban economy.

Cuba was not, of course, unique in this respect. Every exporter of agricultural products experiences seasonal fluctuations. Practically without exception, primary producers have suffered severely from recessions and depressions. They were all affected to a greater or lesser extent by the slowing up of growth in North America, and more recently Western Europe, and by the failure of exports of primary products even to keep pace with this growth rate in the industrial countries. Among the main reasons for this lag in commodity sales were the low income-elasticities of demand for primary products,[1] especially foodstuffs, and the increasing tendency of industrial countries to subsidize their own farmers. These depressing tendencies on demand also influenced prices, so the problems of underdeveloped countries have been aggravated by a downward trend in the terms of trade in the past decade.

While the post-World-War-II boom in commodity exports has petered out, population growth has quickened in countries selling such exports. And under the surface, impatience with poverty and unemployment has grown, gradually but persistently. There is enormous political pressure to create expanding economies, but expansion involves increasing imports of manufactures, especially machinery, and this is precisely what it is difficult to pay for.

Cuba must therefore be seen as one of many backward economies making attempts to break out of this impasse. Industrialization has become increasingly the order of the day. Yet this is not a simple business. One object of setting up new industries is to save foreign exchange by producing at home the manufactures which are currently imported. But this saving is partly offset by the need to import materials, fuel, and spare parts, and in the short-run there are heavy needs for new equipment. Moreover, the new industries are usually rather high-cost producers, and their establishment raises the demand for skilled labor and technicians (which are hard to mobilize), as well as for power and transport (which require imported equipment) and food supplies (which are not easily extracted from the neo-feudal agricultural sectors). So there are upward pressures on prices and a continuous strain on the foreign balance. Since industralization is a rolling process and each year there are more industries to be set up, this strain lasts for decades, rather than merely for years.[2] It implies the need for economic planning and controls, especially on imports, and big loans from abroad.

Sooner or later, it becomes clear that what is needed is the reform of the social structure, especially land reform, to limit the demand for luxuries and to create mass markets, large middle classes, a dynamic farm economy, and an educated and flexible labor force. Such reform has been slow in coming in Latin America.

Most of the larger countries of the region (and indeed of other underdeveloped areas) have by now had experience in coping with this sort of problem.[3] Success has varied. They have all made some progress by setting up new industries and thus becoming less dependent on exports; in several (though not in Argentina or Chile), there has been a continued fast rise in the per-capita national income. But the chronic balance-of-payments crises have been relieved only by periodic injections of foreign aid,[4] and even these have not halted price inflation. Moreover, the great majority of the people, especially peasants and farm workers, still play little part in the political process;[5] and in the past few years, largely because it has proved impossible to satisfy economic aspirations, the public's political role has been reduced rather than increased (through military coups, increasing press censorship, etc.). Social change has been very slow. Recent land reforms have either had a limited impact (as in Chile or Colombia) or have mainly affected public lands (as in Venezuela); in no case has there been a recognizable alteration in the social structure. Indeed, the income distribution may well have become more unequal in many countries, and urban slums remain a very evident social problem in every great Latin American city, as the surplus rural population comes in, searching for work. So far, the prescription for rapid economic growth in the region has involved reliance mainly on private capital, whether domestic or foreign, responding to profit opportunities. The conventional advice (given particularly by the International Monetary Fund) has been to create a favorable atmosphere for this process by stabilizing prices and exchange rates and abandoning controls on payments in foreign currency. This line of solution involves conservative monetary and fiscal policies.

However, the mounting political and social disorder of the past five years led to a drastic, if not agonizing, reappraisal. In 1959, the Inter-American Development Bank was set up to speed the flow of public capital; in 1960, by the Act of Bogotá, a fund was established to cover social investment, and far-reaching reforms, including higher taxation, were agreed to in principle; the Charter of Punta del Este of 1961 required some economic planning, as well as social progress, by recipients of the large sums of public money which were to be made available. These were, however, modifications in a system which continued to rely primarily on the workings of the price mechanism.

The significance of Cuban experience, and its great professional interest, lies in the fact that it represents an attempt to achieve broadly the same objectives as those set out in the Charter of Punta del Este (fast growth and a more equal society) but by different means. Social change has taken place at an early stage of industrialization; an ambitious educational program attempts not merely to educate the labor force of the future but to change the existing one; much of the economy has been taken over by the state, and communal incentives are stressed rather than private self-interest; industrial and agricultural development is attempted with a detailed central plan covering every sector; food is rationed and price inflation is suppressed by controls on wages and prices; the distribution of income has become much less unequal.

ii

Being a sugar economy was not always a burden for Cuba. After the successful revolution against Spain (1896-98), there was a very fast development of sugar for the United States market. During the first quarter of this century, sugar output and exports rose rapidly, with the help of American capital, and this rise led to general increases in activity in other sectors, such as transport, energy, and construction. It seems from the data available that in the years from 1912 to 1924, Cuban living conditions were not low by international standards then current—per-capita income in 1922-25 averaged over $200 in current prices, according to very tentative estimates;[6] this would be at least $400 at the prices of the mid-1950's. From another point of view, this figure was more than 35 per cent of per-capita income in the United States, which was about $600 at that time.[7]

But this upward climb showed signs of slackening even in the 1920's. There was a short but ominously severe break in the sugar market in 1920;[8] after 1924 exports leveled off, with prices settling at 2 to 3 cents a pound. From 1929, prices and volumes both started to slide and sugar exports dropped to very low levels (see Table 1). In 1933 and 1934, the dollar value of these exports was less than one quarter of what it had been a decade earlier. A recovery brought exports up to quite a high level again in the 1940's, but once more there was a lag in the 1950's, relieved only temporarily by sales of $656 million in 1957; in 1958 they had fallen back to $594 million.

Even the apparent rise between the 1920's and the 1940's in the value of exports was partly due to price rises. The physical output of sugar climbed from about 1 million tons a year in 1905 to 5 million in 1925, but a level of 5 to 6 million was typical of the years 1947 to 1958, apart from the quite exceptional crop of 7 million in 1952.[9] There was, in consequence, no need to build any more sugar mills after 1925, and in fact the number of mills in operation declined from 184 in 1926 to 161 in 1958. Production control was initiated as far back as 1927, when, under the Verdeja Act, a maximum (4.5 million tons) was set for the crop, in the hope of preventing price declines, and that aggregate figure was broken down into individual quotas for each producer, based on past performance. These quotas became a familiar feature of Cuban sugar output.

Reasons for the poor performance of exports are not difficult to find. Cuban exports depended very much on what she sold to

Table 1. Sugar and Total Exports and United States Export Prices, 1902-6 to 1952-56, Quinquennial Averages

	Cuban Sugar Exports (in millions of $)	Total Cuban Exports (in millions of $)	Percentage U.S. Share of Cuban Exports	Index of U.S. export prices (1925-26 = 100)	Purchasing power of Cuban sugar exports (in millions of $ at 1925-26 prices)[a]	Purchasing power of total Cuban exports (in millions of $ at 1925-26 prices)[a]
1902-6	52	89	83	56	93	160
1907-11	78	119	82	63	124	189
1912-16	169	214	81	69	244	309
1917-21	426	482	76	155	274	311
1922-26	317	367	81	97	326	377
1927-31	174	232	75	80	218	290
1932-36	86	111	75	60	143	185
1937-41	128	163	80	68	188	240
1942-46	279	371	82	103	269	358
1947-51	612	689	60	129	475	534
1952-56	508	623	66	166	305	374

a. In terms of the volume of U.S. exports which could be purchased.
Sources: Cuban exports: *Anuario Azucarero de Cuba,* 1959. U.S. export prices: *Historical Statistics of the United States* (Washington, D.C., 1960).

the United States, easily her best customer up to 1960. In turn, these sales depended on: (1) the income of the United States; (2) the relation between income and the demand for sugar; and (3) the allocation of U.S. consumption between various suppliers.

The real national income of the United States more than doubled between the 1920's and the 1950's. However, per-capita consumption of sugar did not rise at all. In fact, after being slightly over 50 kilograms (raw equivalent) a head in the 1920's, it fell back in the depression to about 46 and never recovered.[10] This decline occurred despite the fact that, if anything, retail sugar prices rose less than retail prices in general. The interpretation of the Food and Agriculture Organization Commodities Division was that at high incomes the income-elasticity is low, that in the war years there was a structural change in demand (perhaps attributable to rationing), and that dental propaganda, concern with weight, changes in taste, etc., resulted in a downward trend in consumption.[11] The change in U.S. consumption of sugar was about equal to the change in population between the 1920's and the 1950's, i.e., about 40 per cent. By contrast, consumption had nearly doubled between 1906 and 1926, indicating a strong positive income-elasticity in the earlier period.

Table 2. United States Sugar Consumption, Cuban Participation, and Average United States Price for Cuban Producers, by Periodic Averages

	U. S. Consumption (millions of short tons)	U. S. Imports from Cuba (millions of short tons)	Column 2 as percentage of Column 1	Price in United States (cents per lb.)[a]
1906-13	3.9	1.7	44	2.6
1914-18	4.4	2.1	49	4.4
1919-29	6.0	3.2	53	4.2[b]
1930-33	6.5	2.2	34	1.2
1934-40	6.7	1.9	28	2.1
1941-45	6.6	2.8	42	3.0
1946-49	7.0	3.1	43	5.1
1950-53	8.1	3.0	37	5.6

a. Crude price in New York *less* duty on Cuban sugar.
b. For 1921-29: 3.1.
Source: A memorandum by the Banco Nacional, using as sources H. H. Pike and Co., *Lamborn Sugar Market Report,* and *Anuario Azucarero.*

Figures of participation in the U.S. market are shown in Table 2. From before World War I to the 1920's, there was an upward trend in the Cuban share, as Cuban output raced ahead of other sources of supply.[12] In 1930, however, under the Hawley-Smoot Tariff, duty on Cuban sugar rose (from 1.76 to 2.00 cents a lb.) and the share of Cuba fell rapidly year by year, from 52 per cent in 1929 to 25 per cent in 1933.

In 1933, the economic plight of Cuba was desperate, and the island was the scene of guerrilla war, urban tension, and a general strike. President Machado was forced to flee and was followed in quick succession by Céspedes, Grau San Martín, and Batista's nominee Mendieta. United States policy changed. Tariffs on Cuban sugar were cut back to 1.5 cents and then 0.9 cents. The U.S. market was now allocated by quota, and Cuba was receiving nearly a cent above the world price, but her share of this market was only 30 per cent,[13] slightly more than the total of domestic cane and beet producers.

Temporarily in 1939 and again in 1942 to 1947, this system was suspended. There were no quotas and the world price reigned.[14] Because Philippine exports ceased in 1942 (this country had previously had a share of 15 per cent under the 1937 Act), the Cuban share recovered its pre-World-War-I level. However, when the quota system was re-established in 1948, Cuba was allocated 33 per cent (making room for the Philippines to pick up 11 per cent). Price control was re-established, and a gap opened once more between the U.S. price and the world price. In the 1950's, the picture essentially was that U.S. producers were getting rather over 7 cents a lb., and (after deducting subsidy and tariff) Cuban suppliers received between 5 and 6 cents a lb., as against a wildly fluctuating price in a world market that had by now become rather marginal. These price fluctuations were to some extent mitigated by the International Sugar Agreement, which also allocated a quota to Cuba, but prices of sales under the agreement were, except in rare occasions, considerably lower than Cuba was getting from the United States and averaged about 3.5 cents for much of the 1950's.

The net result, therefore, was that the volume of Cuban sales to the United States hardly changed between the 1920's and the 1950's, because she suffered a declining share of a total that was only rising slowly. However, prices rose (if we exclude the abnormal years of 1919 and 1920) by about the same as U.S. export prices, whereas in the period from 1906-13 until 1921-29, there had been a smaller rise in U.S. purchase prices for sugar than in her export prices. The special price paid by the United States in the 1950's mitigated the effect of the long-run depression in Cuban sugar sales.

If we refer to Table 1 again, we can see that Cuba did manage in the 1950's to become less dependent on the United States for exports. Sales of sugar were negotiated with a number of countries, including Japan, France, West Germany, United Kingdom, Canada, Netherlands, and (at times) India and Morocco. The Soviet Union had also become a purchaser by 1958 (buying 182,000 tons then). However, it was hard to sell great quantities since the French and United Kingdom markets were essentially reserved for politically associated territories, and beet production had made further headway during the war. It was also hard for a large producer like Cuba to achieve what would be for her significant additional sales without harming the market. Most sales other than those to the United States were made at the lower world price, so that the average export price for sugar was depressed (rather under 5 cents a pound).

Table 1 shows in its last column the combined effect of these influences. The purchasing power of Cuban exports in 1952-56 was no more than it had been thirty years earlier, whereas in the period from 1902-1906 to 1922-26 their purchasing power had more than doubled.[15]

The stagnation in sugar affected the whole economic picture, for no other major sectors emerged to stimulate the economy. Other forms of agriculture expanded, but not very rapidly.[16] Mineral output fluctuated violently, mainly in response to the U.S. need for imports;[17] output of some minerals (iron ore, manganese, and nickel) rose in World War II but fell back afterwards and only recovered again in the course of the 1950's.[18] The index of manufacturing output rose by no more than 20 per cent between 1947 and 1957,[19] and showed setbacks whenever sugar did.

Although the economic statistics are not firm enough to permit much confidence to be placed in them, especially for the years before 1947,[20] the general impression they give is unmistakable. It is one of chronic stagnation from the 1920's on-wards in real per-capita income. The upward trend in income barely kept pace with the rise in population, which averaged rather more than 2 per cent a year between the censuses of 1919 and 1943. The very tentative estimates of Alienes[21] indicate that the end-of-war boom of 1944-47 hardly brought average real incomes back to the levels of corresponding years for the previous war (1916-19).

There is some confirmation of the general failure of per-capita real incomes to rise from the 1920's to the 1940's in data given in an Economic Commission for Latin America study of consumption trends, based on statistics of local output and imports. The statistical raw material, even on such important, easily measured items, is suspect; but when many series all tell broadly the same story and tell it in a vivid manner, then one can trust this story much more than any of the individual series. (Table 3.) From 1905-1909 to 1925-29, consumption of basic foods seemed at least to keep pace with the population; but, though the rate of advance of population slowed down in the next two decades, the expansion of consumption showed an even greater deceleration. In these 20 years, the consumption only of wheat flour and beans kept roughly in line with the population (and only beer consumption rose faster). The leveling-off in the trends of energy and transport consumption was especially marked. The pace of growth of output quickened somewhat in the 1950's, especially in the Korean war boom of 1951-52, and again in the Suez crisis of 1956-57. But the population growth had also accelerated (to 2.5 per cent a year) and in 1958 per-capita real income was still only about the same as it had been in 1947.[22]

Further information which is consistent with the picture of stagnant per-capita income for more than three decades is the failure of large-scale unemployment to disappear after the depression. There are no figures of unemployment for the 1920's, but it must have been low, for immigration was still considerable then.[23] On the other hand, in the period from July, 1956, to June, 1957, overt unemployment averaged 16 per cent of the labor force, and this was the best year of the middle of the 1950's.[24] Those working less than 40 hours a week averaged 10 per cent of the labor force in the same period, and there was also considerable disguised unemployment, especially in agriculture.[25] Unemployment of this magnitude could hardly have appeared if there had been a big rise in per-capita income (unless there was—which there was not—a great deal of mechanization).

Slowing down of economic growth to a virtual standstill was matched by a similar halt in progress in social fields. Illiteracy, after falling to relatively low levels in the first quarter of the century, failed to decline further. In fact, the proportion of children of school age attending primary school in the 1950's was lower than in the 1920's.

Cuba in the 35 years from 1923 to 1958 showed little progress. The stagnation was more serious and lasted longer than in any other Latin American economy—excepting perhaps the economies of one or two very small and poor nations such as Bolivia and Haiti. Although Argentina and Chile have shown rather slow growth rates since the 1920's, per-capita incomes have certainly significantly increased since then; while exports in these countries too have failed (in terms of purchasing power) to exceed the level of the 1920's, there has been a considerable expansion in other sectors.

Two institutional explanations for this chronic stagnation stand out. The first is that the great majority of the land was held in large estates. Twenty-two large sugar companies accounted for about one-fifth of the agricultural area, and some of this land was held in reserve against a boom in sugar prices. The other main use of large holdings was as natural cattle runs, with low output and small labor requirements per hectare. There are many reasons why this type of organization does not conduce to an expansion of supplies to the domestic market, but for them the reader will have to turn to the chapters on agriculture. Suffice it to say here that the sector was not by any means as dynamic as it should have been. Moreover, the sugar companies insisted on refining the bulk of their output overseas, inside the industrial countries, and Cuba did not therefore benefit much from the quite considerable income and employment generated in sugar processing.

The second reason is the trade treaties with the United States, especially the Reciprocal Trade Agreement of 1934, which was associated with the concessions on Cuban sugar and which re-

Table 3. Long-term Changes in Population and in Apparent Consumption of Certain Staple Goods

	Annual Average for Period			Percentage Increase	
	1905-9	1925-29	1945-49	1905-9 to 1925-29	1925-29 to 1945-49
Population (millions)	2.0	3.6	5.1	78	41
Apparent consumption, final products					
Rice (thousand tons)	102.0	208.0	254.0	104	22
Wheat flour (thousand tons)	73.0	113.0	157.0	55	38
Potatoes (thousand tons)	—	104.0ᵃ	109.0	—	5
Coffee (thousand tons)	—	28.0	36.0	—	29
Beans (thousand tons)	59.0	13.9	18.1	119	40
Beer (million liters)	—	47.0	89.0	—	89
Cotton cloth (thousand tons)	7.3	8.8	9.5	20	8
Passenger transport (million passenger-kilometers)	180.0	524.0	662.0	191	26
Apparent consumption, intermediate products					
Energy (million equivalent KWH)	1.2	3.5	3.9	192	12
Iron (thousand tons)	48.0	84.0	95.0	75	12
Cement (thousand tons)	61.0	306.0	321.0	401	5
Freight transport (million ton-kilometers)	0.3	1.3	1.3	362	0

a. Imports only.
Source: Calculated from tables in *El Desarrollo Económico de Cuba* (ECLA E/CN. 12/218, 1951), based on *Anuarios del Comercio Exterior* and *Memorias del Banco Central.*

mained in force (with some modifications) until the Revolution. Under this agreement, Cuban import duties were lowered on many items; it was specified that duties were not to be raised on a long list of goods; internal taxes on products originating in the United States were to be reduced; quantitative restrictions on imports from the United States were to be limited; and exchange control was prohibited.[26] The consequence was that doors were held open to imports from the United States, including foodstuffs. But the main effect was on Cuban manufactures. The industrialization to be found in other Latin American economies of a similar size was never attempted. Such factories as were established were mostly light consumer-goods industries which traditionally come at an early stage of industrialization (e.g., food and textile processing). Basic metal and engineering industries had already been firmly established in Chile, Colombia, and Mexico by the middle of the 1950's, but not in Cuba.[27]

There were certain advantages for Cuba as well as the United States in this set of arrangements.[28] The question, however, is not whether it was "equitable" but whether there was any conceivable way forward for the Cuban economy within this framework, any way of absorbing unemployment and raising living standards.[29]

As the crisis of the Cuban economy grew worse over the decades, some characteristics emerged which can be explained as reactions to it but which nevertheless made it even more resistant to change. In the first place, a stagnant sugar industry does not have much incentive to spend a great deal on technical improvements, such as irrigation. Yields per acre were in the 1950's only a fraction of those in most other sugar economies.

Secondly, as unemployment increased, so did labor resistance to measures which would raise productivity. The sugar industry itself was affected: mechanized cutting and bulk loading were successfully opposed, although with other sugar producers they had become common practice. Tobacco workers also resisted mechanization. Cuba's exports became therefore less competitive and correspondingly more dependent on the special position afforded by U.S. quotas.

Moreover, despite unemployment, Cuban labor was not cheap by Latin American standards. Successive labor laws made dismissal of workers difficult or in other ways raised costs, and these laws naturally did not stimulate the establishment of new manu-facturing industries. Nor did they facilitate the diversification of agriculture, since high sugar wages during the crop set the pattern for all activities.[30]

By the end of World War II, there was strong resistance to the employment of foreigners in Cuban industry, even as tech-nicians, whereas a significant fraction of Cuba's own rather meager professional and technical staff emigrated to the United States. In both these ways, the diversification of the economy was hampered.

Lastly, the government attempted to alleviate the growing social strains in various ways—for example, by controlling prices and "intervening" periodically in strike-bound industries. But these policies, too, discouraged foreign capital, which in any case was reluctant to enter a country marked by such a deep and chronic economic and political malaise. Back in 1929, the United States had more capital invested in Cuba than in any other Latin American country, but subsequently the value of sugar invest-ments was written down, and some land and mills were sold to nationals.[31] During the war and for some years afterwards,

Table 4. Direct United States Investments in Cuba
(Book value in millions of $)

	1929	1950	1958
Agriculture	575	263	265
Petroleum and mining	9	35	270
Manufacturing	45	54	80
Services	290	305	386
Totals	919	657	1,001

Source: *United States Investment in the Latin American Economy* (U.S. De-partment of Commerce).

direct investment activity was slow, though it picked up in the 1950's. (Table 4.) It can be seen that the main expansion was in petroleum and mining,[32] and there was also investment in electricity generation, telephone communications,[33] and hotels. Virtually no new U.S. investments in agriculture were made, and indeed the total is low compared to the totals for many other Latin American countries in this period.[34]

It should be noted that the payments effect was on balance negative. The increase of $344,000,000 in book value of investments was outweighed by $378,000,000 in remittances to the United States of profits and interest on private investments (apart from another $74,000,000 not repatriated).

There was no significant inflow of public capital to make up for this low level of private investment. (There had been fairly big foreign loans in earlier periods—altogether $400,000,000 up to 1950.)

The economic growth which did occur in the 1950's was due in large part to two forces, a rise in tourism and an expanding program of public works. The contribution of the former was somewhat limited by the fact that nearly all the profits accruing from the tourism were remitted to the United States, and some of the food and drink consumed by tourists was imported. Moreover, tourism is notoriously highly sensitive to income fluctuations at home, to fashions in travel, and to the political climate in the host country.

In the years 1955-57, public investment averaged 6 per cent of the national product, a definite increase over the beginning of the decade. The government was now using various types of development banks to finance investment, including loans intended to stimulate capital formation in the private sector of the economy. The internal public debt rose from $102,000,000 in December, 1950, to $682,000,000 in December, 1957, and $860,000,000 in December, 1958.[35] The counterpart of this rise was a decline in reserves of foreign exchange. It is sometimes possible to use public works as a major means of promoting growth (Venezuela did so in this period), but unless exports are rising or big loans coming in from abroad, the eventual outcome can only be the collapse of a system of freely convertible currency at a fixed exchange rate.[36] In any economy such as Cuba's the "multiplier effect"[37] of public works is small, because a large part of the increased purchasing power spills over into the demand for imports. In any case, much of this investment did little to raise the productive power of the country.

If further progress was almost impossible to achieve, the *status quo* in 1958 was intolerable, especially for a country so close to Florida and receiving through many channels an imposing (perhaps exaggerated) picture of North American levels of living. Income per capita per year averaged about $500[38] or one-fifth as much as the average in the United States[39] (far lower even than in any Southern state there). Yet by international standards this was not so bad. Only Venezuela and Argentina, of the larger Latin American countries, had a higher average income. What was intolerable was, first, a level of unemployment some three times as high as in the United States. In few families were all the male adults steadily employed. The surplus labor force lacked both legal possibilities and sufficient education to emigrate on a large scale (contrast the possibilities open to the surplus populations of two neighbors, Jamaica and Puerto Rico).

Second, in the countryside social conditions were very bad. About a third of the nation existed in squalor, eating rice, beans, bananas, and root vegetables (with hardly any meat, fish, eggs, or milk), living in huts, usually without electricity or toilet facilities, suffering from parasitic diseases and lacking access to health services, denied education (their children received only a first-grade education, if that).[40] Particularly distressing was the lot of the *precaristas,* those squatting in makeshift quarters on public land.

A substantial fraction of the town population was also very poor. Here, too, there were squatters living in shacks, and of course there were slum tenements. In 1953 no less than one-fifth of families lived in single rooms, and the average size of these families was 5, according to the census. Taking the urban and the rural population together, 62 per cent of the economically active population had incomes of less than $75 a month.[41]

Moreover, the population growth had in the meantime been accelerating gradually, and was about 2.5 per cent a year. The labor force was also growing, perhaps at an even faster rate.[42] If the national product was to remain dependent on sugar and yet to increase at 2.5 per cent a year, it would have been necessary to raise the average output of 1951-55 from 6,100,000 tons to over 7,000,000 tons in 1961-65 and well over 8,000,000 in 1971-75, without any deterioration in the terms of trade.[43]

Though the pent-up demand for change was kept in check by repression of political opposition, it was very strong. Political stability can hardly be expected in a country which has fallen far behind a neighbor with which it is in close economic and political relations. In fact (and this is indicated by the surprising speed with which the armed forces of Batista collapsed) the existing state of affairs—in which people were short of food and work but land lay idle and factories were not built—could not continue.

iii

So the revolutionary government took over an economy that was structurally unsound. It depended excessively on exports of a single, not very promising crop. (Table 5.) Even its other leading products, tobacco and coffee, enjoyed markets far from dynamic. As Table 6 shows, the country relied on imports for advanced engineering products as well as for basic sources of energy. In many cases, it would have been feasible to make these products at home (and a number of Latin American countries were making them). Imports of foods were especially conspicuous, including dairy products, eggs, canned fruits, potatoes, vegetables, confections, and even some fish, poultry, and pork. Cuba had even become a net importer of alcoholic beverages[44] and cigarettes. Materials imported included cotton and textile semi-manufactures, chemicals, fertilizers, and containers. Imports of automobiles were heavy, and so were those of electrical household goods. Payments by Cubans for tourism exceeded receipts until 1955 and even thereafter continued to represent a high fraction of gross receipts on the tourist account. Remittances of profits and interest absorbed over 5 per cent of foreign exchange earnings.

Another weakness was the heavy dependence for both imports and exports on one country (the United States). (Table 7.) Moreover, tourists came almost exclusively from the same source.

Table 5. Composition of Cuban Exports, 1958
(In millions of pesos)

Sugar	594
Tobacco	50
Minerals	44
Other	46
Total	734

Source: Memoria, 1958-59 (Banco Nacional de Cuba).

Table 6. Composition of Cuban Imports, 1955-57
(Annual average in millions of $ at 1955 prices)

Food, drink, and tobacco	168
Textiles	95
Paper and its products	32
Wood and its products	12
Chemicals	53
Fuel	55
Basic metals	5
Semi-manufactures	51
Household durables	47
Machinery	125
Transport equipment	17
Automobiles	40
Other	54
	754

Source: Economic Commission for Latin America, *Economic Bulletin for Latin America,* V, Statistical Supplement, Table 36.

Table 7. Geographical Composition of Cuban Foreign Trade, 1958
(In millions of pesos)

	Exports	*Imports*
United States	492	543
Latin America	10	80
Sterling area	48	37
Other Western Europe	57	73
Other	127	44
Totals	734	777

Source: Memoria, 1958-59 (Banco Nacional de Cuba).

This dependence had serious implications. Since most of the equipment came from the United States, the economy depended on a flow of spare parts from North American firms. The distributors in Cuba of both semi-manufactures and consumer goods were in the habit of ordering directly from the mainland (often by telephone); they knew only those sources of supply; they were accustomed to fairly rapid delivery; and customers were used to U.S. brands. The Cuban economy was so wedded to the U.S. economy that the country was in many ways an appendage of it—though without enjoying, as a poor state in the United States does, federal social services or access to U.S. sources of employment. Such lack of independence would have hampered any policy of diversification, however imaginative.

Table 8. Distribution of Output and Labor Force, 1953

	Domestic product		Number occupied[a]	
	($ millions)	(% of total)	(thousands)	(% of total)
Agriculture: Sugar	274	13	819	42
Other[b]	259	12		
Manufacturing: Sugar	130	5	327	17
Other	387	17		
Construction and utilities	113	5	74	4
Mining	28	1	10	1
Transport and communication	121	5	104	5
Other private services	896	34	532	27
Government services	140	6	96	5
Dwelling rent	102	4	—	—
	2,349	100	1,972	100

a. If the census forms were filled in accurately, these figures actually refer to occupation in 1952.

b. Includes forestry and fishing.

Sources: Domestic product: Harry T. Oshima, "The New Estimate of the National Income and Product of Cuba in 1953," *Food Research Institute Studies,* Stanford, II (November, 1961).

Labor force: 1953 Census.

Sugar: *Memoria del Banco Central.*

The trade structure was reflected in an unbalanced structure of production and employment. Table 8 shows that 42 per cent of the labor force was engaged in agriculture and a further 37 per cent in service industries of various kinds (a very high proportion).

The industrial structure was reflected in the geographical distribution of the population. About 43 per cent did not live in any urban grouping in 1953 (and "urban" centers included villages as small as those with 50 people). Yet 21 per cent of the whole population lived in Greater Havana, where such manufacturing establishments as existed, apart of course from sugar mills, could mostly be found.

It would be a great oversimplification to describe social contrasts entirely in terms of capital and labor. The labor force itself was split into two groups, which can be distinguished with a sharpness that is surprising in view of the smallness of the country and the moderately high per-capita income. The rural workers mostly received low incomes and were badly housed and largely uneducated. The proportion illiterate of the rural population,

aged 10 or over, was 42 per cent in 1953. Some indications of
their food and housing standards have been given above. On the
other hand, the urban worker, when he happened to be employed,
was often relatively well paid—leading companies paying about
$1 an hour for unskilled labor and about $200 a month for stenog-
raphers in 1955.[45] Oshima estimates average non-agricultural income from employment at $1,600.[46] Where union organization
was strong (e.g., on docks, in electric works, and in cigarette
factories), many workers received higher than average wages. One
of the defects of the inheritance of the Revolution was that the
wage structure was highly irrational.[47]

The general picture is indicated by Table 9. It should be borne
in mind that this refers to April, 1960, after the revolutionary
government had already raised some wages, especially low industrial wages, and those earned in agriculture. Moreover, it
refers to a period at the height of the sugar harvest, when the
country workers were seasonably well off. Nevertheless, it can
be seen that, whereas most agricultural workers were earning less
than 81 pesos a month,[48] there was a substantial number of industrial workers earning over 121 pesos a month. It can also be
seen that, even excluding property income (and taking account of
the large numbers in domestic service, hawking, etc.), incomes
tended to be noticeably higher in Havana than in the rest of the
country. In Oriente, on the other hand, over half of all incomes
(excluding those not reported) were less than 81 pesos a month.

A word must also be said about the attitude towards work.
Some parts of the labor force had become unfit for more productive work because of the possibility of making money easily out
of various vices associated with the tourist industry or out of
personal services such as taxi-driving. Other sections had a much
more radical, if not revolutionary, tradition, but this often meant
that they had exaggerated ideas of what could be done in a revolutionary climate.[49] All of them resisted labor-saving devices as
hard as they could.

The educational structure of the labor force was another
severe problem. Even in the cities, professional workers (other
than lawyers and teachers) were few—especially engineers, who
numbered less than 3,000 in 1953. There was, in fact, little incentive to educate oneself highly unless one wanted to work over-

Table 9. Income Distribution for Economically Active Population in April, 1960[a]
(Thousands of people in each wage group)

	Total	Not reported	Less than 81	Month's wage or salary in pesos 81 to 101	101 to 121	121 to 151	151 to 500	Over 500
Manual workers:								
Agriculture	461	113	247	60	16	16	8	—
Industry	320	62	99	41	19	39	58	2
Other	144	27	49	19	17	17	13	—
Total	925	202	395	122	52	72	79	2
Office workers	268	31	84	62	9	30	51	2
Service workers	334	49	187	33	15	16	34	1
Others	320	69	71	33	24	50	66	5
Whole country	1847	351	737	250	100	168	230	10
Havana	667	98	211	104	39	79	129	7
Oriente	389	72	199	45	15	28	29	1
Other provinces	791	181	327	101	46	61	72	2

a. Where paid weekly, monthly wage was estimated on the basis of wages in the week of April 4-10.
Source: Censo Laboral, 1960 (Ministry of Labor). Includes self-employed.

seas; underemployment was not uncommon among lawyers, city doctors, architects, and engineers.[50] Many professional people and managers were either foreigners or working for foreign companies (such individuals often enjoyed relatively high living standards). Skilled workers were not scarce for the needs of the time, but they were certainly far too few for rapid industrial advance.

The administrative system was inefficient and notoriously corrupt. There are naturally few authoritative references on this subject, but the examples given by the International Bank for Reconstruction and Development mission may not be unrepresentative of pre-revolutionary practice: "Cubans know that too many of the inspectors who now visit factories expect to be paid for not making bad reports. The factories pay them, moreover, and so they need not even make the inspections. The government, in turn, finds it unnecessary, in many cases, to pay the inspectors more than token salaries, since their income is augmented privately; consequently an inspector is under economic pressure to continue the vicious system."[51] The so-called "public works cycle" is described in these terms: "A new administration comes into power and finds that the public funds have been exhausted by the previous one. For a while, therefore, it does not—indeed cannot—carry out many public works and there are only a few signs of activity. Around the middle of its term, however, the government has to start to think about its political future. So funds are accumulated, meetings are arranged all over the country at which the people are encouraged to explain their public works needs, and the work gets slowly started. When the administration comes to the end of its term, the work, whether finished or not, stops. This wasteful pattern is not, of course, invariable and some projects are brought to completion over several administrations; but it is sufficiently common to be typical of much public works activity."[52] Again: "The consensus is that this coordinated tariff (for transportation) never functioned from the date of promulgation (in 1938)."[53] According to MacGaffey and Barnett, "Until 1959 government was rarely honest and frequently staggeringly corrupt."[54] From our present point of view it is also worth noting that the statisticians and economists working in government offices were few and not very proficient.[55]

In these various respects, Cuba was probably worse off even than other comparable Latin American countries, and these profound disabilities complicated the task of structural change which lay ahead.[56] Yet the Cuban position in 1959 looks rather different if we compare it with, say, the situation in the Soviet Union in 1917. The Cuban Revolution started with advantages unknown to the other socialist regimes on taking power.

In the first place, it did not face the need to repair great physical (and psychological) devastation left by international and internal wars;[57] it even had about $350,000,000 in net foreign reserves.[58] Second—in company with the Soviet Union, Yugoslavia, and China—it achieved its revolution without direct intervention by another socialist country; its success in this regard implied a firmer political base and moreover meant that nationalism could be more easily harnessed. There was a tradition of revolutionary activity which provided inspirational force (the life of Martí and the campaign in the Sierra Maestra were notable legends). Third, because of the very structure of agriculture, a large fraction of the agricultural labor force was, like the sugar mill workers, accustomed to organized and disciplined paid employment. Fourth, the existence of a communications network, especially television, made it possible to convey new policies rapidly to the public (and later to organize extensive adult education). Fifth, a fairly high standard of living, by comparison with other new socialist nations (except Czechoslovakia) gave the government some room to maneuver. Declines in food consumption did not raise the specter of starvation, and it was not out of the question to think of devoting a high proportion of the national product to investment. Last, there were by 1959 other countries with a similar political system, especially the Soviet Union itself; these were economically strong enough to provide considerable quantities of equipment on credit, to supply petroleum, to make technical advisers and training facilities available, and to guarantee a market for the bulk of Cuban exports.[59] The Cuban Revolution coincided rather happily with the turn of Soviet policy towards a greater emphasis on raising living standards. In fact, a tropical economy is obviously to some extent complementary to a bloc situated almost entirely north of Cancer.[60]

Moreover, the relatively low level of economic activity in 1958 meant that there were idle resources which could be mobilized quite quickly. There was spare land, in the senses both of what was uncultivated and what was cultivated more or less extensively. In sugar growing, productivity was low by comparison with virtually all other sugar producers. Much of the labor force was unemployed or underemployed; women were far from fully mobilized. In some sectors there was idle capital, or at least capital being used well below capacity, and quite high inventories. From another point of view, resources which were being used, but used to provide luxury goods or services (such as domestic service), could be diverted to more productive purposes.

Even in comparison with other Latin American governments, the revolutionary government of Cuba had certain advantages. There was not the same pressing shortage of basic social capital in electric power facilities or transport or buildings. Precisely because industrialization had previously been stunted, the immediate steps forward in import substitution were not technically very hard to take. (In Argentina or Brazil, even in Chile or Mexico, further industrialization means the complex and difficult creation of advanced engineering industries). Imports could to some extent be reduced painlessly by eliminating non-essentials which had already almost disappeared from the purchases of the other moderately large economies of Latin America (except Venezuela).

We must therefore judge Cuban performance since the Revolution against the relatively fast increase in output that was physically manageable. Nevertheless, there were some special disadvantages faced by the Cuban government, compared to the other socialist countries. The first was the close proximity to a country which had previously had a dominant position in the Cuban economy. There is no point here in going over all the arguments about who was responsible for the deterioration of relations. It would have taken able statesmanship on both sides for cordial relations to have survived a period when the Cuban economy was swung onto a new course, with diversification of agriculture and rapid growth of industry. Conflicts of interest, which had to emerge as links were broken, were many and acute. In the event, such statesmanship did not materialize, and relations deteriorated to a point not far short of war, with the United States government virtually ending trade with the island and endeavoring to induce its many allies to do likewise.

It is true that the actual military invasions that marked the first years of the Soviet regime have not been repeated in Cuba (except for the abortive landing at Playa Girón, which did not involve foreign troops). Nevertheless, the strategic position of Cuba is clearly extremely weak, and this weakness has economic implications. It would have been difficult for a hostile country to cut off, or even threaten, the trade of the Soviet Union or any of its allies. Moreover, at the time of their revolutions, none of these countries (particularly the Soviet Union and China) relied so much on foreign trade to maintain in operation a partially developed economy. They did not have large sections of the economy so highly dependent on imports of fuel, materials, and spare parts to maintain existing levels of output, nor did their living standards incorporate to the same degree imported food and clothing. What created special difficulties for Cuba was that her machinery and equipment had very largely been made by firms of the same nationality as the sugar estates, petroleum corporations, etc.

Moreover, the effort required to industrialize a country like Cuba is a tremendous one, whatever the specific external and local situation, particularly if the object is at the same time to raise local food consumption. A full-fledged industrial economy, whether socialist or capitalist, requires a technically trained labor force, accustomed to factory or farm discipline, a large corps of professional people, and administrators accustomed to organized routine and capable of intelligent foresight. It needs some set of incentives which will induce people to study and to be willing to forgo immediate consumption for the sake of the future. It implies the creation of organizations in every sector and at every level, with channels of responsibility and the scope for decision clearly defined, and it involves finding people capable of filling top jobs satisfactorily and preparing them to do so. All this cannot be achieved in a few years, or painlessly, in an underdeveloped tropical country where such a small fraction of the adult labor force had received an education which was in any degree complete.

iv

There would be much to be said for leaving considerations of social change out of a work of this kind. This was indeed my original intention, because personal judgment inevitably colors any description, still more any appraisal, of such change. One's view is necessarily personal and subjective. But it soon became apparent that some account of the social change which had occurred was essential if other developments, especially in education, were to be understood and correctly assessed. To leave it out would be less "objective" than to attempt an accurate statement of its significance.

In the first place, there has been a general improvement in the economic lot of the country workers and many peasants. This policy is no doubt attributable to the fact that the rebel army was born in the Sierra Maestra and then developed its campaign with the active cooperation of the rural workers of Oriente. But in any case, the declared intention of the revolutionary regime is to integrate the population by eliminating the great differences between town and country. This policy has been put into effect partly by giving country districts a big share in new housing and roads, by constructing state shops (*tiendas del pueblo*) in these districts, by rapidly electrifying rural areas, and by expanding medical services in the countryside.[61] The agrarian reform, which has given titles to squatters and tenants and eliminated rent obligations, was another means of achieving this end. So was decreeing a national minimum wage of 60 pesos a month in rural districts. Recruiting thousands of workers for the state farms (*granjas del pueblo*) and giving most rural workers year-round employment had the same effect.

Perhaps the biggest psychological impact has been that of the educational program. The campaign against illiteracy sent more than 100,000 people, mostly adolescents, into the countryside in 1961, the "Year of Education," with the declared aim of teaching all adults to read and write. The big expansion in primary education (now almost universal) has mainly benefited the children of country workers, because previously they were largely neglected. It is true that the sharp increase in the numbers enrolled in the secondary and technical schools, achieved partly by boarding students in Havana, and the schemes for training people in the Soviet Union and Eastern Europe have not particularly favored country families up to the present because there are not many with children educated to the necessary standard.[62]   Still, this whole set of developments, together with the planned expansion of the universities, really means for the rural worker or small-holder that there is now, for the first time, an avenue by which his children can rise to the top, and few families are unaffected.

The urban worker has also benefited economically, but not to the same extent.   His family's income probably has not risen as much, though here too the decline in unemployment has had significant economic effects.   The reduction of rents in 1959[63] and the assurance under the urban reform of 1960 that he would become the owner of the house he was living in particularly favored him.

There are some measures, apart from education, which benefit both town and country workers.   One is that holiday facilities are now available cheaply to union members in hotels previously out of his reach—in some cases, they are free as prizes for high production.[64]   Private clubs, including all private beaches, have been thown open to the public,[65] and facilities for tourism and sports have been greatly extended.   Much of the investment, especially in the first three years of the Revolution, was social rather than productive and in various ways raised living stand-ards.[66]

Moves towards social equality have been matched by an egalitarian income policy.   Very few new appointments are made at more than $300 a month, which can be compared with the $60-a-month minimum agricultural wage ($69 on a state farm) and the $85 minimum urban wage.   The new wage structure that was being considered at the end of 1962 (with standard wages set for equivalent occupations in each industry) would give very few people incomes outside these ranges.[67]   It is matched by a pro-posed new pension plan with a minimum of $40 and a maximum of $250 in monthly benefits (rural workers would be brought into such a plan for the first time).   The same social security bill estab-lishes benefits for incapacitation, death (for burial), and widow-hood.   Since taxes are graduated (especially if one includes as taxes the profits made by nationalized industries on luxury products), the measure of equality in Cuba is very high.

The structural and social changes that have occurred have also meant that there are almost countless vacancies in professional, supervisory, and technical jobs. Many of these are being filled by former workers. Large-scale vocational training courses of various types have been created; there are also numerous other programs of instruction of a less vocational nature available to workers.

The "workers' faculty," another of the social innovations announced in 1962, is designed to provide education that will fit workers to take university classes later. Domestic servants (and some of the prostitutes) have received special training to fit them for jobs as seamstresses, clerks, and drivers. Altogether, about a half a million adults were enrolled in 1962 in various schemes. The widespread enrollment reflects a general desire to learn, as well as more specific hopes for personal advancement (and often of helping the Revolution).

A point which must be stressed is the change that has come about in the quality of administrators, from a corrupt and self-seeking clique to a group which evidently cannot be influenced by bribery and which lives modestly and works extremely hard. This is not to say that there are no complaints. The restraint on wages, the scarcity of food (especially in the towns), the shortage of a wide variety of consumer goods, and price increases on some, offset, at least in part, economic gains in other directions. There are political reasons for objection, too, such as the absorption of religious education in the state system (July, 1961), the suppression of organized political opposition, the limitation of trade-union activity, the undoubted problems of dealing with bureaucrats (and such dealings are unavoidable), the lack of news media reflecting a critical point of view, the virtual impossibility of obtaining non-technical journals or newspapers from foreign countries, the use in the schools of a rather narrow form of Marxism. These are common grumbles. I would not attempt to judge whether the working class is in fact better off, for that would involve trying to weigh essentially incomparable changes.

The crucial question is whether wage-earners *believe* they are better off. The nationalization of industry and the collectivization of agriculture, which have proceeded by stages since 1960, impose the necessity for communal incentives, especially now that unemployment is no longer feared. A socialist system requires a degree of cooperation in reaching targets and people who will take seriously campaigns of *emulación,* or competition between individuals or units.[68] It relies to some extent on voluntary labor and study, on personal thrift (at times on economic sacrifice), and on the willingness of people to put national interests first, for instance, when choosing a job.[69]

A careful sample survey among factory workers carried out in 1962 by Dr. Maurice Zeitlin, of Princeton, who kindly showed me some preliminary findings, indicated that rather over two-thirds considered themselves in favor of the regime.[70] Many have good reason to feel this way, particularly if one bears in mind the complete absence of grounds for hope before 1959, especially in the countryside. And the succession of political and social changes, year after year, no doubt helps maintain enthusiasm.

Groups other than wage-earners have more reason to oppose the Revolution. Certainly the former rich are in most ways worse off and feel strongly hostile. They suffer most from the political restraints and yet lose most by the economic changes. Luxury goods are hard to get; meals are difficult to vary; foreign travel is virtually impossible (except to the Soviet Union and Eastern Europe); the nationalization of property has reduced their incomes.[71] Moreover, social changes, such as the training of domestic servants for other jobs and the abolition of private schools and beaches, are directly against their interests.

The middle classes, too, have many possible grounds for discontent. The equalization of incomes is in part at their expense, and they may particularly resent conformist tendencies. The professional often cannot avoid taking a stand one way or another on political questions; many teachers, for example, object to the pressure put to them to adapt their instruction to current political requirements. On the other hand, some in the professions find they have greater scope for work (e.g., in architecture and engineering).

In fact, support for the regime is evidently strongly correlated with former income, as it is also with skin color (though this may be largely a reflection of the income effect, since race was itself correlated with income), and with age.

Large numbers have been leaving Cuba as refugees. The net recorded surplus of departures over arrivals in international travel to and from Cuba was 217,000 from July 1, 1959, to June 30, 1962, according to official data shown me. This amounts to 1 per cent of the population a year and corresponds to the fact that two DC-6's of Pan American Airways used to leave every day for Miami before the "missile crisis." In addition, there were illegal departures, and consequently the actual gross emigration must have been higher than 1 per cent. (There were several thousand immigrants in that period, including many Cubans returning from the United States to help the government, as well as hundreds from Latin America and the socialist countries.)

The policy of the government in permitting emigration had obvious political consequences, since it gradually removed much of the opposition.[72] But it also has economic implications, for it meant a serious loss of professional and technical skill. Yet on the other hand, it provided the government with a supply of large houses and cars, since refugees who ran these had to give them up. It also reduced the demand for consumer goods, and at the same time it changed the composition of this demand, since those who left were in large part consumers of luxuries.[73] The natural increase in population in Cuba is about 2.5 per cent a year, but the net increase was 1.5 per cent, after allowing for migration.

v

One economic consequence of these social reforms has been a change in the balance of the market for consumer goods. According to estimates given me by JUCEPLAN (Central Planning Board), wages and the profits of the self-employed rose by 40 per cent between 1958 and 1961, attributable about equally to the increase in the average income and to the reduction in unemployment (including seasonal unemployment). This figure seems to me quite plausible. There were some more gains in employment in the following year, though little further change in average wages. This suggests that total wages rose by about 50 per cent between 1958 and 1962.

Table 10. Retail Price Index in Havana (Metropolitan Area), 1958-62

	% of total	May 1958	May 1961	May 1962
		(1953 = 100)		
Food	43.1	100	103	109
Rents and house operation	27.4	99	81	83
Clothing and footwear	8.4	99	125	163
Other	21.1	101	95	96
All items	100.	100.9	97.1	103.5

Source: *Costo de vida* (Ministry of Labor mimeographed report, June, 1962).

The Ministry of Labor told me that pensions had risen by more than 70 per cent in the same period; this was partly because pensions were now payable to those injured while fighting with the rebel army (or to widows of those killed) and partly because many workers who had not previously had enough service to qualify under one of the industry schemes now receive a basic pension (usually of 25 pesos a month).[74] In addition, of course, the number of the elderly has been growing.

There have been two offsetting factors. One was the sharp decline in income from property, owing to expropriation. Second, deductions from employment incomes for all purposes (social security, income tax, etc.) rose from about 6 per cent before the Revolution to nearly 12 per cent in 1962 for incomes of less than 250 pesos a month; and for higher incomes the increase in tax rates has been even larger (and evasion has been greatly reduced).[75] All in all, it seems that disposable personal incomes must have risen by about a third in those four years.

We must now allow for price rises. According to the official index, there was at first a decline (due to the decreed reduction in rents and charges for services, such as transport and electricity, after nationalization), but in 1961 prices started to rise (Table 10), so that by the middle of 1962 they were some 2.5 per cent above their 1958 level. Although the index seemed to me soundly constructed and competently run, it understates the true increase for a number of reasons. One is that the goods available have changed beyond recognition in many cases (with Soviet products replacing those from the United States), and there is little doubt that quality has generally declined. Some attempt has been made to allow for this, but it is very hard to estimate quantitatively what the deterioration of quality amounted to.[76] Second, one or two items which have become more costly are not included in the index—rum, for example, which has gone up in price from pesos 1.25 to 3.50 (standard grades). Third, the proportion for clothing looks low by international standards, and this would give the index a downward bias in the years following 1958. Fourth, the decline in rents would be less important to households outside Havana. Fifth, certain items are not readily available (e.g., a shirt in the size required), so people have to buy more expensive substitutes, or only a limited quantity may be available at the controlled price (which is used in the index), the remainder being sold at a much higher price. Chicken, for example, has been sold through INRA (National Institute of Agrarian Reform) at 53 cents a pound, but small farmers can often obtain over 2 pesos a pound (they have to transport the fowl to market themselves). Restaurant meals, which have become much more costly, are a similar case.

Still, food sold at controlled prices accounts for the great majority of purchases. Ignoring quality changes for the moment, the price rise from 1958 to 1962 would not have been more than 10 per cent, so that the increase in the real purchasing power of personal income must have been of the order of 20 per cent. But this rise was not uniform. The increase in both employment and average income has been bigger in agriculture than in other sectors; moreover, a good deal of the construction work, especially in the early years, took place either in small towns or in the countryside. On the other hand, the increase in taxes and decline in property income especially affected Havana and the other large cities. Broadly speaking, total real disposable income rose considerably in the country districts but perhaps hardly at all in Havana.

What happened to real consumption over the same period? Reliable data on consumption are very hard to find. One clue is the rations of food. Table 11 shows the rations in the middle of 1962. These rations were in general honored, as far as I could

Table 11. The Food Rations Established in March, 1962[a]
(Per person)

Whole country
Animal or vegetable fats	2 lbs. a month
Rice	6 lbs. a month
Beans	1.5 lbs. per month

Havana
Beef	¾ lb. a week
Chicken	2 lbs. a month
Fish	1 lb. a month
Ground vegetables	3.5 lbs. a week (5½ lbs. for children under 7)
Butter	⅛ lb. a month
Milk	⅕ liter a day (1 liter for children under 7)

a. There is also rationing of soaps, detergents, and toothpaste in 26 cities, including Havana, and some canned foods can only be obtained from time to time (grocers distributing them to customers in turn).
Source: Regulations of March 13, 1962 under Law 1015.

gather, except for the three items listed first in Table 11 in some small towns and country districts, where organization was weak, though of course there is no way of verifying this point, and there were undoubtedly exceptions even in Havana.

It should not be concluded from the existence of rationing that food consumption standards are on the average lower than before the Revolution. In the first place, the scheme mainly applies to the one-fifth of the population living in Havana. Elsewhere few things are rationed (though many are hard to find). In fact the rationing scheme is in part a response to the difficulty of supplying the capital. Since the countryside is relatively better off financially and since, in addition, supplies of consumer goods that farmers might themselves purchase are inadequate, a smaller surplus of food is available for the cities. Food farmers may well be eating a good deal more; in country districts before the Revolution, the typical rural family hardly ever ate meat or eggs or drank milk. In some cases farmers are apparently dissatisfied with the buying prices offered by INRA. Moreover, INRA has not yet solved the organizational problems of getting foodstuffs to the capital, and sometimes food available for distribution is never collected.

Second, there are several foodstuffs which are not rationed, even in Havana. The most important are wheat and sugar and their products. These are readily available at fairly reasonable prices.[77] The consumption of wheat (including flour) is said to have risen from 169,000,000 kgs. in 1958 to 275,000,000 kgs. in 1961.[78] The ration of eggs and milk in Havana is higher than national average consumption was in 1953. Food is also readily available in restaurants, bars, etc., though usually rather heavy in starch there (rice, spaghetti, etc.), and meals are provided at a considerable number of schools.

In the case of items rationed nationally, however, per-capita consumption has declined by one-half or more since before the Revolution.[79] These used to provide much of the diet.

The *rationed* articles in Havana would provide 1,307 calories a day for somebody over 7 and 2,155 for a child under 7, according to an appraisal made for me by the nutritional research office of a university.[80] These figures can be compared with a national average of 1,860 for the same products in 1953 according to Oshima.[81] Since Havana almost certainly used to be better off nutritionally than the national average, it seems very likely that, even allowing for additional bread,[82] average food consumption must have fallen there. It may well have increased, however, in the countryside.

It is worthwhile digressing for a moment to discuss the absolute level of nourishment in Havana in April through August, 1962. A physiologist tells me that, even without purchasing bread or sugar, an adult could survive for a long time on the ration. Allowing for bread and sugar, there would be no question of acute hunger, though the diet would be monotonous, and it would hardly be adequate for expectant mothers or children aged over 7. The ration for younger children is considered quite sufficient.[83] In fact a daily liter of milk is far above what would be customary in any other Latin American city. As stated above, midday meals are also increasingly being supplied to school children, including those in nursery schools. Evidently, as a whole, the Cuban food supply is considerably better than it was in the United Kingdom for the years 1942-47, say.

What can be fairly confidently said is that there are far fewer people, especially children, seriously undernourished than before the Revolution. One must not forget that the departure of the rich and their partial impoverishment would in itself lower the average food consumption—or, to put this point another way, the average used to be unrepresentative of what the great majority of the people consumed. This would have been especially true of Havana.

Judging from shortages, although prices are much higher, private consumption of clothing and footwear has probably declined, especially of the latter, even ignoring quality deterioration. (In November, 1962, according to press reports, clothing was also put on rationing.) In addition, a large range of consumer durables cannot be purchased (e.g., motor cars and refrigerators) or are now being imported in much smaller quantities than previously (e.g., motorcycles, electric irons); whisky and beer supplies have declined; and foreign travel is greatly reduced. On the other hand, the consumption of books and periodicals, inland travel (including restaurant services), entertainment, soft drinks, and cigarettes has probably increased greatly, and so has the use of dwelling space (through the building of large numbers of new homes and flats) and of electricity. All in all, it may well be that total real consumption has not fallen.[84]

In fact, it would be hard to understand the general condition of markets if total real consumption had fallen significantly. The propensity to spend must have risen about in line with real consumer income—i.e., some 20 per cent (see above). It is true that a big drive to induce workers to save has apparently had some success (thousands have opened savings accounts), and the elimination of consumer credit must have helped reduce consumption. But the much more equal income distribution is a strong influence in the other direction, and so perhaps is the memory of a currency reform in 1961 (which confiscated part of the banknote circulation in private hands).

If there had been a fall in real consumption, then, we would have found in 1962 an acute general excess demand. The general state of consumer's markets is at once understandable if one compares it with markets in the United Kingdom in the second half of 1940, for instance (or about 1948). Queues form rapidly if items in short supply appear (such as razor blades, children's shoes, nylon stockings); these are sold on limited-amount-per-customer basis. Bars, cinemas, nightclubs are usually full to capacity, even on weekdays, and so are trains and buses. But it is difficult to believe that the excess demand signaled by these observations amounted to more than 20 per cent of what people wanted to spend, in view of the level of inventories in the shops, even food shops.

We can get some confirmation of this general conclusion from the balance of savings. In 1962 heavy losses were occurring in many state enterprises, and there was big expenditure on education and health services. In fact, the overall deficit in the public sector (taking account of current and capital items) was likely, according to a planning office official, to be equivalent to a sum not far short of 20 per cent of total disposable personal income. Some of this deficit was covered by the import surplus (i.e., by credits from the Soviet Union and associated countries) and by further inventory liquidation. Still, personal savings must, to balance the deficit, have accounted for between 10 per cent and 20 per cent of disposable income. This is considerably higher than one would expect voluntary savings to be, but again the figures are not consistent with view that there is *very* heavy excess demand or that real consumption fell.

The general conclusion one can reach on this evidence is that there may have been some rise in real private consumption, but it was certainly less than 20 per cent and probably was no greater than the rise in population (which amounted to about 8 per cent in this period). If quality could be taken into account, a rise in private consumption would be more doubtful. On the other hand, the government is supplying a good deal of what would previously have been bought. Examples are meals for schoolchildren—especially for the tens of thousands of boarders (who also receive clothing)—militia uniforms and boots (which are worn off-duty), rural medical services, and new beach facilities.

There is still another way of approaching this problem: by asking ourselves what happened to the supply of consumer goods. Our starting point here would be data on employment (Table 12). A word is necessary on these statistics. Though the 1960 labor census appears to have been carried out in a serious spirit, the figures for the other two years have little factual basis. It is highly unlikely that the population over fourteen years old grew as fast as is indicated (over 2 per cent a year), in view of emigration.

Table 12. Changes in Manpower, 1958-62
(In thousands)

	Estimate 1958	Estimate 1960	Estimate or Target 1962	Estimated increase 1958-62	
				Number	Per cent
Population over 14	4,159	4,346	4,552	393a	9a
Less sick or in prison	90	92	97	7	8
Less students, armed forces, and pensioners	322	391	493	171	53
Less housewives	1,538	1,555	1,561	23	1
Labor force	2,209	2,308	2,401	192a	9a
Less Unemployedᵇ	627	376	215	—412	—66
In employment	1,582	1,932	2,186	604a	38a
Agriculture	598	806	915	317a	53a
Industry and mining	366	431	473	107	29
Construction	54	82	150	96	178
Transport	94	110	121	27	29
Distribution	180	188	188	8	4
Other services	289	315	339	50	17

a. Believed to be too high (see text).
b. Includes partly employed.
Source: Primer Estudio Provisional del Balance de Recursos de Trabajo (Ministry of Labor memorandum, dated May 23, 1962, based in part on the 1960 census of employment). Figures are presumably annual averages.

On the other hand the decline in unemployment, the main source of increase in numbers at work, looks plausible, and the 1962 figure is consistent with the number of identity cards issued to the unemployed in July and August of that year.[85] Some increase has certainly taken place, too, in the proportion of housewives at work (for example, those brought into teaching and wives of those previously enjoying property incomes). Perhaps one-third would be a better estimate of the rise in the number in employment than 38 per cent.[86] A downward adjustment should also probably be made to the numbers employed in agriculture; one reason for thinking this is that the 1962 figure was to some extent a target, and the authorities found it more difficult than they expected to recruit additional agricultural labor in 1962. The increase shown for agriculture might be as much as 100,000 too high (conversely, the rise shown for services may be somewhat too low, in view of the big increase in education). However, looking on the table as a way of showing the effect of the natural growth of the labor force and of the reduction in unemployment, it may not be so misleading.

There must have been some decline in agricultural output by 1962, in view of the low sugar crop. The fall in productivity was sharp. On the other hand, it is now believed by the authorities that industrial output grew by about a third between 1958 and 1962 (rather less if price rises are taken into account). If this were true, it would indicate little change in productivity, because employment rose in about the same proportion; but it must be judged cautiously, since the data are bad and have been quite differently interpreted in the past by Cuban officials. There must have been big increases in some other sectors (e.g., transport). For service industries, at least on national accounting definitions, there has been no change in productivity, so the rise in employment implies higher output. All in all, the total domestic product must have risen, possibly by a moderate amount, though it may well have changed little between 1961 and 1962, in view of the fall in sugar output (which would have reduced the national product by about 5 per cent, *ceteris paribus*).

Because of low exports (mainly due to the fall in farm output), the import surplus in 1962 must have been larger than in 1958, but on the other hand there was probably some deterioration in the terms of trade. Whereas in 1958 the United States paid 5.41 cents a pound for crude 96° Cuban sugar, in 1961 the Soviet Union paid on average 3.93 cents. The average for all crude sugar exports fell from 4.30 cents in 1959 to 3.72 cents in 1961. Evidence on import prices is inconclusive; generally, prices of fuel and capital goods are said to be lower, but those of consumer goods higher; there is unlikely to have been a fall, on balance.

So the total volume of goods and services available, at constant prices, may not have risen much more than the product. The total of investment and public current expenditure rose considerably (Table 13). Omitting public debt interest, and deducting $175,000,000 for social security expenditure (almost all transfers), total public expenditure in 1962 on goods and services, current and capital, was about $1,500,000,000. Since the budget

Table 13. Public Expenditure Budgets, 1957-58 and 1962
(In millions of pesos)

	1957-58	1962
Economic development	45	703
Social and cultural	98	569a
Military	94	247
Administration	83	195
Public debt	40	116
Other	5	24
Total	365	1,854

a. Of which education accounts for 238, social security 175, public health 89, science and culture 33, social assistance 21, and sport and recreation 14.
Sources: *Trimestre de Finanzas al Día*, No. 1 (April, 1962); *Suplemento del Directorio Financiero* (Ministry of Finance).

now contains nearly all the country's capital formation, this figure should be compared with the total of investment (public and private) and government consumption in 1958, which was $747,-000,000.[87] A rise of about $800,000,000 has occurred, then, which must have been nearly all a "real" rise, because salaries in government did not change greatly. The rise in the volume of non-consumption spending must have been equivalent to about one-fifth of the 1958 product, which was possibly less than the rise in available supplies, leaving something for a rise in real private consumption.

In parenthesis, note should be taken of the very rapid expansion of the budget. This has grown since the Revolution from 390,000,000 pesos in 1959, to 756,000,000 in 1960, to 1,330,000,-000 in 1961, to 1,854,000,000 in 1962.[88]

The rise was due primarily to current spending. In 1961 public investment of all types accounted for $427,000,000,[89] though this figure may not be complete (for example, it would not include all the capital equipment imported). Even if there was, as is probable, a big rise in investment in 1962, with an increase in imports of equipment, current spending must still have accounted for most of the increase in spending—owing in part to increased educational outlays.

"Economic development" expenditure is not identical with investment, because some capital outlays are excluded (e.g., schools and houses) and some of the expenditure under this heading is

Table 14. Government Budget for Economic Development in 1962 (In millions of $)

Agriculture	112
Industry	208
Commerce	15
Communication	48
Transport	88
Basic services	233
Total	703

Source: Trimestre de Finanzas al Día, No. 1 (April, 1962).

current-account. Nevertheless, it provides a good clue to the weight of investment, and the breakdown shown in Table 14, is interesting particularly as evidence of rather low investment in agriculture.[90]

Various pieces of evidence are therefore not inconsistent with the picture that there may have been some increase in consumption,[91] but nevertheless disposable income has risen more, so that there is a moderate excess of demand in the economy.

What are in fact seen are the familiar symptoms of suppressed inflation. Partly because of a bad harvest but also because of an inadequate rate of advance in substitution for certain types of imports, particular shortages appeared. The change in economic direction involved a big rise in government current and capital spending, without a corresponding increase in receipts, so that general excess demand also arose. Cuba has therefore not avoided the upward pressure on prices experienced in other Latin American economies. If the problem was not very acute in 1962, it was partly because at an early stage of converting an "open" economy into one where foreign supplies of consumer goods were limited, there were still new equipment and excess capacity. (Note that such pressures are mild so far in Venezuela, which has also only recently pursued an active policy of import restriction.)

Nevertheless, the symptoms are different in Cuba. The prices of all key commodities, including staple foodstuffs, have been frozen at 1958 levels, and wage increases have also been held in check (after initial rises), largely because of official influence in the unions. Broadly, this system of controls has worked. Productivity declines, however, combined with price controls, have meant losses in state enterprises. The consequences, as in the industrial countries in wartime, have been queues for non-essentials, and rationing of basic foods (and now clothing), which was adopted to prevent great inequalities in consumption and also to avert the need to spend time searching and queuing for supplies.

Some cumulative tendencies familiar to Latin Americans have also appeared. Costs have tended to rise, especially in agriculture, because labor has been attracted by the higher wages paid by the expanding industries, so that shortages, especially of skilled farm workers, have hampered production. The attempt to control prices of necessities has meant that the public sector has been involved in heavy losses, while the private sector has at times been unwilling to deliver. These distortions have not, however, been allowed to affect, as is often the case elsewhere in the region, the pattern of investment, which is determined without respect to profit.

One way of easing the excess and stimulating output of goods in short supply would be to let prices rise. This has in fact been done to some extent (Table 10 shows the rise in clothing prices between 1961 and 1962), but so far the authorities have been reluctant to touch prices of essentials, no doubt because this would create demands for wage rises which would be hard to handle.

The experience of Cuba not only shows the pressures other Latin American countries have experienced, it has brought out one additional problem that would face any predominantly agricultural country which adopted collectivization. Suppose there is a bad crop, for whatever reason (e.g., drought). The supply of foodstuffs falls, but wages in state farms continue to be paid as before. Consequently, excess demand tends to appear, unless prices are allowed to rise. The form this problem takes is liable to be a shortage in food supplies to the cities.

Note the difference here between the working of capitalist and socialist agricultural systems.[92] If the value of the crop falls under capitalism, incomes fall, workers are dismissed, and profits of self-employed farmers decline. The agricultural sector will therefore consume less food. There need be no excess demand in general. Under socialism, however, the link between the incomes generated in the farm sector and the value of its output is broken.

The same problem can arise in the export sector, too, but then it does not matter, provided some other country is willing to allow an imbalance in trade to develop (as apparently happened in the case of Cuba in 1962). One might think that the problem of a bad food harvest could be solved in the same way, but the case is not quite symmetrical. It takes time to order and obtain increased imports (months in the case of an isolated country like Cuba), whereas if exports fail, all that is needed to avoid excess demand appearing is that imports should continue as before.

Theoretically, the problem could arise in manufacturing, too, but then it would be the result of disorganization. The difference is that there is no necessary reason why the manufacturing sector should go into deficit in this way—whereas because of climatic fluctuations, if for no other reason, it *is* inevitable at times for collective farms. Moreover, as we have seen, it is much easier politically to let the prices of manufactures than of foodstuffs rise. Where the collectivized agricultural sector is big, this may be a considerable problem.

These considerations do not by any means constitute an overwhelming argument against agricultural countries' adopting socialism. After all, it may well be better that the consequences of inevitable fluctuations in the weather should be shifted to the public as a whole, instead of being borne by the rural population alone. And there is no reason why the resultant excess demand should be unmanageable. Reserves of foods are one obvious answer if they can be built up or imported. In fact, in good years, savings would arise in agriculture, and the surplus could be hoarded (except that the pressure of need for food may make this restraint hard to achieve). The planning authorities might be sufficiently well informed and alert to import food as soon as rainfall data could be read as a warning. But this discussion does have some implications for the controversy of cooperation versus collectivism; personal incomes of a farm sector genuinely organized along cooperative lines would fluctuate with the total revenue of the sector, and the problem need not then arise.

vi

Institutional history since the Revolution falls into four distinct phases. The first, from January, 1959, to June, 1960, was a period in which there was little attempt at state control. Some properties were "intervened" (managed by an appointee of the state)—e.g., the telephone company.[93] Agrarian reform became law in June, 1959, and shortly afterwards expropriations of large holdings and the distribution of titles started, but the agricultural sector remained predominantly private. During this period economic transactions continued along more or less conventional lines. The United States bought, as traditionally, most of the sugar and tobacco crops and provided most of the imports. Despite a growing use of controls, especially of foreign exchange, decisions were still mostly made by private owners.

The next period, from June, 1960, to February, 1961, was one of rapid institutional change. First, the petroleum refineries were nationalized (after the companies refused to refine Soviet oil). In July (following the abolition of the Cuban sugar quota in the United States), U.S. sugar companies were expropriated and cooperatives formed. Shortly afterwards, the same happened to American-owned factories and the electric power and telephone systems; and in October, banks, as well as the bulk of urban housing, were taken over. In the same month, nationalization of businesses owned by Cubans began. Early in 1961, state-administered farms (and some non-sugar cooperatives) were consolidated into large *granjas del pueblo*.

After these expropriations, there at first was no very great change of economic substance. The new state-appointed administrators (often selected on political grounds rather than for their personal capacity) improvised as best they could to keep their units running, more or less as previously; and any dislocation was cushioned by the existence of inventories, which could be run down (at least for a while), and by the labor availability that still remained. The first "people's crop" (*zafra del pueblo*) of sugar turned out, at nearly 7,000,000 tons, to be the second largest in Cuban history.[94]

The most noticeable change was a complete switch in the direction of the island's foreign trade. As relations with the

Table 15. Cuban Foreign Trade, 1958-61
(In millions of pesos)

	1958	1959	1960	1961
Imports, f.o.b.	808	673	580	670
Exports	763	675	618	643

Source: International Monetary Fund, *International Financial Statistics* (for 1958 and 1959), and Ministry of Foreign Trade (for other years).

United States deteriorated (culminating with the U.S. embargo on exports in October, 1960), trade negotiations with the Soviet Union were rapidly expanded. The Soviet negotiators agreed to take 4,000,000 tons of sugar, though at a lower price than the United States had paid. Exports to the Soviet Union, which were valued at 13,000,000 pesos in 1959 and 104,000,000 in 1960, jumped to 301,000,000 in 1961 (the corresponding figures for China were zero, 32,000,000, and 92,000,000, and for Eastern Europe as a whole 1,000,000, 14,000,000, and 65,000,000).[95] Foreign credits were also arranged, and short-term financial arrangements made to cover temporary imbalances. Imports started to rise and approximately regained the levels of 1959 (Table 15).

Although there was no real central direction of the economy in this period, a start was made. One compelling reason was that a national shopping list had to be prepared for discussions with the Soviet Union. But in addition the state had to organize and coordinate the large number of enterprises it had recently acquired and was still acquiring, if it were to solve the island's basic economic and social problems.

The third phase opened with the strengthening of the planning office, the so-called JUCEPLAN, in February, 1961. It was given the task of preparing an annual plan for 1962 and a four-year plan for the period 1962-65. The government modeled its planning techniques on those developed in the Soviet Union and Eastern Europe—indeed, there are no other models for an economy which is mostly nationalized. A number of experts from these countries were invited to Havana to help establish the system,[96] and 1962 was designated as "the year of plan-making" (*año de planificación*). Political statements characterized the country as a "people's democracy," "Marxist-Leninist," etc.

This phase can be described as one of euphoric planning. Thus in August, 1961, at a conference on production, Regino Boti, the Minister of Economics and head of JUCEPLAN, stated that from 1962 to 1965 the total production of Cuba would grow annually by "not less than 10 per cent and probably [!] not more than 15.5 per cent." By 1965 per-capita consumption would have risen by more than 60 per cent in comparison with 1958, and Cuba would be, in relation to its population, the most industrialized country in Latin America. He went on: "I want to affirm that if we raise our eyes and contemplate the picture of Cuba in 10 years' time, we arrive at the conclusion that Cuba will overcome passing difficulties and within 9 or 10 years we shall achieve the highest level of living in Latin America by an ample margin, a level of living as high as almost any country in Europe."[97] At the same conference, Néstor Lavergne, sub-director of planning, referring to the former workers who were now at the head of nationalized firms and factories, said that, though the majority of them had had little previous experience in management, their efficiency was "much greater than that of the former owners." The speech of Guevara at Punta del Este in the same month envisaged a sugar crop of 8,500,000 to 9,000,000 tons in 1965.[98]

In December, 1961, the same general long-term targets were being mentioned by Boti,[99] though the sugar target had been revised: "The annual sugar output will vary between 7,000,000 and 7,500,000 tons in the period 1962-65." Some emphasis was put on statistical and organizational weaknesses, but these, it was stated, were being rapidly overcome. The immediate target for agriculture was "the elimination of queues and problems of supply in 1962."

As will be evident from the analysis above, general excess demand had emerged by this time, and food crops were proving disappointing. As the months passed food shortages grew worse, especially in Havana, and people had to go from shop to shop in search of supplies. A system of registration was improvised, under which people received milk and fats in turn at their grocer's. Despite an apparent rise in industrial output, shortages also grew more severe in clothing and other manufactured consumer goods, although the administration remained optimistic.[100]

In March, 1962, the system of rationing was established, marking a recognition of the seriousness of the problems of supply and thus initiating the fourth phase, one of growing realism. Castro introduced rationing with a television broadcast in which he said, "It is necessary, without any doubt, to speak with complete frankness. The most serious problem the Revolution has had to face is that of supplies."[101] Apart from the increase in purchasing power (and the change in its distribution), he mentioned the following reasons for food shortages: the lack of experienced managers, which could not be easily made good; the inadequate rainfall; and the failure of peasants to deliver food (partly because they no longer needed money to pay rent). The speech was marked by a forthright recognition of the misleading character of earlier statements.[102]

The sugar crop of 1962 turned out to be only 4,800,000 tons, over 2,000,000 tons lower than in 1961 despite the mobilization of much voluntary labor. Moreover, in August the new head of INRA, Carlos Rafael Rodríguez, declared that the target for 1963 would simply be to repeat the 4,800,000 crop of 1962. The failure in supplies of fodder and vegetables in the middle of 1962 drove home the lesson that problems lay ahead, as did the necessity in September to use once more volunteers on a large scale (mostly students) to pick the coffee crop. The final blow was that even the low target for the 1963 sugar crop was not nearly achieved.

One major cause of the difficulties was that equipment which had arrived from overseas was not being brought into production, often because the necessary management and labor had not been found. A good deal of machinery remained on the docks until it had to be removed (sometimes to lie in a field) in order to make way for other imports.

In retrospect, the mistakes of 1961 can be attributed to a number of serious miscalculations. The first was that, in the wave of the self-confidence generated by the successful sugar crop and repulsion of the invasion attempt, the government did not notice the acuteness of certain problems. Equipment was running down, often owing to inadequate maintenance routines, and inventories were getting low. With imports from the United States declining fast, it was necessary to find new sources for materials, spare parts, and goods which were a customary part of the Cuban worker's standard of living. Buyers were not familiar with supply conditions in the Communist countries or even with the needs of the Cuban economy.

The magnitude of the task that Cuba was attempting does not seem to have been understood by the administration. To turn a country like Cuba in 1958 into an advanced industrial economy in a few years would be a most remarkable achievement, especially in view of the continuing departure (or dismissal) of managers and technicians. Everywhere else in the world that change took decades, if not centuries. It was not just a matter of establishing new factories and raising their output (though this is hard enough, especially since the increases in output of various products need to be synchronized). Such drastic industrial expansion meant that services such as transport and electricity had to be adapted to the needs of an industrial economy, rather than a sugar economy, and that the labor force had to be trained and reallocated, preferably without a big increase in the wage bill.

What has been thrown into sharp focus by the experience of Cuba, and this is of wider significance for all development policy, is that organization, rather than capital, is the clue to really rapid structural change.

A planning organization cannot be created overnight. One big snag for Cuba was the shortage of statistics; and such statistics as did exist were of very doubtful reliability. Traditionally, Cuba has been weak statistically, even by comparison with other Latin American countries of the same income level, but in 1960 and early 1961 the quantity and quality of statistics may have become even worse. Following the nationalization of industry, the flow of information stopped from some of the key factories. In addition, the customs administration passed from the Ministry of Finance to the Ministry of External Trade, which had no organization for compiling trade statistics from customs warrants. Import figures by category of merchandise were not tabulated for 1960 (those for 1961 were only tabulated in September, 1962). Agricultural statistics (except for sugar cane and tobacco) have always been so bad that they could hardly have got worse, but their quality was very far short of what is needed for economic planning. During the course of 1961, collection of statistics started to improve in many fields, and many new types of data were being compiled, but this was far too late to yield results that could be used in either the 1962 plan or that for 1962-65.

The consequences of this statistical weakness were aggravated by an overambitious attempt at detailed planning, owing to the uncritical adoption of planning methods being used in the Soviet Union and Czechoslovakia. Some 500 detailed "national balances" (i.e., broadly, plans for the output and input of various branches of industry) were drawn up. These were based either on statements of administrators made in the heat of enthusiasm of production conferences (at various levels) or else represented what someone in Havana, far removed from actual problems of production, thought was possible. For example, the agricultural forecasts apparently took little account of the attitude of private producers, who still controlled about half the agricultural land.

When it came to checking on performance and seeing that units achieved their targets, there were other difficulties. One was the weakness of the planning office vis-à-vis the other ministries. Another was the continued uncertainty about the relations between ministers and the corresponding productive units; there were doubt about where decisions should be made and often long delays in handling correspondence,[103] which were aggravated by the overloading of postal and telegraph services.[104] Financial control was weak because of lack of coordination between the Banco Nacional and the Ministry of Finance. Thus state enterprises were able to escape in part from financial discipline by running down balances (or obtaining advances), or by getting into debt with other state organizations.[105]

In individual productive units, disorganization became severe. Under-utilization of machinery and long periods of labor idleness were by no means uncommon. Often plant layout was changed without good reason, and central policy to increase food production by uprooting cane plants (itself a very doubtful decision) was interpreted in a way that ruined much of the best sugar land. There were many cases, both in agriculture and in industry, in which the manager really did not understand the production process, and he was then likely to resist technical inspection from above or criticism in assemblies of employees. Monthly targets were sometimes ignored.

But above all, no accepted framework for economic policy was created. The regime had inherited structures of prices and wages which, for reasons explained above, were rather odd. These structures have, however, largely been retained. Difficulties were increased by the excess demand that developed. These high incomes in certain sectors[106] helped to attract labor from which it was most needed, especially in some agricultural areas. Adjustments were made to prices and wages from time to time, but there was no general policy on what circumstances justified freezing or raising them, or on how much excess demand could be tolerated. The deficits of various state enterprises meant that many lines of consumption were being subsidized, but whether they should receive subsidies, and how much, was hardly being considered.[107] Nor was there any clear conception of the role of the private sector in agriculture or what stimuli were needed to enable it to fulfill this role.

The problem of seasonality in agriculture had not been tackled either. Spare labor was not going to wait for short-lived (and unpleasant) employment cutting cane when it could get year-round employment on construction projects or in nearby state farms.[108] Moreover, the unemployed were concentrated in Havana and awaited work in industry (Table 16 contains data on unemployment in 1960; even then there had not been much spare agricultural labor during the sugar harvest). The 1962 crop, small though it was, was only gathered at the expense of an enormous effort mobilizing voluntary (and not very efficient) workers. Essentially, the government has used voluntary labor to make up for deficiencies in planning. But this is not without its costs; there may be a reduction in output in the industries from which volunteers come, and students (the main source) are only obtained at the price of lower-quality professional work in the future. Seasonality, then, is another fundamental problem if a specialized agricultural economy is to be run by central planning or, indeed, even if it is organized in any way that involves a high degree of employment of labor.[109]

Table 16. Unemployment in April, 1960[a]
(In thousands)

By province and sex			By last occupation and sex			By duration of unemployment and sex		
	M.	*F.*		*M.*	*F.*		*M.*	*F.*
Havana	104	82	Agricultural			25 weeks and		
Pinar del Río	22	15	labor	75	3	over[c]	68	46
Matanzas	12	11	Labor in			15 to 25 weeks	28	12
Las Villas	46	29	industry and			5 to 15 weeks	64	27
Camagüey	25	11	mining	107	38	Less than 5		
Oriente[d]	97	18	Labor in			weeks	43	29
Total	306	166	transport and			Not specified[b]	73	52
			communica-				306	166
			tions	16	1			
			Selling and					
			office work	32	12			
			Personal					
			service	18	48			
			Not specified[b]	58	63			
				306	166			

a. Those more than fourteen years old seeking work in week of April 4 to 10, 1960, including pensioners, persons never employed, and those previously self-employed.

b. Includes those who had never been employed.

c. Includes 38 and 32 for Havana, respectively.

d. Coverage was not complete in isolated areas of this province.

Source: Censo laboral, 1960 (Ministry of Labor).

At the start, the whole agricultural problem was underestimated, in fact. The view (well-founded) that physically large increases in farm output were possible because of previous underutilization of land and labor led JUCEPLAN to devote its attention to the professionally more exciting task of selecting the new industries to be set up.

The cost of the lag in agricultural supplies has been serious. It has forced workers—not merely town workers but those in the country too—to spend part of their time searching for food. In the case of farm workers, this necessity has affected food output itself; in the case of town workers, absenteeism for this reason (and others) has limited the output of goods which would stimulate the rural population to work harder and eat less.[110] There has therefore really been a breakdown in the exchange of goods between town and country, which evidently has possibilities of being cumulative (though this analysis also implies that any increase in agricultural output would help raise the output of manufactures, and vice versa).

Of course, again these problems must be looked at in perspective. Almost any degree of disorganization would have been preferable to the complete failure in Cuba in earlier years (and in several other Latin American countries) to mobilize the factors of production. The chronic, apparently incurable poverty and unemployment of that period, combined with "feather-bedding" and little technical progress, has given place to what is at least a hope that the direction taken by the economy will eventually yield favorable results, including tolerable living conditions and a degree of economic independence.

And while the Cuban government has made serious mistakes, so have other governments in Latin America. No single error in Cuba's planning seems comparable to that of Brazil in setting up ten motor vehicle manufacturing plants when it is doubtful whether the market was big enough for three. In addition it is certainly better to make mistakes in a drive for food production than to leave arable land unused (as is the case with so much of the land in Colombia, for example).

The mistakes made by the planning authorities appear not to be very different from those made in other socialist countries. For example, John Michael Montias describes over-optimism as typical of the stage when detailed central planning is introduced. The reasons seem to be universally the same: underemployed rural labor is quickly mobilized, big initial increases in output are achieved, non-priority industries can temporarily be neglected, re-equipment can be delayed, etc; on the other hand, statistics are inaccurate and the authorities fail to realize fully what is involved in achieving planning targets.[111]

To some extent, of course, the function of a plan is to hold out to people the vision of rapid improvement rather than appraising what may reasonably be expected. In fact, raising a target may actually increase the chance that it will be achieved, since labor and management are not independent variables but are themselves in part affected by the statements of policy about the results of their own actions. On the other hand, over-optimism, particularly in an open economy where orders have to be placed some time ahead of requirements, may lead to incorrect decisions and eventually to frustration, declining morale, and a fall in output.

vii

There is evidence that the administration is learning from its mistakes. In the course of 1962, attempts were made to cope with these weaknesses. More and more enterprises were brought under the discipline of accounting systems (including the compilation of estimates of the costs of production), and, as a by-product, statistics were gradually improving. Standard statistical questionnaires were drawn up for the monthly reporting of results, and efforts were made at the provincial level to collect returns from organizations that were not making them. Agriculture was given a much higher priority in the course of 1962, as it was realized that the failure which threatened here could be politically dangerous. Guevara, Minister of Industry, became the president of the council of JUCEPLAN, putting his authority behind it, and one of his senior vice-ministers (Ortuski) was made a permanent official in the organization. Reports on weaknesses in individual industries were commissioned and carefully studied in long joint sessions of JUCEPLAN and the Ministry of Industry. Finally, there were drastic changes in personnel. The head of INRA was replaced at about the same time as food rationing was introduced. And the speech of Castro attacking the Communist leader, Aníbal Escalante, for conspiratorial methods, was, it is widely reported, followed by the weakening of the influence of ORI (Integrated Revolutionary Organization, the union of parties supporting the government) in the economic sphere. In many cases, consequently, administrators who had been appointed mainly for political reasons were replaced by people with more technical knowledge, some of whom, for instance, had been foremen before these farms or factories were nationalized.[112]

A number of steps are being taken to tackle the problems of labor supply. A uniform salary scale has been drawn up, under which workers doing the same job in different industries will receive the same wage.[113] Formulation of the uniform scale required a good deal of research to discover what the technical skills needed in various jobs are, and trade tests applying the results of this research were introduced in the second half of 1962 and administered to the unemployed.

Another step to organize the labor market has been the introduction of identity cards showing the grade of skill of each worker and his standard wage. These serve as a source of information on the distribution of labor and on the flows from one sector to another, but they are also apparently intended to provide the means for controlling labor movement so as to prevent shortages in key sectors.

The problem of shortages of labor to harvest particular crops has been tackled in various ways. Plans were drafted for creating a mobile group of young workers who would pass from district to district, as migrant workers used to do on quite a big scale before the Revolution. Then, about 1,000 mechanical cane-cutters (assembled in Cuba) were used in the 1963 harvest. It was hoped that these machines would ease the most acute problem, but they had yet to prove their worth in long periods of heavy work week after week, used by inexperienced operators, and in some cases far from spare parts or skilled mechanics.

"Norms" were established for the output of individual workers or groups of workers so as to raise productivity, and "emulative" competitions are being increasingly used, with prizes (such as paid holidays at the beach) for those who are especially productive. The conversion of sugar cooperatives into state farms was partly designed to make it easier to require a full day's work from cane-cutters. Heavy propaganda was applied to discourage absenteeism, lateness, waste, etc.

As well, efforts are being intensified to provide education at primary, secondary, and university levels and also to lift rapidly the educational and technical standards of adults. This educational drive amounts to nothing less than an attempt to change in a brief time the human resources available for development—a factor normally considered as given, at least in the short run, in most theoretical or practical treatments of economic development planning. One of the chief lessons of the Cuban Revolution is that to change the quality of the labor supply is at least conceivable.[114] However, one can hardly visualize how adults could be induced to study on this scale but for the promise held out by social change and by the publication of ambitious economic goals.

Meanwhile the planning office has struggled to produce a presentable plan for 1962-65, and the numerous revisions necessitated by the setbacks of 1962 compelled frequent postponement of its publication (due originally early in the year). In general, sights were lowered. The most important new factories are not expected to go into production until after 1965;[115] there is no question now of Cuba being by that date very highly industrialized, relative to other Latin American countries.

The details given elsewhere in this study suggest that the plan as now envisaged falls into two clear stages. In the first stage, up to 1965, investment is mainly being devoted to repairs to sugar mills and textile factories and the construction of new capacity in textiles, foodstuffs, mining, and metal products of various types (including household durables). Altogether $900,000,000 is to be invested in the years 1962-65 (of which some 40 per cent would be covered by credits already granted), including $180,000,000 for electricity. Industrial output as a whole would rise by rather over 70 per cent, or 14.5 per cent a year, from 1961 to 1965, and the output of consumer goods would increase rather faster,[116] as also would electricity production. The increase in output in the sector would amount to $1,600,000,000 for 1961 to 1965, suggesting an incremental capital-output ratio of less than 1, which is partly to be explained by the existence of idle capacity in 1961 but which nevertheless looks low.[117]

Towards the end of this period, work would commence on a steel mill with a capacity of 1,300,000 tons (to cost $150,000,000), a nickel-processing plant (to cost $100,000,000), a cobalt-processing plant (to cost $62,000,000), and a motor-vehicle-assembly plant (to cost $90,000,000). These major heavy projects would come into production in about 1967. They are all to be situated in Oriente, where the nickel and cobalt mines are, and this would therefore become the industrial heart of the country. A big ammonia plant (costing $54,000,000) would be set up in Matanzas, to come into full production by 1968.[118]

So, while the first stage of the plan would involve a big increase in the output of light industries producing consumer goods, after 1965 the emphasis would change and the output of heavy industries would rise much more quickly. The picture therefore is of an attempt—unusual in centrally planned economies—to raise consumption standards sharply *before* turning to the expansion of heavy industries. The fact that it is possible to order equipment in quantity on credit (which the Soviet Union could never do itself in its early years) makes it possible to reverse the traditional order.[119] On these plans, consumption of manufactures would rise quite quickly, while there would be considerable savings on imports of consumer goods from the Soviet Union. It is also intended, however, to start exports of manufactures on a considerable scale to both socialist and capitalist countries by 1965.

Table 17 represents, as well as they could be ascertained, the shape of government intentions for the economy as a whole (though these may have been revised since May, 1962, when it was prepared). The table indicates that the expected increase in the numbers of students (school and university) and of housewives will absorb quite a large proportion of the increase in the population, while the decline in unemployment will slow down markedly, so that the total in employment will grow by only 10 per cent,[120] considerably less than in the period 1958-62. It seems that agriculture, industry, transport, and distribution are all expected to grow approximately in line with the total employed. A decline in domestic service and approximate stability in public administration and other services are expected to permit a further fast rise in the numbers engaged in construction, education, and health services.[121]

It is questionable whether the agricultural labor force will grow at the expected rate, since it implies little net movement into the towns as unemployment falls.[122] It also seems doubtful whether an increase of 36 per cent in the number of teachers will be sufficient (even allowing for the fact that the expansion of primary education will slow down) in view of the shortage in 1961. The major meaning of this table does not, however, rest on the exact figures shown in it; rather it is the clear implication that further economic progress, especially in industry, depends very largely on increasing productivity, now that the main labor reserves are believed to be exhausted.

The table implies that productivity in industry and mining would have to rise at over 10 per cent a year. A sugar crop of 6,500,000 to 7,000,000 tons is envisaged for 1965; this would also involve a sharp rise in agricultural productivity, which is required

Table 17. Planned Changes in Manpower, 1961-65
(In thousands)

	Reference Years		Increase	
	1961	1965	Amount	Per Cent
Population "able to work"[a]	3,695	4,010	315	8
Less students	82	181	99	121
Less sick or in prison	38	41	3	8
Less other outside labor force (housewives, pensioners, etc.)	1,210	1,318	108	9
Labor force	2,365	2,471	106	4
Less unemployed	220[b]	118[b]	—102	—47
In employment	2,145	2,353	208	10
Agriculture	915	989	74	8
Industry and mining	456	498	42	9
Construction	116	169	53	45
Transport	114	126	12	11
Distribution	154	175	21	14
Education	45	61	16	36
Health	37	48	11	30
Public administration	86	90	4	5
Domestic service	50	25	—25	—50
Other service	172	172	——	——

a. Ages not stated.
b. Includes 25,000 partly unemployed.
Source: Primer Estudio Provisional del Balance de Recursos de Trabajo (Ministry of Labor memorandum, dated May 23, 1962).

in any case by the objective of creating self-sufficiency in food-stuffs.[123] (The ending of the drought that has plagued Cuba will bring an automatic improvement in food production.) A large rise in productivity in transport is counted on.[124] Only in construction does it seem that the increase in output would be achieved in large part by recruiting labor.

Whether output will climb as rapidly as is planned depends of course in part on international developments. Cuba is by no means released yet from the need to find secure markets for its sugar and to reduce its dependence on a single customer (formerly the United States, now the Soviet Union). The possibilities of a big expansion of sales to the Soviet Union are doubtless limited, even if this were a desirable development, and apparently it is expected that China will purchase much of the increase in output, as its incomes rise.

A good deal also depends on United States policy. The tighter the embargo, the more difficult it is to keep old machinery running, the more severe are the shortages in certain types of consumer goods, and the more resources are absorbed in military activities. But the net effect of such measures as the embargo is difficult to assess. The embargo provides an excuse for almost any economic difficulty, whether or not it is actually so caused. Moreover, the greater the international tension, the easier it is for the government to appeal to nationalism (which has deep historical roots) and to maintain a high level of enthusiasm among the sections of the public which support it.[125] In any case, as the months pass, the need for supplies from the United States diminishes, because purchases from Communist countries constitute a larger and larger fraction of the vehicles and equipment in use.

Perhaps a more important influence on productivity is organization. Will the steps taken to solve organizational problems succeed? In judging this question, one must allow for the fact that solution will take a long time. Years rather than months are necessary before a decision to collect statistics results in usable information or before new administrators learn to be efficient. On top of this, it must be expected that while organizational methods improve, difficulties will also be increasing. The industrial sector will become more complex, and a big problem will be to put at the disposal of each new major industry all the myriad components and spare parts it will need. To find labor for seasonal sugar work will become increasingly difficult as unemployment declines and jobs become plentiful. After the experience of the past two years, we ought not to fall into the trap of mistaking planned for probable developments. What is physically possible is not necessarily organizationally possible.

Another vital question is morale. At root it is a question of whether enthusiasm will prove sufficiently enduring to withstand setbacks, some of which are inevitable, for example, frustrations in factories due to irregular arrivals of materials. More fundamentally, can a tropical country with a largely uneducated labor force, taught in the past to be acquisitive, successfully build its future on highly centralized planning and an appeal to people to work largely for the common good?

This question cannot yet be answered. But there are two relevant points. One is that there are undoubtedly great possibilities of increasing food output, even if only as a consequence of higher rainfall. The other is the emphasis on the expansion of consumer-goods production in the near future. If the supply of consumer goods rises, the exchange of goods between the countryside and the city (the basic economic requirement) will revive, with possible cumulative effects upwards. In fact, unless disorganization continues to be very acute, Cuba may well make considerable progress over the next decade in its attempt to raise living standards and make the economy less dependent on foreign trade.[126]

In view of the great international uncertainties, one must take into account the possibility that any assessment will be upset by a complete political change. It should be clear from what has already been said, however, that severe problems will have to be faced by anyone who proposes a completely different path, because the Revolution, like all social eruptions, is to a great degree irreversible. What has happened economically would be especially difficult to reverse, because new industries have been established and the pattern of employment has changed. Since by now a large part of the equipment comes from the socialist countries, and factories are becoming accustomed to materials from the same source, a switch back to other suppliers would cause almost as much difficulty as the former turn to Eastern sources. Similarly the identity of private units is becoming merged in new productive organs, and different networks of distribution are being established; another wholesale change in administration would create another organizational crisis. And if the people become accustomed to communal incentives, it may prove hard to return to a system based mainly on private gain. To turn the state farms back to *latifundia* or to foreign ownership would scarcely be practical politics, nor could differences in income be easily re-established. It is difficult to imagine the new social security system's being dismantled or former domestic servants' returning to the kitchen. Educational advances, such as the newly acquired literacy, not merely could scarcely be taken away but have brought distinct changes in attitude. Each year tens of thousands of adolescents enter into adult life after a fairly heavy political education.

The expectations of fast industrialization, with an associated major expansion in higher education and the creation of large numbers of new executive and technical jobs, could not easily be extinguished. Nor could the belief that unemployment can be, and will be, eliminated. Any new regime would therefore be strongly impelled to adopt a program the economic content of which would not be very different (though the degree of popular cooperation, and thus the economic success, would also depend on the political form of the program). If awakened aspirations are a strong force anywhere in the world, they are certainly powerful now in Cuba. They could scarcely be held in check.

PART I

Agriculture

BY ANDRÉS BIANCHI

CHAPTER II

Agriculture

The Pre-Revolutionary
Background

In spite of the historical importance of the Cuban agrarian reform, little is known about the development of Cuban agriculture since the victory of the Revolution. The lack of reliable information is especially severe for the period following the break of diplomatic relations between Cuba and the United States early in 1961. This and the following chapter constitute a partial and necessarily imperfect attempt to bridge this gap. My main concern is to describe and to analyze the institutional and economic changes that occurred in the agricultural sector during the first three and a half years of the Revolution. Nevertheless, as a necessary background, I have outlined basic trends of farm output before 1959 and described the structural characteristics of pre-Revolution Cuban agriculture.

Three general limitations of this study must, however, be noted. The first arises from the fact that relatively short time has elapsed since the agrarian reform started. This, together with other factors explained below, made it difficult to assess, at the end of 1962, the trend of total agricultural output after the Revolution. The production changes analyzed here represent primarily, if not only, the immediate effects of a process characterized by the rapid institutional transformation of agriculture and other sectors of the economy and by a drastic shift in the direction of Cuba's foreign trade. Under these circumstances, only tentative suggestions are offered about the probable changes of farm production in the future.

A second limitation is the marginal treatment the study gives to the substantial and largely irreversible changes in the social structure of rural Cuba which have occurred since the beginning of the agrarian reform. The extent and implications of these changes are analyzed, however, in Dudley Seers's Introduction and are implicit in much of Richard Jolly's part. To consider them here would have resulted in unnecessary duplication. Yet my concentration on economic and institutional matters should not be interpreted to mean that I underestimate the impact of social change on the present and especially the future development of the Cuban economy.

The insufficient quantitative information underlying the sections dealing with economic changes is the third limitation. I did not have free access to the statistical offices of government agencies. This inevitably restricted the scope of the analysis and has prevented a more rigorous treatment of economic developments.

The lack of data has also forced me to rely on qualitative information more than I would otherwise have desired. Much of this information was gathered during visits to people's farms in five of Cuba's six provinces and in talks with a number of candid officials at the regional offices of INRA, the National Institute of Agrarian Reform. Several officials at the Institute's headquarters in Havana were also kind enough to discuss frankly with me some shortcomings of agricultural policies and plans, and also certain aspects of the internal organization of the Institute, the people's farms, and other agricultural units. Nevertheless, whenever possible I have substantiated critical remarks with quotations from articles or statements of government leaders and high administrative authorities.[1]

The economic history of Cuba is to a large extent the history of Cuban agriculture—the trends of farm production and the changing structural characteristics of the agricultural sector have played a dominant role in shaping the course of Cuban economic affairs.

1. Basic Production Trends

Ever since the beginning of the nineteenth century, the expansions and declines of Cuban agriculture have been closely associated with the fate of sugar in the international markets. Prior to that time, farm income depended more heavily on the cultivation of tobacco, with the production of cattle, coffee, and sugar cane also making sizable contributions. Toward the close of the eighteenth century, however, foreign demand for Cuban sugar began to rise.[2] Later, the application of steam power to the methods of processing sugar-cane led to considerable mill mechanization.[3] As a result of rising profits in the sugar industry, the number of mills multiplied in the following decades, with sugar output climbing steadily, while production of tobacco and livestock fell in relative importance, and the coffee industry became insignificant after 1860.

The upward trend of sugar production was reversed during the 1870's by the devastation caused by the Ten Years' War for Independence (1868-78). It resumed, however, in the last decade of the century, following the introduction of new technological improvements and the construction of railroads connecting the cane fields with new and larger sugar mills.[4] In the short span of five years, sugar output rose by more than one half, surpassing 1,000,000 Spanish long tons in 1894.

Yet the great expansion of the industry was still to come—beginning after the Cuban Republic was launched in 1902[5] and lasting for more than two decades. The impressive boom, during which the volume and value of sugar output mounted at steep rates, resulted from peculiar circumstances. It was stimulated on the demand side by rising levels of consumption in the United States—in whose market Cuban sugar enjoyed preferential treatment[6]—and by the needs generated by World War I; after 1918, the slump in the European beet sugar industry provided a new stimulus.

On the supply side, the fast growth of production was made possible by large inflows of foreign capital and labor and by vast additions to the acreage under cane. Protected by the Platt Amendment, which provided the basis for United States intervention, United States capital poured into Cuba in massive amounts,[7] helping to finance the construction of the ultra-modern *centrales*[8] and accelerating the revolution in the structure of land ownership begun before the War of Independence.[9] At the same time, large numbers of European immigrants, especially Spaniards, settled in Cuba, while cutters imported from Haiti and Jamaica helped to meet the peak demand for labor during the cane harvest.[10]

Until the end of the second decade, increases in volume were reinforced by rising prices, with the process culminating in the frenetic "Dance of the Millions" in 1920—the year when sugar prices skyrocketed, raising the value of the crop to over $1,000,-000,000 (Table 1). By the end of 1920, however, the price of

Table 1. Volume and Value of Sugar Production in Cuba, 1903-58

Average for Period	Volume (In thousand metric tons)	Value (In million pesos)
1903-7	1211.8	64.3
1908-12	1592.1	96.5
1913-17	2836.3	220.2
1918-20	3856.2	607.2
1921-25	4732.9	321.8
1926-30	4803.6	219.8
1931-35	2578.7	71.4
1936-41	2819.4	107.1
1942-46	3658.5	250.1
1947-50	5673.1	578.6
Annual		
1951	5759.4	662.6
1952	7224.8	764.3
1953	5159.2	461.4
1954	4897.2	425.1
1955	4538.3	390.4
1956	4744.9	418.9
1957	5673.3	653.7
1958	5784.5	554.2

Source: *Anuario Azucarero de Cuba*, 1959.

sugar was less than one-fifth of the May record level, and the market started a spectacular downward spiral. In spite of almost constant production, the value of the sugar crop fell during the following two years to just over one-quarter of the level reached in 1920. Moreover, production in the European sugar beet fields had recovered, and the expansion of the demand for Cuban sugar was beginning to slacken. For some years producers tried to offset the effects of declining prices by increasing production, but, after a short recovery in 1923, the value of sugar output continued its decline. The outcome of several schemes designed to limit sugar production unilaterally was equally futile, and sugar income fell again by almost one-third during the late twenties.

The final blow came, however, when the United States plunged into the Great Depression, and duties on Cuban sugar were raised under the Hawley-Smoot tariff. The sugar industry contracted painfully, pulling along the whole economy in its downward adjustment. During the period 1931-35, the value of sugar output was just over one-tenth of what it had been in the prosperous days of the post-war period; total and per-capita income fell sharply, immigration ceased, unemployment became widespread, and demands for land reform gathered momentum. The sugar industry entered a period of minute regulation.

The decline of the sugar industry had one positive effect, however. It was to make clear the dangers involved in the economy's extreme dependency upon the fortune of one single crop, whose demand fluctuated according to factors which were largely beyond Cuba's control. The need to diversify agricultural production thus became apparent, and to implement the new policy of diversification protective tariffs were imposed in 1927 and again in the early thirties.

As a result of the protectionist policy, a new sector started to develop within Cuban agriculture which, unlike sugar, was oriented toward the internal market. From the point of view of demand, the agricultural sector began to acquire a dual character, although in value terms the export-oriented sugar industry continued to dominate the economy.

As was to be expected, the two sectors behaved quite differently during the thirties. While severe crop restrictions succeeded in cutting sugar output to the low levels shown in Table 1, and production of tobacco fell to about two-thirds the pre-depression level (Table 2), the output of the sector catering to domestic demand rose swiftly from 1927 to 1940.

Protected by virtually prohibitive duties, the coffee industry revived (Table 2), and from being a net importer Cuba became again a net exporter.[11] Similar developments occurred with livestock, enabling demands for meat, poultry, and dairy products to be met internally. As the country became self-sufficient in a number of foodstuffs formerly imported, the ratio of food imports to total imports dropped from an average of 37.8 per cent in 1924-29 to 26.7 per cent in 1935-39.

During the forties the relative rates of change of the production in the two sectors shifted again. Under the stimulus of war demands sugar output rose, although it exceeded the high pre-depression levels only after hostilities had ended. The tobacco

Table 2. Production of Tobacco and Coffee in Cuba, 1904-58 and 1925-58
(In thousands of metric tons)

Average for Period	Tobacco	Coffee
1904-10	25.1	n.a.
1911-20	31.9	n.a.
1921-30[a]	32.2	19.8
1931-40	22.8	29.6
1941-45	24.4	30.8
1946-50	33.6	32.2
Annual[b]		
1951	42.5	39.8
1952	36.0	32.7
1953	33.9	28.7
1954	43.7	35.7
1955	50.9	38.6
1956	48.2	46.5
1957	41.7	36.7
1958	50.6	43.7

n.a. Data not available.
a. For coffee average crop years 1924-25 through 1929-30.
b. For coffee crop years 1950-51 through 1957-58.
Sources: Averages: *Investment in Cuba* (U.S. Department of Commerce, 1956).
Years 1951-56: *Cuba Económica y Financiera.*
Years 1957-58: Jacques Chonchol, "Análisis Crítico de la Reforma Agraria Cubana," *El Trimestre Económico,* No. 117 (January-March, 1963).

industry continued to stagnate during the war years, but large crops were harvested in 1946 and again in 1950, thus bringing output back to the high level of the 1920's.

The expansion of output began to show symptoms of weakness in some branches of the domestic sector, with production increases lagging behind the rise in consumption induced by a faster rate of population growth[12] and the higher incomes generated by the recovery of the sugar industry. The growth of coffee production tapered off during the forties, forcing domestic consumption to be again satisfied partly by imports. Pressures on the balance of payments arose also from unfavorable developments in the livestock industry. The number of cattle declined sharply from 1940 to 1946, and slightly in the following six years. The fall was repeated with some time lag in the case of hogs, the number of which fell almost 20 per cent between 1946 and 1952. Finally, poultry, which had reached a peak in 1935 with 12,500,000 birds, was down to 7,100,000 by 1946 and to an estimated 7,400,000 in 1952 (Table 3).

As a result of retrogression in the livestock industry, imports of prepared beef, salted pork, ham, mutton, lard, milk, butter, cheese, and eggs—all of which had declined sharply in volume between 1922-26 and 1935-39—increased rapidly until the early fifties.[13] Imports of beans also rose at a steady rate as demand increased and production almost halved over the same period.

Table 3. Livestock in Cuba, Selected Years
(In thousands of head)

Year	Cattle	Hogs	Sheep	Poultry
1930	4991	650	112	8563
1935	4651	952a	164a	12540
1940	5335	857	141	n.a.
1946	4116	1622	154	7146
1952	4042b	1286	194	7400
1955c	4500	1395	210	7750

n.a. Data not available.
a. Year 1934.
b. Includes 9,440 on keys off the coast of Cuba.
c. Estimates.
Sources: Investment in Cuba, on basis of data from: P. G. Minneman, *The Agriculture of Cuba; Cuban Agricultural Census,* 1946; *Cuban Livestock Census,* 1952; and estimates of American Embassy, Havana.

Table 4.   Production of Rice, Henequen, Potatoes, and Beans in Cuba
(In thousand metric tons)

Average for Period	Rice	Henequen	Beans	Potatoes
1935-40a	19.8	13.9	43.7	n.a.
1941-45b	32.8	12.6	39.1	n.a.
1946-50c	56.2	14.3	31.3	n.a.
Annual d e				
1951	118.2	16.4	25.3	90.9
1952	127.4	12.5	23.5	90.7
1953	192.0	11.5	21.2	89.7
1954	181.0	14.8	21.2	95.0
1955	215.0	8.7	21.3	99.3
1956	250.0	10.4	n.a.	119.6
1957	256.8	11.2	n.a.	94.9
1958	225.9	9.1	n.a.	79.3

n.a. Data not available.
a. For henequen 1934-40; for beans 1935-39 average.
b. For rice 1940-45; for beans 1940-44.
c. For rice 1945-50; for beans 1945-49.
d. For rice 1951 and 1952 correspond to the quota years 1951-52 and 1952-53.
e. For potatoes crop years 1950-51 to 1957-58.
Sources: All averages, beans, and rice until 1952 from *Investment in Cuba.*
Henequen from *Revista del Banco Nacional* (March, 1960), on data from Ministry of Agriculture.   Rice (1953-56) and potatoes (1951-56) from *Cuba Económica y Financiera.*   For the remaining years from Jacques Chonchol, "Análisis Crítico de la Reforma Agraria Cubana," *El Trimestre Económico,* No. 117 (January-March, 1963).

In contrast, output of potatoes expanded and spectacular gains were scored in the cultivation of rice, post-war production being almost three times the pre-war (Table 4).

With the major exception of livestock,[14] the output of the sector catering to domestic demand rose satisfactorily during the early fifties.   After 1956, however, the trend seemed to level off.   As Tables 2 and 4 show, coffee production stagnated, potato output fell sharply, and the remarkable expansion of rice cultivation seemed to be over.

The failure of domestic agricultural production to keep up with rising demands was promptly reflected in the foreign trade accounts.   Food imports, which had declined between 1952 and 1955, advanced again in each of the following three years, with the value of those items which could be produced domestically rising faster than the overall value of food imports (Table 5).[15]

In the export-oriented sector, production of tobacco expanded with some fluctuations along a rising trend, induced by steadily advancing sales abroad. But exports of henequen fell throughout the fifties, leading to a one-third reduction in output (Table 4).

In the strategic sugar industry, developments during the decade before the Revolution fell into a rather neat three-period pattern that closely followed the successive changes occurring in the international markets. Stimulated by demands generated by the Korean War, sugar sales advanced steadily until 1952, when an all-time peak was reached in volume, although not in value. Production was deliberately reduced one year later in order to facilitate the disposal of unsold stocks accumulated in 1952. As the tensions surrounding the Korean conflict subsided, a glut developed in the world market. In 1953 a new International Sugar Agreement was reached to which Cuba became a party. Crop restrictions were reimposed in 1954, and within a year sugar income had fallen to just over one-half the record level of 1952. Production remained low in 1956, but the Suez crisis and failures in the production of the European sugar beet fields raised the 1957 price in the world sugar market to its highest level since the early twenties. As a result, the value of sugar sales

Table 5. Cuban Imports of Selected Foodstuffs and Total Food Imports, 1955-58
(In millions of dollars)

	1955	1956	1957	1958
Rice	18.7	24.5	38.9	39.9
Beans	6.3	6.6	7.5	10.3
Lard and edible oils	25.7	23.7	25.4[a]	25.4[a]
Pork	7.9	9.6	9.8	11.7
Onions and garlic	3.4	3.4	3.7	4.3
Dairy products and eggs	6.4[b]	6.4[b]	6.4[b]	6.4[b]
Sub-total	58.4	74.2	91.7	98.0
Total imports of food	132.8	134.4	157.9	173.3

a. 1957-58 average.
b. 1955-58 average.
Source: Ministry of Finance, *Resúmenes Estadísticos Seleccionados;* Jacques Chonchol, "Análisis Crítico de la Reforma Agraria Cubana," *El Trimestre Económico*, No. 117 (January-March, 1963).

increased by more than one-half over the 1956 level. The boom was short-lived, however. In 1958, prices fell back to more normal levels, and the value of sugar production once again declined below the level reached during the favorable days of the second post-war period.

2. The Institutional Framework

The institutional pattern of modern Cuban agriculture was shaped largely during the great expansion of the sugar industry at the beginning of the present century. After this boom and until the end of the fifties, the rural scene was characterized by considerable concentration of land in the hands of the owners of a few large cane plantations and cattle ranches, by the prevalence of non-owners among farm operators, and by the high proportion of the labor force who were wage-earners.

i

Table 6 illustrates the degree of concentration of landholdings in the mid-forties. The contrast is striking. At one end of the scale, less than 8 per cent of all holdings accounted for slightly over 70 per cent of the farmland, one-half of 1 per cent controlling more than one-third of the total farm acreage. At the other extreme was the *minifundia* complex[16]—more than 80 per cent of the holdings comprised less than one-fifth of the agricultural land, over one-third of the farms being smaller than two hectares[17] and more than 70 per cent of them less than twenty-five.

These overall measures of concentration largely reflected the situation that prevailed in the sugar and cattle industries, the two principal branches of Cuban agriculture.

The rise of the sugar latifundium had been both a cause and result of the accelerated growth of sugar production from about 1890 to 1925. Until the 1870's, cane had been grown primarily in small and medium-sized farms, operated by their owners, who could sell the cane competitively to a number of relatively small mills. During this period, the area which the mills could serve economically had been limited by the difficulties of transporting the cane to the mills in ox-carts and by

Table 6. Cuban Farms by Size Groups, 1945

Size Groups (Hectares)[a]	Farms (Number)	(Per cent)	Area (Thousand hectares)	(Per cent)
0.4- 24.9	111278	69.6	1021.9	11.2
25.0- 99.9	35911	22.5	1608.0	17.7
100.0-499.9	10433	6.5	2193.6	24.1
500.0-999.9	1442	0.9	992.5	10.9
1000 and over	894	0.5	3261.1	36.1
Totals	159958	100.0	9077.1	100.0

a. One hectare equals 2.471 acres.
Source: Cuban Agricultural Census, 1946.

the need to cut and cart to the mills substantial amounts of timber for fuel.[18] After railway networks connecting the cane fields to the mills were built on a significant scale at the end of the last century, it became technically possible for the mills to serve much larger areas than hitherto. Moreover, it became profitable for the sugar companies to own the surrounding land in order to assure an adequate supply of cane for their mills, now bigger and more efficient. The progressive concentration of the sugar industry and land ownership was the result of the new technological conditions. The number of mills declined from 1,190 in 1877 to only 207 in 1899, in spite of fast-growing production and considerable additions to the area under cane.

Until independence, however, capital limitations imposed a constraint on the expansion of the sugar *latifundia*. Nevertheless, after 1900 the massive inflow of American investments and the rising profits of Cuban and Spanish-owned sugar mills[19] removed these limitations, and the full flowering of the sugar latifundium began.[20] During this period the sugar companies bought or otherwise acquired vast tracts from the former independent cane growers,[21] and by 1912 they controlled more than one-tenth of all Cuban land (Table 7). Concentration in the industry accelerated still further after the crash of the sugar market in 1921. American interests invested heavily in expansion and modernization, and these developments led to further reductions in the number of *centrales* and to new acquisitions of land from the peasants. By 1925 only 184 sugar

Table 7. Percentage of Total Land Area Controlled by Sugar Mills in Selected Years

Year	Owned	Rented	Total Controlled
1860	7.0	n.a.	n.a.
1912	8.2	2.1	10.3
1925	n.a.	n.a.	17.7
1939	19.7	7.0	26.7
1953	16.6	7.7	24.3
1959	14.7	6.2	20.9

n.a. Data not available.
Sources: 1860-1953: *Investment in Cuba.* 1959: *Anuario Azucarero,* 1959.

mills were in operation but they controlled 17.7 per cent of Cuba. A similar pattern existed in the thirties, a decade during which the mills owned a fifth and controlled more than a quarter of all land in the island. After the war, their influence declined somewhat, but in 1959 the mills still controlled nearly 2,400,000 hectares.

Yet even these figures do not reflect adequately the immense concentration which characterized the sugar industry on the eve of the Revolution. The information assembled in Table 8 is more revealing. In May, 1959, the 28 largest sugar-cane producers owned over 1,400,000 hectares and rented 617,300 hectares, thus controlling over 20 per cent of the land in farms and almost one-fifth of the Cuban territory.[22]

The degree of concentration was also significant in the cattle industry. Table 9 shows that the 40 largest firms[23] in the industry owned almost one-tenth the land in farms.[24] Moreover, the livestock census of 1952 showed that 2 per cent of the approximately 90,000 holdings that were raising cattle at that time possessed 42.4 per cent of the national cattle stock. In contrast, farms having under 50 head of cattle represented 84.7 per cent of all holdings but owned less than one-quarter of the total number of head.

Finally, during the 1950's the rapid development of rice cultivation introduced a new type of large-scale farming. By 1958, roughly 5 per cent of all rice producers had control of about 75 per cent of the area under rice and produced an even larger share of total output.[25] As with the sugar estates and cattle ranches, the

Table 8. Land and Sugar Mills Controlled by 28 Largest Sugar Companies (May, 1959)

Firms that controlled: (In thousands of hectares)	Number of Firms	Number of Sugar Mills	Land (in thousands of hectares)			Percentage of	
			Owned	Rented	Controlled	Farmland	Land Area
13.42 to 67.1	17	35	391.9	147.6	539.5	5.35	4.7
67.1 to 134.2	5	15	332.8	146.3	479.1	4.75	4.2
More than 134.2	6	36	712.6	323.4	1036.0	10.30	9.0
Totals	28	86	1437.3	617.3	2054.6	20.40	17.9

Sources: Mills and area controlled by firms: INRA, *Un Año de Liberación Agraria.* Land in farms: *Proyecto de Plan Quinquenal para el Desarrollo de la Agricultura Cubana en 1961-65.*

Table 9. Land Owned by 40 Largest Cattle Firms in Cuba, 1959

Size Groups (Thousands of hectares)	Firms (Number)	Area (Thousands of hectares)	Percentage of Land in Farms
13.42-26.84	31	204.4	2.0
26.84-67.10	7	252.9	2.5
More than 67.10	2	534.8	5.3
Totals	40	992.1	9.8

Sources: Area owned by firms: *Ciclo de Conferencias sobre Planificación Industrial* (Ministry of Industry, 1961). Land in farms: *Proyecto de Plan Quinquenal para el Desarrollo de la Agricultura Cubana en 1961-65.*

large rice farms were, in general, highly specialized, one-crop units. Rice cultivation enjoyed, however, a degree of mechanization which was considerably above national average standards.

ii

The important role played by managers who did not own farms they cultivated is apparent from Table 10. In 1946 only 30.5 per cent of all holdings and 32.4 per cent of the land in farms were directly managed by their owners. Both the number of holdings controlled by different types of renters and their area exceeded the corresponding figures for owners. In addition, one-fifth of the agricultural production units were farmed under share-cropping arrangements.

As Table 11 makes clear, there was also a high number of wage earners in the agricultural labor force. This situation, together with the abundancy of tenants, was closely related to the introduction and expansion of *latifundia* in the sugar sector. As a result of the vast purchases of land by the *centrales* during the first quarter of this century, the number of independent owners of cane farms had fallen considerably. During the heyday of the sugar boom, most of the mills operated primarily on the basis of "administration cane," a system under which the mills themselves grew the cane, with the use of hired laborers. The result was the almost complete "monetization" of the agricultural sector.[26]

Table 10. Number of Holdings and Area by Types of Farm
Operators in Cuba, 1945

Type of Operator	Farms		Total Area		Average Area
	(Number)	(Per cent)	(Thousands of Hectares)	(Per cent)	(Hectares)
Owners	48,792	30.5	2958.7	32.4	60.6
Administrators	9,342	5.8	2320.4	25.6	248.4
Renters	46,048	28.8	2713.9	30.6	58.9
Sub-renters	6,987	4.4	215.2	2.4	30.8
Share-croppers	33,064	20.7	552.1	6.1	16.7
Squatters	13,718	8.6	244.6	2.7	17.8
Other	2,007	1.2	72.1	0.8	35.9
Totals	159,958	100.0	9077.0	100.0	56.7

Source: Cuban Agricultural Census, 1946.

Some of the cane processed by the sugar mills was cultivated, however, under the *colono* system, in which former owners of cane holdings and other independent farmers grew cane on land they leased from the *centrales*. Thus, side by side with the system of administration cane, a special type of sugar production developed, with operators who also relied on wage-earners for harvesting but who depended upon the mills not only for grinding cane but also for land and credit.[27]   The position of the *colonos* vis-à-vis the mills improved, however, after the collapse of the sugar market in the early thirties. The 1937 *Ley de Coordinación Azucarera* favored the *colono* when allocating cane quotas, regulated his rights and obligations in minute detail, and tried to protect him against arbitrary actions by the landowners and sugar mills.[28]

Whereas tenants and wage-earners were common in the sugar sector,[29] administrators predominated in the large-scale cattle industry in which absentee ownership was not uncommon.[30]

On the other hand, the large number of share-croppers indicated the widespread use of this arrangement on the small-scale, more intensively cultivated tobacco farms.[31]   Finally, squatters abounded in the eastern end of the island, Oriente province alone accounting for 84 per cent of them.[32]

Table 11. Agricultural Labor Force in Cuba, 1952

	Thousands of Persons	Per Cent
Farm laborers	596.8	72.9
Paid workers	520.9	63.6
Unpaid family workers	66.7	8.1
Administrators and foremen	9.2	1.1
Ranchers and farmers	221.9	27.1
Agricultural labor force	818.7	100.0

Source: *Censos de Población, Viviendas y Electoral*, 1953.

3. Economic Patterns

Monoculture and serious under-utilization of land and labor were the principal economic features of pre-revolutionary Cuban agriculture. Each reinforced the other in a classic "vicious circle" which, together with inadequate technical standards, kept actual farm output considerably below economic potential.

i

Cuba was, of course, a prime example of the one-crop, export-oriented economy. During the early 1920's the island provided a good fifth of all the sugar consumed in the world, and, although this share declined after 1925,[33] "king sugar" continued to dominate the economy. During the fifties approximately one-fourth of national income[34] came from the sugar industry, which provided also four-fifths of all exports. The agricultural sector of the sugar industry employed 400,000 wage workers and contributed 40 per cent of farm income. More than one-half of all cultivated land was under cane.

Over-specialized farming was not restricted to the sugar estates, but typified the majority of the agricultural production units. As Table 12 shows, the main source of income for every group of farms never provided less than 60 per cent of all earnings and considerably more on farms specializing in sugar-cane, livestock, tobacco, and coffee. Rice production—relatively unimportant at the time of the census and not listed separately—

Table 12. Composition of Farm Income, and Farms Classified
According to Principal Source of Income in Cuba, 1945

		FARMS		
Source of income	Per cent share in total farm income	Per cent of income from principal crop	Number (in thousands)	Per cent of all farms
Sugar cane	41.6	86.6	29.1	18.2
Livestock	20.9	82.2	28.8	18.0
Tobacco	10.2	75.9	22.8	14.2
Cereals and beans	9.4	63.8	26.8	16.8
Root crops	6.7	60.7	15.7	9.8
Coffee	2.7	75.6	9.3	5.8
Tree fruit	2.0	70.6	4.8	3.0
Garden truck	0.9	62.1	1.2	0.9
Other crops	5.0	73.9	11.4	7.1
Forest products	0.6	79.3	0.9	0.6
			9.1[a]	5.7
Totals	100.0	————	159.9	100.0

a. No income reported.
Source: Cuban Agricultural Census, 1946.

later reached a level of specialization comparable to that of the
cane plantations and the cattle ranches.

ii

As already noted, the rapid expansion of the sugar industry
during the first quarter of the century created a labor shortage
which was partly eliminated by considerable immigration. After
the collapse of the industry in the early thirties a sharp reversal
occurred in employment, and Cuba thereafter was burdened by
considerable under-utilization of its available human resources.

Although the number out of work was known to be high
and closely dependent on the seasonal requirements of the sugar
industry, reliable figures about the levels and fluctuations of unemployment were not available until the mid-1950's. The Agricultural Census of 1946 gave, however, some indication of the
magnitude of the problem which affected the more than 400,000
paid temporary workers who constituted about one-half of the
gainfully occupied agricultural population: 52 per cent of them
had worked no more than four months in the year, and only 6

per cent of them had been employed for nine months or longer. In addition, there must also have been an unknown but probably significant percentage of concealed underemployment among unpaid permanent workers.[35]

More information on employment conditions was obtained from a survey of 5,000 families distributed throughout the island, carried out between May, 1956, and April, 1957. Its principal results are given in Tables 13 and 14.

Table 13 shows that during the 12 months considered, 16.4 per cent of the labor force were totally without work and less than two-thirds were fully employed; the remaining fifth fell in intermediate categories.

The strong influence of the sugar industry on the seasonal pattern of unemployment is neatly revealed by the figures in Table 14. The number without work dropped sharply from August-October to November-January as activity in the tobacco industry increased, employment in the coffee fields reached a maximum, and preparation for the sugar harvest was started. A further reduction occurred in the following months as cane cutting and milling reached a peak of feverish activity. But even in this period the unemployment rate was as high as 9 per cent.[36]

The number of unemployed again rose in May through June with an abruptness comparable only to that of its fall towards the end of the year. By the middle of May the cane harvest was practically over and the "dead season" (*tiempo muerto*), made its effects felt throughout the economy. Only maintenance work in the mills and some replanting in the cane fields was then available. Employment also fell in transportation, trade, and shipping, since railway traffic and exports through the ports moved seasonally with sugar. Similarly, domestic consumption rose during the harvest and declined sharply afterwards, providing yet one more channel through which the rhythm of sugar production was communicated to the rest of the economy.

It was because of these forces that at least one-fifth of all workers were totally unemployed between August and October, when the cycle would begin again.

Although no sectional breakdown is available to show the level and fluctuations of agricultural unemployment, it seems reasonable to assume that rural work was even more irregular than the

Table 13. Employment and Unemployment in Cuba, May, 1956—April, 1957

	Thousands of People	Per Cent of Total Labor Force
Fully Employed	1439	62.2
Partially Employed[a]	223	10.1
Employed without remuneration	154	6.8
Unemployed	361	16.4
Other[b]	27	4.5
Total Labor Force	2204	100.0

a. Working less than 40 hours a week.
b. Having a job, but not working.
Source: Symposium de Recursos Naturales de Cuba (Consejo Nacional de Economía, 1958).

Table 14. Seasonal Fluctuation of Unemployment in Cuba, May, 1956—April, 1957

Periods	Thousands of Unemployed	Per Cent of Labor Force
May-June	435	19.7
August-October	457	20.7
November-January	353	10.6
February-April	200	9.0
Average	361	16.4

Source: Symposium de Recursos Naturales de Cuba (Consejo Nacional de Economía, 1958).

national averages suggest. In the cities, on the other hand, the more regular flows of industrial, construction, and service activities cushioned, at least in part, the violent ups and downs originating in the sugar sector. It was therefore the rural population that had to bear the brunt of unemployment, a burden still further aggravated by the concentration of public works in the urban centers and by the relatively small amount of subsistence agriculture.

iii

Table 15 shows how land was used in Cuba during the mid-forties.[37] Pastures covered by far the greatest part of the farmland.[38] Not much more than one-fifth of the farm acreage

Table 15. Cuban Land in Farms by Uses, 1945

Uses	Area (In thousands of hectares)	Proportion of land in farms (Per cent)
Cultivated	1970.4	21.7
Pastures	3897.2	42.9
Woods	1265.7	18.9
Marabú[a]	268.1	3.0
Other uses[b]	1650.4	18.2
Idle[c]	25.2	0.3
Total land in farms	9077.0	100.0

a. Area covered by *Dychrostachys nutans, Banth,* a leguminous, thicket-like growth which is one of the worst agricultural pests in Cuba.

b. Includes roads, buildings, and unproductive land.

c. Land that was not exploited in 1945 and was idle at the time the census was taken in 1946.

Source: Cuban Agricultural Census, 1946.

was devoted to crops—a somewhat surprising proportion considering the value of food imports and of agricultural raw materials which could be grown on the island,[39] the high level of unemployment of the rural labor force, and the abundance of cultivable land. Indeed, it would seem that still only a relatively small fraction of the latter was under crops in 1950 when the International Bank mission reported, "It is estimated that, of the total land in farms, nearly sixty per cent is tillable. At the present time slightly over one-third is under cultivation."[40]

Some of this under-utilized land was apparently concealed by the census classification, which listed land considered unproductive by its owners and areas occupied by roads, ditches, and buildings under the common heading of "other uses." "While much of this 'unproductive land' is considered wasteland," the experts of the bank wrote, "the Mission believes that a large proportion could become productive if put to its best economic use."[41]

Over one-half of this "unproductive land" was controlled by the large estates of more than 1,000 hectares, which devoted to crops only about one-tenth of all their land. As was to be expected for both economic and institutional reasons, the ratio of cultivated to total land rose steadily as the size of the holdings declined, hovering around one-fourth for the farms having be-

Table 16. Area Under Cane and Area Harvested in Cuba, 1952-59

Year	Area Under Cane (In thousands of hectares)	Area Harvested (In thousands of hectares)	Area Harvested as Per Cent of Area Under Cane
1952	1425.0	1405.8	98.6
1953	1604.9	1009.2	62.9
1954	1541.7	957.4	62.1
1955	1444.3	834.7	57.8
1956	1346.4	996.0	73.9
1957	1376.9	1264.8	91.8
1958	1304.1	1047.1	80.3

Source: *Anuario Azucarero*, 1959.

tween 50 and 500 hectares, and exceeding 40 per cent in the smaller units.[42]

In general, the pattern of land use was molded by a number of factors, institutional and economic. Because of the sharp concentration of land ownership, the allocation of land to alternative uses at the national level was bound to reflect the decisions of the sugar mills and the cattle ranchers of the eastern provinces. But allocation was also partly determined by "natural" causes, such as the instability of the international demand for sugar, and by "artificial" ones, such as the vast array of institutions which, being related to sugar, tended to perpetuate monoculture. Finally, the divergence of private and social costs caused by unemployment placed severe limitations on incentives to diversify agricultural production and thus influenced indirectly the pattern of land use.

As noted already, the sugar mills controlled nearly 2,500,000 hectares and operated highly specialized units. Nevertheless, they kept under cane only about half of this area. The remainder was maintained "in reserve" or under low-yield natural pastures which provided the base for extensive cattle grazing. The practice was hardly surprising. Since land was the cheapest and most abundant factor of production, economic rationality recommended that *some* land be kept uncultivated in a sector catering to a market characterized by large periodic fluctuations. Indeed, the data in the first column of Table 16 confirm the predictable—the area under cane expanded during favorable periods and contracted (at times with a short lag) when the situation in the world market deteriorated.

But the figures also prove that the amount of land kept in reserve was clearly *in excess* of what was justified by the insta-bility of the demand for sugar. The maximum absolute variation of the area planted with cane (that between 1953 and 1956) represented, in fact, only about one-fourth of the amount of "reserve land" held by the *centrales* (roughly 1,000,000 hectares).

Moreover, the need to maintain large amounts of semi-idle land was further reduced because the sugar mills used another (and more peculiarly Cuban) method to adjust output to changes in the market. A comparison of the figures in the first two col-umns of Table 16 reveals that during 1953-58 a significant gap developed between the area planted with cane and that actually harvested. Naturally, this margin fluctuated with the variations in the demand for sugar. During the downswing, the gap widened, as the harvested area declined more rapidly than the area planted; it narrowed when market prospects improved, since the companies absorbed the partly unexpected increases in de-mand through cutting a higher proportion of the available cane.

For the *centrales,* concerned almost exclusively with the pro-duction of sugar, this system was extremely flexible and almost costless. For the national economy, however, it represented a costly under-utilization of the best farmland of the island.[43] The system meant in fact that during the period 1953-58 not less than 15 per cent of the total area under crops was, on the average, left unharvested in the cane fields.[44]

The data just analyzed also provide conclusive evidence to support the contention that in pre-revolutionary Cuba it was the level of demand and not the limitations imposed by productive capacity that determined the actual volume of sugar production. They prove further that the possibilities of expanding the area under crops on a significant scale were inextricably linked even in the case of the sugar estates to the diversification of farm out-put. And they prove that in Cuba there was neither a land nor a labor shortage to require that agricultural diversification could only be bought at the price of a reduction in sugar output. In this respect diversification would not have entailed any significant (social) economic cost.

On the other hand, diversification obviously required more capital in the form of higher inputs of seeds, fertilizers, tractors, and other agricultural equipment,[45] as well as investments in the training of agronomists, technicians, foremen, and laborers. *In theory* the former could have been kept at relatively low levels by the employment of labor-intensive techniques.[46] Moreover, to the extent that investments used semi-idle but fertile land and unemployed workers, they would have yielded high rates of net social return. By expanding both output and employment and by making them steadier over the year, investments in diversification would also have increased the average productivity of some of the social overhead capital, which was large enough to meet the seasonal peak requirements of the sugar harvest but remained under-utilized during the rest of the year.

Diversification could have made still another strategic contribution to the development of the economy. By replacing food imports and by increasing exports of agricultural products, it would have saved foreign exchange—one of the essential conditions for increasing imports of capital equipment.[47] Capital imports in turn would have facilitated industrial growth and improvements in agricultural technology, thus reducing still further the under-utilization of resources.

The social and economic advantages of agricultural diversification were thus very considerable. They had been recognized— at least in their broader implications—ever since 1927, when reducing the vulnerability of the Cuban economy to world market fluctuations was given high priority in economic policy. Nevertheless, actual progress in diversifying was slow, and in the 1950's monoculture still dominated the countryside.

A full explanation of this seeming paradox cannot be given here. The prolonged failure to diversify suggests, however, that the factors at work were anchored deep in the peculiar economic institutions of Cuban agriculture.

As indicated earlier, one of Cuba's rural characteristics was a high level of unemployment, which caused the *private* costs of agricultural production to diverge from the *social* costs—unskilled labor was a free resource for the economy but not for the private business organizations. Farm management by entrepreneurs seeking to maximize *private* profits was therefore bound to bring a smaller volume of production than that based on calculations of *true* social costs.[48]   This distortion, although of quite a general nature, in practice affected almost exclusively the output levels of agricultural products other than sugar cane.[49]   It was thus a major obstacle to diversification under the prevailing institutional system.

Moreover, in the special case of the sugar firms, the private profits which might have been made by growing other crops were artificially reduced by the high cost of labor.   The Law of Sugar Coordination of 1937 and subsequent legislation in effect required the *centrales* to pay the same minimum wage earned by workers during the sugar harvest to persons hired during the "dead season."[50] This meant that the wage rate which the sugar companies would have to pay for the cultivation of subsidiary crops throughout the year was set at the level prevailing in the most productive sector of agriculture during the period of peak demand.   Private and social costs of labor were thus driven further apart; labor-intensive techniques became expensive; unemployment did not fall; and investment in diversification was made less attractive to the very firms which had the largest financial resources and the best farmland of the island.

Whether under these circumstances the sugar companies could have increased their profits by diversifying their output remains, in the absence of detailed data on costs and prices, a debatable point.   The fact that monoculture persisted lends support to the hypothesis that it was the high cost of labor which made diversified production sufficiently unprofitable not to be attractive to the sugar companies.

Yet it would probably be wrong to explain this persistence of monoculture *exclusively* in terms of the legally imposed wage rate.   Even the attitudes of the sugar companies towards introducing technical improvements in the cultivation of cane were generally unprogressive.   In this respect, the experts of the International Bank—who were certainly well aware of the artificial level of the wage rate—seem to have had some misgivings about the ability of the sugar mills to maximize their *own* profits: ". . . it is an obvious waste," they wrote, "for the sugar *centrales*—with their power plant and other equipment, communication and transportation system and technical personnel—to be idle, except for making repairs and improvement, during almost two-thirds of the year."[51]

It is therefore not evident that a more realistic wage rate would by itself have led to substantial changes in the production patterns of the sugar companies. Indeed, it seems likely that the companies might have responded rather weakly to the stimulus of potential profits from agricultural diversification, for diversification required from the companies much more than a simple reallocation of land to new crops. It meant adding to a time-tested and traditional pattern of cane farming, new lines of production requiring different techniques, more complex types of knowledge, new managers, less specialized agricultural experts, and a more permanent and skilled labor force. In short, agricultural diversification implied for the sugar firms a shift to a quite different production function and, more generally, a radical change in their organization and methods of operation.

Under these circumstances, a satisfactorily profitable routine may have been more attractive than the pull of higher profits which were only obtainable by rather deep changes in institutions, methods, and attitudes. Past experience and knowledge, and, above all, the all-pervasive "sugar mentality" are likely to have introduced a strong bias in favor of the well-tried pattern of monoculture.[52]

Whereas it was high wages and the weight of routine that prevented diversification of the sugar lands, in the case of cattle farms the same effect was due to the extreme concentration of land ownership, which enabled absentee owners to extract large profits from extensive cattle raising on their administrator-operated holdings.

Yet if individual entrepreneurs could see the profits to be made in food production for the domestic market, it may be asked why they did not rent land from the sugar mills and cattle ranches to grow these crops. Here again the built-in institutional bias in favor of sugar appears to provide the answer. The Department of Commerce reported in 1956 that "habit, experience, and capital, as well as credit and marketing facilities, all favor continued dependence on sugar; other crops, except for tobacco, have few of these long established advantages."[53]

Only at the end of 1950 was the Cuban Agricultural and Industrial Development Bank organized; until then the government had no system of farm credit. Besides, the sugar sector absorbed the largest part of the loans granted by the commercial banks, which meant that producers of other crops had to look to industrial companies, local stores, and merchants for this assistance.[54] And university agricultural training and research were both insufficient and biased in favor of sugar, thereby hindering further the development of other crops.

Thus, the difficulties in changing the pattern of land use reflected to a considerable degree the peculiar nature of the agricultural problems of Cuba. It was necessary to expand the area under crops if land were to be better utilized and idle labor employed. But because of the vast area and financial resources controlled by the cattle and sugar industries, diversification on a significant scale was not possible without their cooperation. Artificially high labor costs, great concentration of land ownership, and the pull of routine and tradition made such cooperation unlikely or negligible. In turn, the bias of institutions and attitudes towards sugar discouraged individual entrepreneurs from supplying domestic needs, an activity in many cases made still more difficult by the ease with which American foods entered the Cuban market.

iv

The previous sections have shown that substantial gains could have been made by removing the institutional obstacles which prevented the full use of available resources. In addition, farm output could have been increased by introducing improvements in technology and organization. Some of these depended on additional investments and, in this sense, represented potentials for future rather than immediate growth. Others, however, primarily required dynamic entrepreneurship in the private sector and imaginative government policies. As the following pages show, neither seems to have been overabundant in pre-revolutionary Cuba.

With regard to sugar cane, in 1950 the International Bank mission had reported that, while other sugar-producing areas of the world were making various efforts to increase per-acre cane yields, the Cuban sugar industry displayed "a conspicuous lack of technological progress."[55] The bank group found that more than 60 per cent of the cane planted was of a variety developed in Java and introduced in the late twenties. There was little irrigation, fertilizers were used infrequently, and research was at a standstill.[56]

The effects of such neglect of technical improvements were still apparent in the second half of the fifties. As Table 17 shows, Cuba, the world's leading producer and exporter of sugar, lagged behind virtually all the main sugar-cane producing countries in cane yield per hectare.[57] Although the high raw-sugar content of Cuban cane changed the ranking and reduced the differential in the case of raw-sugar yields per acre, Cuba in this respect also occupied a secondary position.

A variety of relatively inefficient methods also characterized a large part of the cattle industry.[58] Scientific feeding was, in

Table 17. Yields of Sugar Cane, 1954-55 to 1958-59

Country	Metric Tons of Sugar Cane per Hectare
Hawaii	205.53
Peru	158.34
Indonesia[a]	91.34
British Guiana	89.06
Barbados	86.53
Taiwan	70.34
Union of South Africa[a]	70.01
Australia	62.47
Mauritius	60.81
Puerto Rico	60.66
Jamaica	58.87
Mexico	55.47
United States	52.65
Fiji	47.16
Trinidad	46.63
Brazil	40.58
Cuba[a b]	39.17
Argentina	33.65

a. Average yield for period 1949-50 to 1953-54.
b. For 1954-55 to 1958-59 the average computed from Banco Nacional data is 40.58.
Source: The World Sugar Economy in Figures, 1880-1959 (Food and Agriculture Organization, Rome, 1961).

general, little known, and dependence on pasture meant that it took longer to rear cattle to slaughter weight. Neither natural nor artificial pastures were fertilized. In spite of the fact that during the dry season animals gained little weight and milk yields dropped owing to the shortage of grass, hay was seldom stored, in silos or elsewhere. On the other hand, a great deal of grass was lost during the rainy season through the habit of letting cattle roam freely in land blocks which sometimes extended without fences for as much as 250 hectares. Poor grass management also resulted in considerable sheet erosion and weed and brush infestation.[59]

In sharp contrast to sugar and cattle, tobacco was grown in small plots, using labor-intensive techniques and fertilizers and irrigation. In the rest of the agricultural sector, practices varied widely among the different crops. Rice cultivation, for example, was characterized by modern techniques—grain drills, self-propelled harvester-threshers, power-units for irrigation, and airplanes for planting.[60] On the other hand, coffee and cacao plantations employed fairly backward and primitive methods which gave low yields per acre. Technical standards were quite low also in the small farms producing root crops, corn, and beans.

In general, neither the use of fertilizers nor the irrigation of croplands was common practice. In 1945 only 4 per cent of all farms had land under irrigation; they represented just 3 per cent of the total cultivated area. Irrigation increased, however, during the 1950's, especially for rice, and by 1959 it was estimated that 10 per cent of the cultivated land was under irrigation.[61]

The area fertilized and the number of farms using fertilizers were somewhat higher but still low—12 per cent of all holdings fertilized 7.4 per cent of the total agricultural land in 1945. Besides, the use of fertilizers was scarcely scientific. The 1950 International Bank team thought that application of fertilizers was still done largely by guesswork and explained that "not even the large foreign or Cuban growers had taken the trouble to analyze their soils for specific deficiencies as a guide to the kinds of fertilizers needed."[62]

During the 1950's the situation, it appears, was not greatly changed. Sales of mixed fertilizers reached a peak level in 1951-52, only to plummet by about half in the following years as the situation of the international market forced the curtailment of sugar output. Not until 1956 was the level of the early 1950's surpassed. These larger sales arose from the recovery of the sugar market and the very rapid increases in the use of fertilizer in rice production.

Mechanization made progress during the 1950's, the expansion of rice cultivation again being the main cause. By 1955 the largest part of the sugar industry used machines to clear and prepare land for sugar cane and, to some extent, to haul cane to the mills. Planting and harvesting were still largely done by hand, partly because the workers were opposed to mechanization, but also because the machines could not do quite as good a job as the hand cutters.[63]

Despite these advances, much remained to be done. A study undertaken by the International Harvester Company estimated that the number of tractors in use in 1955 represented only 50 per cent of the market potential and concluded that for other major farm equipment percentages were very much smaller.[64]

Perhaps the principal limitation to raising the technological and organizational level of Cuban agriculture and to diversifying farm production was, however, the weakness of agricultural training, research, and extension programs. Higher education in agricultural techniques was available at the University of Havana, and, on the whole, education standards appeared to have been fairly good.[65] A number of deficiencies, however, strongly reduced the impact of the University program on agricultural practices.

There was, in the first place, a purely quantitative problem. The combined budget of the School of Agronomical Engineering and Sugar and the University Farms represented in 1950 less than 4 per cent of the University budget. The outcome was inevitable: the University could not prepare the number of agricultural engineers and technicians needed to lift and change technical standards in the countryside. Thus, the last population census found that in 1952 there were in Cuba not more than 355 veterinarians and 294 agricultural engineers.[66]

The numerical insufficiency of agricultural graduates was further compounded because only a minority of them—about 10 per cent—actually entered farming pursuits.

Agricultural training suffered also from qualitative shortcom- ings. Too much emphasis was put on sugar and too little on research. Thus, additional barriers to diversification existed pre- cisely at the place that could and should have fostered the tech- niques of farm production. The lack of research generated still another failing: the University had no extension service and so could not transfer its knowledge to the farmers.

In addition to agricultural education provided by the Uni- versity, there were six provincial agricultural schools operated by the Ministry of Agriculture. Their purpose was to provide both practical and theoretical training in actual farming to sons of farmers who had completed five grades of primary education. These schools were considered by the World Bank Mission to have provided the best practical agricultural training available in Cuba in 1950. But they were numerically insufficient, and, as with the University, graduates were reluctant to return to the farms upon completing the three-year course.

The situation was apparently no brighter in agricultural re- search, an activity of the highest priority in which investments would certainly have paid generous social returns. The Depart- ment of Commerce study reported as late as 1956 that research remained one of the most neglected fields of government activity. While the three experimental stations in existence were said to have qualified personnel, they were hindered by lack of funds and frustrated by political interference. These—the study concluded —had combined to make their efforts largely sterile.[67]

The insufficiency of research in turn hampered the achieve- ment of effective agricultural extension services, supposedly the function of Ministry of Agriculture inspectors. In fact, there were but few inspectors, and their possible impact was further nar- rowed by the lack of formal coordination between them and the educational institutions and experimental stations. In addition, it was alleged that lack of travel funds prevented some inspectors from visiting the farms in their districts.

The technological backwardness of Cuban agriculture, then, was even more damaging as a drag on the dynamics of future growth than it was harmful in terms of the static problems of inefficiency and low yields. In fact, it is not unreasonable to think that the notorious shortcomings in both agricultural extension and research were, together with the institutional obstacles already analyzed, the principal causes of the failure to diversify agricultural production—a target which, at least on paper, had been given top priority since 1927.

4. The Socio-Economic Situation of the Agricultural Population

The existence of relatively large differences between living conditions in urban and rural areas is a common characteristic of underdeveloped economies. But in few countries can this difference have been wider than in pre-revolutionary Cuba. Although well paid during the cane harvest, the rural worker earned little during the "dead season," when employment opportunities fell sharply. For this reason his annual income was low both in absolute terms and in comparison to the income of workers in the cities.

The population and housing census, on which Table 18 is based, provided a broad but reliable comparison between the relative and absolute living standards of the countryside and cities. The contrast is so striking that it requires little comment. Three-quarters of the rural dwellings were not houses but huts—the pre-Columbian *bohío*—and two-thirds had earthen floors.[68] Almost nine-tenths of the rural homes used kerosene lamps for light; a similar proportion had to get water from rivers, wells, or springs. Over 90 per cent had neither tub nor shower, and less than 8 per cent of all dwellings had any form of water closet.

In 1958 new information became available when the *Agrupación Católica Universitaria* published the results of a survey conducted two years earlier.[69] The survey involved 1,000 interviews on a wide range of topics with peasant families spread over the entire island and chosen to provide a representative sample of the farm population.

The 1958 results on the housing situation in general resembled those of the census taken in 1952.[70] In addition, the survey included information on income levels, expenditure patterns, food intake, educational and health standards, and other subjects. All

Table 18. Housing Conditions in Cuba, 1953
(In percentages)

	Urban	Rural	Cuba
Buildings			
Masonry	51.8	2.7	33.5
Wood	34.6	16.4	27.7
Palm or wood thatch	9.7	75.4	34.3
Other	3.9	5.5	4.5
Floors			
Tile	53.3	2.6	34.4
Cement	26.9	18.2	23.6
Wood	6.6	7.5	6.9
Earth	9.3	66.2	30.6
Other	3.9	5.5	4.5
Conditions			
Good	53.8	25.7	43.4
Fair	37.6	48.4	91.6
Poor	8.6	25.9	15.0
When built			
Before 1920	36.1	8.1	25.7
1920 to 1945	35.8	46.6	39.8
After 1945	28.1	45.3	39.5
Lights			
Electric	87.0	9.1	58.2
Acetylene	.3	1.9	.9
Kerosene	12.3	87.6	40.1
Other	.4	1.4	.8
Water			
Inside piping	54.6	2.3	35.2
Cistern	5.2	4.6	5.0
Outside piping	22.0	8.1	16.8
River, well, or spring	18.2	85.0	43.0
Toilets			
Water closet, inside	42.8	3.1	28.0
Water closet, outside	18.9	4.8	13.7
Privy	33.3	38.0	35.1
None	5.0	54.1	23.2
Baths			
Tub or shower	64.9	9.5	44.4
None	35.1	90.5	55.6
Refrigeration			
Mechanical	26.5	2.4	17.5
Ice	11.0	1.1	7.3
None	62.5	96.5	75.2

Based on 1,256,594 living units (793,446 urban, 463,148 rural).
Source: Censos de Población, Viviendas y Electoral, 1953.

of these confirmed the squalid living conditions which about 40 per cent of the country's population had to face.

The average annual income of a family of six was estimated to be $590.75, giving a per-capita figure of $91.25.[71] More than half the families had yearly incomes below $500 and only 7.2 per cent were in the $1,000 to $1,200 range. More than two-thirds (69.3 per cent) of expenditures went to food.[72] Almost one-quarter (24 per cent) of the total diet was rice, with beans and root crops[73] supplying much of the rest (28 and 22 per cent respectively). For only 11 per cent of the families did the usual diet include milk; for only 4 per cent meat, for only 2 per cent eggs, and for only 1 per cent fish. Green vegetables were never mentioned.

Health standards were no better. More than one-third (36 per cent) of those interviewed had intestinal parasites; 31 per cent of them had suffered or were suffering from paludism and 14 per cent from tuberculosis; 13 per cent had had typhus. Almost nine-tenths of the peasants had to pay for medical care out of their meager incomes. The government subsidized about 8 per cent of the medical services which were offered, and employers and unions did the same in 45 per cent of the cases. There were no medicines of any sort in 70 per cent of the houses.

Slightly over one-half (53 per cent) of the peasants interviewed could read and write; 4 per cent could read but not write; the remaining 43 per cent were completely illiterate.[74] Forty-four per cent had never attended school, and of those who had, 88 per cent had not gone beyond third grade.

Two of the survey's most revealing findings related to the peasants' own assessments of which factors and institutions could solve the agrarian problem. Seventy-four per cent thought that the best way to improve living conditions was by increasing employment opportunities. More and better education was the choice of 18.4 per cent of those interviewed. A great majority (69 per cent) thought that the institution most capable of solving their problem was the government; 16.7 per cent turned to the employers as the best choice.[75]

The economic and social consequences of the living conditions summarized by these figures were serious.

Economically, low income levels represented an important obstacle to the expansion of industrial output; lack of education wasted potential talent; poor housing and health reduced labor productivity.

Still more negative were the social effects of the adverse conditions in the rural areas. The scarcity and irregularity of employment and the inadequacy of educational facilities meant that the peasant's lot was essentially determined by forces outside his control. Thus, on the average, he had little chance of improving his situation. The odds were heavily against him. Poor and ignorant had been his father and, under the system, the probability was high that basically the same poverty and the same ignorance would be suffered by his son.

5. Conclusions

One basic fact emerges from the previous analysis: in the 30 years between the crisis of the sugar industry in the late twenties and the 1959 Revolution, Cuban agriculture failed to adjust to the new conditions created by the sharp decline and subsequent sluggish recovery of its leading sector. It is true that total farm output rose over the period and that some crop diversification occurred; but, on the whole, expansion was weak and irregular and diversification insufficient. Essentially, the problem was that after the end of the sugar boom, a structural transformation of agriculture was required if its economic resources were to be fully employed. Yet this transformation did not take place; monoculture continued to dominate the farm economy, and, with few exceptions, technical standards remained low.

Thus, during the decade before the Revolution, the Cuban economy was still highly vulnerable to uncontrollable changes in the international demand for sugar. Moreover, food imports were high, notwithstanding the fact that many foodstuffs could have been produced on the island itself, that land was underutilized, and that farm labor was unemployed.

The lack of rapid economic progress was accompanied by basic absence of change in institutions. Although Article 90 of the 1940 Constitution forbade the *latifundia* and provided for the restriction of foreign ownership of land, the supporting legislation was never enacted,[76] and a few large Cuban and American firms continued to control an extremely high proportion of the country's agricultural area. Moreover, non-owner operators managed most of the farms and worked the largest part of the land.

Finally, as a result of the slow growth of agricultural output, of the persistent predominance of sugar monoculture with its highly seasonal demand for labor, and of the uneven distribution of land ownership, the economic, social, and cultural conditions of the peasantry were low by absolute standards and in sharp contrast to the more favorable circumstances of the urban population. Indeed, on the eve of the Revolution, Lowry Nelson's incisive phrase, almost a decade old, still seemed essentially true —the land was rich, the people poor.

CHAPTER III

Agriculture

Post-Revolutionary Development

Agrarian reform was an essential part of the program of those who came to power in January of 1959. Six years earlier —when on trial for leading the assault on the Moncada barracks— Castro had stated that a revolutionary government would enforce the long-neglected constitutional provision which forbade large landholdings and would undertake large-scale redistribution of land to the peasants.[1] In October, 1958, three months before the collapse of the Batista regime, the leaders of the Revolution prepared a provisional law of agrarian reform; within half a year of taking power, they had drafted a definite version, which the Council of Ministers approved on May 17, 1959 at the former headquarters of the rebel army in the Sierra Maestra.

The basic purpose of the Law of Agrarian Reform was the thorough transformation of the institutional structure of agriculture, as a means of accelerating the economic development of the country and the social progress of the rural workers. In compliance with the Constitution, the opening article of the law proscribed large estates. Landlords were permitted to keep 402.6 hectares, but this ceiling did not apply to sugar and rice plantations in which yields exceeded the national averages by 50 per cent;[2] similar exceptions applied to cattle ranches when they met quotas which would be established by the National Institute of Agrarian Reform and to farms devoted to crops whose efficient production required more land than the prescribed amount. Nevertheless, under no circumstances could privately owned farms exceed the absolute maximum of 1,342 hectares.[3]

Other key provisions aimed at freeing the production of sugarcane from the control of the *centrales*. A year after the passage of the law, joint-stock companies would no longer be permitted to operate cane plantations unless their shares were registered, owned by Cubans, and held by persons who were not owners, share-holders, or employees of firms engaged in sugar manufacture. The prohibitions on corporate and foreign ownership of land were wider. Only joint-stock companies with registered shares could possess land devoted to non-sugar agricultural production. Acquisition of land would in the future be restricted to Cuban citizens and to companies formed by them.

Privately owned land in excess of the limits indicated above was to be expropriated; indemnification would be paid in 20-year bonds bearing an annual interest rate not higher than 4.5 per cent, with payments based on the assessed value of the property as determined for tax purposes.[4] Land cultivated by renters, share-croppers, and squatters was also expropriable, even when belonging to owners who possessed less land than the legal maximum.

Public property and expropriated private estates could be distributed in two ways.[5] One was in the form of individual holdings of not less than 26.8 hectares of fertile land, without irrigation, distant from urban centers, and devoted to crops of average yield. This was the "vital minimum" for a family of five.[6]

Renters, share-croppers, and squatters had first priority to free "vital minimum" awards on the land they were cultivating; if this was less than 26.8 hectares, the supplementary land required to complete the legal minimum would be given (also free of charge), in so far as land was available and local conditions permitted.

In order to insure that distributed land was productively used, the law provided for the rescission of the titles in case the beneficiaries neglected its cultivation; moreover, distributed land could be sold only to the state (or with its authorization) and could not be divided, not even for inheritance purposes.

Land could also be distributed to agricultural cooperatives, which INRA would promote whenever possible. Until the law granted the cooperatives greater autonomy, they would be under the control of the Institute, which would also appoint the managers and supply credit and other resources.

Owing to the high concentration of land ownership and the high number of tenants, share-croppers, and squatters,[7] about 85 per cent of the land in farms[8] fell under the provisions of the Reform Law. As can be seen in Table 1, however, close to three-fourths of the area affected was in holdings of more than 400 hectares which belonged to only 2,873 owners.

Of course, not all the land reported in Table 1 would have been subject to redistribution under the law. In the first place, each large landowner could retain 402.6 hectares, and therefore only the area above this limit was expropriable; that, however, would still have amounted to about 5,000,000 hectares (roughly one-half of the land in farms). In the second place, the provisions allowed large estates to retain up to 1,342 hectares if their productivity exceeded national averages. Finally, owners must have managed directly part of the area in the holdings of less than 402.6 hectares which were being cultivated partly or totally

Table 1. Land Potentially Affected by the Agrarian Reform Law

Size Groups (hectares)	Area (1000's hectares)	(per cent)	Holdings (number)	(per cent)	Owners (1000's)	(per cent)
Up to 67.1	628.7	7.4	28.7	68.3	20.2	66.1
67.1 to 402.6	1641.4	19.3	9.7	23.2	7.5	24.5
More than 402.6	6252.1	73.3	3.6	8.5	2.8	9.4
Totals	8522.2	100.0	42.0	100.0	30.5	100.0

Source: Legal Department of INRA. The data are based on the replies of landowners to a request of INRA in which the former were asked to report all the land they held which was affected by any provision of the Agrarian Reform Law.

by tenants, sharecroppers, and squatters, and this would also have caused a decrease in the area which could be distributed under the law.

Nevertheless, it seems clear that, had the different provisions of the law been fully implemented, a large part of the land in farms—probably more than one-half—would have been subject to expropriation, the exact amount depending primarily on the intensity with which the large private estates were cultivated.

In practice, however, the institutional changes brought about by the Revolution were regulated only in part by the Agrarian Reform Law. At first, the government took over the estates of former officials and supporters of the Batista regime. Later in 1959, it "intervened" all the large cattle ranches. Expropriation gathered momentum in 1960;[9] more than 1,250,000 hectares belonging to the American sugar mills were nationalized under Law 851 of July 6 (the day on which the Eisenhower administration eliminated the remainder of the Cuban sugar quota for 1960). Three months later it was the turn of the Cuban *centrales;* under Law 890 of October 13, 910,000 more hectares passed into the control of the government from this source. By the beginning of 1961 about 4,500,000 hectares (just under one-half the land in farms) had been either expropriated or confiscated.[10] This marked the end of what can be called the first phase of the agrarian reform, in which institutional and social changes occurred at a dazzling pace and reflected primarily the deterioration of Cuban-American relations and the progressive radicalization of the Castro regime. The reorganization of the public and private sectors of agriculture early in 1961 introduced the second phase of the agrarian reform: the definite turn toward the organization of the rural economy along socialist lines.

1. The Initial Plan of Agrarian Reform

A. Institutional Changes

i

From the beginning the National Institute of Agrarian Reform became the key agency of the revolutionary government.[11] Under the law, INRA was endowed with considerable powers, which were by no means restricted to the expropriation and re-distribution of land, the organization of cooperatives, and other measures designed to carry out the program of agrarian reform. INRA could in effect propose tax and trade policies aimed at stimulating agricultural production; it was to supervise and co-ordinate housing, health, and education programs for the rural population, and it would have a credit department with whose policies those of other lending agencies would have to be co-ordinated.

In practice, INRA's influence was still wider. In the months following its creation, INRA absorbed numerous autonomous institutions which, like the Cuban Institute for Sugar Stabiliza-tion, the Committee for Tobacco Production, the Rice Stabiliza-tion Administration, and the Institute for Coffee Stabilization, had until then been in charge of promoting and regulating specific lines of agricultural production. Early in 1960, the former Bank of Agricultural and Industrial Development was integrated to the credit department of the Institute. Similarly, when the Bank for Economic and Social Development was abolished, its technical and costs departments were transferred to INRA. Thus the In-stitute became, in fact if not legally, the actual Ministry of Agri-culture, with an unprecedented range of functions and powers.[12]

Internally, INRA included departments concerned with legal, land, production, and trade affairs. Special sections in charge of agricultural machinery and credit were soon added, and the structure of the Institute continued to evolve as new institutional changes in the agricultural sector brought additional functions under government control.

At first, INRA was probably understaffed, at least in relation to the scope of its tasks. This limitation, however, seems to have been the result of a deliberate policy of Castro, who feared that the Institute might become slow, inefficient, and bureaucratic, devoid of direct links with the provinces. For this reason, the number of personnel was kept at a minimum, most of the depart-ments being staffed by a few technicians and some administrative employees. Thus a great burden was placed on high-level INRA officials, whose activity was further strained by the tendency to leave many decisions—including relatively unimportant ones—to the top levels of the administrative hierarchy.[13]

For implementing agrarian reform, the country was divided into 28 Zones of Agricultural Development. The zones were of very uneven sizes,[14] and each encompassed several *municipios*. An INRA delegate—usually a member of the rebel army—was installed, under the title of Chief of Zone, at the head of each administrative unit and was responsible for applying the Law of Agrarian Reform in his region. He had broad authority in all matters related to the economic and social development of the redistributed areas. Funds were placed at his disposal through direct remittances from INRA's central offices, and considerable latitude existed for their allocation. The delegates used them to finance the clearing of weeds and to purchase cattle, to pay the current expenditures of the recently organized cooperatives and for up-keep of rural roads, to set up "people's stores," and for social subsidies.[15] Although the chiefs of zones were in principle responsible to the Provincial Delegates of INRA, they frequently took the zone's problems directly to the national officials in Havana. Coordination was maintained by means of periodic meetings in the capital, attended by the leadership of the Institute, the heads of the principal departments, and all the provincial and zone delegates. High officials of INRA, including its president, also made frequent visits to the provinces.

ii

Between mid-1959 and the end of 1960, 3 new types of production units were organized in the agricultural sector: the agricultural cooperatives, the INRA-administered farms, and the cane cooperatives. Only the latter survived after the early 1961 reorganization until their final conversion into state cane farms in August of 1962.

The Agricultural Cooperatives were the first units established according to Article 43 of the Agrarian Reform Law, which prescribed that INRA would set up cooperatives whenever possible. The economic rationale for their establishment lay in the actual or potential economies of large-scale production which would have been lost if the large tracts of expropriated land had been divided. The revolutionary leaders were well aware not only of this direct economic loss but also of the higher costs involved in supplying social services (like schools, hospitals, recreational facilities, and technical advice) to a large group of small production units.[16]

The internal organization of the cooperatives was extremely loose.[17] None of the boards and councils usually associated with cooperatives existed formally. INRA appointed the managers, who were in charge of maintaining the necessary coordination with the chief of zone; they were often chosen from the peasants who became cooperative members. The members, typically, received a wage of 2.50 pesos for an 8-hour work-day, although a uniform, nationwide pattern did not exist. It was understood that these wages were an advance payment to be supplemented at the end of the year by a proportional share—based on the number of hours worked—of the cooperative's final net benefit. In fact, however, the lack of accounting records prevented the determination of the profits, and it was decided not to distribute any dividends.[18]

By May, 1960, INRA had organized 881 agricultural cooperatives, of which 550 were devoted solely to crops, 10 to livestock, 220 to mixed crop-cattle farming, and the rest to poultry and the exploitation of timber and coal. Most of the cooperatives were in the 200-300 hectare range, although some in Camagüey and Oriente were over 30,000 hectares.

Other farms were directly managed by INRA. These were organized primarily on land which had formerly belonged to the cattle *latifundia*, but they also included some large rice plantations. Although both ranches and rice plantations were certain to be affected by the Law of Agrarian Reform, the actual creation of the INRA farms was apparently prompted by the refusal of many of the owners of cattle *latifundia* to purchase young cattle from the small producers shortly after the promulgation of the Law of Agrarian Reform. The discontinuance of these purchases presented difficulties to the small producers, who, as has been noted, lacked sufficient pasture to maintain the cattle on their farms beyond a certain age. To remedy the difficulties, the government started to buy cattle from the small producers and, lacking its own pastureland on which to bring the cattle up to slaughter age, determined to "intervene" all the farms devoted to the production of livestock of more than 1,342 hectares at the end of June, 1959.[19] As a result, a substantial amount of land, located largely in Camagüey and Oriente, passed into the hands of the state. By the end of 1959, INRA was administering 475 farms with a total area of almost 900,000 hectares.

As with the cooperatives, the advantages of large-scale production recommended that the cattle *latifundia* be kept intact. On the other hand, their very low labor-land ratios influenced the government to administer these holdings directly, rather than to create cooperatives out of them. It was believed that members of cooperatives formed from the few permanent workers of the cattle *latifundia* would have been "privileged," given the large acreage such cooperatives would control. But if more peasants were to join these cooperatives the government would have had to invest heavily in housing for them. Ownership of these new facilities by the cooperatives would again have tended to establish a specially favored group. This the government did not want.[20] It preferred to retain as state property the substantial new investments required to diversify the cattle ranches. Hence these *latifundia*, after they were "intervened" in the second half of 1959, remained under the direct control of INRA until their eventual transformation into people's farms in January, 1961.

By May, 1960, the number of these units had risen to 511, of which 500 were devoted to livestock production. The latter had more than 600,000 head of cattle (over 10 per cent of the national total), most of which were close to slaughtering age. Few of these were cows.[21]

The last of the production units created during the initial period of agrarian reform were the cane cooperatives. As noted earlier, numerous state-administered farms and loosely organized agricultural cooperatives already existed at the end of 1959. The General Administration of Cane Cooperatives, on the other hand, was established only in March of the following year, and three more months elapsed before the first cooperative was actually created, on June 18, 1960. The relatively late establishment of cane cooperatives resulted from the government's decision to postpone agrarian reform for one year in the sugar industry in order not to disrupt the 1960 harvest. As soon as the harvest ended, cooperatives were organized in the areas supplying the sugar mills.

By August, 1960, more than 118,000 agricultural sugar workers were permanent members of the 604 new production units. The number increased to over 122,000 in May, 1961, when a census showed that the cooperatives had a total labor force of almost 170,000 workers and more than 800,000 hectares of land, the distribution of which, by provinces, is indicated in Table 2.

As institutions, the new production units defied easy classification. They were not cooperatives in the traditional sense of an association of independent farmers who unite their efforts to accomplish tasks which—like the purchase and use of costly equipment, the raising of loans, and the marketing and distribution of their produce—can be done more efficiently on a social basis but who retain private ownership of their usually rather small plots of land.

This classical type of cooperative could have been organized in Cuba with the *colonos* who cultivated cane on land they leased from the sugar *centrales*. Instead, the cooperatives were established on the former "administration cane land," that is, on acreage that was both owned and directly cultivated by the major landowners and sugar mills.[22] Similarly, the great majority of the members of the cooperatives were the former permanent agricultural workers of the cane *latifundia*.

These factors determined many of the institutional characteristics of the new units. As noted earlier, the Cuban sugar workers

Table 2. Provincial Distribution of Cane Cooperatives, Associations, and Cane Cooperatives, with Area and Labor Force of Cooperatives, May, 1961

		Cooperatives				
Provinces	Associ-ations	Number	Area		Workers	
			Total	Average	Permanent	Seasonal
			(In thousands of hectares)		(In thousands)	
Pinar del Río	46	29	30.6	1.06	4.7	1.6
Havana	2	29	31.0	1.07	4.1	1.3
Matanzas	3	62	67.9	1.09	8.4	2.0
Las Villas	4	125	120.5	.96	17.9	6.4
Camagüey	10	168	252.7	1.50	32.6	11.7
Oriente	14	209	306.6	1.46	54.7	23.6
Totals	13	622	809.4	1.30	122.4	46.6

Source: Administración General Cooperativas Cañeras.

were used to an environment which in some respects was more like an industrial wage system than the kind of pre-capitalist, semi-feudal, non-monetary *latifundia* which tend to prevail, for example, in the Andean countries of South America. Cuban workers had had long experience with trade unions, were paid in money wages (not through share-cropping arrangements), and were accustomed to working collectively under centralized management. It was therefore relatively easy to group them in entities in which they continued to work very much as they did before, but in whose administration they were offered greater participation, even though they did not themselves elect the managers.

The new production units incorporated some cooperative elements with other characteristics of state farms giving the government the dominant role. INRA was in charge of appointing the managers "until the cooperatives were perfectly organized and their members had acquired the necessary administrative experience."[23] On the other hand, the general assembly formed by all the members elected an annual directing board to aid and advise the manager in the performance of his functions. This seven-man board included officials responsible for production, supplies, education, machinery, housing, and personnel, with the principal member, the coordinator, entrusted with legal representation of the cooperative and allowed to share some administrative responsibility with the INRA-appointed manager.

The hybrid nature of the cane cooperative was apparent in other ways. Thus, while the farms that were directly and totally administered by INRA were financed out of the INRA budget, the cooperatives worked on the basis of annual credits from the Banco Nacional. They were, however, supposed to organize their production so that it fitted the government's plans and, with few exceptions, to sell their output to the state.[24]

Permanent members received "advances" at a daily rate of 2.50 pesos and were entitled to a share of the yearly net profit of the cooperative to which they belonged.[25] During the first 5 years, however, only 20 per cent of this net profit could be distributed among the members, the remainder being used to finance the construction of houses and other buildings in the cooperatives.

Seasonal workers could also be employed and, to the extent that diversification generated new employment during the "dead season," it was expected that they would be brought into the cooperatives as permanent members.

Coordination between the individual production units and the national authorities of INRA was maintained through a series of intermediate administrative offices. Ten to 15 cooperatives formed one association (*agrupación*), of which there were 46 in the country. Each association was headed by an administrator and staffed with an accountant and other administrative personnel; it also maintained repair shops for machinery. The associations were under provincial offices; at the top of the pyramid was the general administrator of cane cooperatives, responsible for all aspects of the agricultural part of sugar production.[26]

iii

In the private sector of agriculture two major institutional changes occurred over the period being analyzed: the issue of ownership titles to farmers cultivating less than the "vital minimum" and the limitation of most private farms to a statutory maximum of 402.6 hectares.

The distribution of land to the peasantry started slowly in 1959. Less than 2,000 titles had been granted by the end of January, 1960.[27] Thereafter distribution gathered momentum. The number of titles approached 16,000 in August, 1960, was just under 20,000 in October, and by the end of the year had climbed to nearly 30,000.[28] By February, 1961, 32,823 peasants had become owners of the land they had previously cultivated as tenants, share-croppers, or squatters. As Table 3 reveals, more than 380,000 hectares had been transferred, almost one-half of them in backward, squatter-heavy Oriente, where most titles were granted.

In the rest of the private sector, the size of the production units was usually reduced to 30 *caballerías*, though in some cases farmers were allowed to retain up to 671 hectares of land. The latter exception was often made in the cattle ranches of Camagüey and Oriente, which were permitted to retain the higher limit as long as they kept 14 head of cattle per *caballería*.[29]

Table 3. Ownership Titles Granted and Land Distributed in Cuba (June, 1959—February, 1961)

Province	Titles	Land (In thousands of hectares)
Pinar del Río	5536	53.4
Havana	2669	37.7
Matanzas	3057	33.1
Las Villas	4508	58.3
Camagüey	2524	27.1
Oriente	14,529	173.2
Total	32,823	382.8

Source: Legal Department of INRA.

B. Economic and Social Developments

The crop production that can properly be associated with the first phase of the agrarian reform occurred during the agricultural years 1959-60 and 1960-61. The crops of 1959 in most cases had already been harvested by the time implementation of the new programs began and were not affected by them. On the other hand, the farm output of the agricultural year 1961-62 was influenced by the institutional reorganization which took place early in 1961; it will therefore be analyzed as part of the second phase.

i

Table 4 shows the physical output of sugar for the period 1957-61. Two factors are immediately obvious. The first is the maintenance of production during the first two years following the Revolution; the second is the big increase in 1961.

As noted, the rise in 1959 cannot be attributed to the agrarian reform. From an institutional point of view, the harvest that year was not different from those of pre-revolutionary days, the 161 sugar mills still being under private management. That harvest does provide, however, at least partial evidence of the ability of the new government to avoid major disruptions in the cane fields during the period immediately following the collapse of the Batista regime. Nor was the institutional setting significantly altered until after the 1960 harvest. During 1959, INRA intervened 7 sugar mills which had contributed only 2 or 3 per

Table 4. Physical Output of Sugar in Cuba, 1957-61

YEAR	VOLUME (In thousands of Metric Tons)	INDEX (1957-58 = 100)
1957	5673.3	⎫
1958	5784.5	⎬ 100.0
1959	5961.6	104.0
1960	5804.9	101.3
1961	6869.7	119.9

Source: 1957-59: *Anuario Azucarero,* 1959, 1960: Jacques Chonchol, "Análisis Crítico de la Reforma Agraria Cubana," *El Trimestre Económico,* No. 117 (January-March, 1963), 1961: *Variedades de Caña, Zafra de 1961* (Ministry of Industries).

cent of the total output of sugar in the harvest of that year; 6 of these 7 *centrales* were operated by INRA during the 1960 crop.

As already noted, cooperatives were organized in the sugar *latifundia* after the end of the 1960 harvest. By October of the same year, all 161 *centrales* had passed under the control of the government. The following year was therefore the occasion of the first "people's crop" (*zafra del pueblo*). It was a remarkable success. In spite of labor shortages toward the end of the harvest, production soared to more than 6,800,000 tons—the second largest crop in Cuba's history, exceeded only by the 7,200,000 tons of 1952.

Three factors caused this steep rise in output. There were, first, very favorable weather conditions in 1960. Average rainfall for the year was 61.9 inches, falling almost exactly between the average annual normal of 54.0 inches and the 72.2 inches "high" for the period 1925-47.[30]

More important, however, were the short-run effects of the institutional changes in the sugar sector. These meant that for the first time in nearly a decade the productive potential of the sugar industry was fully utilized. In effect, the government decided in 1960 to discontinue the practice of leaving a large part of the cane unharvested in the fields;[31] in 1961, whatever cane was available would be cut.[32] In practice, the target was not fully reached, the harvested area being 93.8 per cent of the land planted with cane.[33] This percentage, however, considerably exceeded that of any year since 1952 and led to a considerable rise in the area harvested, even though the area planted with cane had been smaller than in any year between 1953-59, with the sole exception of 1958. In comparison with 1958—the last year for which the 1959 *Anuario* gives a definite figure—the area harvested in 1961 was about 20 per cent higher, which was also the approximate percentage difference between the outputs of the two years.

Finally, the increase in sugar output reflected the delayed expropriation of the lands of the sugar mills, and, in particular, the perennial nature of sugar cane. Taken together, these factors meant that the task of the cooperatives during their first year was primarily, if not only, that of harvesting already existing plantations. This challenge they met successfully—an organizational achievement which appears more remarkable in the light of the simultaneous military mobilization before and during the invasion of Bay of Pigs.[34] Yet, as subsequent events would show, it did not signify that efficient production units had been established in the principal sector of Cuban agriculture.

ii

As noted by Oshima,[35] data on the output of animal products were very inadequate before the Revolution, and a reliable index of livestock production did not exist. A precise quantitative comparison of pre- and post-revolutionary trends is therefore impossible. Nevertheless, the main lines of development in the cattle industry can be assessed broadly by considering, first, changes in the consumption of beef and, second, changes in the size of herds.[36] Enough information is available to estimate the direction and the order of magnitude of the former, and for the latter, the direction, if not the rate of change, can be inferred from subsequent developments.

The first years of the new regime, as we have learned, witnessed increases in employment and production and a drastic redistribution of income in favor of the poor.[37] As was to be expected, the increased purchasing power of the low-income groups induced a sharp increase in the demand for beef. Thus, in May, 1960, INRA claimed that it was regularly supplying the demand for beef of Havana, "in spite of the fact that consumption has increased up to 60 per cent with respect to 1958."[38] Similarly, when discussing the early economic changes brought about by the

Revolution, Dr. Felipe Pazos in 1962 observed that "this rise in the real income of the working class must have brought an increase in the consumption of beef of not less than 50 per cent. . . ."[39] In fact, the rate by which meat consumption rose may have been still higher. For example, data collected by the JUCEI (Council for Coordination, Execution, and Inspection) in Las Villas revealed that while 17,267 head had been slaughtered in that province during the first quarter of 1959, the figure for the corresponding period 2 years later was 41,587, that is, consumption had increased by 140.8 per cent.[40] Similarly, in Oriente the number of cattle slaughtered went up from 22,900 head in the first quarter of 1959 to 47,600 in 1961, reflecting a rise in consumption of 107.9 per cent.[41]

Although some government officials claimed that the higher levels of consumption had been met by corresponding gains in production,[42] it is clear that increases of the magnitude indicated could in the short run only result in a substantial reduction of the cattle reserves. That this was the case was to become evident in early 1962, when rationing of beef was imposed at lower levels of consumption than those of pre-revolutionary days.

iii

The output of crops which together represent somewhat over one-fourth of the total value of crop production in Cuba is shown in Table 5. The figures reveal an unmistakable upward trend. Only for coffee was output in early 1961 below the level of 1957-58,[43] and this fall was largely attributable to the almost perfect two-year cycle observable in recent Cuban coffee production.[44] Even for coffee, however, production in 1961 was only 4.2 per cent below the average level of the years 1957-58, and 1960 had marked the historical peak.

All the other "traditional crops" showed significant increases, ranging from almost 10 per cent over the 1957-58 average in the production of henequen to 26.1 per cent in the output of rice. For both henequen and potatoes, the gains reversed the downward trends in output of the years before the Revolution (Table 4, Chapter II). Production of tobacco, after falling in 1959, rose steadily in the following years, reaching a record level in 1961 which exceeded the 1957-58 average by 13.4 per cent.[45]

Table 5. Production of Selected Crops in Cuba, 1957-61
(In thousands of metric tons)

	1957	1958	1959	1960	1961
Tobacco	41.7	50.6	35.6	45.3	52.3
Rice	256.8	225.9	282.1	304.2	230.0
Coffee[a]	36.7	43.7	29.5	55.2	38.5
Potatoes[a]	94.9	79.3	71.6	97.6	101.4
Henequen	11.2	9.1	8.5	13.2	11.1
Peanuts	4.2	2.5	2.4	5.3	8.0
Cotton	—[b]	—[b]	0.05	0.8	5.5
Soybean	—[b]	—[b]	—[b]	0.3	2.0[c]
Tomatoes	n.a.	n.a.	89.9	102.4	129.9

n.a. Data not available.
a. Figures correspond to agricultural years.
b. Crop was not cultivated.
c. Estimated.
Sources: 1957-60: Tables 2 and 4, Chapter II, and Jacques Chonchol, "Análisis Crítico de la Reforma Agraria Cubana," *El Trimestre Económico*, No. 117 (January-March, 1963), 1961: All products, except tobacco, rice, peanuts, and soybean from Chonchol; tobacco, peanuts, and soybean from INRA; rice from *Castro, Dorticós, Guevara, Rodríguez Hablan para el Instituto Popular de Chile* (1962).

The rates of growth were, of course, much higher for the "new crops," such as cotton and soybean, and also for peanuts, the cultivation of which had begun in the thirties but had stagnated in the decade before the Revolution. These increases reflected the vigorous drive of the government to reduce the dependence of the textile industry on imported raw materials and to replace heavy imports of lard and vegetable oils by expanding cultivation of oil-bearing crops.

There is little doubt, then, that in the first half of 1961, crop output (including sugar cane) was substantially higher than before the Revolution. Indeed even with fairly pessimistic assumptions about the production of crops for which information is not available, total crop output at the end of the first period of agrarian reform must have been about 12 per cent higher than the average of the years 1957-58.[46]

iv

Although the limitations of the available data preclude a precise determination of the factors which caused crop output to rise, a broad interpretation is possible. Some of the relevant facts are fairly well known, and in other cases figures are available which, though not exact, at least provide orders of magnitude of the factors involved.

On the side of demand, expansion was stimulated by the pressures arising from the rise of employment and the rise and more equal distribution of income. In many cases these changes led to increases in the prices paid to the farmers,[47] and even when prices were frozen, as for rice and coffee, the increased demand meant that producers faced a rapidly expanding market.

In terms of inputs, the key role was played by the growth of the area under cultivation and the fuller use of the agricultural labor force. More fertilizers were applied, and, although reliable statistical information is lacking, it would seem that the stock of farm machinery did not decline.

On the first anniversary of the Agrarian Reform Law, in May, 1960, INRA claimed that the Zones of Agricultural Development had added to the area under crops over 175,000 hectares of land formerly idle or covered by *marabú*.[48] Although this amount fell short of the planned target by 24 per cent, it represented an increase of over 20 per cent of the land devoted to crops other than cane in 1945.[49] Most of this new area was allocated to import-substituting crops, like rice, cotton, peanuts, potatoes, and soybeans. Rice alone took almost one half of the additional acreage. The area planted with cotton (less than 150 hectares in 1958) increased to more than 3,600 hectares in 1959 and to 17,500 one year later. Similarly, between 1959-60 and 1960-61 the area planted with potatoes was estimated to have risen by more than one-fifth. In contrast, the area devoted to the traditional crops—sugar, coffee, and tobacco—varied little.

Expansion of the cultivated area continued in the second year of the agrarian reform. At the production meeting of August, 1961, it was reported that until then the amount of land cleared by the bulldozers of INRA exceeded 440,000 hectares.[50] This did not mean that the area under crops had risen by the same amount; at least 73,000 hectares had been allocated to increase artificial pastures,[51] and because of obvious time lags only a fraction of the land recently cleared could have been immediately planted. Moreover, part of the crops planted on the new land would be ready for harvesting only at the end of 1961 and thus could not affect production attributable to the first phase of reform. Nevertheless, it is clear that during this period the area under cultivation was greatly increased.[52] Indeed the expansion may well have been exaggerated: led by what Dumond calls the "hatred of the *marabú*," INRA units plowed up land under the weed, at times with insufficient consideration for the low productive quality of the area being cleared.

The widening of the extensive margin of cultivation was accompanied by a rise in rural employment. The latter was estimated by the Ministry of Labor to have averaged about 600,000 in 1958 and over 800,000 two years later.[53] Although this increase of one third may overestimate actual changes, some significant rise in agricultural employment seems beyond doubt, given INRA's vigorous policy of agricultural diversification.

A third factor contributing to the growth of non-sugar production after 1958 was the increased use of fertilizers, whose allocation also reflected the emphasis on diversification. As Table 6 shows, total inputs of fertilizers rose from 1955 to 1957 and then fell sharply between 1957 and 1958; in these years the changes in the total consumption of fertilizers reflected almost exclusively the fluctuations of sugar production. The pattern changed in 1959, when total use of fertilizers remained practically constant, notwithstanding a reduction of more than 10 per cent in the fertilizer consumption of the sugar industry, and again in 1960, when the rise in the volume of fertilizers used by the sugar industry accounted for less than 40 per cent of the total increase. Use of fertilizers rose sharply in 1960 in the production of tobacco, potatoes, and vegetables and almost doubled for rice; yet the greatest expansion occurred in the cultivation of the "other crops," in which consumption of fertilizers was that year more than three times higher than in the period 1955-58.

It is not clear whether rising inputs of land, labor, and fertilizers during the period 1959-60 were also accompanied by a higher rate of investment in agricultural machinery. In May, 1960, INRA reported that it had spent about 32,000,000 pesos on tractors, pumps, spare parts, and other farm equipment.[54] Of this total, however, almost one fourth had been purchased abroad but had not yet been received. One year later, the Institute re-

Table 6. Use of Fertilizers in Cuba, by Crops, 1955-60
(In thousands of short tons)

Crops	1955	1956	1957	1958	1959	1960
Sugar cane	46.0	122.2	245.9	115.6	98.2	136.0
Tobacco	36.3	30.4	36.5	32.3	40.4	48.5
Rice	36.1	25.6	20.4	22.9	28.7	55.9
Potatoes	25.4	20.7	19.0	26.6	19.9	22.6
Vegetables	15.2	24.5	29.2	30.7	32.3	39.6
Other crops	14.0	13.2	13.0	14.5	23.5	47.4
Totals	173.0	236.6	364.0	242.6	242.9	350.0

Sources: 1955-58: *Anuario Azucarero,* 1959. 1959-60: Production Department of INRA.

ported that its imports of tractors, bulldozers, combines, and other agricultural machinery had reached a value of 81,000,000 pesos, of which 35,000,000 had been spent in the socialist countries.[55] Presumably these figures represented the aggregate purchases made by INRA up to May, 1961. The figure probably included an unspecified amount of machinery which had been acquired but had still not arrived in Cuba at that time. Nevertheless, even after reducing the figure quoted by 25 per cent to 60,000,000 and spreading the latter over a three-year period, the value of imports of capital goods for agriculture would be higher than the 16,800,000 annual average over the five-year period preceding the Revolution.[56]

Two qualifications seem to be in order, however. First, the significance of the comparison above—as of other similar value comparisons—is considerably reduced owing to the host of problems raised by the drastic changes in the sources of imports and the shift from a system of multilateral trade to one largely conducted under barter agreements. In the second place, it is likely that by the end of 1960 the efficiency of the old farm machinery was beginning to fall because of the difficulties of importing American-made spare parts. On the other hand, as a result of the diversification policy agricultural equipment was probably used more intensively, even though less carefully. All in all, it does not seem unreasonable to think that the capital equipment available to Cuban agriculture in the first two years of the agrarian reform was probably no less than in pre-revolutionary days.

More land, labor, and capital are not, however, all that is needed to attain higher output. As, or more, essential for economic growth, especially in countries undergoing rapid structural change, is organization, understood in its widest sense of all effort aimed at combining productive resources. Indeed, it is here where radical agrarian reforms are likely to find the greatest initial difficulties; when the old institutions are discarded, the available supplies of land, labor, and capital do not change greatly, at least in the short run. The greatest scarcity is likely to be of managers and foremen, and, more generally, of personnel with experience in making and implementing production decisions.

Therefore, an analysis of the early growth of crop production must also consider the internal organization of the production units. In particular, it must explain why rapid and massive institutional changes in Cuba did not lower crop output as had occurred, initially, at least, in other countries where radical programs of land reform were introduced.

During the first two years of the Cuban experience, two major factors seem to have offset any short-run reduction of output owing to the institutional reorganization. The first factor was the ability to make wide modifications in the institutional framework of important sectors of agriculture with rather minor changes within the production units themselves. For example, the principal effects of the Agrarian Reform Law in the tobacco industry were the elimination of share-cropping (which, as noted earlier, was very common in this sector) and the award of ownership titles to former tenants. The production process was hardly disrupted by these institutional changes, although the elimination of rents provided greater incentives to the tobacco growers. Nor was the internal structure altered in the coffee industry, where small, privately managed farms continued to predominate. Essentially the same situation prevailed in the 380,000 hectares distributed as "vital minimum" awards to former tenants, share-croppers, and squatters, who continued to work, now as owners, the same land they had cultivated before. Similarly, the government's decision not to divide the large rice plantations after expropriation early in 1960 meant that the internal structure of these units was little changed until their consolidation into gigantic "people's farms" one year later.

The importance of this institutional factor should not be exaggerated, however, since it hardly applies to the land cultivated by the newly established agricultural cooperatives. Instead, the initial success of these cooperatives reflected the single-minded determination of the new government officials and farm managers to raise agricultural output. Chonchol has aptly characterized this drive as "productive enthusiasm."[57] It was productive enthusiasm which led the regional delegates of INRA and the managers of the cooperatives to promise the fulfillment of impossibly high output targets. As was only to be expected, often targets were not reached, but in the very attempt land was cleared and plowed, the area under cultivation expanded, rural unemployment declined, and farm output increased. It was also productive enthusiasm that explains the situation prevailing on the large private farms after the first months of the Revolution; Pazos describes it so well:

As the months elapsed and the revolution became more radical, the landowners began to lose the hopes of retaining their land if they pursued a policy of crop intensification and stopped making additional investments, beginning, on the contrary, to reduce the work required to maintain production. *But the workers prevented the reduction of the work.* When the time came for plowing or planting the fields, the local workers demanded that the owner or manager order (and pay for) the work, and, if he refused, they accused him of being a counter revolutionary before the chief of the rebel army in the zone or before the delegate of INRA, *and the work was promptly done.*[58]

Of course, productive enthusiasm was not free of mistakes— for example, the plowed acreage was not always of good quality, and at times it would have been more economical to concentrate on improving existing pastures than on opening new areas covered by *marabú*. Nevertheless, even though these shortcomings somewhat offset the influence of the powerful drive to increase output, the impression remains that the net impact was positive in the areas of deepest structural change.

v

Agrarian reform, as conceived by the leaders who came to power in 1959, was a revolutionary process of wide scope, in which the social and cultural improvement of the rural masses had high priority. "From now on," said Castro in a speech to the peasants of Santa Clara in June of 1959, "the children of the peasants will have schools, sport facilities, and medical attention, and the peasants will count for the first time as an essential element of the nation."[59]

To fulfill these promises, the government invested heavily in rural housing, schools, and clinics. By December, 1960, the housing department of INRA had built or was building 49 small hospitals in the countryside, of which almost a half were in Oriente.[60] More than 60 rural school centers had been finished by the same time. Construction was started on the Camilo Cienfuegos "school city" in the Sierra Maestra, designed to provide primary education to 20,000 peasant children upon completion. Teams of doctors were periodically sent to the countryside. The government organized courses in sewing, art, and pottery, with students drawn primarily from the agricultural and sugar cane cooperatives, who returned to their places of origin to teach their new skills.

The rural population was also the principal beneficiary of the housing and public works programs of the government. Over 10,000 dwellings and more than 150 commercial developments, social centers, supermarkets, sport parks, and other social projects were constructed by INRA in the first 2 years of the agrarian reform. Nearly 2,000 state stores (*tiendas del pueblo*), said to be capable of serving more than 400,000 peasants, were set up in an attempt to improve the distribution of consumer goods in the countryside. New roads were opened to link cities and towns with isolated rural areas.

C. Conclusions

In the light of this analysis, it is difficult not to conclude that the first phase of the Cuban agrarian reform was characterized by rather remarkable achievements. Overall crop production rose, sugar output came close to the all-time 1952 record, and a start was made in the substitution of agricultural imports. Employment opportunities improved, social development was pushed vigorously, and for the first time a serious attempt was made to integrate the large rural population into the national life.

Of course, government policy and action during the period were not faultless. The failure to control the over-slaughtering of cattle was a mistake which was to exact a high price in the future. It was, moreover, an unnecessary error, since it was clearly predictable that the massive redistribution of income would result in a greatly increased demand for beef.

Also costly for the future, but probably unavoidable because of the rapidity of change, was the failure to keep accounting and statistical records in the cooperatives and zones of agricultural development. The result was that little information was collected on which serious planning could eventually be based. Authorities also had no way of knowing where crops were being produced more efficiently and why, and they were thus obstructed in their attempts to improve the allocation of resources.

It also seems that, in general, too many resources were allocated to social (as opposed to economic) investments in agriculture: the quality of the dwellings built in the countryside was excessive, for it was obtained at a sacrifice of quantity. Politically, of course, there were advantages to presenting to the peasantry a picture of the "new society."

The same tendency toward somewhat wasteful techniques tended to prevail in the construction of new secondary roads, which, according to Dumond, were unnecessarily wide for the traffic. "At the same cost," he writes, "it would have been possible to build longer, more solid, and more quickly finished roads."[61]

Finally, the lack of government concern with the private sector of agriculture was a serious shortcoming in view of the relative importance of privately owned farms in the total agricultural picture.

With the exception of the decrease in the size of the cattle herds and, to a lesser extent, of the failure to collect statistical information, these shortcomings could, however, have been amended easily and quickly. Hence, on the surface the Cuban agrarian reform did not seem to face in early 1961 insurmountable obstacles. Nevertheless, the second phase of the agrarian reform was distinctly less successful than the first.

2. The Second Phase of Agrarian Reform

In Cuban revolutionary terminology, 1959 was the year of revolution, 1960 the year of agrarian reform, and 1961 the year of education. But in agriculture, 1961 was to mark the beginning of a massive effort to diversify and increase farm production.

In order to accomplish its ambitious targets, the government introduced sweeping changes in the institutional framework of agriculture early in the year, which also reflected the growing political radicalism of the regime and the need to establish more permanent agricultural units now that the large estates had almost all been expropriated.

A. Institutional Changes

The two outstanding features of the 1961 reorganization were the creation of about 260 state farms, which became a part of the "socialist sector" of the economy, and the establishment and rapid expansion of the National Association of Small Farmers (ANAP) in the private sector of agriculture.[62]

i

In January, 1961, the loosely organized agricultural cooperatives were consolidated with the INRA-managed cattle ranches to form the *granjas del pueblo*. The new units were state enterprises, similar to the Russian *sovkhozy*. The ideological preference for state over cooperative production was only one of the reasons for their establishment. Other factors were the desire to control large units where agricultural diversification could proceed unhindered by traditional prejudices and where the most modern techniques could be implemented; the need for "factories in the countryside" which would insure a regular flow of foodstuffs to the urban centers; and the belief that redistributive justice would be better served by equal pay for equal work than by division among workers of the cooperatives' profits, which would partly depend on differences in land productivity.[63]

The state farms were run by managers appointed by INRA, with assistants in charge of machinery, cattle, crops, education, and other activities. Expenditures were financed directly out of the Institute budget. The workers of the *granjas* received a net wage of 2.61 pesos for an 8-hour day, initially with no adjustment for differences in productive performance.[64] In addition, permanent workers were entitled to free housing, medical care, and other social services.

At the beginning, administration of the people's farms was considerably centralized. Unlike the cane cooperatives, which were grouped in 46 regional associations, no intermediate level was established for the state farms, which therefore had to refer their financial and organizational problems directly to the central offices of INRA in Havana. "There are 304 farms"—said the Institute's Production Chief Eduardo Santos Ríos during the 1961 national production meeting—"and they are centrally managed, one by one."[65] It later became obvious, however, that exaggerated centralization contributed to wasteful delays, and by 1962 special departments concerned with the problems of the people's farms had been established in the regional offices of INRA.

In terms of the area controlled, the people's farms became the most important units within the public sector, although they lagged behind the cane cooperatives in employment. In May, 1961, 266 state farms extended over nearly 2,500,000 hectares and provided employment to almost 100,000 permanent or seasonal workers. As Table 7 shows, most of the new units were located in the eastern provinces; Oriente alone contained almost one-half of all the farms, although in terms of area Camagüey was a close second.

The gigantic size of the *granjas* is apparent from Table 8, the national average in 1961 being as high as 9,000 hectares. The average size was much larger in Camagüey, and the Gramna farm in Oriente extended over 47,000 hectares.

Most farms typically consisted of half-a-dozen separate pieces of land, often widely scattered.[66] Land-labor ratios were very high—national averages in May, 1961, were almost 90 hectares per permanent worker, and just over 25 hectares if seasonal workers are also considered (Table 8). The corresponding figures for

Table 7. Number, Area, Labor Force, and Provincial Distribution of the People's Farms in Cuba, May, 1961

Provinces	Number of Farms	Total Area (in thousands of hectares)	Workers (In thousands) Permanent	Seasonal	Total
Pinar del Río	29	328.0	4.0	17.7	21.7
Havana	23	172.6	2.9	2.7	5.6
Matanzas	11	106.2	3.0	6.1	9.1
Las Villas	41	328.5	4.3	5.5	9.8
Camagüey	58	700.2	4.3	7.8	12.1
Oriente	104	797.8	8.7	29.3	38.0
Total	266	2434.4	27.3	69.1	96.5

Source: Administración General de Granjas del Pueblo.

the cane cooperatives at the same time were 6.6 and 4.8. The difference, however, is easily explained in terms of the different types of land held by farms and cooperatives. The people's farms were primarily organized on the land controlled by the cattle and rice *latifundia* before the Revolution;[67] in contrast, the cane cooperatives were established on former administration cane land, whose employment (although sharply fluctuating over the year) was considerably above that of the cattle farms or the highly mechanized rice plantations.

ii

In a major speech to the sugar workers in December, 1960, Castro called for the establishment of a nation-wide association of small farmers that would merge the organizations of cane growers, coffee cultivators, and other specialist farmers that existed before the Revolution.[68] Shortly thereafter steps were taken to establish ANAP, and in May, 1961, on the second anniversary of the Agrarian Reform Law, the new institution held its first national assembly, in which its statutes were approved.

According to these, ANAP would organize and orient the small farmers in implementing the agrarian program of the Revolution and, by managing credit policy, would attempt to direct small farm production in accordance with the national targets. It would also cooperate in the purchase of agricultural products and

Table 8. Average Area and Land-Labor Ratio in the People's Farms in Cuba, May, 1961

Provinces	Average Area	Land-Labor Ratio	
	(In 1,000 hectares)	(Hectares/Perm. Workers)	(Hect./Worker)
Pinar del Río	11.3	81.9	15.1
Havana	7.5	58.6	30.5
Matanzas	9.6	35.3	11.7
Las Villas	8.0	75.7	33.2
Camagüey	12.1	161.2	57.8
Oriente	7.7	92.0	21.0
CUBA	9.1	89.1	25.2

Source: Table 6.

help the government with the economic and social development of the rural areas. The new association might "foster the spirit of cooperation, but following always the voluntary principle" (*principio de la voluntariedad*). Membership was restricted to farmers possessing not more than 67.1 hectares, although, exceptionally, peasants having more land than this could join the association, provided "they had a proven revolutionary background."[69]

Headed by a general administrator appointed by INRA,[70] the administrative structure of ANAP was composed of provincial and regional delegations and, at the base, of local delegations of cane *colonos,* the peasant associations, the credit and service cooperatives, and the agricultural societies.

The new institution developed rapidly. Part of INRA's credit department was transferred to it, which gave ANAP significant influence in the shaping of policy for small farmers. In addition, ANAP was compelled to create a department of supplies to fill the vacuum left by the decline of the private system of distribution, and by 1962 it was running almost 1,000 people's stores located in areas populated primarily by peasants.

Small and intermediate farmers were initially organized in Peasant Associations and in Local Delegations of Cane Growers. By May, 1962, there were over 2,000 Associations, almost one-half of them in Oriente, with probably about 100,000 members.[71] There were 160 delegations of cane growers at that time, but no figure was given of either membership or area controlled. Both these institutions, however, were believed to be of declining importance and likely to give way in the future to "other superior forms of organization."[72]

One of these institutions into which the Association and Local Delegation might evolve is the Credit and Services Cooperative, in which individual farmers join together to obtain credit, buy machinery, and sell crops but cultivate their plots separately.[73] Another is the Agricultural Society—which was at one time the most advanced form of organization and production in ANAP. Agricultural Societies are cooperatives of the traditional type, established on land contributed by individual peasants,[74] who cultivate the aggregate on a commercial basis and elect a three-man managing council. Payments to members—either in kind or in money—vary according to the contribution made to production and, unlike the method employed on the people's farms, payment for equal work may vary among the different societies according to overall yields and outputs. For ideological reasons, use of hired workers is strongly discouraged. The societies can obtain financial credit from ANAP, which markedly favors them over the other types of agricultural organization. The societies also receive preferential treatment in the distribution of seeds, fertilizers, and agricultural machinery. In return, they are expected to adjust their production according to the national plan and to determine annually the proportion of their output which will be sold to the government.

In May, 1962, the Agricultural Societies were still relatively insignificant: of the 229 such societies, 220 had just over 2,000 members working an area of only 16,800 hectares.[75]

By mid-1962, the agricultural societies had ceased to be the most advanced form of socialist production in ANAP. A new department of ANAP[76] was in effect managing almost 700 small and intermediate farms extending over almost 150,000 hectares. Close to 8,000 agricultural workers were employed under conditions which closely paralleled those on the people's farms.[77]

Due to ANAP's rapid expansion, it is difficult to calculate its membership. In May, 1961, it was estimated that between 80,000 and 90,000 small farmers belonged.[78] One year later, the administrator general's annual report estimated that about 150,-000 peasants had participated in the discussion of ANAP's output targets for 1962.[79]

Similarly, the area controlled by ANAP members is uncertain. Although the 1962 report does not give any aggregate figure, INRA's 1961 *Informe al Pueblo* stated that ANAP farmers controlled slightly over 3,500,000 hectares in May, 1961. This figure also seems too high.[80] In fact, by 1962 the area controlled by ANAP's members was probably in the neighborhood of 2,500,000 hectares.[81]

iii

In May, 1961, a census of the cane cooperatives and people's farms gave the total areas and provincial breakdowns shown in Tables 2 and 7. Three months later further data on the distribution of land indicated that the public sector of agriculture had made new gains, although it still accounted for only about 35 per cent of the total farmland (Table 9). Hence, in the second half of 1961 Cuban agriculture was still predominantly private. The owners of intermediate and large farms possessed more land than the whole of the public sector, although if the land held by members of ANAP is added to that of the state farms and cane cooperatives, the share of the total farmland under the direct or indirect control of the government rises to almost three-fifths of the total.

Private farmers were also more important than state units in certain key sectors of agriculture. As Table 12 shows, in early 1962 the public sector controlled just over one-third of the 1,200,000 hectares under cane. Similarly, the almost 1,400,000 cattle[82]—most of them on the people's farms—in the public sector represented one-quarter of the total estimated herds;[83] the proportion was below one-fifth in the case of cows.

Although no relevant figures are available, it seems unlikely that the public sector included a predominant share of the land devoted to coffee and tobacco. Thus, among the important crops, only in the case of rice was more produced in the public than in the private sector. In August, 1961, 54 per cent of the area under rice was in people's farms, 6 per cent in cane cooperatives, and the rest in private farms, mostly medium-sized or large.[84]

B. *Economic Developments*

"The next year," said Premier Castro in December, 1960, "must be the great year of diversification in the cane coopera-

Table 9. Distribution of Land in Farms in Cuba by Type of Unit, August, 1961

	Area	Per Cent
	(In thousands of hectares)	
People's Farms	2656.7	26.4
Cane Cooperatives	877.8	8.7
Public Sector	3534.5	35.1
ANAPa	2416.3	24.0
Rest of Private Sectorb	4118.2	40.9
Total	10070.0	100.0

a. Estimated.
b. Obtained by residual.
Sources: People's farms: "Informe de la Administración Nacional de Granjas del Pueblo a la Primera Reunión Nacional de la Producción," *Obra Revolucionaria,* No. 30 (August, 1961). Cane Cooperatives: "Informe de la Administración Nacional de Cooperativas Cañeras a la Primera Reunión Nacional de la Producción," *Obra Revolucionaria,* No. 30 (August, 1961).

tives. . . ,[85] the year of the great development of agricultural production."[86] With ample supplies of machinery, which was beginning to arrive in great quantities, and based on the three large organizations—the people's farms, the cane cooperatives, and ANAP—farm output would increase[87] and agricultural unemployment disappear.[88]

Such were the general directives. In the next few months, as sugar output reached what was almost a historical peak, other crops made impressive gains, and the regime emerged victorious from the Bay of Pigs, the revolutionary leaders developed increased confidence in the possibilities of a "great leap forward." The long-sought desire to escape from the evils of monoculture was to be realized, now that the government controlled a substantial part of agricultural resources.

Ambitious targets were set for almost all crops. Following perhaps too literally the "golden rule" formulated by Professor Dumond in May, 1960—never a crop-farm without livestock, never a cattle-farm without crops[89]—all production units in the public sector were asked to diversify. The people's farms would put 830,000 hectares—nearly one-third of their total area—under more than twenty-five different crops and *pangola.* Plans for the cane cooperatives were perhaps even more radical. They had grown some crops besides cane in 1960, and, following Premier Castro's speech to the cane cooperatives coordinators in August, they had been buying cows to supply their members with milk. But the great shift was to occur the following year. According to the plans, the cooperatives in 1961 would cultivate substantial areas of maize, rice, beans, millet, *viandas,* and numerous other crops on about 165,000 hectares. In addition, they would sow over 40,000 hectares of *pangola* to feed their increasing numbers of cattle.

To allow for this considerable expansion, more than 130,000 hectares of cane land were to be uprooted following the harvest of 1961. This plan was adopted not because cultivable land was no longer physically available at the cooperatives but because of what were thought to be some economic considerations. In a reference to the cane which remained uncut on the land before 1961, Dr. Castro had explained to the sugar workers and cane cutters that they "have left us . . . more than 10,000 *caballerías* of fertile land completely unutilized, . . . land which is suitable for cereals, grains of all sorts, for any type of crop."[90] "How," he had asked, "are we going to spend millions of pesos in buying bulldozers to clear the land if we have more than 10,000 *caballerías* for which nothing else is to be done than to send the cane cutters to clear them, without having to spend millions of pesos in the clearing?"[91] Thus the momentous decision was made. In 1961, wrote Professor Severo Aguirre, "the cooperatives will cease to be exclusively devoted to cane. They will cultivate cane under systems which will permit the use of less land and obtain higher yields per *caballería* of cane."[92]

By August, 1961, the decision was being implemented. "The cane cooperatives"—read the report of the General Administration of Cane Cooperatives to the national production meeting— "are demolishing 10,000 *caballerías* of cane, which," it added, "for their members means the difference between hunger and the satisfaction of all their needs."[93] Some people, it is true, had certain hesitations about destroying cane, but they, said Aguirre, had no basis for their fears after the national production meeting. Had the cooperatives not demolished the cane, they would not be able to fulfill the output targets for 1962.[94]

How much of the agricultural program was accomplished? Did farm production increase? Or did it fall and, if so, for what reasons? The statistical evidence is limited (though the rationing that was imposed in 1962 provides an additional source of production estimates), and thus a precise answer is difficult. Some general conclusions nevertheless can be reached.

i

Table 10 shows the planned and actual production of cane and sugar in 1962. The failure to reach the target is obvious, for actual sugar output was more than one-fifth below planned output. The decline is, of course, much greater—about 30 per cent—with respect to the previous year. In fact, it is necessary to go back to 1955 to find a smaller harvest.

It is not difficult, however, to explain the sharp reversal in the output of the main sector of the Cuban economy. Three factors played major roles. The first was the prolonged drought of 1961. As Table 11 shows, rainfall in 1961 was considerably below the average of the previous year (61.9 inches) and also less than normal. Moreover, the distribution of rainfall over the year added to the detrimental effects of the drought. Although rainfall from January through May was hardly different from usual (total rainfall during those months was only one inch below normal, and in three of the five exceeded the average), for the rest of the year, with the sole exception of August, rainfall was well below normal (by almost 20 per cent in the last seven months). This distribution meant that the drought hit hardest precisely during and after the vital period when the sugar cane sprouts.

Unfavorable weather conditions, although important, do not, however, explain the whole of the decline. As mentioned already,

Table 10. Planned and Actual Production of Cane and Sugar in Cuba in 1962
(In thousands of metric tons)

	Planned	Actual	Per Cent of Goal
Cane Ground	54,588.4	36,691.7	67.2
Sugar	6,141.8	4,815.2	78.4

Source: INRA.

Table 11. Normal and 1961 Actual Monthly Rainfall in Cuba (In inches)

Month	Normal	Year 1961
January	1.7	2.19
February	1.4	1.90
March	2.0	1.85
April	3.4	1.37
May	7.0	7.25
June	7.8	7.35
July	5.5	4.15
August	6.0	6.57
September	7.2	5.47
October	6.8	5.78
November	3.5	0.82
December	1.7	1.17
Annual	54.0	45.77

Source: Normal: *Investment in Cuba,* Table 79.   1961: Ministry of Industries.

the diversification plan for the cooperatives involved uprooting 134,000 hectares of cane—a reduction of almost 10 per cent in the acreage planted in cane at the beginning of the 1961 harvest.   In terms of potential output, however, the uprooting had even greater significance, since the cane that was destroyed was on some of the best cane land of Cuba—the former *cañas de adminis-tración.* Thus, even if nothing else had changed, a decline in sugar output of about 10 per cent could have been expected. Besides, the plan was not always executed in the way that would hurt production least: in some cases, young cane or cane close to the sugar mills was uprooted, and production was further reduced.[95]

In addition, other things had changed.   At least on the co-operatives, it seems clear that the average age of the cane had increased.   Although no precise information is available, it seems unlikely that much cane was replanted in 1960 following the creation of the cane cooperatives and the intervention of the sugar-mills.   Perhaps as early as 1961, then, the average age of the co-operative's cane began to rise.   The process continued after the harvest, for the plan of the cooperatives called for the replanting only of about 4,000 hectares,[96] that is, less than 1 per cent of their land under cane.   Thus not only was the cooperatives' cane land cut from about 600,000 hectares in 1960 to 438,600 in 1962 (Table 12), but it also declined qualitatively as a result of two consecutive failures to replant. At least partial support for this belief can be inferred from the data in Table 12, which shows that in 1962 productivity in cane cultivation in the public sector was 10 per cent lower than on large farms in the private sector, notwithstanding the superior quality of the cooperatives' land and the preference they received in the allocation of capital and fertilizers.

Thus the third and principal cause of the decline was the disorganization of the cooperatives, first evident in the latter half of 1961, when the new units had to turn from the relatively easy task of harvesting already existing cane to cultivation. It became clear that INRA's assumption of a "spontaneous organization of production by the masses"[97] had led to severe underestimation of the need for supervisory personnel; where formerly there had been 4 or 5 foremen concerned with the cultivation of the cane, there was now one manager whose task was greatly increased by the program of diversification and by his role as political leader of the cooperative.[98] Moreover, administrative difficulties were accompanied by a growing labor shortage, as members of the cooperatives were attracted by the higher wages paid in construction, in public works, and on the state farms, which also, since that was the policy of INRA, offered a chance for better housing. The result of these developments was the "general neglect of the cultivation of cane."[99]

ii

In the cattle industry, production and consumption developments followed the lines that could be expected. The indiscriminate slaughter in the earlier period and the sharp reversal of government policy on this score reduced consumption of beef drastically with respect both to the first years after the Revolution and pre-revolutionary days. Before 1959, per-capita consumption of beef—by far the largest component of total meat consumption —was between 65 and 70 pounds.[100] In 1962, the corresponding ration—applying, admittedly, only to greater Havana—allowed 39 pounds of beef per person. Although consumption might have been higher in other cities and in rural areas, the relative size of Havana's population and the large drop in its per-capita consump-

Table 12.   Land Under Cane and Production of Cane by Sectors in Cuba, 1962

	LAND UNDER CANE		OUTPUT OF CANE		OUTPUT OF C/
	(In 1,000 Hectares)	(Per Cent)	(In 1,000 tons)	(Per Cent)	PER HECTAI
Cane Cooperatives and People's Farms	438.6	36.1	12,475.1	34	28.44
Small and Intermediate Farms (up to 67.1 hectares)	452.1	37.2	13,942.8	38	30.84
Large Farms	324.9	26.7	10,273.7	28	31.62
Totals	1,215.6	100.0	36,691.6	100	30.18

Source: Land and percentage of cane output: Alfredo Menéndez Cruz, "Problemas de la Ind▪ Azucarera," *Cuba Socialista,* No. 12 (August, 1962), 2.   Output of cane: Table 10, Chapte▪

tion point to a fall in the national average consumption of beef in comparison to the years before the Revolution.[101]   The decline in consumption also reflected a lower level of production,[102] even though by 1962 the herds were beginning to be built up again, implying that "cattle production" was greater than consumption.

Developments were more favorable in the poultry industry. It seems that production of chickens increased at a high rate until mid-1960, when INRA reported a monthly national output of 2,000,000.[103]   One year later, production had apparently been reduced by half[104] as a result of the reduction of trade with the United States[105] and of early disorganization in the people's farms.[106]   Yet by May, 1962, output, although substantially below the planned target, seemed to have recovered the high level reached 2 years earlier,[107] and the consumption allowed by the rationing in Havana exceeded the national pre-revolutionary average by a substantial amount.[108]

The expansion of the poultry industry apparently led to a rise in egg production.   Before 1959, per-capita consumption of eggs averaged about 50 a year.[109]   The rationing in Havana, on the other hand, permitted in August, 1962, an annual consumption of 60 eggs per person, which exceeds the old national average by 20 per cent.   Consumption in Havana itself in 1962 may not have been higher, however; indeed, because of the large gap between consumption levels in the capital and the rest of the country before the Revolution, per-capita consumption in Havana in 1962 may actually have fallen.[110]   Nevertheless, this assumption is not incompatible with a rise in domestic output. In effect, consumption in 1962 must have been more evenly distributed than in previous years, and a (possible) decline in the consumption of eggs in the capital may have been offset by a rise in the rest of the country (especially in the rural areas). Moreover, domestic production now probably contributes a larger share of total supply,[111] which would imply that domestic output could have increased even if total consumption had not.

iii

Table 13 summarizes the quantitative information available on production of crops other than sugar in the agricultural year 1960-61. The only major advance occurred in the production of coffee, which rose sharply in the upward phase of the traditional two-year cycle, reaching a historical peak. Output of tobacco also increased, but the gain was small both absolutely and in comparison with the rapid advances of the two previous years.

On the negative side, the production of rice[112] and potatoes fell sharply, in both cases to below the 1957-58 averages.

It also seems fairly clear that production of root crops[113] declined. Acute shortages of *malanga* were already reported in the second half of 1961. "We accept full responsibility when [they] tell us there is no *malanga*," said Eduardo Santos Ríos, at the national production meeting held in late August that year.[114] "That we accept," he added, "because it is a criticism deserved, correct, and just." He concluded, "Undoubtedly we are, if anything, satisfying now 50 per cent of supplies."[115] Eight months later, Santos Ríos broadened the scope of his critical comments to include all root crops. "The *viandas* have been our principal failure," he wrote. "Their shortage has caused very serious problems."[116]

Shortages could have arisen because of an increase in demand, of course. Nevertheless, the shift in demand could hardly have been large enough to generate a shortage of the magnitude reported by Santos Ríos in August, without a simultaneous fall in production. That the shortages reflected both an increase in demand *and* declining supplies of *viandas* became evident in March, 1962, when the rationing for greater Havana allowed 3.5 pounds per person each week, with 2 additional pounds for

Table 13. Physical Production of Some Crops in Cuba in 1962

	Production in 1962 (In thousands of metric tons)	Percentage change with respect to: 1961	Percentage change with respect to: 1957-58 Average
Tobacco[a]	52.9	1	14.7
Coffee[b]	58.1	41	44.5
Potatoes[b]	75.1	−25.9	−13.8
Rice	230.0[c]	−24.4[d]	− 4.7

a. Late estimate.
b. Agricultural year 1961-62.
c. Agricultural year 1961-62 *or* calendar 1961 (see Appendix to Part I).
d. Change with respect to 1960.
Source: INRA, and Tables 1, 2, 4, Chapter II, and 4, Chapter III.

children under seven.   These figures imply that yearly per-capita consumption in the capital was just over 200 pounds,[117] which can be compared with an estimated national average of 373.1 pounds in 1953.[118]   Again the fall in consumption must have reflected a decline in production, since with the exception of potatoes, net imports of root crops were negligible.[119]   Yet, as with beef, the decline in consumption may overstate the reduction of output. *Viandas* are grown mostly as subsistence crops in small plots, and consumption may hence have been higher in the countryside than in the cities; moreover, the proportion of total output delivered to the towns almost certainly fell in 1961-62, because the elimination of land rents reduced the need to market agricultural produce, and the shortage of consumer goods weakened the incentive; thus, lower consumption in the cities may have been partly the result of the redistribution of income in favor of the rural population and of the breakdown of trade between country and town.

In spite of these qualifications, a decline in the output of root crops during 1961-62 seems beyond doubt.[120]   Moreover, because the production of *viandas* represents a high share of total non-sugar crop output,[121] the fall in *viandas* production must have had important effects on the total.   Indeed, aggregate production of crops can hardly have been higher in the first half of 1962 than in the corresponding portion of the preceding year (even if sugar cane is excluded from the analysis), since, as shown in the Appendix, the decline in rice output offset almost two-thirds of the combined effect of the increases in the production of coffee and tobacco. Therefore output of all other crops would have had to rise substantially in order to compensate for these various depressive effects.

iv

Even if one assumes that output of non-sugar crops did not fall, it would still be obvious that farm productivity declined sharply in 1961-62, since, during that time there was a considerable expansion of land, labor, and (possibly) capital allocated to non-sugar agriculture. Undoubtedly, lower productivity must have reflected to a certain extent the effects of the drought. Nevertheless, the fact that large reductions occurred precisely in the production of rice, potatoes, and root crops—all crops for which substantial increases in the cultivated area were planned— reveals that other forces were also at work.

Inadequate planning was one such force. As in other sectors of the economy, early agricultural plans were characterized by a high degree of "subjectivism," expressed in widespread overestimation of targets and the tendency to plan the desired outputs but not the necessary inputs. Usually only land requirements were considered, by the rather simple device of dividing the postulated output by the assumed average yield per land unit.[122] The planning of labor inputs was frequently absent, and even when national and provincial labor balances were prepared—as in the sugar industry—the process was not extended to the level of the production unit, with the result that pockets of unemployed rural workers may have coexisted with labor shortages.[123]

The assessment of the needs of equipment and fertilizer was still weaker. Perhaps no stronger criticism can be made of the planning of inputs than that implicitly contained in Aguirre's truism "but the numbers of *caballerías* to be sown and of quintals to be obtained are not enough. We need to calculate also things as important as equipment, seeds, fertilizers, insecticides, transport, and labor."[124]

Because the complementarity of inputs was ignored, workers' efforts were at times wasted and their productivity consequently reduced. In one example, 78,000 hectares were prepared for sowing with *malanga* when there was seed enough for only half this area;[125] similarly, INRA officials told me that in Camagüey a shortage of seeds meant that about 60 per cent of the area planned for yams was never planted; in the case of beans, it was reported that the unchecked rise in consumption had come close to endangering the supply of seeds available for planting;[126] and in Oriente more than 20,000 hectares were left uncultivated because of the lack of peanuts and bean seeds.[127]

Inadequate planning of inputs also led in some cases to the underutilization of available capital. The importation of farm machinery was seriously unbalanced; relatively too many tractors were purchased and too few plows, harrows, and other complementary equipment.[128] The result was that in many cases the absence of this kind of equipment prevented the full utilization of the tractors.[129]

At times, weaknesses in the agricultural plans were compounded by insufficient coordination between the institutions which were supposed to carry out the different parts of the programs. For example, the big reduction in the output of rice was to a certain extent the result of the lack of aerial fumigation, which, in turn, was partly due to lack of coordination between INRA and the armed forces.[130]

In other cases, falls in productivity reflected the indirect effects of developments beyond farm control. The disorganization of the transport and distribution system is the principal example. Subject to rising pressures from all sectors, under new managers since the nationalizations of late 1960, and hampered by equipment deteriorating through lack of imported spare parts, the transport and distribution systems were not able to satisfy adequately the new demands. As a result, the delivery of seeds, pesticides, and fertilizers was seriously hampered.[131] Deficiencies in the distribution of fertilizer were indicated by Santos Ríos as early as in August of 1961.[132] Eight months later he was still more explicit. "We have had many difficulties," he wrote "because of the delay in applying fertilizers, because of the lack of transport, because of not being able to elaborate a great variety of specific formulas, because of sending them out without appropriate directions, because much fertilizer was lost due to the type of container, because it gets too hard due to excessively long storage, or because of applying it at the height of the dry season without prospectives of improvement in the humidity of the soil."[133] Thus, although probably more fertilizer was available, less may have been delivered and much of this may have reached the co-operatives and farms too late to apply or may have been applied after it could have had any effect on yields.

Deficiencies at the level of the production units also lowered output. In effect, the consolidation of more than 500 INRA-managed cattle ranches and almost 900 agricultural cooperatives into 260-odd people's farms early in 1961 meant a great increase in the average size of the agricultural units.[134] This in itself did not need to cause a decline in efficiency; indeed, to the extent that the change made possible economies of large-scale production, an increase could have been expected. In practice, however, there were factors offsetting potential gains—at least in the short run. As noted earlier, the state farms usually constituted administrative but not economic units, since they were formed by numerous separate farms scattered fairly widely. This dispersion had two disadvantages: it considerably reduced the possibilities of large-scale economies, and it made efficient management of the people's farms extremely difficult. The manager of a *granja* had to waste valuable time simply traveling between the different units under his control; vital decisions were delayed, and direct supervision was made difficult.[135]

The policy of agricultural diversification, together with the inefficiency of the average manager of the state farms, made effective administration of them still more improbable. The attempt to shift rapidly from a system in which each farm produced a small number of crops by extensive techniques to one in which much larger units attempted to diversify production, to start raising livestock, and to introduce new, capital-intensive techniques was by itself bound to increase the difficulties of management. The transition might have been accomplished without reducing efficiency, however, if at the same time well-trained and experienced managers had replaced those who were tradition-bound and ignorant. But this did not happen. The managers of the people's farms were usually former peasants, with little, if any, scientific training and with scarce knowledge of the new crops or of administrative techniques. They were frequently chosen on political rather than technical grounds and in some cases were only semi-literate.[136]

Moreover, amid the ideological wave of 1961, the importance of technicians was often underestimated, and, as a result, production standards declined. Mistakes were frequently made in the selection of soil; in some cases the sowing was done on land which had not been sufficiently prepared;[137] the attempt to raise technical standards sometimes clashed with the stubborn resistance of peasants who wanted to continue traditional methods.[138] On other occasions, unwillingness to accept deadlines for planting different crops—frequently because of the desire to fulfill the output targets—meant that seeds, fertilizer, land, and effort were used with negligible effects on output.[139] Sometimes delay in the transfer of funds to the farms caused the abandonment of work which had already been started; and sometimes lack of precise allocation of responsibility led to misuse of farm equipment.[140]

From an economic angle, all these shortcomings had a common element: they were essentially situations in which additional inputs led to proportionately smaller rises in output. How widespread were such cases is, of course, difficult to say; undoubtedly there were farms where work was efficient and output increased. Nevertheless, as Cuban authorities recognized with increasing candor in 1962, the limitations of agricultural planning and organization had lowered considerably the productivity of the public sector of agriculture in 1961.

A word has to be said, finally, about the policy towards the private sector and its effect on agricultural output. With the exception of the small farmers who joined ANAP, independent producers were largely neglected. Again and again, revolutionary leaders affirmed that growth in agricultural output must be based on the efforts of the two large government-controlled organizations—the people's farms and the cane cooperatives—and of the members of ANAP. On the other hand, no attempt was made to integrate the activities of the intermediate and large farms into the national plans, although they controlled about 40 per cent of the land. Moreover, with the nationalization of the banking, transport, and distribution systems, intermediate and large private farmers found it increasingly difficult to obtain supplies,[141] and to deliver their produce to urban markets, thus reinforcing the declines in the public sector of agriculture and leading to a dangerous reduction of the exchange between country and town.

C. Conclusions

One year after the institutional reorganization of 1961, then, Cuban agriculture was facing serious difficulties. The sharp fall in sugar output showed that the decision to divert a considerable amount of land from cane into other crops had been premature, and the low productivity of the units in the public sector indicated that considerable disorganization existed in the cooperatives. Moreover, because of large declines in the production of rice, potatoes, and *viandas*, the volume of non-sugar crop output was at best maintained at the level of the previous year—in spite of vast additions of inputs and of heavy emphasis on agricultural diversification. As the Appendix shows, the aggregate real value of the 4 main crops was lower in early 1962 than in the year preceding the Revolution, and by the second half of 1961 the delayed effects of the excessive slaughtering of cattle in the previous years had become apparent; they were offset only in part by the recovery of the poultry industry in the first half of 1962.

Thus, three years after the agrarian reform was officially started in May, 1959, total farm output had fallen below the level of the years before the Revolution, and agricultural productivity had declined sharply. Although these developments had been strongly influenced by the lack of rainfall in 1961 and by shortcomings in other sectors of the economy, they also reflected the inadequacy of agricultural planning, the neglect of a part of the private sector, and the inefficient operation of the state farms.

It was hence clear that a serious and wide-ranging reappraisal of farm policy and organization was urgently needed. By March, 1962, the revision had been started and, in many respects, a new phase had begun for the agrarian reform.

3. The 1962 Reappraisal

The revision of Cuban agricultural policy begun in 1962 did not imply changes in the long-run goals of government farm policy, which remained the raising and diversification of agricultural output, the substitution of imports of food, and the progressive socialization of the farm sector. Yet, coming in the wake of a decline in production, the reappraisal meant substantial changes in the immediate strategy of government policy and was characterized by severe criticism of past performance. The solution of the problems of agriculture became the target of highest priority in the government's programs.[142]

The reappraisal of agricultural policy strongly attacked "subjectivism" in planning, and the result was a vigorous drive toward improvement in the collection of agricultural statistics and a new (and long-overdue) stress on the need for realistic assessment of production possibilities. Some steps were taken to induce a more rational allocation of resources; INRA began to emphasize the need of keeping accounts, reducing costs, and turning losses into profits in the state-owned farms. Together with the Central Planning Board, INRA started a study of the structure of relative costs and prices of agricultural products. Finally, a sharp reversal occurred in the relative emphasis placed on agricultural diversification in the short-run, and, in an effort to raise sugar production and thus to expand exports, INRA decided to replant more than 200,000 hectares of cane in 1962.

A. The Attack on Subjectivism

It is not difficult to understand why production failures in the second half of 1961 and the initial months of 1962 led to a critical reevaluation of planning procedures. Shortages of some foodstuffs had appeared already in the summer of 1960, when butter was scarce for a brief period, and some months later, when poultry and eggs were short. These scarcities, however, mainly reflected the pressure of vastly increased demand, especially in the rural areas, and of supply deficiencies, stemming primarily from the reduction in imports from the United States.[143]

The shortages became more acute during 1961 as farm production started to slip back, food imports were further reduced, and transport and distribution become more inadequate. By the middle of the year, supply was not meeting the higher demand requirements in poultry, fish, *viandas,* and fats. But in the production meeting of August, the government promised to solve the poultry shortages by the end of the year in Havana and by early February, 1962, in the rest of the country. Moreover, the production of root crops was expected to outstrip consumption requirements by January, 1962. In fish and fats the period required to bring supply up to the level of demand was to be longer;[144] consumption needs of fish would be totally satisfied by June, 1962, and the regulations on the distribution of fats would be abolished at the beginning of 1963.[145]

In spite of strong criticisms by several officials, the general spirit at the production meeting was optimistic, and the rates of growth included in the 1962-65 Development Plan were, on the average, remarkably high.[146] But by early 1962 it was clear that the task promised had not been accomplished. On March 14, Premier Castro appeared on television to explain the introduction of food rationing for three foodstuffs in the whole country and for a few more in Havana alone. Although he stated that agricultural output had increased[147] and correctly pointed to the greater retention of foodstuffs in the countryside owing to the rise in rural employment and incomes and the elimination of rents,[148] his general tone was critical—"at times we forgot that we knew very little of everything, at times there was some sort of a belief that everybody knew a lot of everything. In fact, we knew very little about very few things."[149] In a sense, the speech heralded the new "hard" look at agricultural policy and introduced the attack on "subjectivism." "We are going to be frank," Dr. Castro said and then added, "I believe that among other things we have to learn also to analyze things objectively."[150]

His advice was promptly heeded. For the first time, INRA did not issue any progress report on the occasion of the anniversary of the Agrarian Reform Law. Instead, *Cuba Socialista* carried two articles[151] rich in frank criticisms of previous policies and freely acknowledging past deficiencies. "The Revolution has put in the hands of our organizations abundant economic resources, equipment, land, fertilizers," wrote Eduardo Santos Ríos. "Our failures have hindered the fulfillment of an improvement of the situation promised to the people in the first national production meeting of August, 1961."[152] The concluding paragraph of Aguirre's article had a similar tone. "The third anniversary of the agrarian reform is a propitious opportunity for deepening the critical analysis that we have started and for reviewing our decision in favor of the development of agriculture which we have proposed to reach through agrarian reform."[153]

The implications of these statements become clearer when they are analyzed in the light of the deficiencies of farm policies and organization and of the pervasive overestimation of output targets which perhaps most typified the "subjective" characteristic of agricultural plans from the beginning.

Thus the targets set for expanding the cultivated area in INRA's initial program[154] had been revised downward by as much as 25 per cent in May, 1960, and the increase then considered feasible was a further quarter below the revised estimate.[155] As the economy moved towards central planning, a parallel change in more accurate assessment of production possibilities might have been expected. Instead, in many cases output targets tended to express wishes rather than economic realities, and, as a result, there were frequent failures to reach the assigned production levels. For example, when explaining the 1962-65 target to the production meeting in August, 1961, the Minister of the Economy stated that in 1962 the per-capita consumption of eggs would be more than twice that of 1959—which he estimated as just under 50.[156] The 1962 ration for Greater Havana, however, allowed only 60 eggs per person. Even if it is assumed that the consumption of eggs was higher outside the capital, the national average in 1962 must have been considerably below the level forecast one year earlier.[157] At the same meeting, INRA's chief of production Santos Ríos stated that at that time, "instead of supplying 4,000,000 chickens, [INRA] was supplying only 1,000,000," but he added, "We shall fight to reach [a supply] of 4,000,000 chickens in December and one of 7,000,000 in March [of 1962]."[158] In May, 1962, however, the same Santos Ríos reported that "already 2,000,000 chickens are being supplied to the national market. . . ."[159] He was still more categoric about rice consumption. "Our people," he said, "can be absolutely sure that they can continue to eat 130 pounds of rice per capita."[160] Half a year later, the nationwide rice ration was set at 72 pounds per person.

Overestimation of output targets co-existed with underestimation of consumption requirements. "We were not able to forecast in all its magnitude the increase in consumption caused by the vertiginous rise in the per-capita income of the people after the victory of the Revolution," wrote Aguirre in May, 1962.[161] And Santos Ríos remarked in the same connection, "They had always told us that we ate 100,000 quintals of beans per month. This is not so. *It seems* that the consumption is 150,000 quintals. . . ."[162] And again in the case of root crops: "We did not have until very recently the data on the consumption of *viandas* of Greater Havana."[163]

Shortages in the cities must have at times surprised the planners because of an elementary confusion between total and commercialized production. Said Santos Ríos, "We have erred in concluding that production would correspond to the number of *caballerías* sown among all the sectors of production, without taking into consideration that the production which supplies the markets is the commercialized output—that it is not possible to take into account in calculating national supplies the subsistence production of a small farmer. This was an objective lesson in the production and consumption of beans."[164]

Thus by early 1962 the revision of the organization and procedures of agricultural planning had become an acute need; still more important, it had become necessary to change the spirit in which planning hitherto had been conducted. It is true that some shortcomings were only to be expected, given the inexperience of the new administrative cadres, the novelty of the planning procedures, and the lack of adequate statistics. But they were also attributable to careless and over-optimistic assessments of production possibilities and to other mistaken approaches of INRA personnel. For example, although the inadequacy of statistical data largely stemmed from the past, it also reflected the disorganization created by the swift pace of institutional change after the agrarian reform was started and the belief of some farm managers and administrative officials that statistics were a manifestation of "bureaucratism."[165] This attitude was hardly compatible with the needs of objective planning. Indeed, it is clear that, once the decision to set up a system of centralized planning was made, substantial resources should have been allocated to strengthen the entire system of collecting agricultural statistics. This, however, was not done, or, at least, not to the extent necessary.[166] Plans were therefore bound to be somewhat unrealistic.

The reorganization of the procedures for gathering quantitative data was finally started in 1962. The Central Planning Board produced a complete set of elaborate statistical forms. All production units in the public sector were required to complete such forms regularly and to send them to the provincial offices of INRA, where they would be consolidated for communication to INRA in Havana. In order to facilitate the new plan, INRA started training in mid-1962 a considerable number of young students who would be assigned to all the state-owned production units with the strict responsibility of completing the forms on time.

Although by August, 1962, the new system was still not working efficiently,[167] it is clear that the new methods represent a considerable improvement. Indeed, it is not unreasonable to think that once the new procedures are fully implemented—this, of course, will take time—INRA will have extremely detailed information on which to base its future plans for the socialist sector of agriculture.

Also indicative of the new approach were the changes in the spirit in which planning and production problems were considered after the denunciation of "subjectivism." Following the appointment of Carlos Rafael Rodríguez to the presidency of INRA, the emphasis shifted from the grandiose to the feasible, from the almost exclusive celebration of accomplishments to the careful consideration of mistakes and shortcomings. Thus, at a nationwide agricultural production control meeting in August, 1962, Rodríguez pointed out that "it would be a grave mistake to suffer illusions and to think that everything is solved. . . . the negative factors still outweigh the positive ones." His concluding note was sober and restrained: "With the changes realized, agriculture will move ahead; we shall advance step by step, unspectacularly but securely."[168]

It sounded the requiem for "subjectivism."

B. The Return to Cane

The decision to demolish vast amounts of sugar cane in 1961 was a classic example of "subjectivism." Based on a technically valid proposition—that there was considerable scope for gains in productivity in the cultivation of cane—the decision overlooked the conditions required to achieve higher average yields: more intensive use of fertilizers and irrigation, more frequent replanting, a better selection of seeds, and, in general, a widespread improvement of technical standards. Clearly, Cuba, in 1961, could not fulfill these conditions—well-trained managers and skilled technicians were scarce, the distribution and transport systems were in difficulty, and the cane cooperatives were disorganized. Furthermore, even the successful implementation of some of the measures would have produced results only after a certain period. Any objective analysis would therefore have seriously questioned the feasibility of accomplishing the change in sugar production without a drastic fall in sugar output.

By 1962, attitudes had changed. More realistic assessments indicated that it was not feasible to shift *in one year* from extensive to intensive cultivation of cane and *at the same time* to diversify greatly agricultural output. Faced with the impossibility of fulfilling existing sales contracts with the socialist bloc, INRA officials came to realize that, up to sugar outputs of about 7,000,-000 tons, comparative advantage recommended export promotion over import substitution.[169]

As a result, a shift occurred in the *relative* emphasis placed on the production of cane. Diversification remained the long-run target of farm policy, but the expansion of sugar output became "the first aspiration of the agricultural economy of the country."[170] To fulfill this goal, new institutional changes were introduced in agriculture, and a vast program of cane replanting was started in 1962.

Although determined in part by ideological preferences, the institutional changes were primarily the result of the government's critical evaluation of the performance of the cane cooperatives and of other agencies connected with the sugar industry during the 1962 harvest. The revision revealed not only the organizational mistakes that had reduced productivity in the public sector but also showed that little coordination had existed between the sugar mills—which depended on the Ministry of Industries—and in INRA-managed cooperatives.[171] Accordingly, in 1962 the government created a National Sugar Commission, with boards at the provincial and sugar-mill levels, comprised of representatives of the Ministry of Industries, INRA, ANAP, and the unions of agricultural and sugar workers, whose specific task was to improve coordination between all government bodies involved in producing sugar.

Moreover, on August, 18 the delegates from the cane cooperatives voted in favor of transforming the cooperatives into state farms.[172] Given the preferences of the revolutionary leaders for state-owned production, the change was hardly a surprise. It was explained in terms of a dialectical contradiction in which the permanent members of the cooperatives—former workers themselves —had become the semi-exploiters of the seasonal laborers working in the cooperatives.[173] Nevertheless, it was clear that the poor performance of the cooperatives during the preceding year had accelerated the transformation and that another purpose of it was to give INRA more control of the public units in the sugar sector. By itself, however, the transformation was unlikely to lead to great and rapid changes, although raising the wages of the cooperative workers to the level of those of workers employed on the people's farms was bound to diminish the outflow of labor from the old cooperatives.[174] In addition, the change offered at least the potential advantage of facilitating the reapportionment of land between the people's farms and the old cooperatives in order to create geographically continuous production units.

Increased realism was also shown in the methods chosen to raise sugar production. In future years, the increase was to be obtained by an initial expansion of the area cultivated and afterwards by raising average yields through more frequent replanting.[175] According to the new plans, more than 200,000 hectares were to be replanted with cane during 1962,[176] of which more than one-half would be on the small farms of ANAP, about one-third on the old cane cooperatives, and the remainder on the state farms. At the end of August, however, only 96,600 hectares, or 43.4 per cent of the revised target, had been planted and 72,500 more hectares had been prepared for planting. Thus, the assigned target would probably not be fulfilled before the end of 1962.

C. The Attempts to Raise Farm Productivity

In addition to the attack on "subjectivism" and the new emphasis on cane, the 1962 reappraisal brought a critical reassessment of the performance of the people's farms and an attempt to induce a more efficient allocation and use of resources in the socialist sector of agriculture.

For the first time, INRA started to emphasize the need for profitable operation of the state farms and for careful consideration of costs—two principles which had been largely absent in the previous periods. "At the present," wrote Dumond in May, 1960, "nobody is in a position to predict accurately the real costs of production."[177] And according to what I was told by INRA officials both in Havana and the provinces, this situation continued to prevail in the following years. At least until the second half of 1961, costs were apparently disparaged as unimportant, a shortcoming which was noticed by Carlos R. Rodríguez at the production meeting in August: ". . . I have been very surprised," he said, "that here nobody has talked about costs; I have not heard the word cost one single time, unless it was to say that costs did not matter—but costs do matter decisively."[178]

The lack of concern with cost accounting was unfortunate. On the one hand, it led to deficits in most of the state farms, and although these probably helped at the beginning, because of unemployed resources, their usefulness became more questionable as labor shortages appeared in the countryside and as inflationary pressures increased. More important, however, were the effects of the lack of cost records on the allocation of resources. It was not possible to know which farms produced the different crops most efficiently and which used higher-than-average inputs. Nor was it feasible to investigate the reasons behind the productivity differentials. The gains which could have been reaped from the imitation of good practices and correction of bad ones were therefore largely lost.

Nevertheless, by 1962 the attitude towards costs and profits had been sharply reversed. Reflecting the pressures of imbalance in the overall financial accounts of the government and the influence of Rodríguez in INRA, a systematic campaign was launched to raise profits in the socialist sector of agriculture. The managers of the state farms were requested to keep detailed accounting records and to report periodically not only the output obtained but also the quantities of land, labor, and capital used. Hence an attempt, at least, was being made to ascertain the real costs of production in the different units and thus to enable the planners to shift the cultivation of the various crops to those farms having comparative advantages.

The need to reduce costs and raise productivity was also a principal reason for introducing norms for agricultural labor. INRA officials at last realized that equal pay for 8 hours work with no adjustments for productivity undermined incentives and resulted in high cost production. According to the new plans, which contemplated the introduction of norms by the end of 1962, wages were to be tied to the quantity and quality of output. The government was also planning to use housing policy as an instrument for stimulating workers, both collectively and individually, to increase their productivity. New houses would be built on those farms which best fulfilled the production targets, and allocated to the most efficient workers.[179]

Finally, the new approach was also apparent in the role assigned to technical personnel within INRA. As noted earlier, the importance of technicians had been underestimated in 1960-61 for political reasons—a grave mistake given the plans for radical changes in farm production, and the prevailing scarcity of well-trained cadres. By 1962, the technical departments in the provincial offices of INRA had been given a greater role in shaping policy. "It is necessary to raise the role of technicians," wrote Aguirre in his May article in *Cuba Socialista*, ". . . to place them where they can truly contribute their knowledge, and to surround them with the minimal conditions which are indispensable for their productive work."[180]

4. Prospects

As the previous sections have shown, after the re-examination in the first half of 1962, the government was attempting to establish some of the conditions needed to increase farm output and to raise productivity in the socialist sector of agriculture.

The prospects for a rapid expansion of total farm output in the near future appeared, however, to be severely limited by the slow recovery forecast for sugar. The plans anticipated no more in 1963 than a repetition of the poor harvest of the previous year, and even this only if "work was well done, and mistakes were rectified."[181] Moreover, output in 1964 was expected to be only about 5,700,000 or 5,800,000 tons, notwithstanding the need to produce at least 6,500,000 tons in order to fulfill international commitments.[182]

On the other hand, government programs contemplated high rates of growth for other crops. According to INRA's President Rodríguez, the output of corn would increase fivefold between 1961-62 and 1965, rising from 160,000 to 800,000 tons; over the same period, production of rice was expected to triple (from 230,000 to 690,000 tons),[183] and INRA officials believed that by the mid-sixties, Cuba would be self-sufficient in rice.[184] According to plans, domestic production of cotton would meet all requirements in 1965, in spite of the very rapid expansion forecast for the textile industry.[185] Moreover, in 1962 INRA was preparing a development plan for coffee designed to correct the yearly fluctuations of output and to raise production to 63,000 tons by 1965 and to 92,000 tons by 1967.[186]

The government also expected that the build-up of the herds during 1962 and improvements in the technical standards of the cattle industry would enable it to increase slaughtering by 100,000 head in 1963 and to export beef on a large scale in the late sixties.[187] In the near future, however, a substantial part of the supply increases planned for livestock products would occur in the production of chickens and hogs, to which the programs of INRA gave high priority.

Thus very ambitious targets were envisaged for non-sugar agricultural production, although at least for rice and corn, the extremely high rates of growth forecast probably reflect in part the expectation of a rapid recovery from the low production of 1961-62. Still, the magnitude of the planned increases—although not their direction—seems to be, on the whole, exaggerated, especially since Cuban agriculture will have to grow in new and different ways from those of 1959-61. In coming years it will become increasingly difficult to achieve substantial gains in production simply by enlarging the area under cultivation, as was done in the first years of the agrarian reform. By 1962, much of the economically useful land, under-utilized or idle before the Revolution, had already been brought under the plow, and massive new additions to the cultivated area would mainly require plowing up pasture (thus hurting the cattle industry) or

using land of lower quality, land located in districts with inadequate transport facilities, or land requiring large investments
in drainage and clearing.

Moreover, the slow growth forecast for sugar implies that
until the second half of the sixties the area devoted to cane is
unlikely to be cut substantially, and land for other crops will
hardly be found from this source. Consequently, the large gains
envisaged for the output of non-sugar crops will necessarily have
to come through substantially higher average yields.

It is also obvious that the planned increases in output depended on rapidly rising productivity of farm labor, since by
1962 the vast pool of idle agricultural workers appeared to have
been largely exhausted. Although in 1962 there were still an
estimated 200,000 unemployed in the whole country, most were
in the cities and were reluctant to move into the rural areas. Near
full employment had been reached in the countryside, leading to
acute shortages of labor there in the periods of high seasonal
demand.[188] The exhaustion of labor reserves also meant that
agricultural employment would rise only moderately in the
future—a total increase of 8 per cent was forecast for the period
1961-65,[189] which was a good deal less than the (probably overestimated) rise of 53 per cent reported for 1958-61.[190]

Agricultural growth will in the future have to depend increasingly on more intensive and better methods of cultivation,
which would both raise the average yields of land and the productivity of labor. The new techniques will, in turn, require
increases in capital inputs and, of special importance, considerable
improvement in the organization and operation of the production
units and in the administration of planning.

The future trend of net investment in agriculture is, of course,
difficult to estimate, since it is likely to be significantly affected by
the trend in foreign aid. If this continues at about its recent level,
the total stock of agricultural equipment will grow fairly slowly
at first and considerably faster in the second half of the sixties.
This is because the contribution of imports of agricultural machinery to the sector's stock of capital will be considerably offset for some years by the deterioration of the existing American-
made equipment which is approaching the end of its economic
life. Later, however, the relative importance of this offsetting

factor will diminish, and the net addition to the total stock of agricultural machinery brought about by an unchanged level of imported equipment will be correspondingly greater.[191]

It therefore seems that, at least in the immediate future, additions to the fund of circulating capital in the form of increased use of inputs such as fertilizers, seeds, and pesticides, as well as general organizational progress and investments in irrigation, drainage, and storehouses, should play a more important role than farm mechanization in raising the level of agricultural yields.[192]

The possibilities for gains in productivity are particularly high in the case of organizational improvements, although here the acute scarcity of well-trained planners, managers, and agricultural experts[193] constitutes an important obstacle to the full realization of advantages. A centrally planned economy requires a vast number of able bureaucrats and technicians not only at the top but also at intermediate and lower levels. The need for technical and administrative personnel is even greater when important structural transformations are being attempted. As noted above, the growth of Cuban agricultural output will require precisely this type of organizational change, and acute pressures on the existing administrative and technical cadres can therefore be expected in the future.

In August, 1962, the administrators and technicians still seemed inadequate to the tasks and targets before them. The managers of the people's farms mostly had little technical training; accountants, veterinarians, and agricultural engineers were hard to find; and in spite of the admirable devotion of its officials, INRA's provincial offices generally appeared to be understaffed.

Nevertheless, it is likely that the limitations imposed by the shortage of qualified personnel will gradually, if slowly, diminish. Some on-the-job learning is almost sure to occur, and, as young officials gain experience, the number of mistakes in planning and executing agricultural policies will probably decrease. Gradual improvement in data collection, and the new, and more influential, role assigned to the technicians in INRA should also help.

Moreover, by the late sixties the number of agricultural experts[194] and young peasants with some technical training in farm management[195] should rise considerably; the supply of skilled agricultural workers will probably increase even sooner.[196]

Finally, it appears that in 1962 INRA officials began to realize that some of the people's farms were excessively large and consequently began to make attempts to determine the optimum size.[197] These, together with the possibilities opened by transforming the cane cooperatives into state farms, implied that in the future new, smaller, and less-dispersed production units were likely to be established in the public sector, thus reducing some of the main obstacles to efficient management.

The benefits of many of these changes, however, will be delayed by several years;[198] only moderate progress from better organization can be expected in the immediate future. Even these moderate gains may be offset by new difficulties—further crop diversification and more capital intensive techniques on the state farms will make planning and implementing agricultural programs more complex, and therefore improvements in organization will be continuously needed in order to maintain even relative economic efficiency.

It is also evident that, at least in the years just ahead, government policy toward the private farmers will have considerable influence not only on the growth of total output but also on the pace at which productivity rises on the state farms. In effect, because of the acute shortage of technical and managerial personnel any significant expansion of the area managed directly by INRA would in the near future almost certainly increase disorganization, reduce productivity, and lower output.

By 1962, the government seemed, on the whole, to have realized these limitations—more emphasis was being given to improving the organization of the state units than to extending their area. Yet it is fairly clear that sooner or later INRA expected to expropriate the land of *rich farmers*.[199] The period of transition into socialism has, however, not been defined, and as a result, long-run incentives must be negatively affected. On the other hand, the new government policy, which at present restricts expropriation to land not being worked or to land of counterrevolutionaries, may provide a strong stimulus for higher output from the large private farmers. Moreover, there is some evidence that, after the slump of 1961-62, INRA's policy toward the *rich farmers* was beginning to shift from neglect to controlled economic assistance.[200] How effectively this policy is being implemented is uncertain.[201] Yet its very existence represents an improvement over INRA's rather limited notion of a *national* agricultural policy before 1962.

Finally, the growth of total farm output, and especially of private production, will depend upon developments in the other sectors of the economy. If industrial output rises, and, in particular, if the government succeeds in solving the problems that beset the transportation and distribution of manufactured goods in the rural areas, stronger incentives will exist on the farms, greater deliveries will be made to the towns, and an essential requirement for the growth of industrial production will have been met.

It seems, then, that the prospects for a rise in agricultural output in the second half of the sixties are rather favorable. Today, as before the Revolution, there exist great technical possibilities for increasing agricultural production. To what extent and how fast these possibilities are realized will primarily depend on four factors—the capacity of the regime to achieve considerable progress in organization, particularly in the socialist sector of agriculture and in the distribution and transport systems; the government's ability to reconcile the highly seasonal demand for farm labor with a situation of near full employment in agriculture; the extent to which INRA bases its policies on realistic considerations of economic advantage rather than on preconceived ideological tenets; and, what obviously cannot be ignored, the developments in the international political situation.

5. Conclusions

Clearly, it is not yet possible to evaluate in a reasonable and comprehensive way the economic effects of the Cuban agrarian reform. Production in agriculture, more than in any other sector, is subject to sharp fluctuations of climate, hardly within government control. The assessment of past performance should therefore be based on output trends over a relatively long period, not on the agricultural developments of just a few years. It should be obvious that in the case of post-revolutionary Cuban agriculture the period is still too short. Moreover, during the few years since the agrarian reform started, farm output has not always changed in the same direction.

Nevertheless, on the basis of what evidence is available, a few tentative conclusions about post-revolutionary agricultural developments can be reached. On the side of production, it seems fairly clear that the statement frequently made by supporters of the regime or its leaders that the Cuban agrarian reform would be the first in history to realize substantial transformations in the institutional framework of agriculture and, at the same time, to increase total farm output, even though accurate until early 1961, ceases to be so if account is taken of the poor crops of 1961-62. Moreover, given the very small sugar harvest obtained in 1963 and the low level from which the recovery of the cattle industry started in 1962, it is clear that total agricultural production in 1963 must have been below pre-revolutionary levels for a second consecutive year.[202]

In retrospect, the fundamental mistake of government policy, and an important cause of the decline in farm output, appears to have been the considerable underestimation of the difficulties of changing rapidly from an agricultural system heavily dominated by a single crop and extensive methods of cultivation to one characterized by intensive techniques and diversified production. It was basically the lack of understanding of the magnitude of these difficulties that led to the premature reduction of the area planted with cane in 1961—perhaps the most important single error of agricultural policy since the Revolution. INRA's underestimation (until 1962) of the importance of technicians and experienced managerial personnel—one of the principal causes of the fall in farm productivity—stemmed in part from the same misconception.

The lack of control in slaughtering cattle during the first years of the Revolution and the neglect of cane cultivation in the cooperatives in 1961 were also costly mistakes, although in the case of meat consumption political considerations may have proved irresistible and may hence help to explain government policy. In both cases, however, it will take time to repair the losses.

Nevertheless, the record of INRA is also in some respects favorable. The considerable expansion of the cultivated area and the higher and more stable level of employment of the agricultural labor force are important, both because of their role in the rise of farm output until early 1961 and because of the contribution they can make to the growth of production in the future, if the organizational problems of agriculture are solved. It is also clear that a start has been made in replacing imports of food and some agricultural raw materials like cotton. Moreover—after initial and to a certain extent inevitable failures—a vigorous stimulus has been given to the production of poultry and hogs, and output of both coffee and tobacco reached historical peaks in 1962.

A few words must finally be said about the effects of government programs on the distribution of income between country and town. Unfortunately, the lack of quantitative information is here especially serious. Conclusions must be based on inferences from partial and indirect evidence and should therefore be treated with caution. In general, however, it appears that living standards in the rural areas were in 1962 closer to those in the towns than they were before the Revolution. Of course, this relative change is in part the consequence of the decline in urban food consumption—in the rural areas, on the other hand, consumption of food has perhaps not fallen, principally because the elimination of land rents and the higher levels of agricultural employment and wages have permitted a larger proportion of the output of food crops to be consumed on the farms.

The narrowing of the gap between urban and rural living standards has been more directly determined, however, by the housing policy of the government and, especially, by the increase in the educational facilities available in the countryside. From an economic viewpoint, the significance of the new educational programs is that they not only affect the peasants' present standards of living but also will influence the productive capacity of the agricultural labor force in the future. Moreover, the quantitative and qualitative effects of the educational programs are likely to be particularly significant in Cuba, in part because in the past social and educational policies largely neglected the vast rural population and also because they come at a time when the destruction of the old institutional system by the agrarian reform has greatly increased social mobility in the countryside. Indeed, the new opportunities now open to the rural population may well prove the most fundamental contribution made by the Cuban Revolution to the country's potential for future economic development.

PART II
Education
BY RICHARD JOLLY

CHAPTER IV

Education

The Pre-Revolutionary Background

i

Education deserves a place in an economic study of Cuba for two reasons: first, because it is a prerequisite for economic progress; second, because it is expensive. Education is a form of investment in human resources and can produce economic returns just as tangible as those from roads, factories, and other physical capital. The Cuban government, as this part will show, is expecting specific returns from its educational program and has made education an integral part of its development plan. Education is also a costly use of a nation's resources, with an economic importance directly related to its expense. In Cuba, the size of the burden is indicated by the government's claims to have tripled the educational budget in 3 years and to have mobilized over a million of its adult population for an unpaid 6 months in the national literacy campaign.

In another way, the Cuban program of education may be of special interest. The revolutionary government has treated education as the key to a complete reconstruction of society. Their educational program is designed not merely to raise the skills and abilities of individuals but to create a new system of national goals and values. In economic terms, this is an attempt to use education to alter the institutional framework of the economy and to make the new institutions workable by affecting individual attitudes and incentives.

The economics of Cuban education, however, is only one part of the picture. Although this study is limited to the economic aspects, it will be obvious that many other matters are important for a full assessment. This reservation must be kept in mind in all that follows.

Furthermore, it should not be forgotten that most of the material for this study was collected during a few weeks in Cuba and, in my own case, with the aid of interpreters. The time factor alone prevented more than a partial view of particular aspects of the program of education, and almost inevitably when writing the study afterwards, I wished that more time had been spent on some things and less on others. Fortunately the reports and statistics available to me covered the major sections of Cuban education. But it will be quite clear that the description is thin on many details of the school system (and sometimes altogether silent). This is particularly true of the various technical training programs, especially those outside the responsibility of the Ministry of Education, and of the work of the National Council of Culture, which is active in education in the arts, music, and drama.

An important qualification arises from the emphasis given to statistics in this part. While indispensable for assessing aggregate impact and cost, especially in a controversial setting, statistics are not themselves free from controversy. There will be doubts about their reliability and strong opinions about their bias. In general, what I saw in schools, training centers, and adult classes (as well as in the offices and in the headquarters of the Ministry of Education) of the methods of collection, preparation, and use of educational statistics in Cuba today may be summarized as follows: I have few doubts about the seriousness with which the Ministry attempts to collect educational statistics, seriousness in the sense of intending them for use within their own planning and so attempting as best they can to obtain accurate and representative data. Naturally, this aim is often far from achieved, and the margins of error vary with the different types of statistics in a way I have tried always to indicate. Some figures by the circumstances of their collection are likely to be biased in a particular direction. Where I had reason to believe this, I have drawn attention to it.

But even if the figures were quite accurate, some misrepresentation could remain, first because education is not merely a number of years at school, though many of its economic effects (for instance, costs) are closely related to this aspect. Secondly, school statistics too easily may play down the form and standard of education, which in Cuba today have double significance, both because the future effects of education will be determined largely by the quality of the instruction and also because most people have strong opinions about the nature of the teaching. The avowedly Marxist content of Cuban education today involves some strong antagonisms and a simple dogmatism which are profoundly disturbing to me and will be to many others. To some, such bitterness and dogma may damn all value from the start. But without forgetting the doctrine taught, one also must not ignore the economic effects of the teaching.

In this part, it is these statistical economic aspects which are central, both to keep the study to size and to keep it within the terms of reference. Because of the controversial importance of the political aspects however, I have included some material in an Appendix. This will no doubt displease persons at both ends of the political spectrum. Those persuaded that education within the confines of Marxist-Leninist dogma is so totally evil that it must be economically valueless will be disturbed by the grossness of my misunderstanding when I relegate the political comment to an Appendix. Even more forceful will be the objections from the Marxists themselves, whose convictions on the totality of social change will deny the reasonableness of treating the political aspects of the Revolution apart from its economics. With both these positions I disagree. The direct economic effects of the massive educational program have a significance for the present and for the future of the Cuban economy quite apart from political issues. It is important to investigate these effects. The experience in Cuba of the economic consequences of extremely rapid expansion of educational services is relevant to many developing countries. I believe this experience has a validity beyond the political environment of Cuba.

For such reasons this report is mainly economic. Not, let me repeat, that the economic focus is adequate for a full understanding of Cuban education. I make no pretense that it is. But I find it difficult not to believe that here are economic achievements which will look very remarkable to the eyes of countries where a large fraction of the population are illiterate, many of the children are not at school, and most never go beyond primary school. They, perhaps half the world, cannot afford the detached view which we may permit ourselves. We ignore the lessons of Cuban education not only at our peril but at their loss.[1]

ii

The history of a country's educational system is contained within its people. Two out of every 5 Latin Americans, for instance, cannot read or write. This is a comment on present capabilities and a record of school education in the past. In Cuba before the Revolution, the same two things could be seen more clearly. The educational tables of the 1953 national census analyzed a cross-section of the Cuban population according to age and education. This analysis is reproduced as Table 1. The picture it gave was not encouraging.

Of the population ten years or older in 1953, one quarter had never attended school at all, and less than a quarter had completed primary school. The remainder, just over half the population, had dropped out of primary school sometime during their first 6 years. Of the quarter who had completed 6, 7, or 8 years of primary or superior primary education, 1 in 5 had gone on to further schooling, just three-fifths of them into the *bachillerato* pre-university program of 5 years of general study, and the others into the 4-year specialist training of the professional schools. Thus, of the total 1953 population over ten, just 1 per cent had completed a professional school, and less than 2 per cent their pre-university training. Of these, the proportion who went to University was relatively high in Latin American terms, but the narrow base from which they were drawn meant that the total number of Cubans with the full 5 years of university education was 21,000, about one half of 1 per cent of the total population.

A population educated in such ways was hardly the foundation of a thriving economy. The educational record was in part a cause and in part a result of the economic stagnation which had stifled growth for many years. Schools alone will not produce economic development. But illiteracy or an incomplete primary education might well prevent three-quarters of the population of Cuba doing anything significant to escape the rut into which had fallen the economy, their work, and often their lives.

Secondary and university education in Cuba was also economically inadequate. Here, for the top 6 per cent of the population, education was not so much deficient as it was economically irrelevant and imbalanced. Lawyers and arts graduates abounded, while agriculture went short of advisers and researchers. Industry suffered an insufficiency of engineers and technicians, as Table 2 makes clear.[2] For a country of 2,000,000 workers, 2,500 engineers is hardly enough. Other economic weaknesses of higher education in Cuba are indicated in the same table. The general result was that agriculture—the basis of the economy—was starved of the technical manpower it needed to lead it from the doldrums of dependence on sugar into balanced and diversified growth. Industry and mining—the other foundations of the Cuban economy—were lacking in sufficient engineers, technicians, scientists, and surveyors to provide the technical leadership and initiative needed to raise real per-capita income much above its 1925 level. Table 2, by including non-Cubans and others who were trained abroad, may even understate the practical inadequacies of higher education in Cuba.

Note that doctors, dentists, pharmacists, and professional nurses were in relatively generous supply[3] (roughly 1 doctor per 1,000, 1 dentist, 1 pharmacist, 1 nurse per 3,000 of the population), although largely located near Havana. Teachers were employed in large numbers (roughly 1 per 30 school-age children), although, as will be shown, employment was a poor index of activity. But these more favorable aspects should not obscure the dominant fact of Table 2: that a country whose economy was built on agriculture and which increasingly needed to build on

Table 1. Level of Schooling Attained in 1953, by Age[a]

		Total 000's	No Schooling %	No Schooling 000's	Primary %	Primary 000's	Secondary Bachillerato %	Secondary Bachillerato 000's
	Population—10 years							
	or more	4,377	25.3	1110	69.4	3038	2.0	88.6
	Men	2,244	27.6	619	67.0	1503	2.4	54.1
	Women	2,133	23.0	491	72.0	1536	1.6	34.4
Age	Probable years of primary schooling[b]							
6- 9	1950-53	564	74.5	420	25.5	144		—
10-14	1945-53	668	33.5	224	65.6	438	0.7	5
15-19	1940-52	558	23.8	133	69.7	389	5.4	19
20-24	1935-47	521	21.7	113	70.6	368	2.7	14
25-29	1930-42	454	19.6	89	72.7	330	2.6	12
30-34	1925-37	404	20.3	82	73.3	296	2.2	9
35-39	1920-32	383	20.9	80	73.4	283	1.8	7
40-44	1915-27	347	22.2	77	72.3	251	2.0	7
45-49	1910-22	293	23.5	69	71.3	209	1.7	5
50-54	1905-17	210	24.3	51	70.5	148	2.4	4
55-59	uncertain	139	26.6	37	68.3	95	1.4	2
60-64	"	152	30.9	47	65.1	99	1.3	2
65-69	"	106	37.7	40	58.5	62	0.9	1
70-74	"	67	44.8	30	52.2	35	1.5	1
75-79	"	35	42.9	15	54.3	19		—
80-84	"	21	52.4	11	42.9	9		—
85 or more	"	19	63.2	12	36.8	7		—

a. The number in each group does not include those who have completed a higher level of education.

b. Assuming persons have done their primary schooling between the ages of 6 and 14.

Secondary		University				Primary		Secondary			
Vocational		1-4 Years		5 years Or More		6, 7 or 8th grade		Bachillerato 5th year		Vocational 4th year	
%	000's	%	000's	%	000's	%	000's	%	000's	%	000's
2.0	86.5	0.7	31.5	0.5	21.9	17.4	762.8	0.5	22.1	1.0	45.7
1.4	32.1	0.8	18.4	0.8	17.5	16.4	367.9	0.6	13.3	0.7	14.9
2.6	54.4	0.6	13.1	0.2	4.4	18.5	394.9	0.4	8.8	1.4	30.8
—		—		—		—		—		—	
0.1	1	—		—		6.3	42.3	—		—	
2.7	15	0.6	2	—		18.8	102.7	0.5	2.6	0.4	2.4
3.5	18	1.3	7	0.2	1.3	19.1	99.3	0.7	3.9	1.7	8.7
2.9	13	1.3	6	0.8	3.6	20.6	93.6	0.8	3.7	1.8	8.0
2.2	9	1.3	5	0.9	3.8	21.0	84.7	0.7	2.8	1.4	5.5
1.8	7	0.8	3	0.8	2.8	21.3	81.4	0.5	2.1	1.2	4.6
1.7	6	0.9	3	0.7	2.6	20.1	69.8	0.5	1.7	1.3	4.4
1.7	5	0.7	2	0.9	2.5	20.3	59.5	0.5	1.6	1.1	3.3
1.4	3	0.9	2	0.9	2.0	20.7	43.4	0.6	1.2	1.1	2.3
2.2	3	0.7	1	0.9	1.2	19.9	27.6	0.6	0.8	1.5	2.1
2.0	3	0.7	1	0.7	1.0	17.2	26.2	0.5	0.7	1.3	2.0
1.9	2	—		0.5	0.5	14.1	14.9	3.8	0.4	1.1	1.2
1.5	1	—		0.4	0.3	12.8	8.6	0.4	0.3	1.0	0.7
—		—		0.6	0.2	16.3	5.4	0.3	0.1	0.9	0.3
—		—			0.1	9.5	2.1		0.1	1.0	0.2
—		—		—		7.4	1.4	—		0.5	0.1

Source: Censos de Población, Viviendas y Electoral 1953, Havana, Cuba. ›les 36 and 37, pp. 119 *et seq.* See also Part II, Appendix C, p. 375.

industry required an educated population and a school system far in advance of what Cuba had in 1953. The economic development of Cuba before the Revolution, as it is in the present, was in part an educational problem. This economic function and purpose of education must be borne in mind in all that follows.

In 1959, when the present regime came to power, the picture of Cuban education was little changed. Indeed, by reading Table 1 "forward" 6 years, i.e., broadly by thinking of the population as shifting up an age group but otherwise being unaltered, the education level of the people in 1959 can be seen fairly exactly. If few people add to their formal education after leaving school, the age-education profile of a country will each year show the population over school age growing older but not wiser. In Cuba the same was also true for the population of school age. Because there were few changes in education in the years between the census and the Revolution, persons in the cohorts moving up from the school age groups had, proportionally, little more education than the persons they replaced in the age groups above.

An ill-educated labor force is one sign of inadequate schooling in the past. To see this, the age-education profile can be read "backwards," in the sense of using the educational level of the people of each age group to give a picture of the educational system in the years when they were at school. Therefore, Table 1 conveniently summarizes the main pattern of Cuban education over the last 40 years.[4]

The striking feature of Table 1, when looked at like this, is the lack of variation during the previous 30 years. Indeed, relative to total population, there was more primary education for Cubans in 1923 than in 1953. In many countries, the proportion of the school-age generation reaching each level of education has risen over the years. The implications of the unchanging proportions in Cuba deserve more thought than they require comment. In these years some improvement is noticeable in the proportion at professional schools, although part of this improvement may be due to training abroad and after leaving school. Some expansion in the number of Cubans with pre-university training may be observed. But remarkably little variation up to the fifty to fifty-four age group is shown in the proportions of those who attended school or even of those who graduated from University. Beyond

Table 2. Occupations of the Economically Active Population, 1952
Technical and Professional persons 14 years of age and over.

Profession	Total Number
Dentists	1,934
Physicians and Surgeons	6,201
Nurses, professional	1,763
Pharmacists	1,866
Teachers: college and university	3,137
secondary and vocational	2,361
primary	36,815
Engineers: civil (including architects)	1,468
mechanical, industrial, mining	309
other	449
Technicians: draftsmen	1,109
laboratory	2,021
mechanical, industrial, electrical	1,784
Chemists	1,257
Lawyers	6,560[a]
Surveyors	335
Agronomic Engineers	294
Veterinarians	355
Other professional persons	15,891[b]
Total	85,909

a. Includes 623 judges and magistrates.
b. Includes 258 scientific specialists, 9,914 artists, writers, etc., 2,184 religious and social workers, and 3,535 others.
Source: National Census 1953, Table 54, p. 204.

fifty-five, differences in life expectancy between the more or less educated may lead to significant variations in the proportions surviving[5]—which would be misleading as a commentary on the early school system.

The picture of early advance and later stagnation is confirmed directly by historical records. In 1901-2 the military government of the United States with energetic and rapid development of primary schools had raised enrollments to 46 per cent of children of school age. Twenty years later the Superintendent of Schools in an official report[6] claimed that 63 per cent of the Cuban school-age population in 1925-26 was enrolled in primary school, a larger percentage than in any other Spanish-speaking republic. Comparisons with Argentina, Chile, and Uruguay were given. But two decades later—admittedly after long years of an unfavorable sugar market, world depression, and political and social unsettlement—the percentages were 35.1 in 1942-43, 50.1 in 1945-46, and 58.7 in 1949-50, which was still less than in 1925. By 1955, all but three countries in Latin America were claiming higher primary enrollments than those of Cuba, which, relative to population aged five to fourteen, were 51 per cent. Argentina had 88 per cent, Chile 85 per cent, and Uruguay 89 per cent: the average for Latin America was 64 per cent.[7]

Percentages of secondary and university enrollments in Cuba were more favorable as compared to the rest of Latin America. Only 5 countries were ahead in secondary enrollments, and only Argentina and Uruguay could better Cuban university enrollments. But although relatively advanced, these enrollments in Cuba were only 12 per cent and 4.4. per cent of the respective age groups,[8] and it becomes a matter of appropriate standard whether the figures are used to acclaim the comparative achievements of one country or to decry the educational backwardness of a continent.

It would not be fair to use the standards of today to judge events of the past. Past governments in Cuba on many occasions acknowledged certain standards of education. These can be used to test their performance. Order No. 368 of 1900 in Cuba made school attendance compulsory for children between the ages of six and fourteen. The Constitution of 1901 established the principles of free and compulsory schooling. Laws and regulations of 1909, 1922, 1940, and 1946 confirmed and amplified the original decrees. They were never repealed. The enrollment figures have already shown the large extent to which this legal obligation was unfulfilled.

The urban-rural contrast offers a second standard. The 1953 census showed that the percentage of non-attenders at school was over 50 in rural areas, less than 20 in the towns. The variations ranged from 58.4 per cent in rural areas of Oriente to 12 per cent in urban areas of Havana. This pattern carried through to the higher levels of education. Yet this disparity had long been recognized as a problem which needed treatment. In 1936, Law 620 was passed which would "carry primary schooling to the areas where there is no school nor likelihood of one soon being created." Batista himself quotes this law with approval to praise the

"Sergeant teachers" whom it created.[9] Yet any success it had must be measured against the urban-rural disparities, of education as well as income, still existing 17 years later.

The financial standard offers deceptive encouragement. Annual expenditure by the Ministry of Education rose from $11,400,000 in 1940 to $36,800,000 in 1945, to $54,900,000 in 1950-51, and had reached $74,300,000 in 1955-56. This was an increase from 14.4 per cent to 22.7 per cent of the government budget and from 2 per cent to 3 per cent of national income.[10] In 1949 educational expenditure nearly reached 4 per cent of national income, and only once since 1940 did it fall below 1.5 per cent. In absolute terms, primary expenditure in 1953 per child of primary school age was $36.8, and the expenditure per child enrolled was $77.3. By the financial standards of the time, this appears to be a respectable record.

Unfortunately, in the words of the 1950 World Bank Report, "the Cuban people have not been getting their money's worth for the relatively generous amounts they have been willing to spend on education." According to the report, "Administrative faults have been the most important cause of Cuba's educational deficiencies."[11] The bank illustrated the discrepancy between payments and results by descriptions of shortages of books, pencils, and paper and schoolrooms themselves, of inadequate or ill-chosen desks, blackboards, tools, and buildings—a catalogue of handicaps for child and teacher. Administration of the Ministry of Education was discontinuous, non-professional, and over-centralized.

To the wastes of maladministration were added the costs of graft. Article 52 of the Constitution adopted in 1940 provided that the budget of the Ministry of Education should not be less than that of any other Ministry, except in case of an emergency declared by law. In practice, the World Bank Report explained, "this laudable principle made the Ministry of Education a principal focus of political patronage and of graft." Other laws produced the same effect. "A teacher in Cuba was a government official, with life tenure on full salary, whether teaching or not . . . . even the outright purchase of appointments occurred." As if such frankness were insufficient to establish the case, the report proceeded to quote the Minister of Education describing his own

Ministry as having been "an opprobrium and a shame and, in addition, a dangerous menace to the Cuban nation. It was a cave of entrenched bandits and of gunmen and an asylum of professional highway robbers."[12]

The World Bank Report concluded that not only had enrollments declined and hours of instruction been cut, but "the quality and morale of the teaching and supervisory force have gone down," and "a general lack of confidence in the public schools is reflected in a disproportionate increase of private school enrollment with a tendency to intensify social class divisions."[13]

The decade before the Revolution was not without reform. Rural education was reorganized in 1952 by creating a department of rural education as a higher administrative and technical body for the planning and conduct of rural education. Between February 20 and March 3, 1956, a primary education seminar, meeting in Havana, worked out plans for the reform of primary schooling in conformity with the directions and guiding principles indicated by the Minister of Education.

Schools were built; in 1956 about 400 new classrooms were created. A public university in Las Villas and one in Oriente were established, and the University of José Martí was given "official"[14] recognition in 1954. We have already noted their effects on the relatively high enrollments in higher education. The educational budget remained high, nearly a quarter of total government expenditure and over $12 per inhabitant in 1955-56—higher than in most other countries in Latin America except Panama and Puerto Rico and possibly Chile.[15]

How deep these changes went I have not the evidence to assess. Batista[16] quotes many of the educational laws and decrees which were passed between 1936 and 1958 and gives figures which show enrollments expanding through the two decades: rural primary enrollments from 110,725 in 1944 to 205,809 in 1958; secondary enrollments in the institutes from 12,918 in 1937 to 26,222 in 1944 and to 35,746 in 1958; *colegio* enrollments from 2214 in 1944 to 13,454 in 165 *colegios* by 1958. But population also increased, in total by 33 per cent during the 14 years after 1944, and population of school age by slightly more. Thus enrollments in the institutes only just held their own with the population, and the increase in the number of children attending rural primary schools represented a gain of enrollments over population growth of about 4 per cent a year. The additional 11,000 secondary students enrolled in *colegios*, although representing an absolute increase of less than 1,000 per year, proportionally were five-fold more than in 1944. By 1955, 12 per cent of the eligible population was enrolled in secondary education, which placed Cuba sixth among Latin American countries.[17] It is necessary, however, to consider not only the improvements which were made but the distance yet to cover, judged (as before) by the standards the Cubans set themselves. By this test, the improvements described, though not to be ignored, left much undone.

In spite of Batista's claims, many of the old weaknesses of the educational system persisted. In 1955-56, 20 per cent of the educational budget was still absorbed by central administration.[18] In the same year, technical and vocational education received less than 4 per cent, and of this the strictly technical was very small. The Ministry of Agriculture devoted less than $600,000 to educational work. A U. S. Department of Commerce Report of July, 1956, said that "facilities for technical and business training in Cuba have not kept pace with the growing need of such training engendered by expanding and diversified economic activities. Broadly speaking, students desirous of playing a productive role in the development of their country must seek their training abroad."[19]

In the 1950's, large proportions of the educational budgets were earmarked for primary education (in 1955-56, 61 per cent), usually more than in most Latin American countries. Yet total primary enrollments in public schools, shown in Table 3, increased on average by only 1 per cent a year for the 9 years from 1950 to 1958-59.[20] This increase, as before, must be compared with a rate of population growth of about 2.2 per cent. Enrollments in private schools rose somewhat, but clearly insufficiently to make up the growing gap between the number of children and public school facilities.

In the area of adult education, the Cuban Ministry of Education reported in 1952 that it had "organized a national campaign against illiteracy,"[21] with support from associations representing civic institutions, societies, and corporations in every school district. The financial allocation to all adult education in the same

Table 3. Public Primary Education, 1949-59

	Enrollments[a]			Classrooms in use		
	Urban	Rural	Total	Urban	Rural	Total
1949-50	400,659	187,349	588,008	11,886	4,777	16,663
1950-51	399,506	196,024	595,530	12,340	4,825	17,165
1951-52	388,842	201,928	590,770	n.a.	n.a.	n.a.
1952-53	422,329	212,595	634,924	15,340	5,168	20,508
1953-54	441,419	216,853	658,272	15,439	5,204	20,643
1954-55	418,856	200,374	619,230	15,743	5,204	20,947
1955-56	435,514	210,625	646,139	n.a.	n.a.	n.a.
1956-57	447,440	221,846	669,286	15,539	5,706	21,245
1957-58	n.a.	n.a.[b]	n.a.	n.a.	n.a.[b]	n.a.
1958-59	425,580	217,254	642,834	n.a.	n.a.	n.a.

a. Enrollment in public primary schools, including kindergarten and pre-primary (about 12 per cent) and grades seven and eight (about 4 per cent of total). Rural schools did not include seventh or eighth grade.

b. Fulgencio Batista gives rural enrollments as 205,809 and rural classrooms as 5,591 in 1958 (*Piedras y Leyes* [Mexico, 1961], p. 99).

Source: Ministry of Education files, Havana.

year was $2,120,000, or 2.5 per cent of the educational budget. This sum may be measured against the 1,032,849 Cuban persons aged ten or over registered as illiterate during the census of the following January.

These further reasons make it difficult to believe that the improvements of the fifties were either sufficiently deep or sufficiently widespread to make great changes in the educational structure of Cuba revealed by the national census of 1953. The population remained widely ill-educated or illiterate. The schools remained largely inadequate and inefficient.

CHAPTER V

The Educational Aims
and Program of
the Revolutionary Government

i

What to the observer seems inadequate was to the leaders of the Revolution intolerable. The educational situation revealed by the age-education profile of the 1953 census[1] challenged their declared aims in two ways. It contradicted their declaration that every child was entitled to at least 8 years of primary education as the 1940 Constitution had required, and it obstructed their intentions to develop and diversify the Cuban economy. Furthermore, as a national system it embodied extreme inequalities and tended to intensify class divisions.

Castro himself, 6 years before he came to power, declared that "a revolutionary government would undertake the integral reform of the educational system" and illustrated his meaning by denouncing the poverty of rural education, the illiteracy among the farmers, and the lack of technical and industrial schools in a country which a reforming government "would proceed immediately to industrialize."[2]

This was not a solitary outburst. Castro often repeated his intentions to reform and expand education. Other leaders did the same. The first Declaration of Havana in September, 1960, declared the right of every child to a free education. Armando Hart, the Minister of Education, had a year before quoted calculations showing what this would mean for school attendance.[3] Castro, speaking to the United Nations General Assembly in 1960, explained what was intended for adult education. "Next year," he declared, "our people propose to launch an all-out offensive against illiteracy, with the ambitious goal of teaching every illiterate person to read and write."[4]

Mass education was in the forefront of the government's program. In economic terms, it had been elevated to one of those items of basic consumption which a government declares it will make universally available, whatever the cost and regardless of return. Martí's dictum, "To be educated in order to be free,"[5] may well express all the justification the leaders felt was necessary to defend the high priority they gave to basic education.

But while valuing education as consumption, the leaders did not ignore it as investment. From the start they had declared themselves for agricultural reform and for industrialization. Implementing each of these was in part an educational problem— administratively a matter of finding more technicians, agricultural engineers, directors, and experts of all sorts, educationally (and in practice to a great extent) a matter of training them. For when technicians cannot be found, they must be taught. Thus, the plans for agriculture and industry created immediate demands for higher education, particularly in the technical fields. General education, at all levels and for all ages, was spurred by the same forces. Success in the drive for new forms of agriculture and for new factories would depend on trainable and responsive workers, as well as on informed support from every section of the community.

Within a year and a half (at the end of June, 1960), the requirements recognized from the beginning were reinforced by further needs for Cuban technicians and administrators to replace expatriates in the industries being nationalized. A year later, the Cuban leaders were openly committed to a planned economy, pressed by its special needs for administrators and statisticians, and urgently aware of the widespread needs for skilled labor. By 1962, a 4-year development plan had been drafted which must have made these links between economic and educational development unmistakably clear. The specific demands for more persons with old skills and others with quite new ones were matched only by the general need to mobilize the whole labor force for the task of development.

As the demand grew for people with technical and professional training, so the supply of people who might have been available declined. The first political emigrants left in 1959. Nationalization in 1960 spurred further departures, especially among foreign personnel, many of whom had technical qualifications. The flow continued. By mid-1962 it was estimated that a quarter of a million persons had left the country since 1959. Although I do not have details, it seems likely that 15,000 or 20,000[6] of them may have been technicians or professionals.

These diverging tendencies—rising demand and falling supply of skilled manpower—may be seen in perspective by referring back to Table 2, Chapter IV, which showed the 86,000 persons in Cuba (including non-Cubans) who had professional and technical employment[7] in 1952. The number in 1959 cannot have been much higher. An unrepaired loss of 15,000 from a total of probably less than 100,000 would have raised considerable and widespread difficulties even if the goals had only been to maintain an existing system. In the context of the Revolution, with objectives of economic expansion, of agricultural reform and industrial development, of better public health and increased schooling, the manpower shortages became desperate. Immediate disorganization in many sectors reinforced an awareness of long-run requirements. Upgrading courses and retraining programs became vital for short-run stability. Ambitions for long-run economic development, often set by the standards of the developed economies, were increasingly seen to depend on the labor force having an education comparable to the countries emulated. This meant expanded programs for training specialists in many skills. But the advanced countries are distinguished from the less developed not only in having more technicians but in having a labor force more educated at every level. A universal program of general education was also essential.

The third reason for introducing reform in Cuban education was at first put in terms of the inequalities and distinctions which the old system fostered. Yet, like the other two aims distinguished, so the third has been widened and modified with the changing circumstances and declarations of the government. What began for many as a revolutionary reaction against inequalities within the educational system has increasingly become a political and doctrinaire reform of education as an integral and essential part of Marxist-Leninism. It is not my purpose to detail the phases or the causes of this change, nor to deal here with its distinctly political aspects, which are reserved for the Appendix. But in terms of economic effects, this third aim of the educational program, at least in the 18 months preceding the preparation of this account, has been directed in support of the new economic system, to strengthen incentives for work and saving, to spread awareness of national needs and intentions, in essence to speak directly and specifically to the individuals who make up the system, in an attempt to win their informed cooperation and to fire their enthusiasm for the task of developing a whole country and "of building its peoples into a Socialist Nation." This third aim has tended to make Cuban education wider in coverage, broader in syllabus, more directly concerned with the topical problems of Cuban economic development.

However ambitious their future aims, countries, like people, are largely bound by what they are and by what they possess at the time. The available stock of capital, natural resources, and labor (with its different skills and levels of education) sets physical and human limits on what can be done.

In education for the first few years of a new system, some limitations may be absolute, determined by the numbers of teachers available and by the numbers of students already in the "pipeline" of the old system. Any attempt to force the pace during this stage may raise the numbers of students per teacher, strain school facilities, bring in students who are inadequately prepared, and result in a decline in standards of education.

In time, the restraints become mainly economic, given not by absolute limitations but by the increasing cost of expansion in terms of the other projects which would have to be curtailed in order to make possible the increase in education. These other projects may be non-educational, as when a dam competes with a new school for concrete and building supplies. Or competition may come from other lines of education, as when schools and adult classes both need new teachers.

Manpower shortages may cause the most crucial conflicts of this sort. The age-education profile has already shown the scarcity of well-educated people of working age. The educational system feeds on such people, wanting them not only as teachers but as students at higher levels. But the same people are also urgently required by industry, agriculture, or administration. In this respect, "How much can the country afford for education?" may be asked more pointedly in the form, "How many of the better educated persons can be spared from current production, for how long, and at what cost?" The age-education profile provides a good background for answering this question. The profile shows the total number of persons of each age and level of education who would be available either to the school system or the economy. It thereby also shows the number remaining to the economy when the school system has taken its share.

The choices among different forms of education and between education and other things are matters not merely of relative costs but of the different benefits expected and of how soon these benefits will appear. Most types of education are both investment and consumption, economically productive and personally enriching. But different types of education combine consumption and investment elements in different proportions. They also have different periods of return. Some education—technical training, for example—is clearly of more immediate use to industry than general studies. Technical education in schools will produce investment returns only after a delay. Training on the job or adult education can produce returns at once. Yet while the economic returns from education as investment may seem particularly important in underdeveloped countries, the value placed on primary education as a basic human right or as the basis for political support may be the deciding factor.

Cuba, as will later be made clear, was by the standards of Latin-America relatively well endowed with the resources needed to expand education. The dominant *economic* problem of Cuba before the Revolution was stagnation rather than low income. And the corresponding *educational* characteristic was unused potential. The educational system was well financed but slack and inefficient, teachers were often available but unused or ineffectively employed, students were eager to learn but discouraged by immediate economic difficulties and poor prospects. Supported by the resources of an economy which was not fundamentally poor, a government embarking on education reform in Cuba had quite a lot to draw upon.

The mere availability of these resources and the fact that some expansion, particularly in the initial stages, was possible rapidly and at little cost, did not remove the need for making the basic education choices described earlier. There were still limits on what could be done, and there was still need to establish priorities between different sorts of education and between education and other things. Faced with these alternatives, the revolutionary government has greatly expanded the total resources going to education and has followed a program of education which puts quantity before quality and which emphasizes both long- and short-range benefits. Primary, adult, and technical education were expanded together. Standards inevitably fell. The costs have been tremendous. But to declare these conclusions is to run ahead of the story. Here it is merely noted how some weaknesses were bound to emerge from the available but limited resources and the immense educational aims of a government which had set itself to industrialize a country, to educate a people, and "to build a Socialist Nation"—all at the same time.

Not all the implications of these policies were foreseen, and some choices were made by default. Perhaps the second and third educational objectives, which each call for widespread education, have been dominant. The popular declarations of a revolutionary government, whatever its deeper intentions, are built on a message to the masses. This priority, expressed in declarations, bolstered by the need for political support, spurred by a Marxist ideology "of reeducating the masses for the socialist future and weaning them away from the prejudices of the bourgeois past,"[8] was further influenced by immediate economic needs to produce the mass educational programs followed by Cuba since 1959.

ii

The age-education profile (Table 1, Chapter IV) provides a summary of the manpower and educational problems before the Revolution, and the preceding quotations explain the educational ambitions of those who came to power. The educational background may be called the supply and the ambition the demand. How has the Cuban government attempted to bring the two together? I intend no value judgments when I say that the Cuban government in the educational field has acted simultaneously on a large number of educational fronts, mobilizing economic and human resources with a massiveness seldom, if ever, seen before in a country of this size.

School enrollments by 1962 had expanded at all levels. Matriculation in primary schools had nearly doubled, from 737,000 in 1958 to 1,253,000 in 1961. Cuba was claiming available facilities (and virtually total enrollment) for every child of primary school age. Secondary basic education (grades 7 to 9 under Cuba's new system) had tripled. Technical school and institute enrollments had quadrupled. Only pre-university enrollments (now grades 10 to 12) showed a decline, from 36,000 to 16,000, and that partly because of a change of statistical definition which is discussed later.

At the university level, enrollments had not yet risen, but a plan for university reform 2 years in gestation and in effect since January, 1962, called for an increase in university students from less than 17,000 to 80,000 by 1970.

Outside the coverage of conventional schooling, the Revolution has used a variety of techniques, equally massive. To deal with the problem of illiteracy, broadly the million over school age who had never attended school, 1961 was proclaimed the Year of Education, formal classes were abandoned, and 271,000 school children and adults were sent out as teachers, often into remote areas of Oriente, under the slogan, "If you know, teach; if you don't know, learn." By the end of the year, 707,000 adults had been taught to read or write, "alphabetized," to a level of grade 1 schooling. In 1962, *Seguimiento* (continuation) classes were arranged for the newly literate and for those of low education. By August, 1962, 455,000 adults were enrolled in *Seguimiento* classes, of whom 115,000 had learned to read and write in 1962. For 94,000 men and women of third grade achievement or higher, *Superación Obrera–Campesina* (worker-peasant–advancement) classes were opened to teach the equivalent of up to sixth grade and, in 1963, to begin on post-primary work. The old night schools were continued with a registration of 56,000, a slight decline from pre-revolutionary days.

For particular groups of adults, further special classes were arranged. In many factories *Mínimo Técnico* classes were started to give workers a basic technical understanding of the functions they performed and of the machines they used; by August, 1962, 72,000 were enrolled. Special classes to train domestic servants for a new occupation were running: 19,000 were studying, 10,000 had been found jobs. Several thousands of young workers or students were studying abroad, almost all in countries of the Soviet bloc. A residential school for high-level administrators and a school of statistics were run by the Ministry of Industries in Havana.

Thus, besides school children, by August, 1962, at least a half a million Cuban adults were enrolled in classes which a year before did not exist. The "mass organizations" were strongly supporting these developments and at their third national congress in September, 1962, emphasized the need for ever-growing enrollments. It is likely, then, that future numbers will be even higher.

As enrollments, so also the budget for education expanded. It grew in total from $74,200,000 in 1958 to $237,700,000[9] in 1962. With the non-Ministry expenditure on science and culture, part of which was spent by schools and part of which was included in the former Ministry of Education budget, the total for 1962 was $270,400,000 (Table 1). A change of this magnitude in 4 years is not common. It raises questions of accuracy, of meaning in terms of resources, and of composition.

$237,700,000 is, of course, a budgetary estimate. Financial experience in Cuba is scarce. Structural and administrative changes in education have been great. A revision of the figure and of its composition was made under Resolution 924 of May,

Table 1. Public Expenditure on Education and Culture

Year	Total $ Million	$ per capita
1958	74.2	11.4
1959	88.4	13.2
1960	110.2	16.2
1961	170.0[a]	24.5
1962	270.4[a]	38.1

a. Budgetary estimates.
Source: "*Cuba y la Conferencia de Educación y Desarrollo Económico y Social*," Santiago de Chile: Comisíon Nacional Cubana de la UNESCO 1962, p. 8.

1962, which shifted $27,600,000 of it (everything which had been earmarked for investment in buildings, machinery and equipment, and general repairs) to the control of JUCEPLAN. The remaining $199,000,000 was cut by 4.25 per cent.[10] Yet three-quarters of the amount cut, i.e., about $6,000,000, was taken from central administrative expenditure, and most of this, I was told in the Ministry, was from funds requested but unused, not from projects begun but curtailed.

The estimated $237,700,000 to be spent on education in 1962, which I will continue for convenience to use, mindful of the revisions described, is of course measured in current pesos. How has their value changed? A rough index of the cost of education may be constructed here, not in terms of general consumer prices but as the money-cost government must pay for its teachers, their supplies, and their buildings.

The money increases in teachers' salaries during the Revolution have been relatively generous. A system was adopted whereby the minimum salary for primary-school teachers would be $67.50 monthly, and this would be raised by $20 every 12 months. New teachers would begin at $67.50. Pre-revolutionary teachers would maintain their former salary, and each person would begin receiving increases when the general level reached his own. In 1962 the general level had reached $129, and nearly two-thirds of the primary teachers received it. In addition, the traditional system of awarding bonuses for long service and extra responsibility was retained, and in January, 1962, these were anywhere from $4 to $47 monthly for long service and up to $12 monthly for a teacher in charge of a school with 6 classes. The government commitment to an annual flat rate increase has undoubtedly proved a strain, and in January, 1962, a cut of 5 per cent in all salaries was introduced. This reduced a supposedly $135 basic salary to the $129 mentioned above. After income tax and social security deductions, pay was $113.65 monthly.

For present purposes these increases very roughly imply an average increase in the basic money incomes of *primary* teachers of something like 45 per cent before tax and social security payments. How representative this is of salaries of other teachers is uncertain. In any case, the addition to the teaching structure of many part-time adult teachers receiving $25 or $35 monthly makes comparisons difficult and the calculation dangerous. If building costs have risen 15 per cent and other prices 10 per cent, an average educational price increase of 30 per cent would be implied. That percentage suggests that real expenditure on education in 1962 was about $165,000,000 in 1958 prices, or about two and a quarter times that of 1958. Because the structure of education has altered so much, this figure indicates no more than an order of magnitude of the change.

The large fraction of the national income devoted to education also shows its importance in the plans of the government. Placing a figure on national output in 1962 is a risky speculation. The choice may be avoided by considering the educational budget in relation to several possible levels of income. From 1955, the national income rose,[11] although not steadily, from $2,400,000,000 to an estimated $3,300,000,000 in 1959. If national income has grown since 1959 from $3,300,000,000 to, say, $4,300,000,000 in 1962, that is, by 10 per cent a year, the educational budget after revisions would be taking over 5 per cent in 1962. If national income did not grow by so much, the proportion going to education in 1962 would be even higher: 6 per cent if national income was $3,800,000,000, 7 per cent if it did not grow at all, perhaps 8 per cent if it fell to $2,900,000,000.

These percentages are extremely high, as comparisons with public expenditure on education in other countries in recent years will show: Puerto Rico has spent 7.4 per cent, U.S.S.R. 7.1 per cent, Finland 6.3 per cent. Most other countries spent under 6 per cent. The United States spent 4.6 per cent, Venezuela 4.1 per cent, Costa Rica 4 per cent, Panama 3.9 per cent, British Guiana 3.7 per cent.[12] Adding in private educational expenditure would of course raise some of these percentages in other countries. But by any standards, whatever the level of national income, the proportion of Cuban resources now devoted to educational activity is extremely high.

As a third test, the breakdown of education expenditure may be considered (Table 2). Expenditure on education in 1952-53 is also included for comparison. Both columns, it should be noted, are based on functional classifications, that is, by purpose of expenditure rather than by the agency having administrative or financial responsibility. There is always an arbitrary element introduced by such reclassifications, both in the definition of

Table 2. Budget Estimates of Expenditure on Public Education in Cuba

	1952-53 $ million	%	1962 $ million	%
Central Administration	16.5	19.8	20.1	8.4
Primary and Pre-Primary	50.9	61.2	92.0	38.7
Secondary	5.1	6.1	40.3	16.9
Technical	3.2	3.8	35.5[a]	14.9
Teacher Training	3.2	3.8	8.1	3.4
Special Education	.2	.2	3.3	1.4
Adult Education	2.1	2.5	25.7	10.8
Universities	2.2	2.6	12.7[a]	5.4
Total:	83.2	100	237.7	100
Science and Culture			32.7	
			270.4	

a. $12.7 million is my own estimate for total University expenditures because this item is no longer contained within the Ministry of Education budget.

University expenditure includes $3.7 million under the scholarship program, which is given in the Ministry budget. The rest I have had to estimate on the assumption that the allowance of $9 million in 1961 from the Ministry to the universities is continued in addition to the new allocation under scholarship aid.

Altogether there is $11.3 million expenditure on additional education which is not contained within the Ministry budget. After assuming that $9 million of this goes to the universities, I include the remaining $2.3 in technical education.

N.B. Further details of the budgetary allocation in 1962 are shown in Table 8, Chapter VI, and Table 2, Chapter VII. In the table above for 1962, expenditure on school libraries and physical education is included under 'central administration' and allocations to technical, agricultural, commercial, and vocational schools and institutes under 'technical.'

Source: 1952-53: UNESCO *"Survey of World Education"* I, 1955. 1962: Ministry of Education, Havana. *"Presupuesto por Actividades de 1962."*

categories and also in the total, which usually will not correspond to the exact amount of the Ministry of Education budget.

The main changes in the budget are clear. While every individual category has increased in absolute terms, some, like central administration, have not increased very much. Even primary education, the largest item, although increased by $41,000,000, has in fact grown less in proportion than the total of primary school enrollments, though this is perhaps explained more by the inefficiencies of the past than by the economies of the present. Its total within the budget has fallen from 61 per cent to 39 per cent. The proportion spent on teacher training is little changed, although in absolute terms there has been a considerable rise. All other categories are greatly increased, absolutely and proportionally. Secondary education now occupies second place in budgetary importance, and technical-vocational education a close third. The increased diversity within the latter and the especial emphasis on the mechanical and technical will be discussed later. Note also the new emphasis on adult education. The figure, it should be remembered, refers to the year after the national literacy campaign and, because many teachers for adult classes work voluntarily or for part-time salaries, disguises the real significance of adult education. Special education in 1962 comprised primary schools for the mentally and physically handicapped and centers of social rehabilitation for minors.

An economic classification of the 1962 budget is shown in Table 3 and an administrative classification in Table 4. As mentioned earlier, during 1962 responsibility for general repairs, machinery and equipment, and capital construction passed to JUCEPLAN.

Although the provinces have charge of over 50 per cent of the budget, more than 85 per cent of their share is in respect of salaries and social security payments. I was told that financial initiative from the provinces was neither unknown nor unwelcome, particularly because the national plans were drawn up with inadequate previous experience. An official statement of policy in 1962 read:

> The system of education in Cuba has been decentralized through the delegation of large areas of authority to municipal and provincial departments. In this way the defects of an overcentralized system of

Table 3. Economic Classification of 1962 Budget of Ministry of Education

	$ million	%
Running expenses		
Salaries	128.4	56.7
Travel and sundry meals	2.0	0.9
School food	17.4	7.7
Medical and surgical expenditure	0.2	—
Clothing	5.8	2.6
Scholarships	8.8	3.9
Material and Services	18.5	8.2
Social Security	12.8	5.7
Miscellaneous	4.7	2.1
Sub-total of running expenses	198.6	87.8
Investment		
General repairs	2.9	1.3
Machinery and equipment	10.6	4.7
Capital construction	14.1	6.3
Sub-total of investment	27.6	12.3
Total:	226.4	100

Source: Ministry of Education. "Presupuesto por Actividades de 1962."

the type from which Cuba suffered for many years are avoided. This policy is implemented through the autonomy of each provincial department in matters of organization, supervision, and administration of education but also in economic matters. The new budget, following this principle, provides for the massive incorporation of the people into the revolutionary education system, since it is prepared and decided upon by units at the basic working level that are conscious of essential needs and conditions.

Owing to limitations of time and technical personnel, this year's budget has been prepared with collaboration on the provincial level only. Next year [1963], however, the towns and neighborhoods will participate in its preparation.[13]

There is no point in debating here the sincerity of these aspirations for local decision, the genuineness of the representation, or the freedom of discussion. But the massive incorporation of large numbers of people within Cuban education is an indisputable fact. Television, radio, and newspapers almost daily keep education in the public eye. Increasingly, schools are being brought within the influence of leaders of local groups who have been made responsible for encouraging higher enrollments and

Table 4. Administrative Classification—Expenditure on Education, 1962

	$ million	%
Ministry of Education		
General		
Central Administration	71.2	31.5
Provincial Departments: P. del Río	8.9	4.0
Havana	40.3	17.8
Matanzas	9.2	4.1
Las Villas	18.7	8.3
Camagüey	9.1	4.0
Oriente	27.7	12.2
	185.2	81.9
Scholarship Plan		
Central Administration	32.5	14.3
Provincial Departments: Havana	2.9	1.3
Las Villas	3.4	1.5
Camagüey	0.7	0.3
Oriente	1.7	0.8
	41.2	18.3
Total: Ministry of Education	226.4	100
Universities and Other Ministries	11.3	
	237.7	
Ministry of Culture and Science	32.7	
Total: Education and Culture	270.4	

Source: Ministry of Education. "Presupuesto por Actividades de 1962."

better attendance and who in various ways support the teachers. Six hundred thousand persons apparently discussed in various local committees the issues to be placed before the National Congress of Education in September, 1962; 30,000 sent telegrams to the Congress. Very large numbers of adults and school children attend classes each day. Some estimate must be made, when counting the cost, of the total manpower used within the educational effort.

It is probably impossible to measure in full the cost of all the bits and pieces of human effort involved. But even a rough estimate of the full economic cost[14] must include the labor, paid or unpaid, of teacher and of student. For an hour in school is an hour less at something else, which is as true for the pupil as it is for his teacher. Because students are more numerous than teachers,[15] the total real cost of their being at their desks and away from work[16] may well be greater than the salaries of their instructors.

For the Cuban teachers and other employees of the Ministry of Education, the salaries they earn will be used to judge the effort they put forth and the "opportunity cost" of their services in the economy. For the students and unpaid teachers, bolder assumptions must be made. Cuban education in 1962 embraced 2,000,000 people, of whom a large proportion were of working age. In 1961, the Year of Education, over a million and a quarter were involved, mostly adults engaged for long hours, either as teachers or pupils, in the adult literacy campaign. Even when the education is free, the pupil pays in time, effort, and alternatives foregone. A voluntary teacher does the same. For this reason, summaries of the different lines of Cuban education must include some estimate of the total manpower involved.

CHAPTER VI

The Literacy Campaign
and Adult Education

1

When a fifth of its population over school age cannot read or write, a country is faced with the stark alternatives of living with illiteracy until the unschooled die off or of dealing with the problem by some form of adult education. As contemporary concern with illiteracy is unlikely to have the patience to wait another fifty years, the life expectancy of some young illiterates past primary school age, it is certain that increasing attention will be given to adult education in many countries in the near future.

It is important to see the educational problems of a backward country in terms of these bold options. Adult education too easily raises thoughts of flower arranging for the interested housewife or continuation courses for the ambitious few. Indeed, evening classes in the most developed countries often exist as a pastime or for a specialized purpose. But to an underdeveloped country they are basic. If less than a fourth-grade education is inadequate for a new technology in agriculture or industry, nearly 2,000,000 adult Cubans could not take part. If a full primary education is a necessity, less than a million Cubans, well under half the working force, would have been eligible.

Such figures also indicate the size of the program that is necessary. If Cuba set a long-run target of raising everyone to the equivalent of a ninth-grade education, the number of persons eligible for adult classes would be more than twice the number of school children. Reducing the target to the more immediate aim of sixth grade for all hardly changes the magnitude of required enrollments, although of course it shortens the task.

Although the problem will ease in time as present school children grow to working age and older illiterates reach retirement, the speed of this aging process is hardly commensurate with the urgency of modern ambitions for development. It is true that there is nothing new in the fact that the youth of one generation is spending longer at school than did its parents and grandparents. But the rapid increase in school enrollments and the quickening of new ambitions in the poorer countries create new complications. Wider school coverage raises problems in many families of a degree quite different from those when the "bright" child went a few grades beyond his father. Now many children get some education when father got none. An educational "divorce" divides children from parents.

Outside the home, the handicaps of illiteracy or low education for a peasant can become the basis of his isolation from modern economic development. There is no point in discussing, without evidence, what degree of isolation can occur. It obviously will vary. But in Cuba, neither the economic nor the social ambitions of the regime could tolerate any major degree of isolation. The dependence of Cuban development plans on skilled, informed labor had become increasingly clear, and with it the need for adult education. The desire to bring the whole population, peasant and worker, of low education as of high, within the full strategy of political-social-economic development added a further urgency for stressing a program of adult literacy. Both produced the Campaign of 1961.

ii

The priority assigned to education in the third year of the Revolution made 1961 the Year of Education. In one of those massive mobilizations of whole populations seldom seen except in war, Cuba for 8 months mobilized over a quarter of a million men and women, schoolboys and schoolgirls, into a teaching force, transported half of them the length of the island, supplied them with 3,000,000 books and more than 100,000 paraffin lamps, and declared war on illiteracy. Before the campaign, the official rate of illiteracy was 21 per cent. By December the government claimed that it was 3.9 per cent. Some of the remaining illiterates continued to be instructed in 1962.

Castro officially opened the Year of Education on New Year's Eve at a rally of 10,000 teachers in Ciudad Libertad, Havana. From that moment it became a focus of public information, educational activity, and economic effort until December 21, when it was officially closed. Castro's rallying call was that there should not be one illiterate person left in Cuba at the end of 1961; the more carefully worded aim was to make literate all persons older than fourteen and those illiterates under this age who had had no chance of schooling.

The teaching technique adopted was a nationally organized form of individual instruction, and for this purpose many thousands of *alfabetizadores* (adult volunteers) and *brigadistas* (volunteer members of more mobile student brigades) were enrolled as instructors. As this required an organization considerably beyond the framework of the Ministry of Education, a National Literacy Commission was created, composed of representatives from the Ministry of Education and the revolutionary organizations.[1] The commission was responsible for countrywide coordination and had sections dealing with finance, technique, publicity, and publications. It was linked to the provincial departments of education and to provincial committees and executives of organizations active in the campaign. This structure was carried down to the municipal level, where similar committees were in charge of finance, technique, and publicity.

The campaign had three stages. The preparatory census was started in November, 1960, and attempted to locate and register all illiterates. By February, 412,000 were located; by April, 546,-000; and by June, 684,000. By August 30, when the census was ended, 985,000 illiterates had been registered. In April, after the school year had been terminated early for this purpose and a few days after the invasion at Playa Girón, the first wave of student *brigadistas* (many were from primary school), were sent to Varadero for 2 weeks of training. Following Castro's appeal on Mother's Day, 22,000 more enrolled as *brigadistas,* and the campaign gathered momentum. After training, the *brigadistas* left for the mountain areas, organized in units of 25 or 50 under the supervision of a *campesino,* worker, or other local leader, with a teacher responsible for technique and a third member in charge of political orientation. Each *brigadista* was supplied with a uniform, hammock, blanket, instruction books, and a teaching manual. Besides the badge of the Conrado Benítez Brigade on their arm, they were given cloth pictures of two revolutionary martyrs (Conrado Benítez and Camilo Cienfuegos), a paraffin lamp, and a Cuban flag. In fact, the paraffin lamp became the symbol of the campaign and was used on posters, lapel pins, and the "Here lives a *brigadista*" signs which were affixed to the houses where they stayed. Usually the student *brigadistas* lived in the homes of the people they taught, often helping with the farm work.

Deciding who was literate and who was illiterate was the responsibility of the teacher in charge of technique who was attached to each unit. Three tests were given. The first, given at the time of the census, was to determine whether the person could read or should be registered. The second, given during the time of instruction, was a simple test more to inform the organizers of the quality of the teacher and his teaching than of the progress of the pupil. A small proportion of pupils were assigned new *brigadistas* if necessary. The third test, which may be taken as their definition of literacy, involved reading one of two short paragraphs from *Venceremos,* the basic primer, taking a simple dictation, and writing a letter to Castro.

Meanwhile, in the towns the men and women *alfabetizadores* were teaching the illiterates who lived near at hand. As in the country, the time of instruction was arranged to suit both pupil and teacher. Because many who taught in the towns had jobs as secretaries, shop assistants, or factory workers, instruction was frequently given during the lunch hour or immediately after work. Officially it was hoped that instruction would be for two hours each day.

By August 30, when the Second National Congress of Education was convened, 985,000 illiterates had been registered; of these 895,000 (over 90 per cent) had been enrolled for study, 119,000 had already been successfully taught, and 776,000 were still studying. The large number studying but not yet literate challenged the Congress. While an average of 3 students per teacher does not seem excessive, even when individually taught, there is evidence from the discussions of the Congress that there was as great a variation in the abilities of the "alphabetizers" as in the number of illiterates each was teaching. A call for more careful organization of teaching and supplies was reinforced by the formation and dispatch of the *Patria o Muerte* Brigade to assist the student *brigadistas* with teaching in the rural areas. This brigade was composed of 13,882 workers who were given paid leave from their jobs on the understanding that their fellows would make up for their absence at work. The campaign continued until December. During the last 4 months, 588,000 were reported to have learned to read and write, about three quarters of the number studying at the end of August. The official report of the results announced on December 21 is reproduced as column 4 of Table 1. The figures are impressive: 979,000 illiterates had been located, 894,000 enrolled in classes, 186,000 unsuccessfully taught, and 707,212 made literate. The previous columns show the progress of the campaign at different months during 1961.

To the 707,212 taught to read and write during the campaign of 1961 should be added those taught informally within and by the army and the revolutionary forces since the days when Castro was in the Sierra Maestra. After the revolutionary government took power, both the Cultural Section of the rebel army and the Department of Technical, Material, and Cultural Aid to Peasants of INRA began organizing more formal classes in different regions of the country, relying on the voluntary cooperation of teachers and *alfabetizadores*. Official estimates of the numbers taught in this way vary between 60,000 and 100,000.

Table 1. Progress of the Literacy Campaign, 1961
Number of illiterates located, studying and successfully taught with the number of teachers.
(All figures in thousands)

	June 30	July 31	August 30	December 21
Illiterates				
Illiterates located	684	822	985	979
Illiterates involved in campaign in 1961	487	656	895	n.a.
Persons studying	465	594	776	
New literates: cumulative total	22	62	119	707
Remaining illiterates				272
The Teaching Force				
Brigadistas	47	—	90	106
Alfabetizadores	145	—	178	174
Total teaching force	192	234	268	280
Pupil/teacher ratio	2.4	2.5	2.9	

N.B. The official report of December gives a slightly lower figure for illiterates located than the cumulative total for August given here. The same is also true for the numbers in the teaching force, which the official report gives as 271,000.

Sources: June 30, July 31, August 30: *"Congreso Nacional de Alfabetización,"* Havana, 1961, and various. December 21: "Official Report on the National Literacy Campaign," and sources of Table 3, Chapter VI.

Detailed records of the total expenses of the campaign are not yet available, although the government has a commission working to compile them. Of the 1961 budget, however, $12,-300,000 of central funds were allocated to the campaign.

Many of the administrative personnel and 33,960 teachers from the Ministry of Education worked in the campaign. Their cost was reflected in the closing of all schools from April to December, although this represents a loss of less than 9 months of actual schooling, when one takes account of vacation time and the extension of school terms in 1962 and 1963. The order of magnitude of financial cost of the educational personnel may be assessed as a proportion of the total salaries of the Ministry budget. Such an assessment suggests that actual budgetary costs were roughly $52,000,000, or about $73 per illiterate successfully taught, or approximately $58 for each person studying.[2]

Table 2. The Illiterate Population in 1953
(Of ten years old and above)

	Illiterate Population (Thousands)			Percentage of Illiterates in The Total Population		
	Total	Urban	Rural	Total	Urban	Rural
Total:	1033	305	728	23.6	11.6	41.7
Men	580	151	430	25.9	11.8	44.5
Women	452	154	298	21.2	11.4	38.3
Both Sexes:						
10-14	213	49	164	32	15	49
15-19	126	26	99	23	9	38
20-24	105	26	79	20	9	36
25-29	82	22	60	18	8	35
30-34	77	22	54	19	9	37
35-39	73	21	52	19	9	37
40-44	71	22	49	20	10	40
45-49	63	20	43	22	11	41
50-54	46	16	30	22	12	43
55-59	33	13	20	24	14	46
60-64	43	18	25	28	18	50
65-69	38	17	21	36	24	59
70-74	28	13	14	41	29	66
75-79	16	8	8	44	33	70
80-84	10	5	5	50	39	74
85 or more	11	6	5	60	50	79

Source: *National Census,* Table 40, p. 143 *et seq.*

The government in August, 1962, had not yet analyzed the data it collected about the 979,207 illiterates located in the campaign. In the absence of more recent information, figures concerning illiteracy shown in Table 2 are taken from the 1953 national census.

Somewhat over half the illiterates were men, although this proportion might have been reduced by the time of the campaign by the army classes mentioned earlier. If we assume illiteracy was little changed since 1953, just over two-thirds of the illiterates were of working age (fifteen to sixty-five)—68 per cent of those in the towns and 70 per cent of those in the rural areas. There were twice as many illiterates in the country as in the towns, despite the fact that the rural population was only two-thirds the size of the urban. All the illiterates spoke Spanish, except for about 25,000 Haitians, who were therefore not included in the campaign.

Table 3. The Teaching Force in the Literacy Campaign

Alfabetizadores		
"Peoples' teachers"	126,069	
Patria o Muerte Brigade	13,882	
Professional school teachers	33,960	173,911
Brigadistas		105,664
		279,575

N.B. These figures, taken from the sources listed, may be compared with the rounded totals given in the "Official Report on the National Literacy Campaign," Decembed 21, 1961, which were as follows:

"Peoples' teachers"	121,000	
Patria o Muerte Brigade	15,000	
Professional school teachers	35,000	171,000
Brigadistas		100,000
Grand total		271,000

Sources: Brigadistas: Ministry of Education, Havana. Other figures: *"Trabajo,"* December 1, 1961.

By official count, the teaching force numbered 271,000. The composition is analyzed in Table 3. The "peoples' teachers" were the volunteers who usually worked in the towns or more accessible areas. Unfortunately, I have no details about their age, usual occupation, or sex, little information, in fact, on which to base any estimate of the cost to the economy of their work as teachers.

The *Patria o Muerte* Brigade by its design should not have represented a burden on the economy but only on the fellow workers who made up for the absence from work of those in the brigade. To assess the extent to which production was not maintained is virtually impossible. The 13,882 members of the brigade were absent for 4 months at the most.

In total, about three-quarters of all school teachers, 33,960, were involved. The estimate already given of their "opportunity cost" in terms of the educational budget and the closing of the schools seems a more representative way of assessing the burden than to consider only the number of teachers involved. That assessment incidentally, is a good example of the usefulness of the "opportunity-cost" concept for the alternative foregone (about half a year of a nation's regular schooling) and a reminder that a simple manpower estimate is not always the best way to assess the cost of unpaid labor.

The *brigadistas* are well described by the data the Ministry has made available, which is given in Table 4. About a third were under fifteen, and over half were in primary school. Most of the others were in their teens and in secondary school. Altogether, about 10,000 were over twenty, and most of these would be in the group from teacher training school, commercial college, or university. The tables below give further details. The net flow of *brigadistas* from Havana to Pinar del Río and Oriente is clearly shown. In addition, the urban background of the majority of *brigadistas* suggests that within each province there was also a decided movement towards the rural areas. This was confirmed in conversations with many of the *brigadistas*. For many, this educational service had been their first trip to the end of the island and their first experience of rural life. Some of their personal descriptions of what they did and what they learned during these months leave little doubt that there were many indirect benefits for the *brigadistas* themselves which must offset some of the costs of the *brigadista* force. Popular enlightenment, as described by Galbraith[3] in his discussion of the benefits of literacy, enables the masses of the people to participate in economic activity and opens men's minds to new methods and new techniques. The interaction between peasant and townsman, young and old, Fidelista and non-supporter, during the months of the Cuban literacy campaign when they all were brought together in study, work, and country life must have achieved something of the same widening of horizons which Galbraith mentioned. This was mass participation with effects not to be underestimated. In economic effects, the benefits gained by the *brigadistas* may well be as significant as those gained by the illiterates themselves.

Basic equipment in enormous quantities was used. Two million copies of *Venceremos*, the basic reading primer, were printed, and a million copies of *Alfabeticemos*, the teachers' instruction manual.[4] Supplying each *brigadista* with two uniforms, including shirts, trousers, three pairs of boots, a beret, a haversack, a blanket, and a hammock, meant the issue of these items in hundreds of thousands. Over 145,000 paraffin lamps were eventually issued. In addition to this equipment supplied to the *brigadistas*,

104,000 pairs of spectacles were issued free to illiterates needing them. Altogether, 130,000 illiterates were examined for deficient eyesight, using an eye-test chart with commonplace symbols in place of letters.

A mass movement of this magnitude deserves more about motivation than a paragraph. Professionals in labor theory will want some explanation of so much unpaid effort. Experts in adult literacy will wish to understand the Cuban technique. Others will want their fears of political pressures dispelled or confirmed. In any case, it seems more inadequate to say nothing than to make a few tentative comments.

Basically the literacy campaign was part of the Revolution. In philosophy, spirit, and organization it was an integral part of wider change. Many in Cuba felt this, and they were meant to. With good reason, 1961 had been named the Year of Education. Among the illiterates in Cuba, the desire to learn may have been strengthened by their relative minority (21.9 per cent) as well as by the surge of the Revolution, the pressures of government publicity, and persuasive visits during the preliminary census. An illiterate could scarcely hide his inability; he could merely refuse to learn. Some did, usually the very old; but education today is a widely prized possession in the underdeveloped world. It is fair to ask why the illiterate in Cuba would prefer not to learn. The fiestas, presentations of certificates, television appearances added great prestige. The opportunity to learn was obviously at hand. Any Cuban who had shown little interest in schooling when younger may well have felt that now was the time to change his mind about it. There is little need to comment on the many whose minds were already decided—those who had missed school because there had not been enough places for them or because they had had to start work at an early age.

There was also a proposal of the Trade Unions which should be quoted: "By agreement of the Trade Unions, the Revolutionary Government was requested to enact a law, effective from January, 1962, under which all those illiterate workers who have refused to be taught would not have the right to receive salary increases or promotions, or jobs if they were unemployed."[5] I do not know whether this proposal was actually enacted into law or whether it merely suggests some additional pressures. But I think it would

Table 4. The Characteristics of the Brigadista Teaching Force, 1961
(In thousands)

School background	Girls	Boys	Total
Primary School	28.1	27.1	55.1
Secondary basic	17.4	16.0	33.4
Pre-University	2.1	2.4	4.5
Teacher training	1.7	0.3	2.0
Commercial college	1.8	1.0	2.8
University and school teachers	2.1	0.6	2.7
Other	1.8	3.3	5.1
	55.0	50.7	105.7

	Province of origin			Province of assignment		
Province	Girls	Boys	Total	Girls	Boys	Total
Pinar del Río	2.5	2.0	4.5	4.8	3.4	8.5
Havana	20.0	17.0	36.7	1.8	1.1	2.9
Matanzas	2.4	2.7	5.1	2.0	1.5	3.5
Las Villas	8.7	8.1	16.8	7.6	7.1	14.7
Camagüey	4.8	5.0	9.9	5.5	5.3	10.8
Oriente	16.9	15.9	32.8	33.3	32.3	65.6
Total:	55.0	50.7	105.7	55.0	50.7	105.7

Age		Race		Residence	
Under 10	—	White	51.1	Urban	73.5
10-14	33.4	Negro	16.2	Rural	9.8
15-19	39.7	Mestiza	15.3	Unreported	0.8
20-29	7.6	Chinese	0.1		84.1
30-39	1.4	Unreported	1.5		
Over 39	1.4		84.1		
Unreported	0.6				
	84.1				

N.B. The 3 tables referring to 84,118 *brigadistas* were taken from medical records of those who were examined for tuberculosis (a 0.1 per cent prevalence rate was discovered) when at Varadero for training. This total quite understandably could be less than the 105,664 given elsewhere as the full number of *brigadistas*.
Source: Ministry of Education and Literacy Exhibition, Havana.

be misplaced to overemphasize the importance of legal obligations when the usual reasons why an illiterate might hesitate had
been removed or diminished. Lack of confidence was trumpeted
away in the mass publicity, fear and hesitation before one's
fellows (or one's children) were replaced by well publicized
approval of all who studied and acclaim for those who succeeded.
Doubts about the usefulness of literacy were swamped by the
revolution of new possibilities. I do not argue that all was convincing or that all were convinced. I heard several descriptions
in Cuba to the contrary. But when a nation gives first priority
to bringing teachers and books to people hitherto neglected, it
should not be surprising if many respond with interest. The
hesitations of the distant skeptic are less convincing than the
brigadista with a book at the door.[6]

Among the teaching force, motives varied. The school teachers received their regular salary. Most joined the literacy effort.
Many of those who did not were occupied with training courses
preparing them for 1962. The "peoples' teachers" taught near
their homes with little disruption of their usual life. It should be
noted that the non-*brigadista* section of the teaching force represents possibly a fifth of the adult population eligible for service.[7]

By the time the *Patria o Muerte* Brigade was formed, the
prestige and persuasions of the mass organizations were focused
on the campaign and encouraged recruitment.

The *brigadistas*, 70,000 under twenty, responded to calls for
sacrifice and idealism. There was also the hope of a scholarship
for 1962. An interesting analysis of response is shown by comparing the numbers of *brigadistas* with the numbers of their school
fellows who were eligible (Table 5). The percentages may seem
high or low according to the degree that enlistment was really
voluntary.

Without personal experience in Cuba at the time of the campaign, it is impossible to say more about the motives and the
spirit of the many Cubans involved. There are perhaps fewer
uncertainties about why many joined in than why others did not.
The element of humanitarianism was sufficiently clear, the task
comparatively brief and well defined, and for the *brigadistas* the
opportunity sufficiently adventuresome that it is hardly surprising
the campaign received support. To an important extent, the

Table 5. Enlistment of Eligible Students as Brigadistas

	Total Brigadistas	Total School Enrollment	% Enlisting
Primary school	55,134	151,963ᵃ	36.3
Secondary basic	33,405	71,057	46.7
Pre-University	4,476	18,697	23.9
Teacher training	2,023	6,767	29.9
Commercial college	2,818	14,634	19.3
University and school teachers	2,728	— ᵇ	
Other	5,080	— ᵇ	
	105,664		

a. Primary school children over eleven of grade 4 and above (to correspond to the actual grades and ages of the *brigadistas* given in Table 4).
b. It is impossible to say how many were really eligible.
Source: Ministry of Education.

sheer magnitude of the effort may have kindled further support and enthusiasm. Indeed, to have mobilized a teaching force of such size without developing any pride, loyalty, or sense of mission would in itself have been remarkable.

Statistical Comment

The nature of the personnel involved, the rapidity of the effort, and the newness of the administrative structure inevitably affected the accuracy of the statistical data. There appears to be some confusion over the number of *brigadistas*, about which no less than 3 different figures have been published. The original estimate of the number of illiterates, given as 2,000,000, was wildly overstated. But the forms used for the literacy census and for final assessment, while not comparable with those of a national population census, did have the style of a detailed questionnaire which might be criticized more for ambiguity than for lack of comprehensiveness. If there has been overstatement, it is more probably the result of the poor quality of returns at the local level than of deliberate inaccuracy or exaggeration in the Ministry of Education headquarters.

Table 6, a full progress report of the campaign as of August 30, 1961,[8] indicates something of the accuracy of the data. The table shows the number of illiterates the campaign census located and compares it with the number recorded in the official census of

Table 6. National Literacy Campaign—Provincial Results on August 30, 1961

	Oriente	Camagüey	Las Villas	Matanzas	Havana	P. Del Río	Total
	(000's)	(000's)	(000's)	(000's)	(000's)	(000's)	(000's)
Illiterates Recorded in National Census of 1953	440	127	193	58	116	99	1,033
Located in literacy campaign 1961	411	127	186	53	116	92	985
Studying	318	106	146	40	88	78	776
Not studying	64	8	30	13	11	12	138
Successfully taught	58	13	17	5	17	10	119
Teaching force							
Brigadistas (students)	56	8	14	2	1	8	90
Alfabetizadores (adult teachers)	50	20	36	11	46	15	178
Total teaching force	105	29	50	13	48	23	268

N.B. The numbers studying, not studying and successfully taught add to the numbers recorded in the 1953 census.
Source: Literacy Exhibition, Havana, 1962.
Note: As all figures are shown to the nearest 1,000 the additions of the total teaching force in certain instances do not agree exactly.

1953, which included illiterates ten years old or more, by province. Undoubtedly, the 1953 census is a useful guide. Its figures are, however, several years outdated. During the 8 years following, the population in total grew 19.1 per cent, and of course there were changes in age and geographical location. If the number of illiterates in 1953 is increased by the same percentage that population grew, bearing in mind the assumptions this kind of projection involves, the figure would rise to 1,230,000. However, the campaign was defined as including adults above fourteen and those younger but with no chance of schooling. These criteria would reduce the comparable number of illiterates from the 1953 census to 820,337, or if increased by 19.1 per cent to 977,000.

The nearness of this projection to the 979,207 illiterates actually located in 1961 should not be taken seriously. The projected figure makes no allowance for the 60,000 to 100,000 adults made literate during 1958-60. It depends on a proportionally static assumption of adult illiteracy. Moreover, the campaign figure, despite intentions, must have included some people under fourteen.

It should be noted that by the end of the campaign, government officials were treating the 1953 census as too outdated for use. The rate of illiteracy in 1961—said to be 3.9 per cent—was therefore based on the campaign census and refers to the number of illiterates located but untaught (or unsuccessfully taught) expressed as a percentage of estimated population in 1961. It makes no allowance for the possibility of there being illiterates the campaign never discovered. If there should have been a significant number of illiterates not counted in 1961 (which does not seem likely), the percentage of current illiteracy would be higher.

Summary

In the realm of adult literacy, comparisons with school education can be misleading. An illiterate adult needs to learn to read and to write. It is sometimes forgotten that he does not need to learn to speak his own language or to be taught to understand it. Furthermore, he has the maturity of an adult, not of a child. His obstacles are rather lack of confidence and difficulties with written symbols.

These points, with many others, are well appreciated by work-ers in the field. For present purposes, they may help explain how 4 months of study under an inexperienced teacher has proved sufficient to teach the basic ability to read and write to illiterates in many countries. Of course, in this time an illiterate can learn little more than the bare fundamentals. He may have crossed the psychological barrier to literacy, but he is far from practiced in the new skill. Some authorities suggest that the equivalent of a fourth-grade education is necessary before literacy is really functional. This implies a good deal of actual reading and per-haps 150 hours of instruction in all. But the Cuban government itself claims no more than that the successful literates were brought to a first-grade level of literacy. Other studies have shown this to be quite possible within the time. In fact, an analysis[9] of the basic primer *Venceremos* suggests that the book, with only 15 lessons, could scarcely have taken more than 2 months to complete.

Experience elsewhere shows that first-grade literacy is only a beginning. Further study is thus of crucial importance, and failure to continue is perhaps the most frequent reason why early gains are not consolidated. The continuation classes in Cuba will be described in the next section. But first, in summarizing the literacy campaign, the boldness and scope of this remarkable project should not be ignored. Undoubtedly there were major errors. Was it really necessary to close all the schools for almost 9 months? Did planning, organization, and coordination of sup-plies always match the dedication of those in the teaching force? Did people learn all they could? But the campaign does show the advantages of one brief, concentrated effort, coordinated at the national level, directed to an appropriate national goal. When relying heavily on the enthusiasm and perseverance of voluntary workers, a short campaign of only a few months may have great advantages. The literacy campaign may prove to be the most successful achievement of the first 4 years of the Cuban Revolu-tion.

iii

The pressing needs which gave rise to the literacy campaign in 1961 were scarcely less urgent in 1962. With the Year of Education concluded and the Year of Planning just commencing, a widespread program of adult education was started. The 3 broad aims of Cuban education may be distinguished in the problems which the program of adult education was designed to tackle.

Planning, with its new emphasis on rational objectivity, needed administrators, statisticians, and clerks with specific training for their new tasks. Agriculture required competent administrators as well as specialized experts on the "peoples' farms," which by December, 1961, were just completing their first year of operation. The government at that time was running enterprises which contributed three-quarters of the nation's industrial output. General coordination in these industries required many persons who understood and could implement a common system—competent clerks, accurate statisticians, well-briefed principals. All of these needs were urgent. School education could provide only the long-run solution. Specific training was also required for people who already had some experience of work but who were needed in new jobs or for more advanced tasks. For these reasons a program of adult education was a short-run economic necessity.

The literacy campaign had meant a shift of more than one-sixth of the adult population from illiteracy to literacy, swelling the number of Cubans with the equivalent of a first-grade education to over a million. As literacy, by the standards of the Cuban campaign and according to the pledges of the Cuban government, was only a beginning, a continuation program was needed for this vast group. In addition, another one and two-thirds million—those who had completed more than 2 years of primary school but less than 6—were in need of basic education under the government's commitment to raise everyone to the equivalent of a third-grade level and half a million workers to the equivalent of a sixth within 3 years. In total, these 2 groups of adults contained almost double the number of children eligible for primary school.

Finally, by the beginning of 1962, 7 months had elapsed since Castro had declared that Cuba was to be a "socialist country." A general understanding of what Cuban socialism meant for the ordinary Cuban and his family could be conveyed in televised[10] speeches by Castro and other leaders of the Revolution. More thorough explanation could be given in the program of adult education, which could also include discussion. But ideological

specialists were wanted who would be the builders and loyal supporters of the "new society," who understood the basis of Marxist-
Leninism and could influence its development in Cuba. Schools
of Revolutionary Instruction to teach the theory and practice of
Marxist-Leninism in 3 months of intensive evening courses were
established in many places throughout the country. These
schools, whose enrollments were said to be 10,000 at the beginning of 1962 and to include many regular school teachers, were
dependent on ORI (the integrated party of the revolutionary
organizations) and outside the control of the Ministry of Education. Instruction within these schools was almost entirely
political. They were allocated $666,000 in 1962 from the Ministry
of Education budget.

The needs for adult education did not suddenly appear, although perhaps they were increasingly recognized to be of economic and political importance. It seems clear that the programs
of adult education in countries of the Sino-Soviet bloc provided
examples to follow. Certainly, experience of the classes held in
the Cuban army for continuing its own early work on literacy
encouraged and guided the creation of the national program of
adult education in 1962.

The needs of the new national program were far in excess
of anything possible within the structure of the traditional evening classes for adults which had functioned for many years. The
literacy campaign had dealt in hundreds of thousands, but enrollments in the evening classes in 1953-54 were 50,000. Furthermore, as Table 7 shows, the classes before the Revolution were

Table 7. Enrollments in Evening Courses for Adults in 1953-54

	Number of Institutions	Teaching Staff Total	Teaching Staff Female	Students Enrolled Total	Students Enrolled Female
Night schools: urban	326	1,332	877	28,618	11,949
rural	27	27	9	533	173
Centers of English, evening courses	65	337	275	20,650	12,355
Centers of manual arts, evening courses	3	18	15	276	276
	421	1,714	1,176	50,077	24,753

Source: UNESCO, "*World Survey of Education II*," Primary Education 1958,
p. 285.

almost entirely in the towns, mainly non-technical, and largely concerned with teaching English.

If the needs for adult education were enormous, there were compensations, in that economic costs and returns could each take a favorable turn. Costs could be lower than for regular schools, for all the obvious reasons. If the adults studied part-time and did not reduce effort in their daily work (an important consideration in assessing the effects of a widespread scheme), there would be no hidden losses to raise the real economic cost of their study, even if the students were of working age. Nothing would be lost,[11] and something could be gained. Because the students already had experience in their jobs, study could be more specific and practical. Because they were of working age, any benefits to productivity could have immediate impact on the economy, unlike returns from school education, which would mostly be delayed until the school children started work.

Requirements for technical training were too widespread and diverse for the Ministry of Education to handle alone. Various ministries organized instruction and on-the-job training, part-time and full-time, formal and informal. Of these, the courses run by INRA and the Ministry of Industries were probably the most important.

In 1962, for instance, the Ministry of Industries had full-time courses planned for 5,870 persons, who would study subjects from statistics and accounting to lathe-turning and carpentry, with students drawn from every section of industry. Classes lasted from 3 months to 2 years. Courses for 1,820 of the students were residential. Most courses covered a good deal of basic work in mathematics, physics, geography, and such, as a background to the main subject. In addition to these students, 8,000 others were also studying in full-time courses of the Ministry of Industries. These courses, held in "peoples' schools," lasted 18 months and covered arithmetic, physics, chemistry, grammar, geometry, and line drawing, in addition to the special subject.

In 1962 an attempt was made to develop piecemeal courses run by individual ministries into a wide program of practical instruction designed to equip workers with a minimum technical understanding of their work and machines. The program was called *Mínimo Técnico*.

Mínimo Técnico classes for business, factory, or agricultural workers were held at the place of work. Their aim was to teach those who already had the basis of reading, writing, and arithmetic,[12] what went on inside the machines they used. The classes were intended to boost productivity, responsibility, and morale by explaining the importance of an individual's work in the whole process of production. Besides fulfilling these purposes, the classes were intended to be an integral part of the construction of the "new economy." They were largely influenced by experience of workers' preparation in countries of the Soviet bloc. The classes were run and financed by INRA and the Ministry of Industries. Expenses for the latter, like other matters of planning and execution, were basically the responsibility of directors of the "Consolidated Enterprises" and of the administrators and social organizations within each factory. Both ministries, in August, 1962, were producing a series of instruction manuals of about sixth-grade level to be used in *Mínimo Técnico* courses to explain particular jobs.

A typical course for factory workers would include 50 to 200 hours of classroom theory, held outside working hours, and some practical training on the job. The workers were formed into groups of 5 to 8 or in larger groups of up to 25 which both worked and studied under their instructor, who might himself be one of the better workers. The classes in theory were to be given once or twice a week by a special teacher, often one of the technicians. Preparatory classes were run for both teachers and instructors. At the end of the *Mínimo Técnico* courses, exams were arranged with the factories. Certificates were given by the Ministry of Industries.

Enrollments in industrial courses in September, 1962, were 72,000, but classes were held in only 30 per cent of factories. Plans then existed for a rapid expansion of both classes and enrollments.

The Ministry of Education was active in the field of part-time technical training and ran schools for former domestic servants. According to the 1953 census, 69,874 women over fourteen were in domestic service, of whom fewer than 6,000 were in laundering or some specialized service. The others must largely have been employed by Cubans who have now left the country.

The domestic schools may well have been started as much to meet an economic need arising from curtailment of domestic work as they were to implement a new philosophy. At any rate, at least a quarter of former domestics appear to have been enrolled in them.

Two types of domestic schools existed in 1962, both admitting girls who were domestic servants but the first offering evening courses of general education (though with particular emphasis on sewing, homecraft, and such) and the second offering full-time courses as retraining for a specific occupation. Common to both was a zealous philosophy of *superación de los humildes* (raising the downtrodden), and something of this philosophy pervaded the instruction and the place the schools occupied in the educational structure.

In the part-time evening courses, the girls studied a full range of primary school subjects, with possibly less emphasis on the school book and rather more on the immediately practical. Many students hoped this would give them the education necessary to take a business or factory job. Classes were given in shorthand and typing. In the metropolitan area of Havana, 19,100 were enrolled in 91 schools in 1962. Altogether, 10,646 students in the domestic schools were registered in the *Seguimiento* (continuation of study after literacy) program. Each student was given a $5 monthly subsidy for transportation to class.

Two other courses, both full-time and residential, were run by the Ministry of Education for domestic workers. The first lasted 8 months and gave training for administrative and commercial work in offices and shops. Its 1,050 students were housed in the Hotel Nacional in Havana and given a monthly allowance of $30 for food and accommodation. Three hundred recent graduates had been found employment, the majority in banks.

The other course, arranged with the Ministry of Transport, trained girls as drivers, many for the *transporte popular* taxi-bus service in Havana. Fourteen hundred were enrolled, and they also received $30 monthly. These students, according to a report of March, 1962, were expected to graduate soon and to join 250 others who already were working.

An important factor in assessing the work of the domestic schools may be the sense of morale and purpose they created.

A number of students were former illiterates taught to read and to write in the 1961 literacy campaign. Many had dropped out of primary school when younger. The opportunity to learn with an object in view, the confidence of finding employment, and the patriotism of working for the future of the country probably contrasted a great deal with their general experiences and personal discouragements of earlier days.

In response to the demand for mass education, the Cuban government in 1962 started continuation classes and family circles, classes for the army, classes for the advanced, and classes for the newly literate. Most classes were entirely new, a few were older. At the end of August, 589,000 adults were enrolled in the 6 different types of part-time schools, mostly in *Seguimiento* elementary continuation study but a quarter in classes studying the equivalent of work in the fourth to sixth grades. Of the 456,000 studying in all forms of *Seguimiento* classes, somewhat over half were new literates who had "graduated" during the recent campaign: they represent only about a third of the 707,000 successful literates. The others in *Seguimiento,* representing by my calculation a slightly larger proportion of those eligible,[13] were students who at some time had studied in school but had not gone beyond second grade. Most of these classes relied upon part-time teachers. The night schools, continued from pre-revolutionary days, were more formally organized and were taught by full-time paid staff. The "family circles" relied on unpaid leaders.

Popular interest in the classes was aroused, using many of the techniques of the literacy campaign. The revolutionary leaders made frequent references to adult education in speeches, the mass organizations urged higher enrollments and attendance. Posters, displays, and banners in shop fronts, on street corners, and on roads brought to the attention of almost every Cuban the importance and patriotic value of evening study. "Work, study, fight" was made a popular slogan. In September, 1962, the Third National Congress of Education, with a thousand delegates, met in Havana to plan means of attracting higher enrollments and better attendances.

A special school for adult teachers, the Makarenko Institute, was started in Havana and in 1962 had 1500 secondary students enrolled, all with boarding scholarships. These students taught

Table 8. Allocation of Ministry of Education Funds for Adult Education, 1962 Budget

	$ million	%
Continuation classes	9.9	39
(includes both *Seguimiento* and		
Superación Obrera-Campesina)		
Traditional night schools	4.3	17
Classes for domestics: *Seguimiento*	4.0	15
re-training	1.0	4
Seguimiento classes of MINFAR	0.6	2
(continuation classes in the		
armed forces)		
Voluntary teachers for schools for adults	0.9	3
Correspondence courses	4.8	19
Miscellaneous	0.2	1
Total:	25.7	100

Source: Ministry of Education Budget, Havana, 1962.

in some of the adult classes in addition to their own full-time study.

A total of $25,700,000, 11 per cent of the 1962 educational budget, was devoted to adult classes. Allocation of this money is analyzed in Table 8.

Three points should be noted before we turn to descriptions of the different classes. The budget for the continuation classes, I was told, had later been increased—$9,000,000 for *Seguimiento* and $7,000,000 for *Superación Obrera–Campesina* were mentioned on one occasion as the new figures. The allowance for the correspondence courses had been eliminated because it was not possible to start them in 1962. The intention was to begin them in January, 1963, with some courses especially designed for teachers in the mountain regions of Oriente as part of a wider plan.[14] The budgetary allowances for the *Seguimiento* courses and for classes for domestic servants were both new. The other items all appeared in 1961.

The *Seguimiento* program (continuation-to-literacy) was started on February 24, 1962, and grew from an enrollment of 300,000 in the first month to 420,517 by the end of August. Three-quarters of these students were studying in the specially created *Seguimiento* classes, mostly taught by *aficionados,* non-profes-

Table 9. Students and Teachers in Continuation (Seguimiento) Classes, 1962

	May	August 30
Classes functioning for *Seguimiento*	13,330	14,386
Registration in these classes	285,742	313,569
Average daily attendance of students enrolled in classes	40%	45.9%
Teachers in these classes	13,328	13,821
of which Professionals	3,703	2,291
Non-Professionals	9,625	11,530
% Professionals	27.8%	16.6%
% non-Professionals	72.2%	83.4%

Source: Ministry of Education, Havana.

sional part-time teachers (sometimes of only fifth- or sixth-grade education) meeting in an informal classroom—a hall, schoolroom, office, or shop, according to what was available.[15]

Seguimiento classes provided continuation studies for adults of fourteen or older who were made literate during the campaign and for those who had attended less than three years of primary school. Classes usually met five nights a week for two hours or more, concentrating on Spanish and mathematics and aiming to impart the equivalent of the first three grades of primary school.[16] On average, 23 students were enrolled in each of these classes and attendance was 46 per cent. Table 9 shows other relevant data.

In addition to these classes, family circles were begun in July to reach the newly literate who did not attend classes but who might come to an informal meeting with 2, 3, or 4 others and a volunteer "teacher" in someone's house. Ninety thousand persons were enrolled in such classes by the end of August, with an average of just over 3 to a class and with 25,370 teachers and 553 *activistas* responsible for supervision.

In the night schools described below, 16,907 persons were enrolled in grades one and two, the equivalent of *Seguimiento*. In the armed forces, 24,668 were enrolled in their own special *Seguimiento* classes, which were in some respects the forerunners of the general *Seguimiento* program. Started to provide further instruction for new literates in the armed forces, these classes

Table 10. Persons in All Forms of Continuation (Seguimiento) Study, August 30, 1962

Type of class	No. of classes	No. of enrollments
Seguimiento classes	14,386	313,569
Night schools	849	16,907
Family circles	27,945	90,041
Army courses		24,668
Domestic schools		10,646
	TOTAL:	455,831
No. of students who had completed *Seguimiento* (3rd grade equivalent) (cumulative total)		19,821

Source: Ministry of Education, Havana.

developed their own techniques and publications. *Arma Nueva,* originally the monthly study pamphlet used in these army classes, was adapted for the *Seguimiento* classes in 1962.

Thus by August, 1962, as Table 10 shows, nearly half a million Cubans were enrolled in the 5 different types of continuation classes, and each evening an average of more than 200,000 were studying. By August 30, almost 20,000 had completed the program and had graduated from the equivalent of third grade; by December, 1962, the number was expected to be 150,000.

Future enrollments, according to the targets set in September, 1962, at the Third National Congress of Education, were to increase by 85,000 by January, 1963. Just over half of these were to be in 15,000 new family circles, a third in existing *Seguimiento* classes, and 11,000 in new *Seguimiento* classes.

The pre-revolutionary night schools still offer part-time evening study to people over fourteen, though they are now incorporated within the educational program of the revolutionary government. They have a full-time teaching staff, a wider curriculum, and higher standing. Probably their educational standards are better than those of other evening classes.

As Table 11 shows, 56,231 persons were enrolled in night schools at the end of August, 1962, of whom a third were in *Seguimiento* courses and two-thirds in more advanced study. One-sixth of the latter group, 6,576 persons, had passed the equivalent of sixth grade by the end of August.

Table 11. Number of Schools, Students, Teachers in Night Schools, 1962

	June	August 30
Schools	664	657
Teachers	2,241	2,511
Students enrolled	55,790	56,231
Average attendance	34,560	33,872
Average attendance as percentage of enrollment	61.9%	59.6%
Students in *Seguimiento* classes	17,965	16,907
Students in more advanced study	37,825	39,324
Students completing equivalent of 6th grade level (cumulative total)		6,576

Source: Ministry of Education, Havana, 1962.

Nearly all the teachers had been teaching since before the Revolution and received salaries comparable to teachers in primary schools. Nearly half of them were receiving long-service bonuses.

Superación Obrera-Campesina (worker-peasant improvement) classes are for adults who have completed the first 3 grades of primary school but not the sixth grade. Classes are similar in organization to *Seguimiento* classes, although the proportion of professional teachers on the staff (nearly half) is higher. The other teachers are non-professional and untrained, of seventh- and eighth-grade education or above. Often, pre-university and university students teach to earn money to finance their own study. The syllabus is wider than *Seguimiento* and includes "the teaching of elementary arithmetic, functional language, based on reading and writing exercises, elements of geography and history having bearing on the study of political economy directly related to Cuba and to the projects and accomplishments of the Cuban Revolution, and general elements of science presented in a practical and attractive form and emphasizing research for term papers. This program also includes reading the daily press, the preparation of current-event reports and bulletin boards, and stimulating an enjoyment of the arts."[17] The classes are intended to cover the equivalent of primary school work from the fourth to the sixth grade.

Table 12. Number of Classes, Students, and Teachers in Superacion Obrera-Campesina Classes, 1962

	Feb. 23	May 11	July 11	Aug. 30
Total classrooms functioning	1,418	2,833	3,422ª	4,059
Registration	80,184	78,221	80,855	93,741
Average daily attendance as percentage of enrollments:	n.a.	37.7%	47.3%	52.0%
Teachers working:				
Professional	n.a.	1,247	n.a.	1,737
Non-professional	n.a.	1,542	n.a.	2,022
Total	n.a.	2,789	n.a.	3,759
% Professional	n.a.	44.7%	n.a.	46.2%
% Non-professional	n.a.	55.3%	n.a.	53.8%
Classes with:				
Television sets	600	n.a.	n.a.	600
Radio	432	n.a.	n.a.	424
"Newspaper murals"	n.a.	n.a.	n.a.	3,003

a. Ignores 224 classrooms which did not report registrations.

Source: Ministry of Education, Havana.

Table 12 shows enrollment growing from 80,000 in February to 94,000 at the end of August, 1962. The very large improvement in average daily attendance, with the dip in enrollments in May, suggests that the original enrollments may have been overstated. By August 30, 1962, 6,500 persons had graduated from the equivalent of sixth grade in these classes, and the number was expected to grow to 30,000 by February, 1963.

Provincial breakdown, with its rather curious fluctuations, is shown in Table 13. In February *Superación* classes were notable for a greater success in the "urban" provinces than in Oriente and Pinar del Río, which often were especially favored by the Revolution. After February, enrollments in Pinar del Río, Las Villas, and Oriente each increased. While the number of classes elsewhere also grew (in Havana classes tripled), enrollments fell.

Although the classes are encouraged to use radio and television, on which there exist special daily programs at both *Seguimiento* and *Superación* levels, relatively few classes have sets. The "murals,"[18] which three-quarters of the classes use, are current-affairs notice boards containing clippings from newspapers, magazines, and government posters.

Table 13. Enrollments and Number of Classes, by Provinces, in Superación Obrera-Campesina Classes, 1962

	February 23		July 10		August 30	
	Enrollments	Classes	Enrollments	Classes	Enrollments	Classes
Pinar del Río	6,245	116	8,755	266	10,292	370
Havana	33,125	452	26,161	1,256	28,609	1,489
Matanzas	6,635	151	4,673	214	4,311	212
Las Villas	12,300	300	14,559	622	19,836	771
Camagüey	11,982	258	8,671	329	10,138	372
Oriente	9,897	141	18,066	735	20,555	845
TOTAL:	80,184	1,418	80,885	3,422	93,741	4,059

Sources: Figures for July and August supplied by Ministry of Education, Havana. Figures for February published in Ministry of Education, *La Superación Obrera* (March, 1962).

The Third National Congress of Education in September, 1962, called for a 40 per cent increase of enrollments, 19,500 of the new students to be brought in by creating 1,000 new classes and 17,500 students by expanding the enrollments in the existing 4,000 classes.

Statistical Comment

I had free opportunity to check the statistics on adult education at a number of provincial and municipal offices, and on the basis of this check, together with frank comments from some of the officials concerned, I must add certain qualifications to the statistics given in Tables 9 to 13. The adult classes were mostly new, having a new administrative structure and being staffed mainly by persons with no professional teacher-training. The basic recording of data at the lowest levels, despite the special design of data forms and instruction courses in statistics, is likely to be less accurate than data recording for formal school education. In some cases enrollments recorded on summary sheets declined by 15 or 20 per cent within the first 2 months, which suggests an over-statement in the original figure. In another case that came to my attention, summary sheets were compiled with 29 per cent of the classes failing to make any attendance return at all. Minor inconsistencies between supposedly comparable forms were spotted.

These blemishes may well be mainly the result of shortages of time and of qualified personnel. Because the pressures for *emulación* are very strong in the field of adult education and expansionist ambitions very pronounced among the organizers, there may have been some bias in recording the basic data. There was no reason to believe any figures were deliberately altered. Some figures—for instance, the attendance rates—are sufficiently low to suggest that if the central authorities had wanted to tinker they would have begun with them. On the other hand, the very low attendance rates may indicate somewhat exaggerated enrollment figures, either because some half-hearted students enrolled but later dropped out, or because the teacher overstated the initial enrollment. What is really needed, of course, is something besides an average attendance rate—for instance, the percentage of students with better than 80 per cent attendance.

There are reasons for expecting improvement in the statistics. Non-completion of returns was sufficient ground for withholding pay. The mass organizations paid close attention to any movements in the statistics and used the figures in their enrollment drives. Ministry officials were designing better forms for returns and stressing the need for promptness and accuracy.

The preceding tables include basic figures for several months, not only to show how enrollments have expanded over a period of time but also to give the reader an impression of the consistency of the data. (I have avoided making any adjustments merely to remove minor discrepancies between supposedly comparable series.

Summary

In summarizing adult education in Cuba, five points stand out. First, it is a very large program. Adult class enrollments of over 650,000, nearly half the total of Cuban school enrollments and about 15 per cent of total adult (over fourteen) population, are impressive.

Second, the relatively low percentage of enrollments among persons who successfully completed the study program of the literacy campaign and the higher percentage among others of less than three years schooling are noteworthy. More evidence is needed to know whether the phenomenon points to a temporary or permanent saturation among new literates or to the keenness and interest of first- and second-grade level students, who may have felt left out during the 1961 campaign. (It may also reflect upon the accuracy of the campaign results.)

Third, there are many doubts concerning the quality of instruction. Many teachers were non-professional and untrained. Almost all the students had little formal education. Attendances were low, although noticeably higher in night schools and *Superación* classes than in *Seguimiento* classes. Although equipment and supplies in vast quantities have been made available—over 5,000,000 books and pamphlets, for instance—it is not certain how well they have been used. The success of the family circle, in particular, depends greatly upon its leader.

Fourth, the economic value of the classes depends on the type of student as well as the quality of instruction. The students appeared to be mostly under forty, with an average age in the late twenties. Their jobs, to judge by their low level of previous schooling, were likely to be manual and unskilled. Thus, any economic benefits of their study should be considered in this light and judged perhaps as much for their impact on incentives for work and the general understanding of a new system as for their effect on skill and efficiency.

Fifth, the economic returns from *Mínimo Técnico* and the other classes directly related to training for specific jobs may well be significant and important for production. The program deals with particular needs arising from a change of organization and from plans of expansion. Besides the direct effects of improving individual skills, there may well be economic benefits from the understanding and support for the new system in farms and factories which the classes may develop.

CHAPTER VII

School
and University Education

i

The task of providing basic education to adults is largely a once-and-for-all problem. School education, in contrast, is continuing. In countries with rapidly growing populations, it can present an annual crisis year after year, a challenge to administrators and those holding the purse strings to find teachers, accommodations, and money enough for an ever-increasing number of children reaching school age. In Cuba in 1958 there were 1,491,000 children aged five to fourteen (a wider age-range than that specified officially for primary school). By 1960 the number had increased by 60,000. Further growth at a rapid rate is anticipated in the next decade, as is recorded in Table 1, which also gives projections for other age groups.

In 1958, when the school-age population was 1,491,000, primary school enrollments (up to sixth grade)[1] were about 735,000 (public schools about 615,000, and private schools

Table 1. Estimates of Population of School Age in Cuba

Category of school and age	1955	1960	1965	1970
		(thousands)		
Primary school (5-14)	1415	1550	1705	1880
Secondary education (15-19)	600	670	730	805
Higher education (20-24)	546	607	672	742

Source: UNESCO, *"Proyecto Principal de Educación,"* Boletín Trimestral, No. 14—especial Abril-Junio, 1962, p. 142.

120,000). Enrollments in secondary and higher education, as we have already noticed, were by Latin American standards high. But secondary enrollments covered less than 12 per cent of the relevant age group in 1958, and higher education in 1955, the year before the universities were closed, had absorbed only 4.4 per cent of those aged twenty to twenty-four.

The problem of a school-age population increasing each year by over 2 per cent was compounded, then, by the need to catch up on past under-enrollments. Given the Revolution's general aim of mass education, both problems required long-range plans for training teachers and building schools. Because, under any realistic estimate, primary school was all the formal education that three-quarters of the Cuban children were likely to receive in the near future, the political and economic ambitions of the government gave added impetus to primary expansion and influenced the character of the new primary program.

At higher levels, the needs for the skills already mentioned dominated the priorities of reform. Here the size of the program was less a question of the size of the population within the secondary and higher age-groups than of the number with sufficient basic education to justify further study and of the ability of the economy to spare them from production. This was the input-output problem mentioned earlier when discussing the limitations on change imposed by the numbers of students (and teachers) already in the education pipeline. The limitations on education expansion already existing in Cuba became more acute when many of the better-educated children left with their parents as refugees. This loss, together with that of teachers and professors (of whom possibly the better qualified left in greater proportions) seriously diminished the resources at the disposal of the government to fulfill its three-fold educational task.

In the 4 years after 1958 there were several lines of major development in Cuban school education. Most noticeable was the expansion of enrollments at almost all levels: primary school registrations increased over 80 per cent, secondary school over 200 per cent, and technological schools and institutes by 300 per cent. There were corresponding increases in school construction and the conversion of buildings for school purposes. Many of the new schools had to be staffed by volunteer teachers with a minimum of professional training.

The increases in enrollments reflected two other developments: an increasing emphasis on science and technology at intermediate and university levels and the awarding of 70,000 scholarships in 1962 to add food and board to an education which was already free. The scholarships were used to reinforce the swing to technology, to reward the *brigadistas* of the literacy campaign, and to bring further education to many who previously could not afford it.

The reform in syllabus embraced more than a change of subject. It was a change in educational philosophy, frankly admitted, largely but not only political, affecting all levels of education. It has been implemented by a number of short teacher-retraining courses and by a wholly new program in the training schools for primary teachers. In the latter much of the future pattern of education can already be seen. But in the schools themselves, at all levels, the picture in 1962 was still one of transition and improvisation: many rural primary schools were staffed by volunteer teachers of little professional training, secondary and technical schools were operating with staff of inappropriate qualification, universities were relying upon foreign recruitment. This was the price of rapid expansion—the result of a deliberate choice of expansion at the cost of standards. One informal but well-informed estimate, I was told, suggested that present standards at the end of primary education might be two grades[2] below their usual level.

In administrative matters there were four major changes: the seventh and eighth grades of the traditional "superior primary" schools were made into the bottom two grades of the new secondary schools for general education; the old five-year *bachillerato* program was replaced by two consecutive programs of three years each, in both of which there are academic and vocational alternatives; there was a far-reaching university reform which in late 1962 was just completing its first trial year; the private schools were all nationalized at the beginning of 1962. Each of these reforms embodied more than just a change in administration. Secondary reform was really a broadening of coverage to embrace far greater numbers. The university reform ended the traditional independence of higher education, bringing it within both the planning and philosophy of government. Nationalization represented the abolition of independence, distinctions, and differences in basic education.[3]

A schematic outline of the new educational system is given in the diagram below. The normal ages at which a student should pass through each level are shown despite the wide deviation existing among students at present enrolled. The first two years of "pre-school" primary education are optional. Thus, six years of basic primary schooling can lead directly into the general or the professional stream, or indirectly into the professional after a further three years of secondary basic education. The university may be entered from either the general or the professional stream.

As Table 2 shows, nearly $180,000,000 was allocated by the Ministry of Education to the various types of schools in 1962. Of this, just over half went to primary and pre-primary schooling, a fifth to the general stream of secondary schooling and most of the remainder to the various sorts of technical and vocational training. Teacher-training received $8,000,000. Of the $32.6 million earmarked for training of more direct economic benefit, over half went to the industrial-technical schools, an eighth each to agriculture and to commerce, and the remainder to various smaller schools. Most of the $4,000,000 allocated to agricultural schools was later transferred to the INRA budget.

ii

In 1958 about 737,000 Cuban children, less than two-thirds the number aged seven through fourteen, were attending public or private primary school in all grades up to the sixth. Because some of those who did attend were outside the normal age limits,

Diagram: National System of Education, 1962

University Level
(normal ages
18 and above)
{
Faculty of humanities
Faculty of science
Faculty of technology
Faculty of medical science
Faculty of agriculture
and veterinary science
}

General Stream   *Professional Stream*

Grades 10-12
or
equivalent
(normal ages
15-17)

Pre-university
institutes

(age 15) Technical-industrial
institutes.

(age 14) Institutes of administration and commerce.

(age 14) Agriculture-veterinary
institutes.
Center of physical
education and sport.

Language institutes.

Secondary Level

Grades 7-9
or
equivalent
(normal ages
12-14)

Basic secondary
schools

(age 15) Technical-industrial
schools

(ages
12-21)
Schools for primary
teachers' training
(3 or 5 year program)

Primary Level

Grades 1-6 and
2 pre-school grades
(ages up to 11)

{
National primary
schools

Infant schools
}

Normal ages of entrance in brackets.

Source: compiled from "*¿ Y qué puedo estudiar ahora?*," Ministry of Education (Havana, 1962).

the actual proportion of children between seven and fourteen in school was nearer five out of ten. In 1962, four years later, primary enrollments were estimated to be 1,350,000, and about eight in every ten Cubans aged seven through fourteen were enrolled. Enrollments had increased, as Table 3 shows, from 737,000 in

Table 2. Allocation of Ministry of Education Funds for School Education, 1962 Budget

	in millions of dollars	per cent
Primary level		
Primary schools	84.9	47.5
Infant centers	7.1	4.0
Teacher training[a]	8.1	4.5
Secondary level		
Basic secondary schools	31.7	17.7
Pre-university institutes	8.6	4.8
Technical schools and institutes	18.5	10.3
Agricultural schools and institutes[b]	4.0	2.2
Institutes of administration and commerce	4.1	2.3
Other technical or vocational schools[c]	6.0	3.3
Special		
Centers for rehabilitation and social re-education of minors	1.9	1.1
Schools for the mentally and physically handicapped	1.4	0.8
General		
School libraries	0.6	0.3
Physical education	2.1	1.2
TOTAL:	178.9	100

a. Includes expenditure on teacher advancement courses run by the Institute of Higher Education.

b. Includes institutes of farm mechanization and animal-husbandry centers.

c. Includes language and secretarial schools, institutes teaching computation, aeronautics, electronics and communications, and industrial and agricultural schools of the rebel army.

Source: Ministry of Education, Havana. *Budget for 1962.*
Total does not add because of rounding errors.

1958-59 to 1,075,000 in 1959-60 and to 1,253,000 in 1960-61, the school year which was ended early by the invasion and the literacy campaign.

Thus, within two school years enrollments in primary schools had increased by about 70 per cent and in three years by over 80 per cent. Lest 1958-59 be thought an unusually bad year, comparisons can be made with other enrollments of the fifties. For instance, in 1956-57, when public primary enrollments were the

highest of the decade, their total (642,897)[4] plus private enrollments (116,903) was just under 760,000.

With respect to primary school enrollments, this increase had
again placed Cuba in a position comparable to other countries
in Latin America with high enrollments at primary level. In 1961,
the total primary enrollments (of any age) as a percentage of
total population aged seven through fourteen was 91 per cent in
Argentina, 78 per cent in Chile, 87 per cent in Uruguay. In Cuba,
where rapid expansion had brought into primary school many
outside the normal age limits, it was 101 per cent.[5] In Venezuela,
which like Cuba had nearly doubled primary enrollments between
1956 and 1961, it was 87 per cent. Enrollments in the same year
were less than two-thirds of the seven through fourteen year old
age group in Bolivia, Brazil, Colombia, El Salvador, Guatemala,
Haiti, Honduras, and Nicaragua, although only in Guatemala and
Haiti were enrollments under half the age group.[6]

Table 3 shows other details of the expansion in primary schooling. The greater increase in rural areas is particularly significant,
not only because of previous neglect but for its implications for
new school construction, the location of teachers, and the syllabus
of instruction. The number of inspectors was sharply chopped in
line with the reaction against the entrenched bureaucracy of the
former administration.

The number of teachers, often the bottleneck to rapid expansion, had increased by 1962, but by less than half the increase in
the number of schools. The explanation of the Ministry on this
point is that very many of the staff before the Revolution were
employed as "specialists," who were not responsible for a classroom, nor for basic instruction, and often who taught for short
hours. Employing this staff more productively and recalling to
their profession others who were unemployed (of whom there
were 9,000 according to a Ministry estimate) provided the teachers needed for many of the new classes in 1959-60.

In addition, Castro made several appeals for volunteer teachers to staff the new rural schools. These schools were often remote
and scattered and consequently unpopular among many of the
older teachers trained in provincial capitals. Castro's first appeal
for volunteer teachers in 1959 was directed to *bachillerato* and
university students, the second in 1960 to less qualified volunteers.

Table 3. Primary Schools in Cuba

	1958-59	1959-60	1960-61	1961-62
Primary[a] students enrolled	736,606	1,075,485	1,253,375	1,350,000[b]
of which:				
government schools	616,606	960,485	1,138,942	1,350,000[b]
private schools	120,000[c]	115,000[c]	114,433	—
and				
rural	217,254	457,126	595,353	n.a.
urban[d]	519,352	618,359	658,022	n.a.
Teachers total	24,355[e]	24,443	29,924	33,916
of which:				
principals	800	884	1,081	1,498
classroom teachers	15,500	23,559	28,843	32,311
inspectors	1,054	n.a.	406	n.a.
Schools	8,232	11,746	12,773	12,843
Students[f] in first grade	185,560	441,727	472,023	457,544
sixth grade	32,035	34,649	43,575	48,703

a. Pre-school and first through sixth grades only: enrollments in the seventh and eighth grades have been transferred to secondary.

b. Government estimate; an actual figure of 1,166,264 in August, 1962, was based on incomplete returns.

c. Official estimates are 100,000. I have preferred to use an approximation to private enrollments in 1956-57 (116,903) and actual figures for 1960-61.

d. All private enrollments included under urban.

e. Includes 8,055 auxiliary teachers.

f. National schools only.

Source: *"Cuba y la Conferencia de Educación y Desarrollo Económico"* (Santiago de Chile, 1962), pp. 74-75, with certain adjustments from other sources and figures from Ministry of Education, Havana.

Apparently 5,000 responded to the first appeal and 3,000 were chosen. These and their successors were given a few months of intensive training, generally emphasizing administrative and political matters, and were based at San Lorenzo in the Sierra Maestra. From the ruggedness of mountain conditions in San Lorenzo developed the new system for training teachers in conditions comparable to those of many rural schools in Cuba. Further training courses for the same teachers have been run in subsequent vacations, concentrating especially on the problems of multiple grade teaching.

In April, 1960, the Institute of Higher Education was established and attached to the Ministry of Education in Havana. Besides other activities it has run 33 courses for up-grading and retraining teachers. In total, 24,027 student-teachers had enrolled in these activities by August, 1962. Much of its emphasis was ideological.

Without direct evaluation, certain indications must be used to judge the quality of instruction. The number of pupils per teacher, the syllabus and duration of schooling, and the previous experience of the teachers are discussed below. The special problems of multiple grade schools are also mentioned.

In spite of the increase in teachers, enrollments have risen faster. The number of pupils per teacher had risen from 37 in 1960-61 to 40 in 1962.[7] Comparison with the situation before the Revolution is difficult because of the "inactive specialists." In 1956 the number of pupils per teacher was 35, which was comparable to ratios in Brazil, Peru, and Venezuela. The current 40 students per teacher is a national average and the proportion in many rural schools is much higher. Most Latin American countries appear to have more favorable ratios.[8]

The duration of instruction has been lengthened in possibly 80 per cent of the urban schools to 5½ hours a day, organized in two sessions. In the rural and other urban schools one session of 4½ hours was still the rule in 1962. Despite the daily increase of hours in urban schools, the total time of instruction in the school year has fallen because of the literacy campaign, when schooling at all levels was closed from April to December, 1961. Thus the 1960-61 year was only seven months, the 1961-62 term did not begin until January, ending for primary schools in August (129 school days) and the 1962-63 year was to begin in October, 1962, and end in July. By 1963-64 the disruption will have worked itself out and the usual school year from September will be resumed.

The official syllabus for the first two grades of primary schools in 1962 allocated to basic reading, writing, and languages nearly half the time and to arithmetic nearly a quarter. Science, social studies,[9] and health and safety each received two hours a week. At higher levels the three-R's received less time, and science and social studies more.

A great advantage of inheriting a reserve of teachers is that many of them already have some experience. In Cuba in 1962 nearly half the teachers had more than five years of teaching experience and, according to the budget, 20,835 had taught before the Revolution. Naturally the favorable effect of this on the standard of instruction may be offset if many of the former teachers were recruited through the privilege of the old system or (for quite different reasons) if they are dissatisfied with the new.

The one-room primary school, with several or all six grades studying together, causes particular difficulties. As Table 4 shows, three-quarters of all rural classrooms and, in three provinces, over 10 per cent of urban classrooms had this arrangement. To deal with this problem, the Ministry of Education ran training courses in the special techniques of dividing the students into three groups (based on their ability to read) and teaching one group while the other two work independently. Roughly the three groups correspond to non-readers (first grade), poor readers (second through third grades), and satisfactory readers.

The need for new school buildings and facilities has arisen not only from the large increase in enrollments but also from both the location and technical nature of the expansion. Rural facilities cannot be expanded by using urban school rooms on double shift any more than machine workshops can be adapted from a former music room. Before the Revolution few school buildings were owned by the government, most were rented or borrowed free of charge from individuals.[10]

During 1959 and 1960, the immediate additional needs were met by using further buildings on loan, by converting a number of former army barracks into schools and administrative head-

Table 4. Multiple Grade Classrooms, 1960-61
Number of Multiple Grade Classrooms as a Percentage of all Classrooms in National Primary Schools

Province	Total	Urban	Rural
Pinar del Río	44.0	5.7	60.7
Havana	14.2	3.6	83.6
Matanzas	44.1	11.2	90.5
Las Villas	48.1	10.1	81.4
Camagüey	58.4	16.9	88.6
Oriente	50.7	9.5	72.5
	41.3	7.7	76.1

Source: Ministry of Education: Statistical Department.

quarters, and by new construction. Shortages of building materials, cement and steel in particular, led to the use of brick and to some curtailment of the overall program. But during the first three years the government claims to have built 671 rural primary schools with a total of 1700 classrooms, and 339 urban primary schools with a total of 3400 classrooms. An earlier report adds that 300 rural and 500 urban primary schools have been repaired and adapted. These figures are, however, only a small fraction of the 18,000 increase in the number of classrooms. It seems that the use of shops, meeting halls, and houses vacated by Cubans who left the country must have provided a large proportion of the new facilities. For the Cuban economy, the savings of resources by switching old buildings to new purposes was important. As publicity, a primary class in a shop or a technological school in a converted barracks was effective.

The conversion plan has transformed 7 regimental or major army barracks of the Batista regime into school centers and 35 barracks or police stations into primary and secondary schools. Some of the conversion and new construction is architecturally very impressive. Where the program has been curtailed, it seems to have been cut in terms of capacity rather than quality of accommodation.[11] The "school city" at the former Camp Columbia in Havana is quite naturally a show piece. Liberty City, as it is now called, will when completed accommodate 20,000 students in three nuclei of 6500 students at all levels from pre-primary to basic secondary. Dormitories, dining rooms, classrooms, an auditorium, and a library of the first nucleus were brought into use during 1962. The Ministry headquarters, including special buildings for the National Commission Against Illiteracy, the continuation classes, and the scholarship program are located here.

The lavishness of model school construction is also well illustrated by the multi-colored, modern design of the Camilo Cienfuegos "school city" on the edge of the Sierra Maestra. Planned to provide facilities for children from the more inaccessible areas of the mountains, the "school city" will eventually include 40 units of 40 buildings each, dormitories, classrooms, teachers' houses, play-fields, hospitals, and a school farm. The two units completed by September, 1962, accommodated 800 students, with surroundings and facilities for study and recreation (television in every dormitory, table tennis, etc.) which would cause less surprise in the suburbs of Marianao than they do thirty miles from the mist and mud of rural life and homes. Army units had been heavily committed in the construction and the project had high financial priority. Yet after the first three years the foundations only had been laid for half the units, and accommodation was actually ready for only 2 units housing 800 students, less than 5 per cent of the total planned for 1965. This apparent priority of quality before quantity, and fairly lavish quality at that, contrasts with the reverse preference evident elsewhere in the educational program.

Resourcefulness has also been shown in the provision of text books. Books have been printed on the magazine presses of *Revista Bohemia,* and syllabus outlines for teachers have been produced like newspapers. In total over the first three years half a million pre-primary books and 4,500,000 primary text books were supplied. There seems to have been no general shortage of paper, pencils, and such in schools, though distribution may have raised problems.

Cuban statistics clearly reveal certain other difficulties which arise when a school system is rapidly expanded. Table 5, which shows primary school enrollments by age and grade, illustrates four of these problems.

First, the bunching of students in the earlier grades: over half a million in first grade, 58,000 in the sixth. If the system were settled, the normal intake would be the six-year-old age-group, i.e., under 200,000. Much of the present imbalance is the result of formerly inadequate facilities in the upper grades together with a long tradition of dropping out of school. But to the extent that facilities are now expanded and there is a change of attitude towards schooling, so the enlargement of the first few grades will cease to be a characteristic of the early grades and become the result of expansion at a particular time. To a large degree, then, the disproportionate enrollments may become a lump swelling the pipeline of the educational system like the baby bulge of the 1940's in other countries, although proportionally far larger. The lump, as it works its way along the pipeline, will cause difficulties for teaching, administration, and long-range planning. Already it has raised problems in Cuba, and acceleration courses have

Table 5. Primary School Enrollments, 1960-61
(By age and grade in rural and urban sectors)

Grade		Total	\<AGES\> 4	5	6	7	8	9	10	11	12	13	14	15	16 and more
Pre-escolar	U	91444	37550	43636	7897	1731	630								
	R	19120	1317	5399	5571	3953	2880								
	T	110564	38867	49035	13468	5684	3510								
I	U	185945	486	5420	47742	43290	31322	21079	15155	9218	6362	3241	1316	432	882
	R	326576	579	8319	47361	54889	50404	42354	37294	27467	22940	15749	10327	4783	4110
	T	512521	1065	13739	95103	98179	81726	63433	52449	36685	29302	18990	11643	5215	4992
II	U	108344			4385	19012	22117	19540	16192	11212	8362	4700	1844	539	441
	R	112493			1373	5638	11541	15277	17798	16454	15966	12454	8876	4128	3188
	T	220837			5758	24650	33658	34817	33990	27666	24328	17154	10520	4667	3629
III	U	89307				3899	14797	18001	16767	13665	10792	6993	2984	905	504
	R	63974				888	2942	6189	9542	10352	11364	9870	6797	3535	2495
	T	153281				4787	17739	24190	26309	24017	22156	16863	9781	4440	2999
IV	U	76476					3466	12521	15698	14769	13414	9660	4852	1541	555
	R	40931					660	2025	4747	6842	8697	7644	5674	2767	1875
	T	117407					4126	14546	20445	21611	22111	17304	10526	4308	2430
V	U	59686						3068	10416	12769	12721	10866	6452	2505	889
	R	21030						466	1266	3052	4551	5084	3583	1946	1082
	T	80716						3534	11682	15821	17272	15950	10035	4451	1971
VI	U	46820							2494	8699	11299	10552	7774	4080	1922
	R	11229							318	931	2015	2869	2526	1551	1019
	T	58049							2812	9630	13314	13421	10300	5631	2941
Total	U	658022	38036	49056	60024	67932	72332	74209	76722	70332	62950	46012	25222	10002	5193
	R	595353	1896	13718	54305	65368	68427	66311	70965	65098	65533	53670	37583	18710	13769
	T	1253375	39932	62774	114329	133300	140759	140520	147687	135430	128483	99682	62805	28712	18962

U—Urban sector includes National, private, nationalized and non-reporting schools.
R—Rural sector includes National, INRA, and non-reporting schools.
T—Total enrollments.

been started to spread the lump. These classes have special syllabuses that attempt to cover two years' work in one and lead to promotion by two grades at the end of the school year. Nearly 150,000 primary students were expected to be in acceleration classes in 1962-63.

Second, the high ages of many junior students: well over half of all students two years older than appropriate; over 10,000 students starting primary school when, or even after, they are fifteen. Table 6 illustrates the problem more clearly. Such age differentials produce classes with students of widely varying ages, leading to problems for both teacher and student. The rate of drop out from school is high and (other statistics show) clearly higher for the older student in the lower class. Acceleration courses were also designed with this problem in mind. But note that rapid promotion of the older student on a basis of age only exacerbates the problems of varying abilities. Already classes involve students of different educational levels, and promotion by age widens the gap.

Table 6. Median Ages of Primary School Children by Grade in Cuba, 1960-61; Percentage of Children at Least Two Years Older than the Established Age in Cuba and Other Countries of Latin America

	GRADE					
	1st	2nd	3rd	4th	5th	6th
Actual Median Ages:						
Urban	7.9	9.4	10.5	11.4	12.3	13.1
Rural	9.0	11.3	12.2	12.7	13.2	13.8
Total	8.6	10.3	11.2	11.9	12.5	13.2
Age established for grade	6	7	8	9	10	11
Percentage of students at least two years older than established age:						
Cuba 1962	59	71	70	67	62	56
Cuba 1955-56	38	48	47	45	37	32
Colombia 1954	48	62	57	54	n.a.	n.a.
Chile 1954	39	49	50	47	39	36
Haiti 1954	n.a.	62	n.a.	58	n.a.	47
Panama 1954	21	34	34	40	35	42

Sources: 1960-61 data, Ministry of Education; other data, UNESCO, "*Situación Educativa en América Latina.*"

Third, high rates of drop out and also absenteeism: this problem is suggested by Table 5, but shown in Table 7. Over 11 per cent of those who register have given up before the end of the year. In the rural areas this rate is higher, sometimes almost 20 per cent. This has been a traditional problem of education in Cuba (and in many other countries). The government is attempting to improve the position by mobilizing the support of local leaders and of the mass organizations—by making absenteeism and drop out a focus of concern of those with a "revolutionary conscience."

Fourth, the striking drop out between years—those who complete one grade but do not register for the next. Unfortunately, Table 8, by using figures of initial enrollment, does not separate the effect of drop out during the year from drop out between years. The combined effect produced a decline from 189,374 to 43,575 between 1955-56 and 1960-61. In part, this was the result of inadequate school facilities before the Revolution, and recent expansion will remedy much of this problem. Even by 1960-61, 43,575 in the sixth grade was nearly 11,000 higher than the highest pre-revolutionary enrollment of 32,779 in 1956-57.

The number of graduates from sixth grade was less than enrollment, but clearly growing as the policy of expansion at lower levels took effect. In 1958-59, about 15,000 graduated from sixth grade from public schools; in 1959-60, 20,000; and in 1960-61, 38,329 (about 80 per cent of those enrolled in sixth grade). With private school graduations the total in 1960-61 was 52,782. In 1962, after the private schools had been nationalized, and with the help of the acceleration courses in lower grades, the total for all schools was 60,000. Future numbers are expected to be much larger.

Plans for future expansion mean that more students will be staying longer in primary school. It was said in 1962 that the target should be 80 graduates from sixth grade from every 100 who start primary school, instead of the 20 as then. Intentions are for 130,000 to graduate from sixth grade in 1965. This will not only require more teachers but a large proportion qualified to instruct the upper classes. Many of the volunteer teachers, who were hastily trained in 1959 or 1960, will need more training; some, who themselves wish to return to study in school or univer-

Table 7. Initial and Final Primary School Enrollments for the Year 1960-61[a]

GRADE	TOTAL				URBAN				RURAL				Percentage of students initially enrolled who discontinued		
	Beginning of course		End of course		Beginning of course		End of course		Beginning of course		End of course		Total	U	R
	Number	%	Number	%	Number	%	Number	%	Number	%	Number	%			
TOTAL	1,005,809	100.0	889,603	100.0	469,695	100.0	433,005	100.0	536,114	100.0	456,598	100.0	11.6	7.8	14.8
I	472,023	47.0	415,122	46.7	168,182	35.8	151,871	35.1	303,841	56.7	263,251	57.7	12.1	9.7	13.4
II	195,979	19.5	174,495	19.6	91,318	19.4	85,421	19.7	104,661	19.5	89,074	19.5	11.0	6.5	14.9
III	131,725	13.1	116,376	13.1	72,206	15.4	67,133	15.5	59,519	11.1	49,243	10.8	11.7	7.0	17.3
IV	97,991	9.7	86,168	9.7	59,910	12.7	55,445	12.8	38,081	7.1	30,723	6.7	12.1	7.5	19.3
V	64,516	6.4	57,270	6.4	44,951	9.6	41,573	9.6	19,565	3.6	15,697	3.4	11.2	7.5	19.8
VI	43,575	4.3	40,172	4.5	33,128	7.1	31,562	7.3	10,447	2.0	8,610	1.9	7.8	4.7	17.6

a. National schools only—excluding private and INRA schools.
Source: Ministry of Education, Havana.

Table 8. Primary Enrollments in Consecutive Years in National Schools—Courses 1955-56 to 1960-61; Percentage of Original Class Who Continued at Each Grade in Cuba and Other Countries of Latin America

COURSE		I	II	III	IV	V	VI	Percentage of original class who discontinued
	U	98,876						100.0
1955-56	R	90,498						100.0
	T	189,374						100.0
	U		71,300					27.9
1956-57	R		46,650					48.5
	T		117,950					37.7
	U			56,758				42.6
1957-58	R			32,021				64.6
	T			88,779				53.1
	U				48,029			51.4
1958-59	R				21,170			76.6
	T				69,199			63.5
	U					37,651		61.9
1959-60	R					12,765		85.9
	T					50,416		73.4
	U						33,128	66.5
1960-61	R						10,447	88.5
	T						43,575	77.0

Percentage of original class who continued

		I	II	III	IV	V	VI
	U	100.0	72.1	57.4	48.6	38.1	33.5
	R	100.0	51.5	35.4	23.4	14.1	11.5
	T	100.0	62.3	46.9	36.5	26.6	23.0

Comparative percentages

	I	II	III	IV	V	VI
Costa Rica (1946-51)	100.0	68.6	41.2	31.6	22.5	18.1
Chile (1945-50)	100.0	60.8	47.8	34.4	25.4	18.8
(1951-56)	100.0					24.8
Peru (1945-50)	100.0	54.8	43.2	35.4	25.4	19.8
Venezuela (1953-54- 1958-59)	100.0	n.a.	n.a.	n.a.	n.a.	22.7

Source: Cuban statistics, Ministry of Education, Havana; other statistics, UNESCO, *"Situación Educativa en América Latina,"* and Boletín Trimestral, No. 14 (1962), p. 192.

sity, will need replacing. An estimate by the Minister of Education made at the end of 1961[12] suggests that there will be only one teacher for every 50 primary pupils from 1962 to 1965, 45 in 1966, 40 in 1967, and 35 in 1968. These figures are presumably related to the anticipated output of the new primary teacher training centers, and to the time when the primary school system will have caught up on the past and settled to a steady growth related to population increases, but not to a backlog of education. Those who started primary school during the surge of new enrollments in 1959, 1960, and 1961 will be leaving primary school in the mid-1960's. The "lump" will have worked its way through. The primary schools will have a first-year intake larger than in the 1950's, though smaller than in 1959 or 1960. The school structure will be more balanced and total enrollments, though large, may be less than the peak in the early 1960's.

By 1965 the first graduates of the new five-year teacher preparation course will join the schools. Under the new system, started in 1961, students who had completed sixth grade began a five-year course involving a first year in the mountain school of Minas del Frío, two years in Topes de Collantes, and a final two years in a training school which will be established in Havana. Some students will begin teaching (up to fourth-grade children) directly after graduating from Topes de Collantes in 1963. The others will study for two more years in Havana and start teaching in 1965.

The new system is based on the success of the rough training methods used for volunteer teachers in 1959 and 1960 and emphasizes preparation for rural schools. It replaces the old provincial training centers which in 1962 were being closed. Enrollments in these older centers were 8,087 in 1958-59, 10,111 in 1959-60, but had dropped to 7,511 in 1960-61 and to something over 4,000 in 1962. Graduations in the corresponding first two years had been 1,403 and 1,902 but increased to 3,700 in 1961 under the intensive courses designed to terminate this type of study.

Teacher preparation is at present the most distinctive, almost dramatic, feature of formal education in Cuba. Minas del Frío is a mountain school in the Sierra Maestra, where the first battles of the Revolution were won. The students relive something of this revolutionary heritage by climbing the steep paths to the rough buildings of the school, sleeping in hammocks, studying outdoors under the trees, and graduating by climbing the Pico Turquino, Cuba's highest point. The tough romanticism is deliberate. Its originators think of it as a way to win dedication to the Revolution and to prepare teachers hardened to difficult assignments anywhere in Cuba's many rural schools. Many of the students respond with enthusiasm. Those who do not may leave. Of the 3,000 students who had begun the course in January, 1962, about a third had left before August. Of those who left 600 were physically not up to an education in the clouds, 350 were not acceptable to the school authorities, and 80 left for family reasons. Of the students remaining, 1,600 were girls, 350 boys. The staff at first numbered 76 and during the year grew to 88.

After a year the students move to the near-lavish ex-hospital school at Topes de Collantes for two years of more conventional training. While the syllabus to the eye is little changed, the presence of laboratories and blackboards, desks and dormitories give the observer the confidence that mathematics and Spanish, science and biology begin to reassume their usual meaning. Yet the authorities are convinced that the rough beginning is the guarantee of competent loyalty among the teachers of tomorrow.

In Topes de Collantes in 1962, 1,645 students (1,345 girls, 300 boys) were enrolled. With the intake from Minas del Frío in 1962-63 the number will rise to between 3,000 and 4,000. The 103 members of the staff were organized in departments of science, mathematics, social studies, with about twenty-five teachers in each and possibly a dozen in all having university degrees.

Plans existed in 1962 for using San Lorenzo, another center near Minas del Frío, as a preparatory center for up-grading third to fifth grade primary school students to enter Minas del Frío.

The special attention thus given to the particular problems and discouragements of teaching in rural areas may be underlined in summary of the whole program of primary schooling. Not merely has the system of primary teacher training emphasized rural work—revolutionary 'conscience' and enthusiasm has been directed towards rural needs. A "Frank País" Brigade has been created of teachers pledged to teach wherever wanted, which will largely mean in rural areas. In Oriente, there were plans in August, 1962, for building a trial center at La Plata, where teachers from the inaccessible schools in the mountains nearby could go for a weekend of relaxation, discussion, and instruction every two weeks. The center would be run in conjunction with a national program of correspondence courses for teachers designed so they can continue their own studies as well as improve their teaching ability. It would largely bypass the need for a rural postal service because teachers would exchange their papers at the center. The center was also expected to be a means of maintaining enthusiasm and spirit among the teachers. In a similar way, the whole system of scholarships and higher education has been used to encourage secondary and university students to serve as rural teachers before themselves continuing with higher education. And finally, the large and lavish hotels of the resort at Varadero, suffering from the decline in the tourist trade, have been turned to serve the schools. During the summer vacation of 1962, many teachers of rural schools went to Varadero accompanied by their families. Rates were subsidized. The teachers studied during the mornings on specially arranged "refresher" courses. The rest of the day was free for them to enjoy, in beautiful surroundings, a vacation which contrasted greatly with the rigor of their rural assignments.

iii

Secondary education in Cuba in 1962 was straining against the leash—ambitious plans of expansion in all fields being held back by an insufficiency of prepared and suitable students. The sixth grade of primary school, though itself rapidly expanding, was outpaced by the hungry demands of the plans for secondary and technical expansion. These plans were, in turn, derived from immediate needs for persons of some technical training and from future needs for university trained specialists. The need for more entrants to universities impinged on the intermediate stages of the school system by demanding larger outputs from the secondary schools.

These basic drives were as unfortunate for standards as they were successful for enrollments. The urge to expand, itself well justified by long-range intentions, was only satisfied by lowering standards of entrance, not only by taking into the seventh grade persons not very successful in the sixth, but often by dipping into lower grades and sometimes by accepting persons without knowing their ability. The problems which emerged from the diverse and low standards of preparation among the beginning class were countered by acceleration and leveling-up courses.

The expansion was assisted and directed by a widespread system of scholarships, about 70,000 of which had been promised by Castro to the *brigadistas* in 1961. These scholarships were awarded to students in almost every type of school in 1962: 401 to nurses training in three hospitals, 1,743 for a school for fishermen in Varadero, 125 for agricultural accounting, 70 for the national school of sugar cooperatives, 300 to the school of artificial insemination, to name only a few. Usually scholarships carried full board and lodging and included a uniform and books. Most scholarship students lived in the special scholarship hostels, which were often obtained by converting the houses of political refugees (who had been required to surrender them to the government when leaving). The hostel matrons were in many cases former domestic servants.

The schools themselves needed teachers, equipment, and buildings. Often the need for teachers was even more serious than in the primary schools. An appeal was made to university students to take special courses in the universities to prepare them to teach in secondary schools. (2,676 persons were on education courses in the three universities in 1962, of whom 347 were on a special secondary school teacher course in Oriente). In the field of technical education the scarcities of teachers were more acute. It was necessary to withdraw skilled workers from the production lines, from garages, etc., and to use them as instructors in the school workshops. Qualified technical personnel from Latin America and from countries of the socialist bloc were used to guide and train teachers of technical education. In spite of these efforts, the loss of teachers in some cases has exceeded the gain, and the total staff has fallen while the number of students has increased. In the technological schools there has been a large rise in the number of students per teacher, and generally there seems to be a high proportion of new teachers, with little experience and perhaps little training. This and the inadequate preparation of many students raise serious problems (and doubts) about the quality of education.

For buildings the pattern was similar to the primary schools—some new building, some conversion of ex-barracks, some repair, and the use of makeshift housing. A particular need arose in the technological schools for heavy equipment, and about a third of their budget was earmarked for investment.

"Basic secondary" is the new system started in 1959 covering grades seven to nine, taking over the instruction which used to be given in the "superior grades" (seventh and eighth) of the old primary schools and some of the first years of the former *bachillerato* program. Basic secondary is essentially a further step of non-specialized education, both for students who will afterwards turn to professional training and for those who will continue with general studies in the pre-university program. Most of the schools are in cities. Those in rural areas are boarding schools and emphasize agricultural instruction. Table 9 shows how enrollments have increased. A detailed comparison with pre-revolutionary figures is made difficult by the change in definition. But by 1962 secondary basic enrollments, covering three grades instead of the former two, were greatly in excess of 1956-57 figures. Even clearer was the margin by which the total of

Table 9. Enrollments in Public Secondary Education—General Stream, Actual 1956-57 and Planned 1962-63 to 1964-65

Year	Basic Secondary Schools		Pre-University Institutes	
	Students	Teachers	Students	Teachers
1956-57	26,389a		35,745	
1957-58	19,858a		37,543	
1958-59	27,278a	1400	35,893	1244
1959-60	35,100	2401	24,588	1263
1960-61	71,057	4055	18,697	1169
1961-62	91,482	5510	16,266	1062
1962-63b	120,000		33,000	
1963-64	135,000		50,000	
1964-65	160,000			

a. Enrollments in superior primary grades 7 and 8.
b. 1962-63 to 1964-65 figures are according to 1962 plans.

Source: Ministry of Education, Havana. Literacy exhibition and "*Cuba y la Conferencia de Educación, Desarrollo Económico y Social.*"

secondary and pre-university students (107,748 in 1962) exceeded the 57,000 to 63,000 "superior primary" and *bachillerato* students enrolled in public schools in the three pre-revolutionary years.

In the pre-university institutes, which provide the second half of the six-year general studies program, enrollments have declined from 36,000 in 1958-59 to 16,000 in 1962. This decline is partly for the same reason that basic secondary schools showed a sharp increase: pre-university enrollments cover fewer grades than the old *bachillerato*, just as basic secondary now covers more. But there is more than a change in definition. Since 1959 there has been a loss of students abroad and a decided shift in studies. Many former *bachillerato* students, when they leave or graduate, are not being replaced. Increasing numbers are enrolling in technological institutes. Others have changed courses in mid-stream. Within the pre-university institutes there has been a shift of emphasis from humanities and law towards the sciences and more specialization.

In 1959, 189 superior primary schools were converted into basic secondary schools, and within three years most of them had undergone or were under reconstruction. By 1961 there were 261 urban and 30 rural secondary schools. A year later, there were 10 more urban schools, and hostels provided accommodation for 18,000 secondary students.

The number of students per teacher apparently fell in both secondary and pre-university classes—from 19 and 29 respectively in 1958-59 to 17 and 15 in 1962. In the basic secondary schools this was the result of nearly doubling the numbers of teachers in the first year of the Revolution and by a further doubling in the next two years. Many of their teachers must have been up-graded or had formerly been unemployed, for even in 1962 half the urban secondary teachers (according to the budget) had more than five years' teaching experience. Some may have transferred from *bachillerato* institutes.

In the pre-university institutes in 1962 the proportion of teachers with more than five years' experience was nearly two-thirds. As the total teaching staff had decreased since 1959-60, it seems that a number of the original staff left and were replaced. Yet the favorable proportion of teachers to students may not continue, with the ambitious target for doubling pre-university enroll-ments in 1962-63 and tripling them by 1963-64. To keep the same teacher-student ratios would require an extra 2,000 teachers, nearly as many as the total 1962 university enrollment in educa-tional courses for teacher training. The targets will also require a doubling and tripling of capacity. In the first three years of the Revolution the number of institutes increased by only three or four a year.

iv

As an alternative to the general studies program at secondary level, students may pass from primary school directly into some vocational training. Or they may continue for three years with general secondary studies and enter the professional stream at a more advanced level.

Students may enter a technical school when they have com-pleted sixth grade or a technical institute when they have passed ninth grade in either a secondary or technical school. The range of possible studies in the technical schools includes linotype, ty-pography, photography, bookbinding, welding, electricity, con-struction, carpentry, cabinet-making, molding, hydraulic installa-tion, foundry-casting, forging, automobile mechanics, and general mechanics. Pupils study the theory and practice of their special subject with general courses in languages, mathematics, and sciences. The institutes aim higher: more technical courses with more theory in mechanics, electricity, engineering, chemistry, electronics and communication, and architecture.

Enrollments in technological schools first declined from 6,883 in 1956-57 to 5,300 in 1958-59 and to 5,063 in the first year of the Revolution. Thereafter enrollments have risen: 8,356 were enrolled in schools and institutes in 1960-61, and possibly 21,524 in 1962. Expansion has undoubtedly been assisted by the scholar-ships, of which over 6,500 were awarded in 1962, including 3,526 to the 5,000 students in the institutes. There were ambitious tar-get figures for future expansion over the next five years.

Of 11,565[13] students in technical schools in 1962, two-fifths were in general mechanics, one-fifth in electrical studies, and the remainder equally divided among welding, foundry training, automobile mechanics, and a miscellaneous group. Detailed

Table 10. A. Enrollment in Technological Schools, 1962

	Students	Workshops	Teachers Needed	Teachers Available[b]	2nd year[a] Graduates 1962	1963[c]	Student-Teacher Ratio	Per cent All Stud
General Mech.	4,550	17	182	85	179	3640	54	39
Welding	1,050	17	42	31	22	840	34	9
Electricity	2,515	17	101	79	298	2012	32	22
Automobile	1,250	8	46	45	161	1000	22	11
Foundries	150	3	9	9	—	120	17	1
Carpentry	675	7	27	26	18	540	26	6
Hydraulics	450	3	18	16	15	360	28	4
Painting	100	1	4	4	23	80	25	1
Masonry	450	5	18	17	79	360	26	4
Forging	150	1	6	1	1	120	150	1
Moulding	175	2	7	6	—	140	29	2
Technology	—	—	62	47	—	—	—	—
Others	50	1	1	1	—	40	50	—
TOTAL:	11,565	82	523	367	796	9252	32	100

a. Assumed to be second year, although not actually stated in the original table.
b. Teachers work double shifts.
c. Assuming 20 per cent drop out.

B. Machine Availability in Technological Schools in
General Mechanical Engineering, 1962

	Needed	Available	Ratio to 50 Students[a]
Lathes	400	190	4
Drills	250	91	1.75
Milling machines	100	20	0.4
Saws	50	29	0.5
Grinding wheels	50	13	0.25
Furnaces	17	13	0.8/workshop
Others	50	39	0.75

a. Raised by double shifts to 8 per 50 students, etc.
Source: Ministry of Education.

figures are given in Table 10. As explained earlier, there was a serious shortage of staff, and the ratio of staff to students deteriorated with the rapid expansion of enrollments. In the technical schools the number of students per teacher rose from 6 to 32 between 1958-59 and 1962. But the general averages disguise even worse difficulties. In the technical schools in 1962, as Table

10 shows, two sections, including general mechanics with nearly half of all students, had over 50 students per teacher. Less than half the teachers had teaching experience before the Revolution. Many were workers withdrawn from production to teach in the school workshops. Even with the teachers working double shifts, the teaching ratio was in every case worse than in 1959. Availability of equipment is indicated by the second section of the same table.

In the more advanced technical institutes, enrollments had grown from under 2,000 in 1960 to about 5,000 in 1962. Two of these—the Hermanos Gómez Institute in Havana and the Abel Santa María Institute in Camagüey—together accounted for over half of total enrollments.[14] The following notes, made during our visits to these two schools in September, 1962, may, therefore, not unfairly indicate the general scope, difficulties, and quality of much of the technical instruction at this level.

Instituto Tecnológico Hermanos Gómez, Havana, is the largest of the technical institutes, probably the one of highest standing, and it is housed within the rich Spanish architecture of the former *"Colegio de Belén."*

The 1,450[15] students, average age about eighteen, varied in educational background from sixth to twelfth grade, which apparently was the result of rushed organization and no entrance exam. A number were girls, some of whom were unaware when they applied of the nature of heavy engineering and had subsequently left. Five hundred of the students were studying either automobile mechanics or electricity and the other 900 were in two streams of up-grading as preparation for technical studies beginning next year. In 1961 all students had been on preparatory courses. Up-grading courses, I understood, were a transitional measure.

There were 75 professors (a student-teacher ratio of 19.3), of whom 14 were workshop directors and 8 engineers from Cuba and from abroad.[16] The others were mainly giving lessons in background theory.

The workshops were well supplied with heavy machinery from Spain, China, and Bulgaria,[17] although some of it was not yet in use because of inadequate amperage-capacity in the electrical cables of the school. The Cuban military was occupying one workshop as a dormitory while the machinery stood in crates outside. The Motor Repair Workshop was not yet ready but in active process of establishment with instructional engineers and a small hand-tool shop. Students in the foundry and hand-tool classes were fully occupied.

Printed textbooks were in short supply and as substitutes the teachers had been producing a complete series of carefully mimeographed selections from the basic texts. This was described as a good way to obtain a textbook with little trouble and effort.[18]

The standard of the practical work in the hand-tool shops, we were told by one Polish instructor, compared equally with work of first-year students in Poland. Laboratories and equipment were worse.

The other, Instituto Tecnológico Abel Santa María, Camagüey, was started in January, 1962.[19] There were 472[20] students, all scholarship holders—231 girls and 241 boys. All had secondary basic preparation but not all had reached ninth grade. There were 27 teachers, one for every 18 students. Of the teachers, four possessed university degrees, two had completed a year at electrical engineering school, and 21 held the *bachillerato*.

In 1962, physics, mathematics, chemistry, English, and technical drawing were being taught. Because the machine tools were not installed, practical courses had not yet begun. There were practically no hand tools available, only the few which remained from the previous year. Textbooks for mathematics and physics arrived so late that lectures during most of the year were given without them. When 500 mathematics and 200 physics books eventually arrived, the physics textbook was the wrong one for the course.

The impression gained from visiting these two schools bears some striking similarities to the descriptions of technical instruction in Cuba given in the World Bank Report of 1950.[21] There appeared to be the same lack of hand tools co-existing with heavy machinery (not always ready for use), a similar variation of standards among the students and a good deal of ordinary and elementary school instruction in consequence. Old traditions apparently die hard.

This is not to argue that everything is the same. Much new machinery has been installed, besides smaller items like work benches and drawing tables. The budget in 1962 allowed $18.5 million for the technological schools and institutes alone, and of this nearly a third was earmarked for investment in machinery, equipment, and building. The drive for improvement is on, and perhaps more than in the past, linked to the specific requirements of industry. But expansion in numbers has not meant comparable improvement in standards.

Plans for future expansion of technical instruction are as ambitious as those already implemented. Table 11 shows the growth of enrollments as envisaged in the middle of 1962—nearly 20,000 in the less advanced schools in 1962-63, nearly 30,000 in 1963-64, and an intake of over 15,000 the following year. In the technological institutes enrollments are expected to increase to nearly 11,000 by 1964-65, when the annual new enrollments in both institutes and schools will be almost 20,000. By 1963-64 the interim measures of leveling-up courses and abbreviated courses (1962-63 in the technological schools) should be terminated.

Inevitably there will be delays before the expanded intake will produce qualified graduates ready to enter industry. The comparative trickle of graduates during the first years of the Revolution until 1962 were largely products of the old system of technological training. Lengthening the technological school course from two to three years (shown in Table 11) will make 1963 a barren year—no graduates from the schools and only 450 from an accelerated course in the institutes. But by 1964, if plans work out, the output will flow fast: over 10,000 from the schools and 700 from the institutes. The annual flow from the schools will afterwards become somewhat less and some of the graduates will enter the institutes for further training before becoming available to the economy. The regular yearly output from the institutes was expected to reach 2,000 by 1965.

The major weakness of pre-revolutionary agricultural instruction was that there was not enough of it. Six secondary-level agricultural schools existed in 1950, one in each province, but usually less than 100 boys were enrolled in each. Few of the graduates became farmers after their three-year course, preferring to use their training as a stepping-stone to a better life in business or as agricultural advisers. (The same was true of the University of Havana, where not more than 10 per cent of the gradu-

Table 11. A. Plan for Enrollments in Technological Schools

	Actual				Planned		
	1958-59	1959-60	1960-61	1961-62	1962-63	1963-64	1964-65
New entrants	n.a.	n.a.	n.a.	13,967	7,000	10,500	15,500
Leveling up	n.a.	n.a.	4,888	726	500	—	—
1st year	n.a.	n.a.	1,958	13,241	7,500	10,500	15,500
2nd year	n.a.	n.a.	1,796	1,646	12,000	7,000	9,500
3rd year	—	—	—	—	—	11,000	6,300
No. Enrolled	5,300	5,063	8,642	15,613	19,500	28,500	31,300
Graduates	558	1,066	1,754	1,137	—	10,500	6,000
No. of Schools	11	11	13	21	23	25	26

B. Plan for Enrollments in Technological Institutes

			1960-61	1961-62	1962-63	1963-64	1964-65
New entrants			1,654	3,586	2,500	3,000	4,000
Leveling up			1,654	3,586	2,500	—	—
1st year			—	1,420	3,000	5,000	4,000
2nd year			—	—	1,200	2,700	4,500
3rd year			—	117	—	750	2,400
No. Enrolled			1,654	5,123	6,700	8,450	10,900
Graduates			—	104	450[a]	700	2,000
Institutes			2	6	6	7	9

a. Accelerated course.
Source: Ministry of Education.

ates from the school of Agronomic Engineering and Sugar were thought to enter farming pursuits.)

In 1962, six agricultural training institutes (officially 9th-12th grade) were operating, at first under the Ministry of Education but later transferred to the direction of INRA. Enrollments had grown to an estimated 3,000 by 1962, from 300 in 1958-59, 480 in 1959-60, and 529 in 1960-61. The large increase was assisted by the 1400 scholarships awarded in 1962, although it needs to be remembered that full scholarships had always been the tradition in the provincial agricultural schools.

More specialized instruction was given in agricultural mechanics at Holguín and Matanzas, where in 1962 there were over 100 staff and nearly 500 scholarship students, and in the seven schools of surveying which in 1961 had enrollments of 1,014. At a less advanced level, the rural secondary schools emphasized agricultural training, and usually had a small farm attached to the school. In 1961 1,288 students were enrolled in these, and the total cultivated land amounted to over 200 *caballerías.*

Without a thorough knowledge of the whole program, standards of the teachers and students, and such things, it is not possible to assess by how much these schemes are an improvement on the past or how well they will meet the needs of the new plans for agriculture. The World Bank Report drew attention to the need for teaching a diversified technology (i.e., less emphasis on sugar and sugar chemistry) and for training which would reach the man with the plow. The new emphasis given to rural needs in all types of education and, for instance, the courses run by the rebel army in agriculture (and industry) with their 1500 scholarship students in 1962, indicates some move along these lines.

v

The Institutes of Administration and Commerce have continued from before the Revolution giving courses in accounting and administration, but the syllabus in 1962 included instruction in statistics and the principles of "socialist planning." Courses lasted four or five years and accepted, officially, students who had completed ninth grade. Enrollments had dropped considerably—from 13,496 in 1956-57 to 8,897 in 1958-59, but thereafter rose from 13,933 in 1959-60, 14,634 in 1960-61, and to 15,702 in 1962. Twenty-four schools were running in 1962. The number of teaching staff apparently fell from 743 in 1958 to 570 in 1961, which raised the number of students per teacher from 12 to 26. The 1962 budget of $4.1 million allowed for 46 additional staff, the increase over 1961 being mainly the result of the new Playa Girón school in Havana for boarding students. Of all teachers in 1962, just over half had more than five years of teaching experience.

Language courses were offered to students of eighth or ninth grade at seven institutes, four for external students and three for boarders. Before 1962 the schools were privately financed but in January they were nationalized and allocated a $2,000,000 budget, three-quarters under the scholarship plan and $447,000 under the general budget. 750 students had scholarships in the "*Pablo Lefargue*" institute and 2,000 in the "*Máximo Gorki*" Russian language institute.

The Schools of Fine Arts taught the various arts and handcrafts, music and drama. Enrollments in these courses had increased from 726 in 1958-59 to 1,105 in 1961. The staff in the five schools had dropped from 103 to 98. In 1962, the budget of $593,000 was shifted to the National Council of Culture.

Of the four schools of journalism functioning in 1958-59, only one was operating in 1961 with a budget of $309,000. Enrollments had dropped from 525 to 385, and teaching staff from 134 to 25. At the end of 1961, the school's finances were transferred to the University budget. Apparently 87 students were studying in Havana at the beginning of 1962. The decline, of course, reflects the closure of most of the 58 daily and 16 non-daily newspapers, together with many of the 750 different periodicals which were published in Cuba (in 1956) before the Revolution.[22]

Study abroad is important in Cuba, for educational and political reasons and significant economically because its costs are often no more than the loss of the student's potential contribution to production and the cost of his transport. Unfortunately my information is patchy and, except for the figures obtained from the Ministry of Industries, only in rough aggregates.

In 1961 about 1,700 persons were sent by the Ministry of Industries to study in countries of the Soviet bloc. About a third were students and the remainder workers. The countries where they went are shown in Table 12. Many of them may have stayed until 1962, when the total on such courses abroad was 1,600.

INRA has also sent people to Soviet countries to study. In July, 1961, about a thousand went for a year and in August and

Table 12. Students and Workers Sent by Ministry of Industry to Soviet Bloc Countries in 1961 (Second Term)

Countries of Study	Students	Workers
USSR	207	400
Czechoslovakia	194	235
Poland	40	174
Rumania	73	90
Hungary	28	80
Bulgaria	13	59
East Germany	19	50
China	—	47
North Korea	—	9
	574	1144

Source: Ministry of Industry Report.

September, 1962, another 2,000. Many were young and of low education. I was told in INRA that a considerable number of the 2,000 were only of second or third grade, some of sixth grade, a few illiterate. Their ages varied between sixteen and thirty.

About half would study organization and administration, presumably in preparation for work on the *granjas del pueblo,* 40 to 50 would be in universities, and the remainder would study agriculture, animal husbandry, and farm mechanization, the latter being largely practical mechanics.

Statistical Comment

As explained, there is a great diversity of training schemes and my information on these is far from complete. For basic schooling under the Ministry of Education, I am inclined to treat earlier figures with caution and to rely more on those for 1961 and 1962. Certainly for 1961 the statistical department of the Ministry of Education had prepared some fairly detailed analyses of primary school statistics, e.g., age enrollments, drop out, attrition, percentage of students over age, costs, etc., and the information was used for their planning. How accurately the basic data had been collected I had no way to judge, although the records were usually kept by the teachers themselves, which guarantees a literate hand. There do seem to be several supposedly comparable totals which do not agree (for instance, numbers of teachers and the numbers of technological students), and some estimates (as the one mentioned in footnote 6 on page 418) seem wildly exaggerated. But, used with caution, the order of magnitude usually seems about right.

Budgetary figures are taken directly from the 1962 Ministry document and (although prior to revisions later in the year) are, I believe, an accurate statement of intentions at that time.

No summary of this diversity of school education will be attempted but it may be useful, in conclusion, to make four general points related to what has been attempted.

Primary school has already been expanded to the point when it is probably correct for the Cuban government to claim that some primary school facilities exist for virtually every Cuban child. The drive for enrollments undertaken with the aid of most of the revolutionary organizations means that the vast majority of eligible children were enrolled by 1962. The dominant need is now for improvements in standard to accompany the expansion.

Coordination among the secondary programs appears to be improving, and within a year or two the expansion of sixth grades at primary level should remove the need for taking students from lower grades and for up-grading and acceleration courses. When hardly more than 50,000 graduated from all forms of sixth grade, as in 1961, it was almost inevitable that the various secondary schools would be short of qualified entrants. If the plans of 1962 work out and the number of sixth-grade graduates grows— strengthened also by expansion of the adult education program— not only will the shortage diminish but there should be opportunity for more careful selection from those who wish to study further. There will also be more persons of sixth-grade level available to industry or agriculture or ready to start practical training.

While most attention and effort is concentrated on the major programs of education, some of the smaller schemes are worth mentioning: the schools for cripples and those for the mentally defective, the day nurseries for the small children (economically useful in enabling their mothers to take jobs), and the *José Martí* school for children of expatriates; there are also the various smaller lines of technical training—like the institute of aeronautical instruction which has expanded fourfold since 1956-57, and the schools of seamanship. Physical education has greatly expanded, being allocated three times as much in the 1962 budget as in 1961. Many school libraries functioned under a newly created department which was allocated over half a million pesos.

The future value to the economy of the tremendous expansion in technological instruction is difficult to assess. As pointed out, there has been a clear tendency for plans to outrun capabilities, not merely in the standard of students, teachers, and instruction, but numerically as well. This exaggeration should not disguise the very large increases which have already taken place, but it does raise uncertainties about the realism of future plans. There should be beneficial effects from the increased numbers of primary school graduates and of university science teachers, which can be expected in the future on the basis of those already enrolled in schools and universities. Some, but not all, of the basic difficulties at present restraining secondary expansion will be eased when these new students and teachers join the secondary schools. But there are many other problems of organization and supply, efficient administration and careful selection, and of course, basically good teaching, proper examinations and such, all of which will need attention.

For these reasons, not only is 1964 the earliest date when students from the expanded programs in the technical schools and institutes can join the economy but it may be several years later before there is a chance of real improvement in the technical standards of those who graduate.

vi

In Cuba before the Revolution there had been three state-controlled universities, one private university, and several private colleges of lower academic standing. The largest and most important of the universities was Havana, in existence since the eighteenth century. The University of Oriente was founded in 1949 and the University of Las Villas in 1952. Total enrollments in these three institutions was nearly 20,000 in 1953-54, with most students enrolled at the University of Havana.

By the standards of Latin America, such enrollments in higher education were large. In 1955 only Argentina (with 9.2 per cent) and Uruguay (with 7.0 per cent) had higher percentages of their 20-24 year old age-group in study. The Latin American average was 2.7 per cent. Cuba's enrollments in higher education were 4.4 per cent of the age group.

But although strong in numbers, the universities were weak in other respects, particularly in preparing students who could meet the needs of the economy. Courses were largely theoretical. Of the 17,527 students in Havana in 1953-54, only 1,502 were in the school of science; of these, 409 studied civil engineering, 463 electrical engineering, 404 agricultural and sugar studies, and 226 pure science and mathematics. Attendance was often halfhearted. Standards, in many cases, were low among faculty and so among students. Many students deserted courses before the year had ended. The state of affairs in the universities reflected social attitudes as well as the condition of the economy.

The prospect of employment after graduation was often uncertain and discouraging.

Yet these universities, adequate or inadequate, had largely to provide the educated foundation of the economy and of the future; university graduates were a main source of technicians and professionals, as well as of school teachers at higher levels. Failures in numbers or in quality at the universities meant undermining the school system, the education of the next generation, research and technical skills in the years to come.

After a student strike at the end of 1956, the universities were closed, so on the eve of the Revolution there was no university education at all.

The revolutionary government re-opened the universities in 1959. During the first three years various changes were made, culminating in a widespread reform[23] implemented at the beginning of 1962. The reform is thorough, sometimes radical, detailed in syllabus, and well aware of the crucial economic (and political) role of the universities. It means the abolition of the traditional independence of the universities and the coordination of the universities with the economic plans of government. (JUCEPLAN is represented on the Higher Council of the universities.) All university instruction is now given in the universities of Havana, Oriente, or Las Villas. Former private institutions were abolished or nationalized and used for other purposes.[24] The numbers of students in each faculty are becoming more closely related to the manpower requirements of the future economy. Science and applied technology are greatly emphasized. The syllabus and style of teaching are designed to be more 'practical' than before.

Table 13 gives the total enrollments in all subjects in the three universities in 1962. The total number of students has decreased by about 3,000 since 1953-54. Enrollments in Havana have, in fact, declined by over 4,000 in the same period, although it clearly retains its dominance over the other two universities. The decrease is probably explained by the loss of many students (and potential students) abroad, the absence of young people who volunteered for teaching in new schools in 1959 and 1960, and the basic shortage of suitable students prepared by the old education system. By 1970 it is planned that 80,000 students should be at university. But it is yet too soon for the expansion of education at lower levels to have produced more students for university entrance.

Table 13. University Enrollments, 1962

| Faculty and School | Enrollments by University | | | |
	Havana	Las Villas	Oriente	Total
School of Humanities				
Accounting	—	440	298	738
Economics	2639	—	298	2937
Education:	1691	438	200	2329
Secondary Teacher Training	—	—	347	347
History	98	—	41	139
Journalism	—[a]	—	—	—[a]
Law	535	—	—	535
Literature	148	24	40	212
Modern Languages	—	19	13[b]	32
Music	—	—	7	7
Philosophy	86	—	13[b]	99
Political Science	732	—	—	732
Sociology	—	7	42[b]	49
Total Humanities	5929	928	1299	8156
School of Science				
Biology	69	—	—	69
Chemistry	129	13	—	142
Geography	63	—	—	63
Geology	65	—	—	65
Mathematics	156	20	—	176
Pharmacy	146	—	—	146
Physics	79	—	—	79
Psychology	154	—	—	154
(faculty not known)	—	—	55	55
Total Science	861	33	55	949
School of Agriculture and Veterinary Science				
Agronomy	558	125	—	683
Veterinary	166	19	—	185
Total Agriculture and Veterinary	724	144	—	868
School of Medicine				
Dentistry	257	—	—	257
Medicine	3071	—	63	3134
Total Medicine	3328	—	63	3391

Table 13 continued.

| Faculty and School | Enrollments by University | | | |
	Havana	Las Villas	Oriente	Total
School of Technology				
Architecture	478	—	—	478
Chemical Engineering	228	167	130	525
Civil Engineering	363	—	—	363
Electrical Engineering	851	100	79	1030
Engineering intensive				
preparatory course	—	—	60	60
Geological Engineering	—	—	12	12
Mining Engineering	—	—	20	20
Industrial Engineering	521	20	30	571
Mechanical Engineering	147	84	154	385
Sugar Refining Chemistry	—	—	35	35
Total Technology	2588	371	520	3479
Grand Totals	13430	1476	1937	16843

a. 87 apparently were enrolled at the beginning of 1962.
b. Course being terminated.

Source: Universities of Havana and Oriente: from University Statistical Departments, referring to August-September, 1962. University of Las Villas: from "*Investigaciones del Departamento de Resümenes Globales de la Dirección de Planificación Sobre el Plan de Cuadros.*"

The decrease in total enrollments should not disguise the reforms which have already taken place within the universities. The numbers studying electrical engineering, for instance, have greatly increased since 1953-54. Enrollments in the University of Oriente have grown from 1,177 in 1956 to nearly 2,000 in 1962: over a quarter of these students were in technology, another quarter in teacher training, and nearly a third in accountancy or economics. The University of Las Villas also specializes in the technical subjects: over half its students in 1962 were in accounting or teacher training, a quarter in engineering, and a tenth in agriculture or veterinary science. Of the 3,400 students in Oriente and Las Villas, only 206 studied history, literature, languages, music, philosophy, or sociology: almost a third of the students in these studies were on courses being terminated.

Comparing enrollments in 1962, the first year of the new plan, with enrollments before reform shows the trends in detail.

Of the 13,430 students in Havana, shown in Table 14, just over two-fifths were in their first year. But in agriculture, veterinary science, dentistry, industrial, mechanical and chemical engineering, virtually all forms of science, and in teacher training, the number enrolled in 1962 (column 2) exceeded the combined totals of all other years (column 3). The emphasis on technical and scientific subjects was reinforced by awarding scholarships, largely to first-year students, in these priority fields. Over a quarter of those studying technology received scholarships (43 per cent in mechanical engineering), nearly a quarter of those in medicine, scarcely one in twenty studying law or political science. No first-year students were accepted and no scholarships were offered for philosophy.

Expansion in the first years of the Revolution was almost certainly hindered by a lack of suitable students, for the reasons already given. It seems that a number of students enrolled in 1962 were those who originally started university some years ago and either dropped out or had to terminate their studies when the universities were closed in 1956. Other students in 1962 were of less than twelfth grade or *bachillerato* standing, possibly prepared on some up-grading courses. The government attaches great importance to students from poor families, who are helped by scholarships to attend university in apparently much greater numbers than before.

It seems from articles in the press, from official university notices urging enrollments, and from the shortage of fully qualified students, that many applicants have been accepted with lower academic qualifications than before. Admission policy appears, however, far better than in the technical institutes, where there was no entrance exam. For instance, in Havana 2,500 applicants to the university were examined in September, 1962, in technology and 40 per cent passed. Some of those from eighth, ninth, or tenth grade were then started on a leveling-up course before being examined again in December. A similar 10-week course in medicine was being held in Oriente for more than 100 students.

Two other sources of new students are worth mentioning: foreign countries and the factories. Over 100 students from abroad were studying in Cuba in 1962, 91 with scholarships in

Table 14. Enrollments in University of Havana in 1962

Faculty and School of Study	Total	New Plan Total 1st Year	Transitional Plan					Males %	Sch... Stu...
			Total 2nd-5th Years	2nd Year	3nd Year	4th Year	5th Year		
Humanities									
Economics	2639	1181	1444	258	505	428	253	73	
Education	1691	638	336	—	164	172	—	15	
History	98	103	—	—	—	—	—	38	1
Law	535	72	354	45	89	136	84	66	
Literature	148	99	42	—	—	42	—	24	
Philosophy	86	—	93	—	29	64	—	15	—
Political Science	732	237	565	137	428	—	—	53	
	5929	2330	2834	440	1215	842	337	51	
Science									
Biology	69	38	22	2	14	6		54	1
Chemistry	275a	114	115	1	48	66		32	
Geography	63	59	—	—	—	—		49	2.
Geology	65	71	—	—	—	—		85	1.
Mathematics	156	129	45	5	19	21		44	
Physics	79	66	12	2	4	6		81	1
Psychology	154	153	—	—	—	—		21	2
	861	630	194	10	85	99		42	
Technology									
Architecture	478	122	369	141	54	104	70	67	1
Chemical Engineering	228	165	64	25	34	5	—	75	2
Civil Engineering	363	171	208	105	52	25	26	92	2
Electrical Engineering	851	331	542	288	142	57	55	97	2
Industrial Engineering	521	400	101	71	30	—	—	78	3
Mechanical Engineering	147	124	30	30	—	—	—	96	4
	2588	1313	1314	660	312	191	151	85	2
Medicine									
Dentistry	257	128	118	32	26	35	25	47	1
Medicine	3071	678	2357	550	494	424	889b	74	2
	3328	806	2475	582	520	459	914	72	2
Agricultural and Veterinary Science									
Agronomy	558	338	208	45	84	59	20	79	
Veterinary	166	136	27	—	—	—	27	78	1
	724	474	235	45	84	59	47	79	1
Grand Totals	13430	5553	7052	1737	2216	1650	1449b	64	1
Probable Year of Enrollment		1962.		1961.	1960.	1959.	—		
Probable Year of Graduation[c]		1966.		1965.	1964.	1963.	1962.		

a. Includes 146 students in pharmacy.
b. Includes 401 sixth-year students and 40 students whose year is not known.
c. Assuming a five year course.
N.B. Details by year (as of May 30, 1962) do not add to enrollments, which are later figures
tember, 1962) and include foreign students and enrollments in miscellaneous courses.
Source: Department of Statistics, University of Havana.

Havana and 11 in Oriente.[25]   Secondly, the number of students will be increased by the *"Facultades Obreras,"* the special program to prepare industrial workers aged eighteen through forty for university study.   Workers who have distinguished themselves for their practical ability and who have been at work at least two or three years will be eligible; those of eighth or ninth grade will have two years of preparatory up-grading courses, those of only sixth grade, three or four years.   The preparatory courses will be held, I was told, within the universities, and several hundred were expected to begin in 1963.   This program is, in part, a social reform of the universities as well as a method of raising the standards of technicians and workers in industry: the universities, it is said, should no longer cater to a privileged group, nor be divorced from the practical experience of the working man.

The question arises as to where professors have been found to teach these new students.   The answer obviously has great bearing on the quality of the students who will graduate, which in turn will indicate their potential contribution to the future economy.   There is the problem of estimating the loss from former professors going into exile.   A large proportion of the medical faculty in Havana left or were removed from their posts in 1960. In many faculties teachers have been replaced by persons from abroad, sometimes by less qualified colleagues at home.   In some instances replacements have not been found and the number of students per professor has risen.   Persons of practical experience but little academic qualification have been widely used for teaching in technical institutes.   The same may be true in the universities.   Besides 155 graduate instructors, 71 non-graduate instructors are teaching in Havana, mostly in science and technology.   The 1962 staffing position in Havana and Oriente is shown in Table 15.   The ratio of students to faculty (excluding instructors) was apparently over 25 to 1 in both the humanities and in technology.   Even allowing for instructors, this appears very high.   The long-run intention for the school of technology is a ratio of ten to one.

Flexibility in the salary scales is quite sufficient to permit an attractive offer to be made to professors from abroad.   The post-reform range of university salaries[26] runs from $330 to $750

Table 15. University Teaching Staff in Havana and Oriente, August and September, 1962

	Professors	Invited[a] professors	Auxiliary professors	Total professors	Instructors[b]
University of Havana					
Humanities	72	6	109	187	6
Science	27	12[c]	65	104	82
Technology	13	5	84	102	43
Medicine	87	14[d]	133	234	91
Agriculture and Veterinary Science	10	3	39	52	4
	209	40	430	679	226

Source: Statistical Department, University of Havana.

	Professors	Invited[a] professors	Auxiliary professors	Total professors	Instructors[b]
University of Oriente					
Humanities	13	4	42	59	5
Science	7	—	9	16	22
Technology	4	10	10	24	2
Medicine	1	2	5	8	3
Agriculture and Veterinary Science	—	—	—	—	—
	25	16	66	107	32

Source: University of Oriente.
a. From overseas, or local professors on special appointment.
b. Mostly graduates, some non-graduates.
c. Includes 1 consultant professor.
d. Includes 3 consultant professors.

monthly for a full professor and $245 to $575 monthly for an assistant professor, according to the number of hours of university assignments (between 10 and 40 weekly). The "hours of commitments" for which a teacher is paid are, I understand, interpreted generously and include research. But the possibility envisaged of professors' teaching as much as 40 hours weekly may indicate a further solution to the shortage of staff.

How much a lowering of standards is indicated by this sketchy evidence is hard to say. Comments from a few staff members in Oriente and Havana may be far from representative. From some I was told of "disappointing standards," of involuntary absenteeism (through militia duty or other work), of little attention to homework. "Often students do not complete more than 18 of 30 weeks' work." In Havana, the official policy towards absenteeism is strict: unless a student maintains 80 per cent attendance, he is not eligible for the exam.

Such individual impressions are quite inadequate for a proper assessment of the present status of the Cuban universities, and they may be misleading for judging the future. The abolition of the traditional independence of the universities, besides its political implications, has meant more careful coordination with the economic planning departments of government. Higher standards may be pressed from this source. The plans outlined in *La Reforma de la Enseñanza Superior en Cuba* were, I was told, two years in preparation. It would be very misleading to dismiss these reforms as nothing more than a subordination of university independence to political control. (That they are this as well is clearly explained in the Preamble.) A whole new organization, extending from the *"Consejo Superior de Universidades"* down, including representatives of each university, of students, and of the Ministry of Education (the Minister is chairman of the council), has been created and has been functioning since March, 1962. Its powers and aims are considerable. It is directly under the government and naturally has direct support. No organization by itself can replace the need for good teachers and good students. But within the limits of its control and the confines of its ideology, the council can do much to remedy the university disorganization of the last few years. It could help in other ways. If it did, it would contribute greatly to raising and maintaining the standards of scientific and technical study. In the longer future, because the quantity and quality of graduates from the technical schools and institutes will probably rise, some will be entering the universities with better technical preparation. Seven hundred are expected to graduate from the technical institutes in 1963-64, 2,000 in 1964-65.

The future of the other faculties is more in doubt. It will be greatly influenced by ideology. Does the present lack of emphasis on the arts suggest new priorities or a basic neglect? The publication of non-political works by Cuban authors by the National Council of Culture may be indicative. Certainly the detailed syllabuses for humanities given in *La Reforma de la Enseñanza*

Superior en Cuba show considerable attention.   Only in modern languages (French and English in particular) and in philosophy were courses being terminated in 1962.   The decrease in French and English is probably associated with the expansion in teaching Russian at, for instance, the *Máximo Gorki* Institute.[27]

vii

The delay before the new emphasis on engineering, medicine, and agriculture will contribute to the economy is indicated by the probable year when the students will graduate.   The year of graduation is shown at the bottom of Table 14.   Doctors are apparently the only group from whom a steady outflow from the university into the economy can be expected in the near future. Agronomy, dentistry, architecture, law, economics, and some engineering and science will provide a small and varying number of graduates until 1964 or 1965.   Not until 1966 will the major increases in the numbers of university students in technology, agriculture, and veterinary science be translated into increases in the number of engineers and agricultural experts ready to take jobs.   Until then, the supply already in the pipeline must suffice. And, of course, as a measure of future supply, the number of students already in each year of study (columns 2, 4, 5, 6, and 7 of Table 14) overstates the number who will be available for production.   Some in study now will fail to complete the course, some fail to graduate, some stay on for research or teaching, and others, for various reasons, be unsuitable for employment.

Yet the future aims are high.   The 80,000 students, mentioned already as the target for university enrollments in 1970, is apparently based on a rough deduction from Soviet experience that 1 per cent of the total population should be receiving university training.[28]   The general target envisages enrollments in technology growing from 10,000 in 1965 to 25,000 in 1970, with a staff of 1,000 and 2,500 respectively.   The economics faculty will be expanded to provide more economist-engineers, trained for practical work as consultants, planners, and industrial administrators.   The school of medicine—according to the plan—must aim to increase the number of doctors to the 10,000 or 12,000 required for the public health needs of 1970.

The five-fold expansion envisaged in these plans is very large and may be greatly beyond the capacities and capabilities of the new system. The targets quoted above were published at the beginning of 1962 and may later have been revised. But, in summary, it is fair to note what has already been done to link the universities with the economic plans.

Enrollments in science, technology, and agricultural studies have already been expanded. New workshops and laboratories have been constructed (as well as four new dormitories for scholarship students in Oriente). Programs of study have been designed which stress matters of direct importance for production in the near future. Whether these changes are generally desirable or appropriate or mark an advance over the former university system is not for discussion in this study. But in terms of *economic* effects, the new links established between the future needs of the economy and the design of training in the universities could well make a significant contribution to industry and agriculture in the new economy.

CHAPTER VIII

Education

Analysis and Implications

i

It is a brave man who predicts the future—too often it is an unwary economist. This summary makes no attempt. It will, however, review some of the data which might indicate what the chances could be.

In giving a broad summary of Cuban education in 1962, three questions will be asked. Will Cuban education produce economic returns in the future? What is Cuban education costing, taking the program as a whole? Finally, is Cuba spending too much on education? At the end, a few notes will be added about the general problems arising from the rapidity of expansion undertaken.

Table 1 shows the *number* of persons involved in Cuban education in 1962. The form of Table 1 is closely related to the age-education profile given at the beginning of this study. Each entry within Table 1 refers to a section of the Cuban population defined by the level of education already attained and by age. Only two age divisions are used: of working age (fifteen or more) and below. Within each entry are included all persons of that age and education who were involved in schools or technical study in 1962, as teachers or students, full-time or part-time. Each type of school or class is listed and total enrollments within them are shown in thousands. (A few educational activities organized

Educational Background[a] (All figures in thousands)

Age	Less than Grade I	Completed only Grade I, II or the literacy campaign course	Completed Grades III, IV or V, but no higher	Completed Grade VI of Primary School or more	Total
Under 15	Primary Schools 349	Primary Schools 622	Primary Schools 281	Secondary-basic Schools 45	1,297
15 and over	Primary Schools 6	Primary Schools 40	Primary Schools 52	Secondary-basic Schools 46	1,029
		bFamily circles 90	bDomestic Schools 9	Pre-University institutes 16	
		bSeguimiento classes 314	bNight Schools 39	Technological schools and institutes 22	
		bMINAR (army) 25	bSuperación Obrera-Campesina 94	Teacher training 9	
		bDomestic schools 11	bMínimo-Técnico 72	Various Vocational Courses 29	
		bNight schools 17	Overseas study 2	Universities 17	
			Domestic retraining courses 2	Overseas study 2	
			Ministry of Industry courses 12	Ministry of Industry courses 2	
Total, 15 and over	355	497	282	143	
Total, students	355	1,119	563	188	2,225
Teachers total	—	—	39	62	101
full-time	—	—	—	51	51
part-time	—	—	39	11	50

a. The Ministry of Education estimated that total primary school enrollments in 1962 were 1,350,000. The breakdown of this total, used in Table 1, is derived from the age and grade of primary school students in 1961 (Table 5, Chapter VII) and assumes (1) that 80 per cent of each group of 1961 had graduated to the next higher grade by 1962, (2) that the other 20 per cent of each group had continued in the same grade, (3) that the new students in 1962 (142,000) had the same age distribution as 1961 students of grade 1 and pre-primary, and (4) that all new students started in pre-primary or grade 1.

An estimate of the age distribution of secondary students was also required, and difficult to make because many were over-age. Allowing for the median age being possibly two years above that appropriate, and for the larger proportion of students in the bottom grade, suggested an equal division of total secondary basic enrollments between those of fifteen or more and those below. While this possibly overstates the number under fifteen, any exaggeration is somewhat offset by assuming those in other types of secondary education are all fifteen or more.

While these assumptions obviously mean that Table 1 can indicate only within limits the sub-division of total enrollments, the emphasis given to mass education in Cuba and the very large enrollments of persons of working age seemed to justify summarizing the results in this broad if tentative form.

Leaders of family circles are included under part-time teachers and the administrative staff of the Ministry under full-time teachers.

b. Indicates part-time activity.

Source: Ministry of Education, Ministry of Industry.

by INRA, other ministries, trade unions, or revolutionary schools are not included.)

Thus 349,000 (row 1, column 1) persons under 15 who had *not completed* grade I were enrolled in primary schools. These persons were *in* pre-school classes or *in* Grade I in 1962. Similarly, the other corner of the table (row 2, column 4) refers to the most educated quarter of the Cuban population, those who have completed Grade VI of primary school and who are of working age; of these, 205,000 were within the education system in 1962, 62,000 as teachers and 143,000 as students. In this way, Table 1 summarizes the *number* of persons enrolled or teaching in classes and schools run by the Ministries of Education and Industry in Cuba in 1962.

Thus, according to Cuban estimates, in 1962 about 1,300,000 Cubans under 15 and nearly 1,000,000 of working age (over fifteen and members or potential members of the labor force) were *studying* in some form of organized education; of these 188,000 were in secondary or higher education and 563,000 in Grades IV to VI of primary school or its equivalent. In terms of total population (7,000,000) and by the standards of Latin America, such figures are impressive. The number of persons in the program of adult education is, as far as I can tell, larger (in proportion) than ever before in a Latin American country.

Table 1, when used with the age-education profile given at the beginning of this study, also indicates the *proportion* of the different groups of the population involved in education. Although the profile refers to 1953 and Table 1 to 1962, the two may be usefully, if cautiously, compared together, particularly in the upper age group and at higher levels of education. Thus, although the total number of Cubans who had completed Grade VI probably increased since the census of 1953 (when it was about 990,000), the increase has been offset, particularly in this education group, by the departure of many as refugees. Thus, of the number remaining, the 188,000 in full-time study were undoubtedly a very high proportion of those under 15 and a significant proportion of those above—perhaps a sixth. The proportions studying among other groups of working age (15 or over) were also high, especially among the illiterates during the campaign of 1961 and among persons of first or second grade level in 1962.

Although it is not clear exactly how many persons under 15 have passed each level of education, the number of them enrolled in primary schools (shown in the first three subtotals of row 1) may be near to the total eligible.

Thus it appears that the *proportion* of Cubans who attended some form of organized instruction during the 15 months from June, 1961, to September, 1962 (a period which includes the literacy campaign in addition to the classes and schools of 1962) was more than one-third of the total Cuban population: of the order of 35 per cent of the population aged 14 years or older, 40 per cent of the population aged 10 years or more, almost 45 per cent of total population over 5 when school children are included.

ii

Consumption Benefits. If schooling is valued for its own sake, these high enrollments in themselves represent a form of return, a benefit in consumption which, while naturally qualified by the quality of the education, is not to be lightly dismissed—and may well be judged by its recipients to be a significant addition to their standard of living. It would reveal a dangerous misunderstanding of the basis of such valuation if the "consumption" benefits of literacy were ignored merely because 3 months' studying of the Cuban primer cannot match a secondary school education. It is for the consumer to judge whether or not it is an improvement on the past. In this respect, at least one and a third million Cubans got some form of organized education in 1962 who in 1958 got none. Including those in the literacy campaign of 1961 more than a quarter of all Cubans over 14 had been enrolled in classes which 18 months before had not existed. Many of these were from poorer families which previously had little hope of education beyond literacy, if that.

Economic Returns. But our main question concerns education as investment. Will there be returns to the new economy? For this also, the overall percentages, even when undifferentiated by quality or grade of education, are significant. To have established a link of basic communication with the equivalent of at least one person over fourteen in every Cuban family (although coverage has, of course, not been distributed in this way) is a fact of importance, certainly for the social and political framework, possibly for individual productivity. The government has clear intentions of using education for building the new society. Time will show better than political pre-conceptions what success they will have. National goals have also included higher production and classes have not been negligent in trying to strengthen incentives to raise it. Whatever the new skills learned, the students will have heard proclaimed the economic needs. Some may have been fired to action. Many will merely understand better the national importance of their daily work.

All of these general influences can mean a great deal for bringing support to the plans and institutions of a new economic structure. They also may contribute something to changing an individual's productivity, both by improving skills and by strengthening (or possibly, of course, weakening) incentives.[1] As the designers of Cuban education clearly had high and quite concrete ambitions in training technicians, administrators, and skilled workmen, it is well to be cautious before dismissing all these efforts as without effect on productivity or on growth of national output.

The future economy. In a more specific way, how much will Cuban education contribute to the future economy? This will largely depend on the number of persons with higher education, the quality of their training, and the economic framework within which they will work. Because the last will be determined by internal and international politics, as well as by a host of other economic factors, its discussion is well beyond this paper. Anything that can be said here is really background to these wider issues. But even as a purely economic question, the available information about the future plans for different sectors of the economy is insufficient to assess how well the future supplies of skilled manpower (to be produced by the education system) will suffice. A forecast of the Cuban labor force in 1965 is given in Table 17 of Dudley Seers's part. Yet without more detail, it is difficult to judge how adequate will be the numbers of technicians, chemists, veterinarians, and such. Some general insights may, however, be gained by seeing what improvement there is on the past.

Table 2. Number of Persons in Professional and Technical Occupations in 1952 and in Training in 1962

Profession	Total Number 1952	Number in Training in 1962	University	
		Non-University	Enrollments	Per Cent in First Year[a]
Dentists	1934		257	54%
Physicians and Surgeons	6201		3134	22%
Nurses, professional	1763	401[b]		n.a.
Pharmacists	1866		146	24%
Teachers: college and university	3137		} 2676[c]	43%
secondary and vocational	2361			
primary	36815	9095		
Engineers: civil (including architects)	1468		841	32%
mechanical, industrial, mining	309		976	81%
other	449		1042[d]	39%
Technicians: draftsmen	1109			
laboratory	2021	5123[e]		98%
mechanical, industrial, electrical	1784			
Chemists	1257		702[f]	72%
Lawyers	6560		535	13%
Surveyors	335	1014[g]		n.a.
Agronomic Engineers	294		723[h]	62%
Veterinarians	355		185	83%
Total	70,018	15,633	11,217	

a. Percentages of university students in first year refer to Havana University only.

b. Scholarship students only.

c. Includes 347 secondary teachers on special training in Oriente.

d. 1030 studying electrical, 12 geological engineering.

e. Technical institutes only.

f. 142 studying chemistry, 525 chemical engineering, and 35 sugar refining chemistry.

g. 1961.

h. Agronomy: includes 40 studying in universities abroad.

Sources: National Census, 1953: Ministry of Education and University Departments of Statistics, 1962.

Table 2 shows the number of persons in high-level training in 1962 compared with the number employed within the Cuban economy in 1952.

The 11,000 training in universities and the numbers studying professional and technical subjects outside the university, compared with the 70,000 who were in employment in 1952, seems low when set against the new ambitions, the urgent need to make up for emigration and to replace those who retire. Many of the students are still in first year and some may never take up employment in their field (though the government is trying in many ways to encourage this). To a large extent the present shortage of students is the result of the delay before sufficient secondary students are available to expand university and technical enrollments. If plans work out, the picture in five years will be very different.

In individual categories the picture is better. For instance, the number of doctors in training is nearly half the number in employment in 1952. Because about the same number of medical students enrolled in each year of study, they should provide a steady flow into the economy. Dentists in training are fewer, but the large intake in 1962 was (in proportion to dentists employed in 1952) comparable to the intake of doctors.

The number in agricultural or veterinary studies, although very large relative to the numbers once in employment is, in fact, not very different from the number studying in the late forties, when so few who graduated went into agricultural work. Will the proportion entering agricultural work be higher now? Note, however, that the high percentage in first year means that many will not even be ready to join the economy until 1966. The same delays are likely in the program of technical expansion. The number of civil engineers and architects in university training is over half what employment was in 1952. For other types of engineering the proportion is almost double. But the number in their first year is very high, and even higher among technicians in secondary training.

In fact, as was clear when looking in detail at both secondary-technical and university plans, the years until the mid-sixties are likely to be fairly barren, with most of the education effort going to build up the supply of students *within* the pipeline, but with little to show in output. By 1964 the technological schools will turn out men for the economy, and a year later the technical institutes. University output will vary according to subject and training, but by 1966 the first graduates who studied entirely under the new system will emerge and general expansion will be under way. Such at least are the plans and the shape of present enroll-ments: naturally, however, many things can upset them.

How adequate will these numbers be in five years' time? Some rough attempts at quantitative manpower estimates have been made for engineers by the planning authorities in Cuba[2] and further estimates to be linked with the 1962-65 development plan were under discussion in September, 1962. In the absence of information about these recent plans, some calculations by Altshuler in *"Cuba Socialista"* may be quoted. Working from the number of engineers per 10,000 inhabitants in Russia (which he gives as 46.5 in 1959) and in the United States (28 in 1958), Altshuler places a target figure for Cuba of 40 by 1975. As the actual ratio in Cuba was less than 5 per 10,000 in 1952 and as Cuba during the 20 years before the Revolution apparently produced only just over 1500 *"títulos"* of engineering, the target is ambitious, economically as well as educationally. So ambitious, in fact, that Altshuler gives short-run targets as meeting 35 per cent of the economy's engineering and architectural needs in 1967, and of increasing percentages thereafter to reach 85 per cent by 1970. If "35 per cent of needs" in 1967 means about 11,000 engineers and architects, it is a very high aim when meas-ured against the present scarcity and the 3,479 engineering and architectural students in the three universities during 1962 (of whom about half were first year, and therefore unlikely to grad-uate before 1966). In fact, such a target for 1967 is clearly not possible with present enrollments and within the time. Even to meet the 1970 target would probably require an annual intake of over 6,000 students (allowing for attrition), which is four times the present first-year enrollment. Thus the shortage of students and teachers may well delay even a modified plan. Of course, to the extent that the projections of economic needs are unrealistical-ly ambitious, so a failure of the educational system to meet these targets will be less serious. But in the absence of further informa-tion, either on the projected enrollments of the future or the estimated demands, it is difficult to say more.

What about the quality of the education? Here the picture is very sketchy. This is particularly disturbing in areas where quality need not have been sacrificed—where weakness is un-necessary. In adult education, the literacy campaign was from appearances and within its objective very successful. Its success will be closely followed by other countries with many illiterates. Yet quality is again the crucial test, less in qualifying the success of the basic campaign than in emphasizing that only with further work can basic literacy be consolidated and become worthwhile; despite many successes in continuation classes, the small enrollment of last year's successful literates must give cause for question. In primary and secondary education quantitative expansion is remarkable. The many uncertainties concerning the ability of the full-time primary teachers cannot detract from this basic achievement. But at higher levels, expansion must be more seriously questioned in terms of its meaning in technical and educational standards.

Descriptions have already pointed to signs of a lowering in standards—rising numbers of pupils per teacher, crash courses for teachers, up-grading courses for students, shortages of certain books, disruption of timetables. Some of these are the inevitable costs of rapid expansion. Some are the results of bad planning and poor administration. Some are what must be expected with understaffed education in a developing country. Lower standards are not inevitably foolish or wasteful if they make possible a very much wider spread of education, particularly if the education imparts basic skills in practical ways. As one economist has suggested in India, it is not entirely clear "if medical education has been really adapted to the situation of the poor country. In the United States and Europe and, indeed, also in New Delhi, we yearn for doctors who are trained and totally trustworthy. The provision of such total training is the *sine qua non* of modern medical education. But in the developing country, with scarce resources, if we insist on these high standards for the few, may we not deny medical assistance to the many? Do we not get good doctors in the capitals at the price of having no one to set a broken leg or prescribe some morphine in the villages?"[3] The point may be relevant to other lines of education.

There may well be economic returns from mass education in Cuba, particularly from the *Mínimo Técnico* classes for workers of some but not great skill, and from the middle levels of technical education—from the technical and rural schools (producing garage mechanics, electricians, machinists, better farmers, agricultural mechanics), and from domestic schools and commercial colleges. But whether half-trained students can become adequate teachers, or factory managers become effective administrators, on a course far from comprehensive is another matter. Undoubtedly some do and others, in every field, learn a great deal on the job. But I would feel more confidence in the economic returns from education if more effort were paid to selection of students for ability and economic potential and less to other (sometimes to hardly any) considerations. Poor administration, delays in receiving books and supplies, inadequate coordination, minor disruptions of teaching schedules, an emphasis on enthusiasm and spirit sometimes at the cost of emphasis on standards—I feel that in some cases these could have been avoided simply by more careful planning at the top. A general decision for quantity before quality is no reason for less emphasis on the best possible quality once the quantity has been fixed.

Time may to an extent remove some of these weaknesses. Since the higher levels of education (and it is the higher levels which give more cause for doubt) require more years of study, so there may still be time for real improvement, even among those who will be graduating within a year or two. Some handicaps arising from inadequate teaching of fundamentals and, possibly worse, from the difficulties of teaching those students who at the beginning received no examination or proper tests will remain as long as the students themselves. Other failings can be corrected. But time is against the planners because it is the present shortage of administrators which is so very crucial, and it is the present output of adult courses, full-time and evening, which largely must tide over the next few years. School and university expansion can pay only a delayed dividend.

These final remarks should not be taken as a negative judgment. The picture is too big for such a definite conclusion to be reached with inadequate evidence. Rather they are basic questions, uncertainties which a full evaluation would need to answer. That the implications are not entirely negative is shown by the fact that many of these questions have already been investigated by the Cuban Ministry of Education. Reports and statistics are not only thorough and improving, they are used in detail—both in the beginnings of manpower planning and in arousing popular interest and concern in the basic educational problems. Furthermore, in adult, technical, teacher training, and university education, 1962 was virtually the first year of operation within the new plans. The need for improvement was recognized; leveling-up courses were seen to be only temporary. It would be shortsighted to judge the prospects of relatively good and far-reaching plans by weak execution in the first year.

What Is Cuban Education Costing?

In terms of the revised budget, the cost of education in Cuba in 1962 was running at an annual rate of $229,000,000 or between 5 and 8 per cent of the national product. In terms of pesos per student it was costing about $60 for a primary school child, three to six times as much for a general or vocational secondary student, over ten times as much for technical students, and possibly fifteen times as much for some of the students under the scholarship plan. Adults in part-time continuation classes were costing $25 or $30 each, about half what was paid per primary child or per illiterate during the literacy campaign. Table 3 assembles the other figures.

But a full assessment of the economic burden dares not consider only money costs. How can a figure be placed on the economic sacrifice of time and energy which arises when pupils or volunteer teachers are busy with education when they might be at something else? A summary of the total manpower used is a first step and it is given in Table 4. Naturally the degree of estimation in a table of this sort is fairly considerable. Some enrollments are imprecise, attendance rates have varied over the year, the estimate takes no account of things like travel time to and from class. More serious problems arise when trying to place an economic figure on such a table. Many of the people included, although able-bodied, might be unemployed; for them, attendance at class is not an economic sacrifice. Or the hours of class might entirely fall within leisure time. Indeed there is considerable stress in the organization of *Mínimo Técnico* on classes being held when they will not cut into production, which is the government's way of saying that it considers the opportunities being missed at these times should be negligible or unimportant.

Table 3. Average Costs Per Student by Type of Education

Average Cost per Student

	$ per annum	
	1961	1962
Full-time Study or School Education		
Primary	54	63
Primary teacher training		
Minas del Frío		800
Topes de Collantes		1168
Makarenko Institute	270	941
Secondary, Basic Urban	139	222
Rural	1353	
Scholarship Students		757
Pre-University, General Students	218	383
Scholarship Students		1948
Technical Schools and Institutes		
General Students	748	831
Scholarship Students		873
Commercial Colleges		
General Students	140	182
Scholarship Students		3611
Institute of Higher		
Education (short courses)	50	
Part-time Adult Education		
Literacy campaign	58	—
Seguimiento classes		32
Family circles		2
Army classes		25
Superación Obrera-Campesina		43
Night Schools		76

Sources: 1961 figures are taken from an analysis made by the Statistical Department of the Ministry of Education, Havana. They refer to actual expenditure; 1962 figures (and the figure for the literacy campaign 1961) are estimates based on 1962 budget allocations and on assumptions and often incomplete data explained in Appendix B, Part II; the 1962 figures must accordingly be treated as tentative approximations.

Are such opportunities, in fact, unimportant? Of course it depends on the scale of values. The present discussion sticks broadly to the values usually considered by economists, although care must be taken not to get caught pretending that only the range of activities measured by Gross National Product are worth considering. The Gross National Product omits many important things and unmeasured economic quantities like unpaid housework and the rental value of public property; neither does it take into account less tangible, non-economic costs like losses of liberty and nervous strain, which have an important influence on human welfare. Secondly, without our being sure of the capabilities of men when fully stretched, it is not possible to say what opportunities are being missed. Most economic concepts of alternatives are framed within some social system. When this is upset, as in Cuba, the hours men will work, the things they could be doing are all quite changed. To measure the availability of manpower in terms of an eight-hour day is all a little irrelevant. The Revolution has never been an 8 o'clock to 5 o'clock business. The more appropriate question is: to what extent and for how long can revolutionary fervor persuade people to work beyond their usual limits? For many people and many tasks, such days may long be passed. But not for all. In education well over 200,000 adults were at class for two hours on most evenings in mid-1962. If they were not there, would they have done something else of economic value? When a government has unlimited ambitions and few hesitations about encroaching on private hours for national purposes, it is not entirely clear that manpower used out of working hours should be valued at zero. If the government had not chosen to use the "leisure hours" for education, might it not have used them for something else?[4]

All these uncertainties lead to several alternative statements of the economic cost of the manpower. They are all based on the persons of working age (fifteen or over) male and female, engaged in educational activity as students or teachers in 1962.

Table 4. Manpower Used in Education in Cuba, 1962

Number of students and teachers of working age (fifteen or over) in thousands

| | Previous educational background | | | |
	Less than Grade I	Grades I, II, or literacy campaign	Grades III, IV or V	Grade VI or completed primary school	Total
Full time	6	40	68	194	308
Part time	—	457	253	11	721
Total	6	497	321	205	1029

Source: Taken from Table 1.

1) The total manpower involved in education activity was just over one million adults, nearly one quarter of the adult population, and almost a third of the labor force. Of these, more than 700,000 were in part-time, and over 300,000 in full-time, study or teaching.

2) Those in full-time activity represented about 2 per cent of the total eligible persons with Grade I or II education, nearly 5 per cent of Grades III to V, and possibly 20 per cent to 25 per cent of those who had completed primary school or more.

3) Those in part-time activity represented about a third of the total eligible persons with Grade I or II education, about 15 to 20 per cent of Grades III to V, and probably about 1 per cent of those who had completed primary school.

4) The part-time persons spent in total about 14,000,000 manhours at class each month, after allowing for absenteeism and such; 8,000,000 hours by students of first or second grade education, 6,000,000 by others.

5) The economic loss owing to the absence from production of the full-time students may be strikingly illustrated in money terms. The following rough assumptions will be made: the potential contribution of primary students of working age (15 and over) is negligible; the potential earnings of workers on Ministry of Industry courses is $60 monthly, and the earnings foregone by full-time students in the top educational group (those with primary school completed in an economy short of educated manpower) is $90 monthly. Under these rough but hardly exaggerated assumptions, the total earnings foregone would be nearly $110,000,000 during a school year of 8 months. The annual loss to the economy from those in post-primary study would be about $100,000,000. This, in effect, would suggest that the real cost of further education among the post-primary group was double the budget cost (not $105,000,000 but over $200,000,000 per year) and that the full economic burden of Cuban education in 1962 would have been nearly $350,000,000, or 7 to 11 per cent of potential national income.

By all the tests considered, the economic burden of Cuban Education since the Revolution, and particularly in 1962, has been very heavy.

Is Cuba spending too much on education? This is basically a question of how large will be the returns to Cuban education in relation to its costs. If the economic returns per unit of expenditure on education are higher than for other investments, there would seem to be an (economic) case for having more of it, and if one type of education gave a smaller return than another (in relation to cost), this might be a reason for having less of that type. However, as explained in the previous two sections, without a great deal more information it is not possible to calculate either the precise returns or the full costs of Cuban education, except on the most heroic assumptions. For these reasons any precise ratio of returns to costs and any general answer to the question cannot yet be given.

There is, however, the question of whether the Cuban program of education could have been obtained more cheaply. The inefficiencies summarized when discussing the quality of education and, in contrast, the fairly resourceful use of fixed capital (houses for the scholarship students, magazine presses for school books, hotels for teachers' conferences) would both need weighing in the light of what would have been reasonably possible, given the resources available.

Some lines of education, shown in Table 3, seem unduly expensive compared with others. The scholarship program may well use up public resources without a corresponding saving of private. Rural secondary education seems very costly. Over a third of the total cost per student in technical schools or institutes is for capital expenditure, which reduces the amount by which its current costs exceed those in other forms of secondary education.

It is noteworthy that the literacy campaign cost more in budgetary terms per successful literate than a year of primary schooling. Adult classes, with the exception of family circles and the night schools, cost about half as much as a year of primary school. Because Table 3 is tentative and refers to total cost (i.e., including capital expenditure) and represents only average costs (and not the marginal costs of increasing enrollments), more detailed conclusions are unwarranted.

Of particular interest is the question whether the enormous programs of mass education—primary or adult—have been bought at the cost of restraints on technical and university expansion. To some extent this has been true. For although the universities are short of suitable students (and applicants), some university students have been employed as full-time teachers before completing their studies. From this source alone the universities or technical institutes could have obtained several thousand more students and, in this respect, expansion of higher education or primary schools was a genuine option. There are other cases where mass education has been given priority over more specialized schooling; the closing of all schools for the sake of the literacy campaign is perhaps the clearest example.

A final point is important when considering whether too much has been spent on Cuban education: the enormous inefficiencies in the use of unpaid human labor and, equally important, in the employment of unpaid human emotions. Of course, supporters of the regime will argue that arousing these emotions has paid a double return—not only material benefits to economic development but benefits to society, a sense of brotherhood and a solidarity, a national purpose for the individual. But the widespread use of voluntary labor (and, for instance, of mass media to arouse support) carries economic obligations to ensure that the volunteers are efficiently supplied with the other things they need for the task, and which they require if they are to find the satisfaction of completing it. Quite apart from moral considerations, there is an economic criticism to be made on this count.

iii

When confronted with the enormous and rapid expansion of almost all types of education in Cuba, it is helpful to ask what special factors made it possible. First, there were the initial advantages possessed by Cuba. Though educationally backward by the standards of Europe, the United States, or Russia, Cuba was more advanced than many developing countries. The Cuban education system, like the Cuban economy, was stagnant rather than poor. In number of teachers, school finance, available buildings (at least in the urban areas) Cuba was relatively well off. Television and radio were available for new methods of adult teaching. The desire for education was widespread, though dampened by immediate economic difficulties, poor prospects, and a demoralized school system. Cuba's rate of illiteracy was 21 per cent. This is higher than the rate of literacy for many countries. Cuban education before the Revolution held great possibilities. The problem was that the potential was unused.

Given the education resources available, revolutionary reform could produce rapid results. When money was needed to divert these resources into education, a large increase in the Ministry of Education budget could pay for school materials, for new teachers and old teachers recalled to their profession, and for building rural schools. Revolutionary fervor could be particularly helpful for reviving the demoralized system. Local volunteers could be recruited; young people spurred to enroll, to attend more regularly and to study with purpose; older students stirred to enlist for teaching; teachers persuaded to accept assignments in the neglected areas. The literacy campaign relied heavily on widespread support, not only from those with revolutionary fervor, but from others who thought rural poverty and illiteracy were wrong. Even those strongly opposed to the Revolution have, in ironic fashion, made some contribution to educational expansion. Although teachers and professors (and others) have left the country, their homes have remained. These have provided hostels for the scholarship students.

Third, schooling (in contrast to education), unlike agriculture or industry, was particularly amenable to rapid expansion. Teachers could teach larger classes and facilities be more cramped without the system breaking down or the schooling becoming completely useless. Improvisation was possible. Adult education at an elementary level is at first as much a matter of persistence as of a well-educated teacher (though a student's persistence is not unrelated to his progress). But the point is that considerable expansion was possible, even though quality would fall—as, indeed, happened. Some advocates will argue that a little schooling for all is preferable to better schooling for fewer—and to some degree this choice is always made in plans for mass education. Mass education was, indeed, an important purpose of the Cuban government, and their social and political aims may be greatly advanced by the sort of education already provided. But whether this education will be sufficient foundation for a new agriculture and industry remains to be seen.

PART III

Industry

BY MAX NOLFF

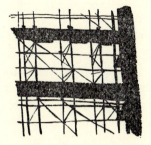

CHAPTER IX

The New Industrial
Organization

i

An analysis of the industrial development of Cuba must take into consideration the Latin American framework and relate itself to the characteristics common to the so-called underdeveloped countries, or those just beginning to undergo development. The basic problems that Cuba has met with in the past and those with which it is faced at the present time are, to a greater or less degree, the same problems as those that are the concern of the nations mentioned above.

The greater part of the underdeveloped countries have chosen industrialization as the way to reduce the increasing differences between their standards of living and those enjoyed by the more advanced countries. The necessity of this step becomes insistent when one considers the rapid increase in population and the contradiction, which becomes more acute every day, between the enormous potential of modern technology to raise the standard of living and the present antiquated economic and social structure which prevents taking advantage of any rapid advance of this same technology. The process of industrialization in the Latin American countries cannot follow the same course as that followed by the more advanced countries. In these advanced countries the acquisition of capital necessary for economic growth preceded in some cases the redistribution of income, and in others it took place at the cost of a regressive distribution. On the other hand, in the economy of the underdeveloped countries the acquisition of capital and its redistribution tend to present themselves as simultaneous aspects of the same problem, because of the generally low level of income and the accentuated inequalities that its distribution presents. The accelerated increase in population, the political maturity of the people, the power of the labor unions, the extension of communications, and the social aspects of development, all produce different conditions that affect industrialization today.

Furthermore, modern technology demands a more extensive accumulation of capital and an efficient utilization of this technology and this capital. In short, it can be asserted that the Latin American countries are now faced with the need of finding formulas for attaining a rapid industrialization suitable to the special conditions existing in each one of them.

In recent years new standards in the field of international cooperation have been explored, and these have tended to bring about developments in different regions rather than in individual countries. This is shown in common markets, zones of free trade, attempts at economic integration on the part of some countries, the coordinated development of countries with central planning, increasing technical assistance, and changes in attitudes toward foreign investments.

The Marshall Plan for European countries can be considered as one manifestation of this change. The Alliance for Progress, in spite of the fact that it has not been able to make its full effectiveness felt in the two years of its existence, is an alternative presented to the Latin American countries. The basic problem, however, is still the necessity of an accelerated and specialized industrialization and, if it is possible, to have this kind of industrialization worked out along with other types of international aid, in order to reduce the sacrifices of the countries that undertake it.

Cuba has chosen, among several alternatives, a way to obtain an accelerated industrialization through the mechanisms offered by a centrally planned economy. This country had no opportunity to decide upon the formula of the Alliance for Progress, since it can be said that the character and the direction that the Cuban Revolution took was what caused the United States to present this plan to the Latin American countries.

It is my purpose in this part to give in the most objective manner possible a picture of Cuban industry under the direction of the revolutionary government. The institutional changes, the new industrial organization, its results, the most important events in industry in the first four years, and the prospect for industrial development will constitute the framework of the picture.

Owing to a number of circumstances, this study must be incomplete in some aspects. In the first place, I did not have access to all the official sources of information that I might have desired. Those directing the Junta Central de Planificación (Central Planning Board), JUCEPLAN, did not furnish me with all the antecedents that I sought. On the other hand, the Ministry of Industry collaborated to a high degree and gave me an opportunity to visit representative industrial plants. I selected a score of factories of different kinds and different capacities. Although visits to such a limited number of industries are not enough to put together a complete picture of the real Cuban industrial scene, I was permitted to talk with the workmen and appraise the new working conditions and the principal problems confronting industry.[1]

Second, at the time when I was carrying out the investigations, the goals of the new plan (Plan Perspectivo, 1962-65) were being revised. I believe, however, that I succeeded in grasping the most important changes that have been instituted.

Third, insufficient statistics and certain incompatibilities hindered an analysis of what happened in the first four years of the new regime.

Needless to say, the opinions expressed here are my own. The organizations and individuals mentioned above have no responsibility in them.

ii

For more than a century the basic support for Cuban economy has been sugar. Cuba produces more sugar than any other country in the world. The importance of the sugar industry becomes evident when one considers that it represents more than 40 per cent of the entire industrial production of the country, that it gives employment to one-fourth of the labor force in industry, that more than one-half of the active agricultural population depends upon sugar. These figures were even greater in the past, especially in the period of the great expansion of sugar production that took place in the first two decades of this century.

In the nineteenth century, great changes occurred in the sugar industry as the industrial revolution extended to this field of endeavor. As a consequence of technological advance, there came about larger units of production, more mechanized methods, and increases in the pay scale.

In the middle of the last century, there were 1,500 sugar factories in Cuba, with a capacity of 1,000,000 metric tons a year. At the present time there are 161 factories, with a capacity greater than 7,000,000 tons. The most significant expansion and concentration in the sugar industry took place in the first two decades of the present century. At the end of the last century production reached 1,500,000 tons and in 1920 it had reached 5,000,000 tons. This notable increase coincides with the first years of the independence of Cuba and with an increase in population, caused in part by immigration.[2]

The expansion of the sugar industry resulted in large measure from a greater demand in the United States and from the necessity abroad of finding a substitute for beet sugar during the First World War when European producers were forced out of business. In 1920 Cuba reached the highest per capita level of exportation in the world and had an income level higher than any other Latin American country.

In the twenties there occurred in the sugar industry a slump that was to become a determining factor in the later stagnation of the Cuban economy measured in terms of per capita income. Yet this slump in the sugar industry, brought about by a reduction in the demand abroad, resulted in a modification of the ownership structure of the industry. The failures of the less efficient sugar mills and those in a weak financial situation permitted a number of them to pass into the hands of United States banks, a situation that was unfavorable to the creation of a Cuban managerial class and that accentuated foreign participation in the sugar industry, with the result that 40 per cent of the production of raw sugar passed into foreign hands.

The great depression of the thirties accentuated the slump in the sugar industry and Cuban economy in general. Cuba, perhaps next to Chile among the Latin American countries, was faced with the sharpest reduction in its import capacity, along with the highest rate of unemployment.

The road taken by Cuba after the world-wide depression was diametrically opposite to that followed by Chile and other Latin American countries. They tried to find in internal development a way out of their economic difficulties. Industrialization became one of the basic objectives of their development, and to attain this objective they turned to protective tariffs. Cuba, on the other hand, reduced its tariffs in exchange for a sugar quota in the United States market. It abandoned any attempt to diversify its production and transform the structure of its economy. In this manner Cuba aligned her destiny with international market fluctuations and thereby accentuated its single crop economy.

The acquisition of capital depended to such an extent upon the exportation of sugar that when they fell, the whole level of the Cuban economy fell and was subject to deflation. This fact prevented the development of other types of production, which under other circumstances would have constituted an internal compensation mechanism against outside fluctuations in the price of its principal export—sugar.

Only after the Second World War did there take place a change in the orientation of the Cuban economy, as expressed in an acceleration of its development. This fact did not have the same favorable effect upon its industrial development as it did with other Latin American countries.

In Table 1 we can see the unfavorable rate of increase in manufacturing industries in Cuba, as compared with the other Latin American countries.

Table I. Annual Accumulative Rate of Increase in the Gross Manufacturing Product in Various Countries in Latin America (Average percentage annual growth)

Countries	1950-55	1955-60	1950-60
Argentina	2.0	—0.8	0.6
Brazil	7.1	16.5	11.7
Colombia	6.3	5.4	5.9
Chile	7.4	3.6	5.5
Cuba[a]	—	—	3.4[d]
Mexico	6.0	7.3	6.6
Peru	5.8	5.5	5.6
Venezuela[b]	14.3	8.9	11.6
Latin America[c]	5.4	8.4	6.9

a. *Revista del Banco Nacional de Cuba* (May, 1959).
b. Figures corrected by OCCP.
c. This figure includes the seven Latin American countries (not including Cuba) mentioned in the table above. They accounted for 87 per cent of the industrial production of Latin America.
d. 1953-58.
Source: ECLA (Economic Commission for Latin America), "Some Characteristics of Industrial Development, 1950-60."

We must keep in mind that the figures on the rate of increase in manufacturing in Cuba are based upon an index prepared by the Banco Nacional and that possibly some objections can be raised to them. But even if this index underestimated the increase in industry, the fact remains that this rate was very much lower than that attained by other Latin American countries.

Slow industrial advance was manifest in all fields, except in the production of gas and electricity, as can be seen in Table 2.

The observation made above of a possible underestimate in the increase in manufacturing industry can be extended to mining and construction. If we examine the indexes corresponding to some of the most important lines of production, as they appear in Table 3, we find that only in oil, cement, and electric power output were significant advances made in 1951-58.

Accordingly, we arrive at the first conclusion: Cuban industrial development was slow in comparison with that of other Latin American countries.

If we compare the increase in the industrial sector with that of the economy in general, we come to the conclusion that industry did not take full advantage of prevailing conditions. The

Table 2. Indexes of Industrial Production
(Base: 1953 = 100)

Years	Industrial Total	Mining	Gas and Electricity	Construction	Manufacturing Industry
1952	97	59	91	93	104
1953	100	100	100	100	100
1954	103	87	109	125	102
1955	104	79	119	111	105
1956	112	79	132	118	112
1957	121	89	148	122	122
1958	120	80	168	121	118
Accumulative annual rate, 1953-58	3.7	4.6	10.9	3.9	3.4

Source: *Revista del Banco Nacional* (May, 1959).

rate of the increase in industrial production relative to the increase of income was very unfavorable to Cuba, as compared with an important group of underdeveloped countries. This may be seen in Table 4.

The rate of increase in income in Cuba for the period 1955-58 was 4.3 per cent annually, while that of its industrial production was only 3.4 per cent. The relation is less than 1 per cent; that is to say, the economy in general increased more rapidly than industry, a phenomenon exactly opposite to that which characterized the underdeveloped countries. Venezuela, with character-

Table 3. Indexes of Physical Production in Some Industrial Lines
(Base: 1951 = 100)

	1957	1958
Sugar	98.5	100.3
Beer	102.9	98.2
Cigars	112.4	103.8
Cigarettes	117.6	122.4
Textiles and rayon fiber	100.0	60.0
Sulphuric acid	118.5	—
Refining of petroleum	590.6	779.2
Cement	174.3	188.7
Electric power output	162.0	175.0
Gas	113.5	113.5

Source: *Statistical Yearbook*, United Nations, 1960; Appendix, Part III, Table 1.

Table 4. Relation Between Changes in Industrial Production and in Income
(Income-elasticity of industrial production for the period 1950-1959)

Countries

Underdeveloped countries[a]	1.89
Venezuela[b]	1.62
Cuba[c]	0.79
All countries[d]	1.37

a. Includes ten countries from ECAFE, eight from Latin America, five from Southern Europe and North Africa, two from the Middle East, and two from Africa.

b. Instead of the rate of increase in the national income, we took the rate of the gross national product. In case one took the period 1950-1960, the ratio would be reduced to 1.51.

c. Figures representing national income, taken from the *Statistical Yearbook,* United Nations, 1960. For the industrial product of Table 2, the ratio corresponds to the period 1953-58.

d. Includes 27 countries with a per capita income less than $200, in addition to the group of underdeveloped countries.

Source: Table 1.3, "Formulating Industrial Development Programs," United Nations, 1961. "Income-elasticity of industrial production" is the rate of increase in industrial production expressed as a multiple of the rate of increase in national income.

istics very much like those of Cuba, showed a rise in industry over 50 per cent faster than in the economy as a whole.

If Cuba had had a ratio similar to that of other underdeveloped countries, its rate of increase would have been 8.1 per cent yearly. Although some objection can be raised to this sort of comparison, it is incontestable that it brings us to a second conclusion: industrial development in Cuba was slow in relation to the possibilities offered by the general economy.

After the depression, and especially in the post-war period, industries of various types were established. They were almost exclusively limited to the production of consumer goods (food and textiles, principally). There was almost no development in the production of intermediate goods, with the exception of cement, rayon, and recently, paper made from bagasse, and still less in capital goods.

Lesser markets, like that of Chile, for example, have shown that it is possible to have a development of a variety of industries in these fields. Cuba, with a high per capita income compared

Table 5. Stock of Automotive Vehicles

Years	Automobiles (Thousands)	Commercial Vehicles (Thousands)
1948	48	30
1951	84	39
1952	98	43
1953	103	42
1954	112	44
1955	126	47
1956	139	51
1957	158	56
1958	159	51

Source: *Statistical Yearbook*, United Nations, 1960, p. 334.

with other Latin American countries, and with a population of 7,000,000, constituted a market suited to many industries. A clear example of the potential of the Cuban market is its large number of automotive vehicles, as may be seen in Table 5.

Table 5 indicates that in the years immediately preceding the Revolution, there was a ratio of approximately one automobile for every forty people. Of the Latin American countries only Venezuela[3] had a higher ratio, and that country had a much higher per capita income than Cuba.

The same table shows how the number of automobiles increased in ten years by 231 per cent, that is, at an annual rate of 12.7 per cent. The increase in the number of commercial vehicles was only 70 per cent in the same period, or 5.4 per cent yearly. In other words, the demand for automobiles in the class of consumer goods rose much faster than that for vehicles as capital goods. Furthermore, the large number of vehicles represented an important potential demand for replacements and parts, something which meant nothing in Cuba at any time.[4] Cases like this one can be repeated in different industries. The third conclusion is that industrial advance in Cuba was slow in relation to the possibilities presented by the development of the domestic market.

In regard to the presence of natural resources that could be utilized in industry, Cuba is in a favorable situation. It is an easily accessible country with a high percentage of level land; it has a good highway system, covering the entire territory; it has

Table 6. Mining Production
(In Thousands of Metric Tons)

Years	Crude Petroleum	Iron	Manganese	Copper	Chrome	Nickel	Salt
1948	13	13	5	15	17	2	55
1951	2	16	42	20	6	–	51
1952	1	30	116	18	6	8	57
1953	1	92	165	16	22	13	52
1954	3	9	123	15	25	13	53
1955	48	73	143	18	27	14	64
1956	71	4	110	15	19	15	64
1957	52	8	66	14	40	20	68
1958	45	6	31	13	26	18	68

Source: *Statistical Yearbook,* United Nations, 1960.

abundant extractive and agricultural resources. The only resources that are scarce are those of energy. That is to say that in Cuba there were no obstacles of a material nature that could explain the backwardness that is sometimes found in underdeveloped countries. Nevertheless, Cuba's resources were utilized only to a very limited extent before the Revolution.

In Table 6 are statistics on the volume of mineral production for the period before the Revolution.

The industries that transformed minerals and farm products were very few in Cuba. Among them we can only mention those making paper out of bagasse, a cement industry, the tobacco industry, and a few wood and food industries' products. As a consequence, the fourth conclusion that can be drawn is that industrial development was slow in relation to Cuba's natural resources.

The contribution of industry to the creation of new types of jobs was very slight. We can assert that the slow increase in new jobs prevented the absorbing to any appreciable degree of the growing number of workers which, as Dudley Seers has shown in the first part, reached a very high rate. In the period from 1955 to 1958 only 8,000 new jobs were created in industry, whereas some 150,000 young men reached the working age in that same period. Therefore, another conclusion can be drawn—industrialization was slow in relation to human resources.

Finally, investments in industry did not keep pace with the availability of domestic savings. As it is pointed out in Part I, the most substantial amount of savings was directed to works of social overhead capital, to housing of a general luxury type, and to commercial and speculative activities. Similarly, a considerable amount of capital was transferred to other countries through profits on foreign investments in Cuba and through Cuban deposits in foreign banks.

As a consequence, industrial development was slow in relation to the increase in other Latin American countries. It was incapable of meeting the potential of the domestic market, of utilizing in extenso its natural and human resources, and allowing savings to be directed to investments in this area. In spite of the slight increase that has been pointed out, there was in process of formation a clear awareness of the need for industrialization. Nevertheless, the policy that was devised to attain it took the form of financing authorized by the state and by a variety of organizations, whose decisions, most of the time, were dispersed and contradictory.

The efforts made by such organizations as the Comisión de Fomento Nacional (Commission for National Development), Banco de Desarrollo Económico y Social (The Bank of Economic and Social Development), Banco de Fomento Agrícola e Industrial (The Bank of Agricultural and Industrial Development), Financiera Nacional (The National Financing Board), Fondo de Regulación de la Industria Textil (The Textile Industry Foundation), Fondo de Regulación de la Industria del Calzado (The Footwear Industry Foundation), Comisión Nacional de Defensa y Propaganda del Tabaco Habano (The National Tobacco Commission), Instituto Cubano de Estabilización del Azúcar (The Institute for the Stabilization of Sugar), and others, met with very limited results in stimulating industrialization, giving rise, on the other hand, on many occasions, to serious irregularities in the authorization of loans. The extensive bureaucratic apparatus created to industrialize the country only succeeded in establishing a limited number of industries of a certain importance, some of which did not even correspond to the demands of the market. In many cases their capacity exceeded domestic requirement by a wide margin.

The fact that local industry had to face strong foreign competition, with no, or slight tariff protection, discouraged the establishment of new enterprises, and those that were undertaken were forced to make installations of high productivity. There was also competition from branches of United States firms established with the idea of holding the Cuban market, if ever restrictive measures prevented its being supplied from the outside.

Along with the enterprises of high efficiency there proliferated a great number of small industries that profited from their location relative to centers of consumption. Finally, there were a great number of establishments of an artisan or domestic type, called *chinchales*, with a very limited production.

More than 50 per cent of the production was concentrated in Havana, and the highest percentage of industrial workers was located in that area, producing, in consequence, a high rate of industrial concentration. This persisted in 1962, as can be seen in Table 7.

Another characteristic of the Cuban industrial development was that many of the newly created industries required most of their raw materials in the form of imports. This brought about an element of rigidity in Cuba's balance of payments, and brought the level of employment and domestic demand to an even greater dependence upon exports.

One last important characteristic is that in many branches of industrial production a monopolistic type of structure had developed. This was owing to the fact that the high technological level that any competition required meant extensive financing

Table 7. Number of Factories in the Consolidated Enterprises of the Ministry of Industry, by Province, 1962

Provinces	Heavy Industries	%	Light Industries	%	Total Industries	%
1. Havana	143	30.0	810	61.1	953	52.8
2. Pinar del Río	37	7.7	46	3.5	83	4.6
3. Matanzas	49	10.2	84	6.3	133	7.4
4. Las Villas	92	19.2	159	12.0	251	13.9
5. Camagüey	61	12.7	48	3.6	109	6.0
6. Oriente	97	20.2	179	13.5	276	15.3
Total	479	100.0%	1,326	100.0%	1,805	100.0%

Source: Appendix, Part III, Table 5.

only available from a limited group of high income investors, or from abroad.

This, in general terms, is the picture of industrial development in Cuba, before the Revolution.

iii

From the moment when the Revolution triumphed in January, 1959, there occurred successively and in an extraordinarily rapid manner substantial changes in the Cuban economy, and within it, in industry. In addition to agrarian, urban, educational, and administrative reforms, the government decreed the nationalization of public services, foreign companies, and later, the principal Cuban companies.

This whole process took place in less than two years. In this space of time a capitalistic type of economy was replaced by a system of highly centralized planning, which first took the form of agrarian reform and control of foreign exchange by the Banco Nacional.

The Revolution, which had made itself felt with extraordinary force in agriculture in the first two years, did not reach such intensity in industry. On the contrary, the first steps in this direction were hesitating and ill defined.

As a result of the process of the recovery of ill-gotten gains, many of which had been used to finance private industry, a number of factories were taken over by the state. At the end of 1959 a Department of Industrialization[5] within INRA (The National Institute of Agrarian Reform) was created to administer these factories.

The state, however, utilized existing financial and administrative mechanisms to stimulate industrial production, to orient development, and to control directly or indirectly this economic sector. In addition, the new Department of Industrialization of INRA initiated in 1960 the purchase of a number of industries considered essential to the general economic development of Cuba.

The exodus of managers, technicians, and professional men which became accentuated, as the character of the Revolution became defined, the increasing demand for manufactured goods, the problems of supply, and even sabotage by some managers and counterrevolutionaries—all these gave rise to a vast number of problems of difficult solution for those directing the Revolution, especially since they had had little or no experience in the industrial field. Thus there began the development of a new industrial policy, destined to produce a profound change in the social relations of production in industry, just as in agriculture.

In the second half of the year 1960, the industrial situation changed abruptly. In July the United States holdings in Cuba were nationalized.[6] This measure was adopted immediately after the government of the United States suspended its sugar quota. Twenty-one sugar companies, three oil companies, one electric company, and one telephone company, with a total investment of $800,000,000,[7] passed into the hands of the Department of Industrialization of INRA.

In October of the same year the revolutionary government took a second decisive step in its policy of nationalization, promulgating two new laws. The first of these[8] permitted the expropriation of 287 industrial establishments,[9] 61 commercial establishments, 6 railway and 13 maritime companies. The second law brought about the nationalization of all the banking institutions.[10] These laws were passed immediately after the government of the United States decreed an embargo on raw materials and machinery destined for Cuba.

The administration of the 300 establishments that were nationalized was entrusted to the Department of Industrialization of INRA. Thereby, this department came into control of more than 50 per cent of the industrial production in the country. This proportion was increased by the expropriation of industries owned by Cubans living outside the country, and of those which had been seized on account of misappropriation of funds under the dictatorship of Batista, and by the acquisition of a number of small or medium sized industries.[11]

The accelerated rhythm that characterized the process of nationalization can be appreciated when we consider that state industries at the end of 1960 constituted more than 50 per cent of the total production of the country, and that in the second semester of 1961 this proportion had increased to no less than 75 per cent. At the present time 95 per cent of industrial production is from government-owned factories.

Table 8. Participation of the Private Sector in Industrial Production, 1961

1. Heavy Industries	Per cent
a. Power output and metallurgy	6.3
b. Heavy and extractive chemistry	0.1
2. Light Industries	
a. Foodstuffs and light chemistry	20.0
b. Mechanical, textiles and leather	32.6

Source: Ministry of Industry.

Participation of the private sector in industrial production in 1961 is shown in Table 8.

Although participation of the private sector in industrialization was limited, the number of industrial establishments belonging to this sector was high, as appears in the next table.

On the same date, January, 1962, there were 1,805 factories under public ownership, 479 of which were in basic industries and 1,326 in light industries.

The rapid progress of nationalization, added to the problems inherited from the former regime, presented the revolutionary government with many varied and complex tasks of an administrative, organizational, and politico-economic nature.

In the first place, the efforts of the revolutionary government were directed toward avoiding paralyzation of the nationalized industries, and then to maintaining—and in some cases raising—

Table 9. Number of Privately Owned Factories, January, 1962

Types of industries	
Wood	2,529
Automotive repair	2,091
Tobacco	1,078
Clothing	421
Manufacture of parts	389
Leather and derivatives	1,616
Total	8,124

Source: Ministry of Industry.

the level of production. Especially complex were the problems relating to the supply of raw materials and replacements, when the traditional sources of supply were closed off. The lack of technicians and administrators made the situation especially difficult.

In the second place, it became absolutely necessary to create an organism that could direct and administer the government-owned industries efficiently. In the third place, there arose the necessity of devising an economic policy that would widen the industrial base of the country, consolidate the objectives of the Revolution, and satisfy the increasing necessities of the population.

Finally, the nationalization of the means of industrial production defined the socialist character of the Revolution and accentuated the need for devising a new economic organization.[12]

The change brought about by the Revolution in the ownership of the means of industrial production necessitated substantial modifications of an organizational type. The promotional activities inherited from the former regime were taken over by the Ministry of Industry; companies of the same type were consolidated (*empresas consolidadas*); training of skilled labor, carried on up to that time on a limited basis, began to be practiced on a very large scale; systems of financing, distribution, and encouragement of labor acquired new forms. In short, a new industrial organization began to emerge.

Many of these changes were effected by following the example of other socialist countries; others took on a spontaneous character, and to a certain extent improvisation was characteristic of others. So it is that the organizational structure presented by Cuban economy today can in no way be considered as definitive. On the contrary, some of it is again in process of transformation, and the rest will be modified and perfected as the period of transition from capitalism to socialism accelerates, or not.

The Ministry of Industry was created in 1961 to "govern, direct, supervise, and carry out the policy of industrial development of the Nation and administer the industrial companies belonging to the State."[13] The new ministry straightway became one of the most important economic organisms in the country.

Only INRA and JUCEPLAN are as important in the field of production.

The importance that the revolutionary government attached to the Ministry of Industry can be measured by the fact that it was put in charge of Comandante Ernesto Guevara, who gave up the Presidency of the Banco Nacional to take charge of the Ministry.

The Ministry of Industry has a highly centralized organization which has undergone a number of changes recently. At first it functioned with four assistant secretaryships. At the present moment these have been changed into vice ministries, and the number increased to five. In August, 1962, some 240 people were working in the Ministry, and it was estimated that this number would be increased to more than 500 in 1963. These two facts show the increasing importance of this organization in the Cuban economy.

The new organization of the Ministry of Industry at the end of 1963 was headed by a Minister and five Vice-Ministers, concerned with basic industry, light industry, economy, industrial construction, and technical development.

The first two vice ministries have as their principal function that of directing, coordinating, and facilitating the activities of the consolidated industries, to collaborate with the Vice-Minister of Economy in drawing up industrial plans and seeing to the fulfillment of established goals. In short, these two vice ministries have as their duty the efficient administration of the consolidated industries over which they have charge.

The Vice-Minister of Economy has a responsibility that is essentially that of planning. He is supposed to draw up the industrial plan of the Ministry and oversee its execution; to prepare and distribute directives for the formation of annual plans and long-range plans in accordance with JUCEPLAN; to see that necessary reserves are established in the plans for supply; to set salary policies in accord with the general orientation of the government; to oversee the application of price policies; and rationalize the activities of the Ministry.

The duties of the Vice Ministry of Industrial Construction are to insure an increase in production, after determining the nature of the expansion in the particular factory, draw up a plan for investments and industrial projects, and control the construction of new industries.

The Vice Ministry of Technical Development is responsible for technological research for the evaluation of natural resources, for elaboration and control of the applications of norms, for the organization and direction of the scientific activities of the Ministry, for coordination in this field with other departments, and the training of a labor supply.

To carry out their functions the Vice Ministries of Economy, Industrialization, and Technical Development can count on different "desks." Thus, for example, the planning desk of the Vice Ministry of Economy coordinates partial plans drawn up by other desks, and controls their execution. The supply and delivery desk draws up the plans for supply; the work and wages desk does the same with regard to plans for work and wages.

In the Vice Ministry of Industrial Construction the investment desk draws up the plan for investments, has control of the factory in question, selects and determines the best alternatives for the investment of available funds, and examines the projects that are to be carried out. The projects desk draws up the projects, determines the location of the factories, evaluates technically the execution of projects, and, through the investment desk, requests any investigations in this field that it deems necessary. Finally, the projects desk executes the investment projects and delivers appropriate funds to the proper industrial branches.

Directly connected with the Ministry are various other offices and "desks," most of them of an administrative character. Likewise, there is a Consejo de Dirección (Directive Council), in which the vice ministers, directors, and other high functionaries of the Ministry participate, and which meets weekly with the minister to deal with the most urgent matters. This council constitutes the principal advisory board of the Ministry.

The Ministry of Industry operates through six provincial delegations charged with controlling the regional execution of the programs and with lending technical assistance to the factories of the consolidated enterprises.

iv

In July, 1961, the *empresas consolidadas* (consolidated enterprises) were formed. They constitute the basic nucleus of production in the industrial sector. All of the state companies with similar activities are grouped together for their operation and administration into these consolidated enterprises.

Before the creation of these consolidated enterprises all of the factories in the public sector were grouped into a single "consolidated industrial," which was under the Department of Industrialization of INRA. The consolidated enterprises thus represent an effort toward decentralization. Nevertheless, the organization of the consolidated enterprise responds in a general way to the centralized conception of the Ministry of Industry, and in its turn this organization is repeated in the factory concerned. Naturally, the difference lies in the importance and the form in which the functions are grouped. The factories are not subject to any department, but directly to the director, who is responsible for their operation to the director of the consolidated enterprise.

The director of the consolidated enterprise is assisted by various administrative offices and by an Administrative Council made up of the heads of departments and technicians. The enterprise has three basic departments: production, economy, and interchange.

The Department of Production supervises, coordinates, and facilitates production in the enterprises, it collaborates with the Technical Department in formulating the plan of production, it has to do with technical conditions making for greater efficiency, it controls the quality of raw materials and finished products, and it looks out for the proper maintenance of the machinery, equipment, and buildings.

The Economic Department develops planning functions. It directs the formation of the industrial plan of the enterprise, and has control of its execution, it prepares and distributes statistics of the enterprise by regions and by factories, it has charge of the statistics and the accounting of the enterprise, and it draws up the financial statements.

The Department of Interchange draws up the plan for the supply and delivery of products, it advises the enterprise in regard to transport and warehousing of raw materials and finished products, and it represents the enterprise judicially.

When this study was made, there were in Cuba 46 consolidated enterprises of an industrial type. Two of them were in mining and two were in electricity and gas; the rest belonged to the manufacturing sector. These enterprises were made up of more than 1,800 factories located throughout the country, and gave employment to 170,000 workers.

There are 19 enterprises in heavy industry and 27 in light industry. In the classification of basic industries the most important is, of course, that of sugar, which comprises a total of 188 industrial establishments, among them 161 sugar mills. Next in importance are the consolidated enterprises of electricity, nickel, petroleum, paper, cement, heavy chemistry. Among the light enterprises the most important are the manufacture of common textiles, leather goods, pharmaceutical products, flour, beer and malt, cigars.

Some of the enterprises, such as cement, ceramics, paper, beer and malt, paint, glass, nickel and petroleum, have only a few factories.[14] Others, like sugar and electricity, textiles, leather goods, wood, and flour, have many.[15]

When the number of units justifies it, the enterprise can establish provincial delegates, after approval by the Ministry of Industry. These coordinate their efforts with those of the other provincial delegations of the industry.

Table 10. Employment in Consolidated Enterprises of the Ministry of Industry

Industrial sectors	1961	1962
	(In thousands of persons)	
Extractive Industries	6.6	6.3
Petroleum	1.5	1.9
Other, mining	5.1	4.4
Manufacturing Industries	137.7	154.2
Traditional industries	106.9	115.7
Intermediate industrial goods	25.6	29.5
Mechanical industries	5.2	9.0
Electricity and Gas	6.5	9.1
Totals	150.8	169.6

Source: Appendix, Part III, Table 4.

Table 11. Employment by Type in Consolidated Enterprises under the Ministry of Industry

	1961	1962
	(In thousands of persons)	
Basic Industries	88.8	93.3
Workmen	70.1	72.3
Technicians	4.5	5.7
Salaried Personnel	14.2	15.3
Light industries	61.9	76.3
Workmen	49.9	65.8
Technicians	2.2	2.9
Salaried Personnel	7.8	7.5
Total Enterprises	150.7	169.5
Workmen	122.0	138.1
Technicians	6.7	8.6
Salaried Personnel	22.0	22.8

Source: See Appendix, Part III, Table 4.

Information furnished by the Ministry indicates that on March 31, 1962, the fixed assets of the enterprises amounted to nearly 800 million pesos, and the circulating assets to 1,100 million. Of the fixed assets 69 per cent was in machinery, equipment, and installations, 25 per cent in buildings, 2 per cent in furniture and office equipment, 3 per cent in land, and 1 per cent in other assets. (See Appendix, Part III, Table 3.)

The consolidated enterprises are regulated by a special financial mechanism. When the Department of Industrialization of INRA took charge of the nationalized enterprises, it found that some of them had adequate financial resources. Others were in a difficult financial situation, and many were completely lacking in resources. Faced with this situation, a common fund was established called the "centralized fund," in which all the enterprises deposited the proceeds from the sale of their products, receiving through a budget the resources necessary for their operations. These operations were handled entirely through bank accounts.

When the Department of Industrialization of INRA was replaced by the Ministry of Industry, a change took place in the financial mechanism of the consolidated enterprises. They had to deposit their proceeds in the "General State Fund" through an account in the Banco Nacional.

On the other hand, the enterprise makes up its annual budget of operations and, in accordance with this, is assigned the funds necessary to attain the goals of production set forth in the plans, and to make any investments needed for expansion. These funds are channeled through two accounts in the Banco Nacional: one for operations and the other for investments, with no funds transferable from one account to another. In other words, the financial mechanism prevents the holding or accumulating of funds on the part of the enterprises and permits a planned assignment of profits through the general funds of the state.

The income of the enterprises is determined by the value of their production. It is in turn determined by the unit prices established in the planning. An outstanding feature of the financial administration of the enterprises is that they are not authorized to fix the wholesale prices of their products. This is the prerogative of the government, or of special boards. The prices of all goods are generally fixed for periods of five years.

The enterprises, on disposing of their own funds, liquidate their obligations by means of checks against the Banco Nacional in accordance with the availability of credits previously approved for the whole period that has been planned. The availability of credit is authorized every three months by the Ministry of the Treasury. The enterprises are allowed to request modifications in the three months' distribution, as long as these do not change the total amount that has been approved and provided that the reasons for the modification are sound.

The balances that are not expended at the end of each trimester can be spent during the rest of the year. In case of the necessity for additional funds for good and sufficient reasons, the enterprises can obtain these funds by petitioning the Ministry of Industry and obtaining its approval.

v

The techniques of central planning which are being applied in Cuba are similar to those developed by other socialist countries, and are based upon the fixing of itemized balances of materials, available labor supply, and finances. The plans adopted in the early years were practically the same as those developed in Czechoslovakia, though with appropriate modifications.

The Industrial Plan includes the following tentative plans:

1) The Production Plan—includes the complete program of production of the consolidated enterprises belonging to the Ministry of Industry, indicating what products are to be turned out and within what period of time.

2) Plan of Supply—here are consigned all the raw materials and materials necessary for the fulfillment of the goals established in the production plan.

3) Plan for Labor and Wages—fixes the number of workers necessary for the fulfillment of the production task, as well as the wages the workmen are to receive. It fixes the increase in productivity in relation to the previous year.

4) Expense Plan—comprises all the costs necessary for the fulfillment of the production task.

5) Finance Plan—specifies the financial measures necessary to attain the production goals.

6) Investment Plan—sets forth what investments are necessary to renew and extend the industrial plants that have already been installed and determine what new plants need to be constructed within a specified period of time, this in accordance with the development of the production that has been planned.

In the elaboration of the industrial plans, three levels, or phases, may be pointed out: 1) the preparation of politico-economic directives; 2) the preparation of control estimates, or specified goals; and 3) the elaboration of the plan itself in all its complex details, based upon the control estimates.

The process of drawing up the plan involves a two-way action —discussions from the top executives down and from the lower echelons up.

The first phase is developed at the level of the Council of Ministers, which makes the fundamental decisions about what direction and at what rate the economy will go in its first years. The politico-economic directives, which may be very general, take a more concrete form in regard to figures and indexes at the level of JUCEPLAN. The goals or directives are established by JUCEPLAN in greater or less detail, depending upon whether it is a question of "basic," "centralized," or "non-centralized" products.

Basic products are those that have a special bearing on the economy in general, such as sugar, cement, minerals, electricity, different types of machinery, etc. The considerations that determine the amount of production are the province of a higher level than the ministries. JUCEPLAN spells out for the basic products the supply, labor force, financial resources, and investments necessary for the fulfillment of the production goals. The number of basic products has, of course, to be limited.

The centralized products are those that are planned by the Ministry of Industry. The non-centralized products are those planned out by the consolidated enterprises. The Ministry, as well as the enterprises, carries out the planning within the framework fixed by JUCEPLAN for each industrial branch, in accord with a proportional development in the national economy.

The directive estimates of JUCEPLAN are handed on to the Planning Division of the Vice Ministry of Economy, which works out the production plan. This contains in detail the proportions of the basic and centralized products, as well as the non-centralized products and their production value.

The Supply and Delivery Section plans the delivery of raw materials, machinery, and other articles needed for the fulfillment of the production plan and their delivery to the proper parties. The Labor and Wages Section analyzes the requirements of labor and its productivity, and works out a labor and salary plan. The Cost and Price Section draws up the plan for costs and prices. And finally, the Section on Investments of the Vice Ministry of Industrial Construction prepares the Investment Plan. The Finance Section studies financial needs.

Once the partial plans are drawn up by the above-mentioned sections, they are further analyzed and divided up according to the consolidated enterprises by the Planning Section. The plans are then delivered to the Vice Ministries of Basic and Light Industry to be distributed among the respective consolidated enterprises.

The figures are sent to the enterprises, and are discussed in the consolidated enterprises, in the factories, and in the production sectors. When this process is finished, the enterprise prepares a preliminary budget, pointing out modifications in the goals previously received. This proposal is studied in the Ministry, and then definite goals are sent to the enterprises. From these goals the production units draw up their operational plan for the next period. This operational plan is submitted to the judgment of the Ministry, which prepares a digest for all the enterprises under its supervision. This is transmitted to JUCEPLAN, where it is reconciled with the other economic sectors. JUCEPLAN then submits the National Economic Plan to the revolutionary government for its final approval. Once these requirements are complied with, the plan becomes a law of the Republic, and from that moment all the production force of the country is set in motion to fulfill the goals which have been set.

Insufficient statistics, a phenomenon common to Latin American countries, constituted one of the principal stumbling blocks in the elaboration of the first industrial plans in Cuba. Estimates for the 1962 Plan were based upon incomplete research. Furthermore, consultation at the lower levels was not fully effected. The directors attributed these errors to the fact that the goals established for several industries were too high.

The preparation of statistics at the factory level, the preparation of manuals of "balances," and the creation of economic departments in the consolidated enterprises, together with the experience that has been acquired, make it fairly clear that when the next programs are drawn up, a great deal of information will be available that will facilitate the task of planning.

Around the month of September, 1962, the 1962 Plan had been prepared and preliminary estimates drawn up for the Four Year Plan 1962-65. We were assured that the process would be continued in the same way in the future, and that the plan would be adjusted annually. Similarly, in some sectors plans would be drawn up for longer periods, say, for fifteen or twenty years. At the time when our report was drawn up, the 1963 Plan had not been finished, and neither had the 1963-65 Plan.

The reason for selecting 1965 as the final date for these plans was that other socialist countries have plans terminating in that year. The Cuban planning was conceived within the context of an international division of labor among the countries belonging to the socialist bloc. Previous to this, contacts had been made with the group charged with coordinated planning for the European socialist countries, namely, COMECON (the Council for Mutual Economic Assistance).

vi

In addition to the problems of an organizational and politico-economic type mentioned above, the directors of the Cuban economy were faced with related problems stemming from industrial development. Among them the most important were the training of a labor force, the creating of mechanisms for financing, the devising of systems of incentives, and necessary technological changes.

The preparation of plans for the industrialization of Cuba brought out in its full significance the scarcity of skilled labor, and this fact constituted one of the principal bottlenecks in the development process. This situation was especially aggravated by the considerable number of professional men and technicians who had left the country, a serious development owing in part to underestimating the value of technicians. Many of them had been harassed when they had been suspected of being counterrevolutionaries. This mistake was finally recognized by those directing the Revolution, and attempts have been made to rectify it.

The requirements of specialized labor for industrialization have forced the adoption of certain extraordinary measures that exceed the traditional range of the Ministry of Education. The Ministry of Industry has had to provide intensive and extensive training for industrial workers. Of the several programs, the following are the most important:

Mínimo Técnico training. This process of massive instruction was initiated in the second trimester of 1962. In August of that year approximately 70,000 industrial workers participated in it, that is, 35 per cent of the total number of workmen enrolled in the industries. Briefly, this program consists of giving the workmen sufficient knowledge to enable them to handle the machinery and to produce most efficiently and at the lowest cost.

The programs are both practical and theoretical, and their length depends on the specialty involved. They may extend from one to six months. The practical part is carried out in the factories themselves during working hours, when groups of workmen receive from an instructor the norms and procedures of their particular specialty. The immediate objective is to have the workmen learn correct procedures and an intelligent use of the equipment, tools, and materials. The theoretical courses are given once or twice a week after working hours. They may take from 50 to 200 hours, depending upon the nature of the specialty.

The instructors in the practical courses are generally the older, most experienced workmen. The theoretical courses are given by technicians in the enterprise, professors from the technical schools, and the more advanced students in the university.

After finishing the *Mínimo Técnico* training courses, the students are required to take a proficiency examination. Those approved by technical commissions receive an appropriate grade that accredits them for their particular specialty. The minimum courses are the responsibility of the consolidated enterprises. The teaching is planned and controlled by the Training Department of the Ministry of Industry.

Because of the brief period that this program of instruction has been in effect, it is premature to judge its results. Nevertheless, on our visits to the factories we could see that the principal drawback was the lack of teachers and instructors. In some of the factories we could see that the instruction was being carried out in a systematic and efficient manner; in others, it was not. In setting up this program, its directors profited from the experience of the Soviet Union and other socialist countries that had been faced with problems involving the rapid training of workmen in an accelerated program of industrialization.

Estimates furnished us by the Ministry of Industry indicate that at the end of 1963 probably almost all the workmen will have finished their *Mínimo Técnico* training. There was general satisfaction at the results obtained thus far, considering of course that there were not enough teachers.

People's Schools. In its industrial plans the Ministry of Industry contemplates the mechanization of handicrafts such as the manufacture of shoes and clothes. In this way the costs of production will be considerably reduced, though the measure would result in unemployment for a considerable number of workmen. To solve this problem, "people's schools" were created in which displaced workmen can learn a new job. During the period of instruction, which has been set at about eighteen months, the workman will continue to receive the wages he made in his previous occupation. This new type of instruction was initiated in September, 1962, in 30 schools distributed through the island. It is estimated that about 8,000 workmen matriculated, principally shoemakers.

Other Training Courses. There are also a number of other special courses conducted by the Ministry of Industry. For example, for the third semester of 1962 a course in mechanics was planned for 2,000 workmen in the sugar mills. In other industries of lesser importance it is estimated that some 600 workmen will be enrolled.

Courses for Specialists. Along with the training of workmen, the Ministry of Industry has taken up the preparation of experts in other specialties. The most important of these is the School for Administrators which is preparing administrators technically and politically on the factory level. In 1962 there were 300 full-time students in this school. These were people who had distinguished themselves in factories and who had been selected for administrators. During their period of study they receive their salaries, with instruction and maintenance free. In these schools the students receive a general knowledge of the organization of the enterprises, techniques of production, and other general information, as well as political sciences.[16]

Finally, the Ministry of Industry has sent about 600 workmen to socialist countries, notably to the Soviet Union, to take certain specialized courses.

As can be seen, the work which is being carried out by the Ministry of Industry in the training of labor is most extensive. New programs will undoubtedly be arranged soon, as requirements demand. The Ministry of Industry assured us that in the future the greater part of these courses would probably be transferred to the Ministry of Education. The intervention of the Ministry of Industry in this field of endeavor was owing to the great necessity of a wholesale preparation for industrial workers in a short period of time.

According to the customary procedure of the Ministry of Education, technicians are also being prepared by it for industry.

There are 14 technical schools and 5 maritime schools under its supervision, with a total registration of 8,400 students.

Furthermore, the university is preparing industrial engineers, chemists, and other specialists. According to the estimates of the university, there were 2,500 of these professionals in 1961. The requirements for 1970 call for some 25,000 engineers and technicians.[17]

vii

The principal sources of financing industrial development before the Revolution were undistributed profits, loans from foreign firms, credits extended by national institutions of development, and investments of foreign capital. The National Treasury is now the only source of financing, except for loans for special programs advanced by the socialist countries.[18] Any profits or surplus go to the National Treasury to be distributed as needed in the economy of the country.

The budget of the state constitutes the fundamental financial plan of the nation, and includes all branches of its economy. In it the state concentrates its net income, which it employs in economic development, financing the social and cultural necessities of the country, and the expenses of administration and defense. In this way the budget is, in effect, an instrument of redistribution of the financial resources of the country.

The most important part of the country's fiscal income comes from the deposits of income made by the state enterprises—agricultural, industrial, commercial, and others—which turn over the total amount of their surplus. In this way the administrative process of the collection of taxes, which existed in the former regime, is eliminated.

Other income for the budget comes from taxes imposed upon the private sector, or direct taxes on goods. The principal items provided for in the budget are operating expenses and investments in state enterprises. After these come expenses of the administrative offices and those of education, culture, and defense. Reserves are set aside for unforeseen expenses.

The total amount of investment required for the development of the industrial plans of Cuba for the period from 1962 through 1965 is 909,000,000 pesos. This represents an average of around

$230,000,000 annually. For a country like Cuba, this amount is considerable. The greater part of these investments are for imported capital goods.

To finance and carry out its ambitious plans for industrialization, Cuba has resorted to foreign aid on a large scale. Credits for moderate and long periods have been extended by a great majority of the socialist countries. These credits cover the delivery of equipment and machinery, and technical assistance.

The foreign aid which Cuba is receiving differs in many respects from what it received in the past. In the first place, the extent of credit granted specifically for programs of industrial development exceeds anything previously recorded. According to official and other sources it amounts to $357,000,000, as can be seen in Table 12.

In the second place, the conditions of payment, interest, and amortization are different from what is usually the case in the capitalist world. The rate of interest is set at 2.5 per cent annually, except for a credit of $60,000,000, in United States currency, from the People's Republic of China, interest free. Any interest, when it is charged, is reckoned from the date of delivery of the industrial plants, machinery, or equipment, or the beginning of the technical assistance. The length of time for amortizing these credits is ten years, except for one case of technical assistance where the limit is five years. Another innovation is that Cuba can amortize the credits extended by the Soviet Union and by China with products from the installations financed by the foreign aid.

In the third place, these credits were granted by almost all the countries which belong to the socialist world. As is natural, the Soviet Union has done most in granting credits—$200,000,000. China comes next, with $60,000,000,[19] Czechoslovakia, with $40,-000,000, and the other socialist countries with lesser amounts.

The process of nationalization of the means of production brought with it a profound change in the circumstances characteristic of production. Profit motive, the basis of economic development in the previous regime, was replaced by emulation; labor unions lost their former meaning; and systems of remuneration and social security underwent profound changes. It is difficult to appreciate fully the complex changes brought about by

Table 12. Credits Extended to Cuba by the Socialist Countries

Countries	Credits Millions $ US	Annual Interest %	Use	Years for amortization
East Germany	10	2.5	Industrial plants, shops, and varied equipment	10
Bulgaria	5	2.5	Industrial plants, refrigerating plants, hydraulic installations	10
Czechoslovakia	40	2.5	Machinery and industrial equipment, electric plants, automotive industries	10
China	60	0.0	Industrial plants and equipment, machinery and tools	10
Hungary	15	2.5	Industrial plants, machinery and equipment, tools	10
Poland	12	2.5	Industrial plants and equipment, shipyard	8
Rumania	15	2.5	Machinery, industrial plants, and equipment, electric installations	
U.S.S.R.	100	2.5	Petroleum refineries, iron and steel plants, electrical installations, geological surveys, services	From 1966 on
U.S.S.R.	100	2.5	Technical and scientific assistance in the nickel and cobalt industries, with equipment, instruments, machinery	12
Total	357			5

Source: *Bohemia* (August 17, 1962).

the Revolution in this field. Nevertheless, an analysis of the industrial development of Cuba would be incomplete if it did not include, even in a fragmentary manner, some of these changes.

Emulation. Just as profit constitutes the principal incentive in the capitalist type of economy, so emulation is the basis for an improvement in production in the socialist type of economy. Emulation springs from the social character of the work and from collective ownership of the means of production.

In general, emulation may take two forms, individual and collective. The first can be defined as "the opportunity each worker has, with his efforts and constant labor, in fraternal competition with other workers, to attain the most distinguished honors and titles available to a workman."[20] The second is "in fraternal competition between one group of workers (section, department, shift, factory, etc.) with another group and in which the honors are attained collectively."[21]

Emulation is not generated spontaneously. It is directed, organized, and stimulated by labor and state organizations.

The results of individual and collective emulation extend over four levels: the unit or work center, the consolidated enterprise, the ministry or corresponding superior organization, and on the national scale. A system of rewards and punishments forms a part of the emulation system. The rewards can be moral or material. The moral awards take the form of publicly honoring the winners in an emulation campaign, either through the press, or in a public ceremony in which medals, diplomas, flags, or pennants are bestowed. The material awards consist of sums in cash, vacations for the worker and his family, scholarships, or travel abroad. Just as publicity is given to the most efficient operatives, similarly attention is drawn to those who commit faults or who fail to fulfill their quotas. Reductions in pay are also contemplated for tardiness or absences.[22]

A complicated system of tables was devised to determine the individual or the collective winner in the emulation campaigns, but this did not work out as well as was expected. At the end of 1962 the Ministry of Labor was studying a new scheme of simple indexes that would permit an evaluation of different levels of work.

Labor organization. Before the Revolution there were around 2,000 local, municipal, or industrial unions in Cuba. The "Law of Syndical Reconstruction" brought about a series of changes in these labor organizations.

At the present time there are only 25 industrial unions, and these are integrated in the Central Syndicate of Workers of Revolutionary Cuba (CTCR). The membership runs to about 1.4 million persons,[23] or about 60 per cent of all the workers in the country.

The largest of the national unions is the sugar union, which has a membership of 316,000 workers. Next in importance are the agricultural union, with 140,000 members,[24] the construction union, tobacco union, and the commercial union. These each have more than 100,000 members. The smallest are the air transport union, with 2,100 members, and the telephone union, with 6,600 members.

The national unions, in their turn, are organized into locals (*secciones sindicales*), which are established in the different work centers.

The new law of syndical reorganization, which took effect at the beginning of 1962, established the principle of voluntary affiliation in the unions, the elimination of compulsory dues, and provision for the removal of the officers in case they do not fulfill their duties, or violate decisions or agreements made by the union assemblies.

The collective agreements likewise took on a different character, both in content and in form. Under the former regime collective agreements represented a clash of interests between the workmen and the employers, a situation which often gave rise to violence. Under the new system, as the Cuban officials told us, the state administrators and the unions "have the same interests and the same objectives." They added that the collective contracts "have been converted into a very important measure, designed to guarantee the fulfillment and the surpassing of the production plans and an increase in productivity."

In the collective contracts the political and economic tasks which the revolutionary government has set for each branch of the national economy are set forth. Then comes the obligations of the enterprise and the union in regard to the fulfillment and the surpassing of the state plan of production, development of the plan for emulation, the norms of work, hours, and quality of the product. In these contracts the salaries and wages are fixed in accordance with the qualifications of the workers. Other technical and administrative details, with rules for vacations, are included.

The collective agreement is drawn up with the officers of the enterprise and the national union participating. Any eventual differences between these parties are settled by the Ministry of Labor, the CTCR, and the union that is involved.

After the collective agreement has been drawn up, it is discussed in a general assembly of the workers in each unit of production. Any decisions or suggestions are then passed on to the Ministry of Labor for consideration and final approval. In accordance with the planning system of the economy, the duration of the agreements is fixed at one year.

An important prerogative exercised by the unions is the distribution of housing, in accordance with a priority rating approved by the workmen themselves in full assembly. Similarly, the union has charge of the Social Circles and the Children's Circles. It also arranges for sports and cultural activities in the work centers.

Other significant provisions:

1) *Advisory Technical Councils*[25]—were to function on a consolidated enterprise level, and its members were chosen by the director of the enterprise from among the workers and technicians. Two years after their establishment the membership was modified "because their practical functioning turned out to be inoperative."[26] According to the new regulations these technical advisory councils, whose purpose is to advise in the tasks of production, will function on the factory level, and the membership will consist of one delegate for each section or department into which the unit of production is divided. They are to be elected in the assembly for a period of one year.

2) *Grievance Procedures*[27]—grievance commissions are set up in the working units that have ten or more members. When there are fewer than ten, the complaints are made directly to the appropriate delegation of the Ministry of Labor. The membership of the commissions consists of two representatives from the

workers, one regular and one alternate; two from the enterprise; and one from the Ministry of Labor, who presides over the meetings. When centers of more than 25 persons are concerned, the number of representatives is doubled. The commission hears and settles individual and collective differences, whether they be of an economic or judicial nature, as they are presented by the workmen to the secretary of the commission. The sessions are public, and the decisions are made within five working days, according to a majority vote. If the opposing parties agree to the decision, the case is settled. If not, an appeal can be made to a committee of the Ministry of Labor, which may render a new decision in the light of new evidence. A final appeal may be made to the Ministry of Labor.

3) *Evaluation Centers*—are boards designed to check the qualifications of unemployed workmen and assign them to productive labor in accordance with their ability.

4) *Wage Policies and Social Security*—as was pointed out in Chapter I, a study of a pay scale for all the workers in the country was initiated in 1962. We were informed by the government officials that the new scale would have two or three categories, depending upon the type of work—light or heavy—and modifications within these scales would be established according to the specialty. They added that they wanted to put an end to the anarchy of the wage system inherited from the previous regime and apply the socialist principle of remuneration "from each man according to his capacity, and to each man according to his work." The scale under discussion would also try to reduce the differences which still existed between the different occupations.

In any case, one of the most equalitarian systems of remuneration in the world is now in effect in Cuba. The minimum wage has been set at 65 pesos a month and, according to a labor census conducted in 1960, only 10,000 persons receive more than 500 pesos a month.

In regard to the systems of social security, profound changes were announced in a measure published in September, 1962. This measure recasts and modifies the numerous laws relating to social security that had existed previously. The main items follow:

1) The establishment of a single system of social security to cover all workers, including agricultural workers and their families.

2) Provision for services, in kind and in money. The first includes medical and dental assistance, hospitalization, and rehabilitation. Assistance in kind consists of furnishing medicines, food, artificial limbs, and orthopedics. Monetary services include aid in maternity cases, retirement owing to disability or old age, life insurance, and help toward funeral expenses.

3) Life insurance benefits are to be not less than 40 pesos a month, nor more than 250, and maternity, sickness, and accident benefits from two pesos to 9.61 pesos daily.

4) For retirement a rating sheet had been established which stipulates that a person with 25 years of service shall receive a pension equal to 50 per cent of his salary, this amount to be increased by 1 per cent for each additional year of service, depending on the kind of work in which the worker has been engaged. The age of retirement is fifty-five for men and fifty for women with 25 years of service. With less than 25 years of service the age of retirement in the case of men is sixty-five, and women at sixty.

5) To enjoy the benefits of social security, it is necessary for the worker to have an identity card, upon which his labor record has been recorded.[28]

viii

The rapid institutional changes in the economic structure in general and the industrial area in particular, brought about by the Revolution, make any analysis of the results difficult. Furthermore, the statistics that are available are sometimes incomplete and sometimes contradictory. It is, then, risky to try to give any definite judgment of the experience of the Revolution in the industrial field.

As for the consumption of industrial products, the figures are generally limited to its qualitative aspects, and on the side of supply it is only possible to secure fairly reliable figures beginning with 1961, when the state controlled most of the industries of the country. Similarly, there are only partial statistics for the importation of manufactured goods.

The tasks of production and labor supply with which the Revolution was faced in the industrial area were not only to maintain or raise the rhythm of production which was characteristic of the old regime, but also to create a new structure of organization and production, and give the Cuban economy a solid base, capable of satisfying the increasing needs of the population. Similarly, the Revolution found itself faced with the necessity of changing the technical norms of production at a time when it was unable to have access to the equipment and raw materials that formerly were furnished by the western world.

All this represents a task of great and long-range proportions. The problems of organization and supply, together with the task of creating a system of highly centralized planning, had the highest priority. All these problems had intrinsic features of great complexity and of difficult solution. Many of these have not yet been solved. In the case of others, mistakes of great import were committed, the rectification of which was made at great social cost.

To understand the process of the Cuban industrial development, it is indispensable not to lose sight of the magnitude of the change brought about by the Revolution and the international tension that accompanied it. It is also necessary to keep in mind that in industrial production, especially along manufacturing lines, important qualitative changes have taken place. These, in many sectors, distort any possible comparison with the period before the Revolution.

We can distinguish two well-defined stages in the experience of the first four years. The first covers the years 1959 and 1960, during which time industrial development was carried out by employing existing instruments of the previous regime. The second stage brought with it nationalization measures and was characterized by a profound change in the production set-up and by efforts made at all levels to adjust the industrial sector to these changes. One can say that this stage is still in development and will continue so for several years more.

The domestic demand for manufactured goods before the Revolution reached high levels, owing to a per capita income of $500 a year, higher than that of the majority of the other Latin American countries. Only Venezuela had a higher per capita income. Nevertheless, the demand per family could have been greater if there had been a better distribution of income, if the rate of unemployment had not been so high, and if masses of country people had not been tied to a subsistence economy.

One of the typical characteristics of the Revolution was the extensive redistribution of the national income. As the interchange between the country and the city improved, there occurred a sudden rise in the income of the country people (*campesinos*), and this generally meant an increase in the demand for manufactured goods. Again, although it is not possible to establish reliable figures in the reduction of unemployment, there is no doubt that this occurred. It is shown by an increase in the scale of collective farming, by new construction, by additions to the rebel army, and by the creation of new jobs in industry. To these factors must be added the establishment of a great many scholarships[29] and extensive plans for education, both of which tended to lighten the burden of unemployment. In confirmation of this fact is the recruitment of volunteers for the harvesting of the sugar and the coffee crops. A lowering of rents and in the prices of certain public services also brought about an increase in the demand for manufactured goods. Finally, the establishment of a minimum wage for all workers and increases in the salaries of some groups that were underpaid in relation to others[30] resulted in additional demand for manufactured goods.

The combined effect of these factors brought about a violent increase in the demand for manufactured articles of popular consumption. However, there occurred a reduction in the demand for manufactured goods of a luxury type, because of a decline in incomes of bond holders, contractors, and top salaried officials. (This reduction, however, was really very slight in comparison with the increase caused by the redistribution of income.) In other words, a notable change in consumer structure occurred.

Before the Revolution, the supply of manufactured goods came by way of imports, chiefly from the United States. Only a relatively small part was produced by national industry.

In consequence of the violent increase in demand, those directing the Revolution were faced with two alternatives: to reduce consumption or increase the supply of manufactured goods. They adopted the second alternative. This meant either an acceleration of national production or stepping up imports, which, in its turn, would have limited the acquisition of capital goods.

It was finally decided to attempt an accelerated program of industrialization, utilizing foreign aid, with the hope that in the course of eight or ten years the country would be in a position to supply the greater part of its needs for imported goods, and to export enough products to increase and diversify its sources of income.

Accelerated industrialization presupposes great efforts and sacrifices and the solving of serious problems of organization. In effect it means setting up an efficient organization in each sector and at each level, having labor and technicians available in sufficient numbers and with adequate training, the training of capable administrators, and an economic policy suited to the new situation.

The greater part of Cuba's industrial equipment and machinery came, as we have seen, from the United States. Consequently, the Cuban economy depended on the same source for replacements. This dependence was accentuated by the proximity of supply. Orders were placed by telephone, and consequently large stocks of replacements were not necessary, as was the case with other Latin American countries. A somewhat similar situation prevailed in the case of the supply of raw materials and semi-finished products, and to a lesser degree finished products.

During the years 1959 and 1960, the supply came in with a certain degree of regularity and no great problems arose. When relations with the United States and other countries were broken, the situation became critical, and in many cases Cuban industries were paralyzed.

A typical example of this sort of difficulty is to be seen in the case of rayon factories. These work with imported pulp and their machines need highly specialized replacements. When the supply of pulp and replacements from the United States came to an end, the rayon factories had to close and remain closed for some time. Finally, a supply of pulp was secured from a Canadian firm,[31] but the problem of replacements still persisted. This made it necessary to dismantle some of the machines in order to secure parts for others. We saw this situation in some of the plants we visited.

Since the production of tires and tubes was the concern of four United States firms (General, U.S. Tire and Rubber, Goodrich, and Firestone), operations in this field were paralyzed when relations were broken. The necessity of standardizing the formulas of these four factories created serious technical problems. The production of nickel concentrate was likewise paralyzed. Finally, Cuba turned to the technical assistance of the Soviet Union, but the trouble was that this involved a different process from that used by the United States firms. After some months of study this problem was solved and the work was not only resumed but, according to reports of Soviet experts, the largest nickel plant in the world will be constructed, with an annual capacity of 70,000 tons.

Other problems came up on account of this change in the source of supply. For example, the adoption of the metric system, used in the Soviet countries, occasioned difficulty in the placing of orders. To these difficulties was added the different terminology applied to the products.

In some cases the lack of replacements was solved when the Cuban workmen made these parts themselves. The results, however, were not always satisfactory. The rigid industrial norms employed in the manufacture of these replacements were not always followed and consequently some of the machines were injured. We were able to observe that in some factories there were idle machines, especially machine tools, on account of a lack of replacements. A foreman in one of the factories told us that in other plants, instead of repairing the machinery bought from the United States, there had been a tendency to order machinery of European origin (from Czechoslovakia, Russia, or East Germany principally). If this practice becomes common, it will mean a real diminution in the fixed capital of industry. To the above difficulties we must add that it seemed to us that equipment and machinery were not receiving proper maintenance.

This entire situation has been frankly recognized by the Cuban authorities,[32] and measures are being taken to remedy it.

What has been the effect of these difficulties upon production? Information on this point is deficient, and the indexes of production are computed at current prices and not at a constant valuation. This makes analysis difficult.

Some sources indicate an increase of 17 per cent and 25 per cent in industrial production in the years 1959 and 1960 respectively.[33] Other information indicates a rate of 8 per cent in the first triennium of the Revolution (1959-61), and a similar rate for 1962.

In any case, it seems clear that there has been an increase in industrial production, although not to the extent hoped for in official circles. This increase seems possible, if one takes into account that in most of the industrial sectors there were formerly wide margins of "idle" capacity whereas new installations have been now put in operation (and the sugar production in 1961 reached one of the highest levels in recent years).

If the volumes of production which appear in the Appendix, Part III, Tables 1 and 6, are compared, the following indicators are obtained:

The following table shows that production of intermediate and mining products has increased significantly, but consumer goods, except for cigarettes, have decreased.

The goals for the 1962 Plan established a total increase in production of 10 per cent over that obtained in 1961, implying 20 per cent for the public sector, while in the private sector a reduction of 50 per cent was contemplated.

Table 13. Indexes of Production for Some Industrial Products (Base: 1957 = 100)

	1958[a]	1962[b]
Sugar	101.2	84.9
Beer	95.4	69.9
Cigarettes	104.0	148.9
Textiles and rayon fiber	60.0	51.9
Sulphuric acid	—	518.8
Refined petroleum	131.9	181.7
Cement	108.3	133.6
Electric power	108.1	166.9
Copper concentrate	—	142.3
Nickel and cobalt	—	165.0

a. *Statistical Yearbook*, United Nations.
b. Ministry of Industry, September, 1962.

Table 14. Value of Gross Industrial Production, 1962
(In millions of pesos, at factory prices)

Industries	Plan	Estimated
Power output	248.7	259.1
Metallurgic	87.9	67.4
Heavy chemistry	542.8	509.4
Extractive industries	93.3	79.2
Foodstuffs	279.7	271.7
Light chemistry	199.7	149.3
Light machinery	85.8	98.2
Textiles, leather	270.5	202.6
Totals	1,807.9	1,636.9[a]

a. The statistics refer to the consolidated industries controlled by the Ministry of Industry and do not include new plants that began production in 1962, in accordance with the 1962-65 Plan.

Source: Ministry of Industry. (Provisional estimates made in August, 1962.)

In regard to the industrial production in the public sector for 1962, one can say that, based upon the facts and figures furnished us by the Ministry of Industry, the results were expected to be 7.2 per cent below the goals fixed.

From Table 14 it is evident that in the power industry and in light mechanical industry it was expected to attain an advance of 4.2 per cent and 14.7 per cent respectively over the levels that had been fixed, while in the rest of the branches the results would be below them, especially in metallurgy (−23.2 per cent), light chemistry (−25 per cent), and textiles and leather goods.

The Ministry of Industry also furnished us with an estimate of the physical production for 1962 for a variety of products, which is summarized in the Appendix, Part III, Table 6. According to this source, the goals would be exceeded in only four lines: refined sugar, wheat flour, fuel oil, and gas oil. In four others the goals would be reached. These are beer, cigarettes, superphosphates, and detergents. In the rest it would not be possible to attain the goals. These estimates reflect with the value of production registered for the first half of 1962 for industries in the consolidated enterprises, as is indicated in the Appendix, Part III, Table 7.

In short, one can say that in 1962 there was an increase of around 7 per cent for the total of the industrial sector, and approximately 12 per cent for the public sector. If these increases did in fact occur, they seem relatively rapid in view of the enormous difficulties which industry had to face in the supply of raw materials and replacements. Nevertheless, both rates of increase were less than the goals set by the Cuban authorities.

According to figures cited in the first part of the present study, employment in the industrial and mining sector between 1958 and 1962 increased from 366,000 persons to 473,000, or 29 per cent. In other words 107,000 new jobs were created in the period mentioned. This represented an average of 26,750 a year.

On the other hand, if we consider that, in 1953, 337,000 persons were employed in these same sectors, in the period 1953-58 only 39,000 new jobs had been created, or some 8,000 a year.

As compared with the earlier period, employment has increased significantly, but it is not possible to establish how much of this increase corresponds to genuine employment. Part of the employment figures registered for 1961 and 1962 corresponds to the opening up of 30 new plants, principally in the sectors of foodstuffs, machines, mining, textiles, and chemicals.[34] Another part is owing to additions to existing plants, and finally, an indeterminate proportion probably owing to an increase in disguised employment.

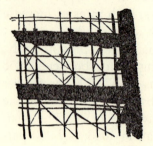

CHAPTER X

Industrial

Perspectives

i

In the first chapter of this part, the principal characteristics of Cuban industrial development before the Revolution were set forth, then followed a sketch of the institutional changes which occurred in industry, and of the new organization existing in this field, pointing out the principal problems encountered in this economic sector. The purpose of this chapter is to analyze the short-range and the long-range prospects of development.

1) *The first efforts at planning.* The preliminary efforts at planning on the part of the revolutionary government were carried out by a mission of experts sent to Cuba in 1959 by the United Nations and ECLA (The Economic Commission for Latin America). Presided over by a Mexican economist and made up of experts of several nationalities,[1] the commission carried out a number of projects that were later utilized in the economic planning.

During the year 1960, tentative bases for a Five Year Plan were established, and these served to draw up the plan for 1962, and later the 1962-65 Plan. In the first Five Year Plan a rate of increase for industry of 19.5 per cent yearly was established for 1961-65.

A report drawn up by Professor M. Kalecki dealing with the first Five Year Plan[2] stated that the high rates that had been fixed could possibly be attained, and the reasons given were: the extensive possibilities of agriculture, the "idle" capacity of present industry, and favorable conditions in the construction industry. This rate of growth was conditional upon a considerable increase in sugar exports, the adoption of various measures in the industrial field, among them "systematic recruiting" of foreign technicians. In his opinion, the problems could not be solved just with programs of education and training.

The Five Year Plan contemplated an investment of 1,930 million in fixed capital, besides a maintenance investment of 140 million for the five years. Approximately 50 per cent of this investment would be in industrial development.

The first plan had a very tentative character and only applied to a few economic sectors. For the rest, estimates were made on very preliminary bases. Goals were established only in agriculture,[3] and many of these goals were kept in later plans. In the industrial sector there were only long-range plans for a limited number of industrial branches, such as paper and cellulose, electricity and textiles.[4]

2) *The 1962-65 Plan.* At the beginning of 1961, a series of institutional changes occurred which included the creation of the Ministry of Industry, Ministry of Foreign Trade, Ministry of Domestic Trade, Consolidated Enterprises, and others. These changes also affected JUCEPLAN (Central Planning Board), to which a new structure was given in accordance with the new situation.

In 1961 JUCEPLAN concentrated its efforts on drawing up the 1962-65 Plan and the Plan for 1962, making the figures of the earlier Five Year Plan more definite.

In the new plan high goals for production were set up. For gross production there was postulated an annual increase of 16 per cent, and for industrial production an increase of 18 per cent.

A report by Professor Charles Bettelheim dealing with the 1962-65[5] Plan considered as reasonable a total gross production increase of 16.4 per cent and 17.8 per cent in the special case of industry. In his judgment, investments ought to reach 5,100,000,-000 pesos in four years. Among these investments those in the industrial sector ought to increase through the period up to 2,135,000,000, or 42 per cent of the total investment. Professor Bettelheim also estimated that complimentary external resources to the extent of 753,000,000 pesos would be necessary. Owing to the imbalance which such a violent expansion would create, it would only be in 1968 that Cuba, provided the plan was realized, would be able to attain an equilibrium in the balance of payments, and only then be able to initiate the refunding of the credits that had been extended.

It is evident that the goals established in the first plans were extremely ambitious. Some of the high officials were too optimistic when they made statements like the following: "In 1965, Cuba, in relation to its population, will be the most industrialized country in Latin America, and per inhabitant will be leading in production of electric power, steel, cement, tractors, and the refining of petroleum."[6]

The most significant increase in industrial production was postulated for the sectors of construction, mining, construction materials, transport equipment, and mechanical industries, all with rates of annual increase above 26 per cent. Lesser increases were predicted in the sectors of consumer goods—tobacco, food, textiles, and clothing, though these were high, as can be seen in Table 1. At the same time an annual increase of 4.5 per cent in productivity was contemplated.

The decline in sugar production in 1962, which is set forth in detail in the part on agriculture, and the fact that the goals fixed in the 1962 Plan were not attained in many industrial fields, brought about an extensive revision of the economic and social plans which were being carried out first, with the assistance of experts from Czechoslovakia, and later from the Soviet Union. The Minister of Industry, Comandante Guevara, assumed the presidency of JUCEPLAN at the end of 1961, after criticizing the goals in the following terms: "In general our ambitious plans were

Table 1. Industrial Production—First Plan, 1962-65ᵃ
(In millions of pesos at current prices)

Industrial sectors	Gross Production 1962	1965	Index of Production 1962 = 100	Annual Percentage Increase, 1962-65
Mining	80.0	160.0	200	26.0
Mechanical industries	147.2	292.3	198	26.0
Transport equipment	62.0	124.0	200	26.0
Construction materials	86.1	172.2	200	26.0
Petroleum and derivatives	164.0	270.0	165	18.2
Chemical industries (not including plastics)	270.0	486.0	180	21.8
Textiles and clothing	306.0	482.0	140	11.9
Sugar	305.0	845.0	167	18.7
Other foods and drinks	755.6	1,000.0	132	9.7
Tobacco	159.0	190.0	119	6.0
Other industries	146.2	217.3	149	14.1
Construction	389.0	843.5	217	29.5
Electric power	84.0	148.0	176	21.0
Total industrial production	3,154.1	5,176.3	164	17.8
Total industrial product	1,310.7	2,195.0	164	17.8

a. These figures were revised and adjusted later, lowering the 1962 base and the rates of increase.
Source: Charles Bettelheim, *Sketch of the 1962-65 Plan for Cuban Economy* (September, 1961).

not fulfilled. We made plans for production that were based upon the prospect of having all the raw materials that were necessary and all the necessary products."[7]

The revisions in the industrial field were made by the Ministry of Industry on the basis of information which it received from the consolidated industries under its supervision. In general the projection base—the year 1962—was rectified in accordance with the results obtained in the first semester of that year, and the rates of increase were lowered.

The Ministry of Industry furnished us with a projection of the value of the industrial production (Table 2). Not included in it was any additional production which might result from the new factories which would become operative during the period of the plan.

Table 2. Value of Production and Gross Industrial Product for the Established Industries—Revised Plan
(In millions of $)

	1961		1962[a]		1965[b]	
	Production	Product	Production	Product	Production	Product
Basic Industries	1,004.1	356.7	980.8	371.6	1,271.0	467.2
Power and Metallurgy	273.1	157.5	341.6	197.1	395.5	228.2
Extractive and heavy chemistry	731.0	199.2	639.2	174.5	875.5	239.0
Light Industries	575.7	311.8	910.6	433.8	1,078.8	577.6
Food and light chemistry	362.7	210.0	481.0	278.5	613.5	355.2
Mechanical, textiles, leather	213.0	101.8	429.6	155.3	465.3	222.4
Private Industry	213.0	150.0[c]	100.0	70.0[c]		
Totals	1,792.8	818.5	1,991.4	875.4	2,349.8	1,044.8

a. Preliminary estimated 1962 Plan (revised figures of the 1962-65 Plan).
b. Revised figures.
c. Estimates made by the author on the base of a coefficient 0.7.
Sources: JUCEPLAN and Ministry of Industry. Reference is made only to established industries. Not included is the production of the new enterprises that would begin operations during the period 1962-65.

If Table 2 is reduced to indexes and the rates of increase in the different sectors are figured out, the following results are obtained:

Table 3. Indexes and Planned Rates of Growth in the Industrial Sector
(Base, 1961 = 100)

	1962 (Provisional)	1965 (Planned)	Annual rates of increase
Basic Industries	104.2	131.0	7.0
Power output and Metallurgy	125.1	144.9	9.7
Extractive and heavy chemistry	87.6	119.8	4.6
Light Industries	139.1	185.2	16.6
Food and light chemistry	132.6	169.1	14.0
Mechanical, textiles and leather	152.6	218.5	21.6
Private Industry	46.7	——	——
Total Industrial Sector	107.0	127.6	6.3

Source: Table 2.

From Table 3 it may be deduced that an increase of 27.6 per cent in the value of production is postulated for the period of the plan, which means an annual rate of increase of 6.3 per cent. We must keep in mind that this increase only refers to the industries that were functioning in 1961. Consequently, we must add the production resulting from the new factories in process of installation during the period. This production can be estimated in a very preliminary manner as 630 million pesos. Industrial production would rise in 1965 to 2,980,000,000 pesos, which represents an increase of 66.2 per cent over 1961, and an annual rate of 13.5 per cent. It is presumed that all industry would be in the hands of the public sector in 1965.

Consequently, the increase in the value of production will originate in two ways: 630,000,000 through new factories, and 557,000,000 through better utilization of the capacity and extension of the industries existing in 1961. In the basic industries a greater utilization of 31 per cent is contemplated, while the proportion for light industries is much greater—85.2. In these there existed a significant "idle" capacity.

If we take all the industrial sectors, that is, if we add to the industries controlled by the Ministry of Industry, the plants that make food products which belong to INRA, and the firms that manufacture construction materials, which are under the Ministry of Public Works, we obtain the following results:

Table 4. Value of Industrial Production
(In millions of pesos)

Industries	1961	1965	Annual rates of increase
Ministry of Industry	1,793	2,980	13.5
INRA (Rough Estimate)	500	732	10.0
Ministry of Public Works (Rough Estimate)	80	166	20.0
Total Industrial Sector	2,263	3,878	14.4

In this manner an annual rate of increase of 14.4 per cent would be attained for the period 1962-65. This would be four times greater than that registered for the period 1953-58.

The rate of annual increase which is postulated in the revised plan is lower than those set in the first two plans and seems to be possible of attainment, provided that the new industrial plants which are planned begin to function on the specified dates, and provided further that no changes occur in the supply of raw materials and replacements, and in working hours, as a consequence of difficulties, as happened in 1961 and 1962.

The only country in Latin America which postulates a similar rate of increase is Venezuela, with 13.5 per cent for the period 1963-66 per year.

The necessary requirements for the fulfillment of the production goals have been estimated in Table 5:

Table 5. Summary of the Industrial Investments Planned for the Period 1962-65
(In millions of pesos of 1962)

Manufacturing Industry		
New plants	363.9	
Extensions	144.4	
Replacements	122.8	
		631.1
Mining	70.0	70.0
Electricity		
New installations	170.0	
Replacements	10.0	
		180.0
Other investments		
New installations	13.0	
Replacements	15.0	
		28.0
Total		909.1

Source: Ministry of Industry, and Table 6.

The orientation of investments puts its emphasis on industries that produce intermediate goods. As is shown in Table 6, more than half the investments which will be made in the manufacturing industry correspond to sectors producing intermediate goods, with particular emphasis on basis metals, chemical products, and non-metallic minerals. On the other hand, the investments in the sector producing consumer goods are in lower proportion.

In the plan, investments covering 134 new plants are contemplated. The details of each of these and the source of equipment

Table 6. Industrial Investments for the Period 1962-63

Industrial sectors	Number of New Plants	Millions of pesos, 1962 prices				Per Cent of Total
		New Plants	Extensions	Replacements	Total	
Food industries[a]	47	19.2	35.5	44.2	98.9	15.5
Drinks[b]				5.0	5.0	0.8
Tobacco				2.5	2.5	0.4
Textiles	7	43.5	26.2	4.2	73.9	11.8
Clothing and shoes	3	3.3	0.2	1.1	4.6	0.7
Wood and cork	3	4.8		1.3	6.1	1.0
Furniture and accessories[b]				0.8	0.8	1.3
Paper and cellulose			4.0	4.5	8.5	1.4
Graphic arts[b]				1.0	1.0	0.2
Leather	1	1.5	1.9	0.2	3.6	0.6
Rubber	1	3.0		1.6	4.6	0.7
Chemical products	20	32.1	9.1	8.8	50.0	8.0
Derivatives of petroleum	1	11.0	0.9	12.8	24.7	3.9
Non-metallic minerals	9	31.8	9.5	4.3	45.6	7.3
Basic metallurgy	7	110.8	57.1	19.5	187.4	29.9
Metallic products	14	25.5		4.7	29.5	4.7
Machinery	6	21.7		4.0	25.7	4.0
Electrical equipment	3	5.3		1.5	6.8	1.1
Transport materials	9	49.0			49.0	7.8
Miscellaneous	3	1.4		0.8	2.2	0.3
TOTAL MANUFACTURING INDUSTRY	134	363.9	144.4	122.8	631.1	100.0
MANUFACTURING INDUSTRY		363.9	144.4	122.8	631.1	69.3
MINING		70.0			70.0	7.7
ELECTRICITY		170.0		10.0	180.0	19.9
OTHER INVESTMENTS		13.0		15.0	28.0	3.1
GRAND TOTAL		616.9	144.4	147.8	909.1	100.0

a. Includes preserves and other foodstuffs of INRA.
b. Estimates.
Source: Ministry of Industry.

and machinery can be seen in the Appendix, Part III, Table 8. An interesting fact is that the greater number of the new factories will be set up away from Havana, and this arrangement shows a decided effort at decentralization. According to the plans the province of Oriente will become an important industrial center.

In regard to the goals for employment, it is foreseen that 42,000 new jobs will be created in four years, or an average of 10,500 each year. Thus, 498,000 people would be employed in the industrial sector in 1965.

3) *The principal industrial programs.* From an analysis of the industrial plans it is evident that greater specialization is intended in sectors which offer more favorable conditions for accelerated development. These are iron and steel industries, nickel and cobalt industries, and serum chemicals. Capital goods are also a part of the plan.

In the iron and steel field the idea is to exploit the extensive iron deposits in Oriente province and in other regions, where reserves have been estimated at about 4,000 million tons. These deposits are of a lateritic type, with an iron content that fluctuates between 40 per cent and 45 per cent, and which contain nickel and cobalt. The Cuban authorities have come to an agreement with the Soviet Union on financing and assistance, according to which Russia will install a complex iron and steel plant with a capacity of 1.3 million metric tons a year.

According to the plan, the design of this plant will be finished in June, 1963, and orders will immediately be placed for equipment. The plant will be in production in 1967. A new process will be employed whereby the iron will be obtained with a by-product of nickel and cobalt.

While this plant is being installed, an increase in the present production of iron is to be effected, raising it from 100,000 tons in 1962 to 350,000 in 1965.

With this increase in production and the new iron and steel plant, Cuba would be in a position to supply all its needs and to export certain surpluses, especially special types of steel.

The production of nickel and cobalt will also undergo a notable expansion. Cuba would take second place in the world in the production of nickel, once a fourth plant has been installed in which a new refining process is employed. It is estimated that by

1967 or perhaps earlier, annual production will reach 70,000 tons of nickel, and 12,000 tons of cobalt.

In the field of serum chemistry Cuba will develop an ambitious program of technological research with the idea of making full use of its sugar production. Important results have already been obtained in the production of yeast and alcohols. Similarly, the production of paper, including newspaper stock, is obtained from bagasse. Under experimentation is a process of making raw materials for the production of rayon from bagasse. Research has already met with success in the laboratory and a pilot plant is already in operation. Cuban experts assured us that possibly in the course of 1963 it would be produced industrially. Interesting experiments are likewise being conducted with the hope of obtaining hormones from cane wax. If this is successful, an important advance in this field will be achieved. Finally, the industrial production of butane will permit installation of a synthetic rubber factory.

In the field of mechanical industry the program contemplates an automotive branch for the production of a considerable number of automobiles. Also in the plan are a bicycle factory and railway equipment shops. Some time ago there was initiated a program for shipyards capable of constructing small fishing boats, with the possibility of making boats larger than 5,000 tons. Also under construction are agricultural machinery and farm implements. We were told that, in the sugar harvest for 1963, 1,000 mechanical cane cutters and 500 elevators constructed in Cuba would be used. This would compensate in part for the lack of labor which characterized the last two harvests.

In the field of the supply of power, several programs are contemplated. A new petroleum refinery will be constructed with a capacity of one million tons a year, which will satisfy the necessary requirements for some time. The generating of electric power will be increased with the installation of two new thermo centers (*centrales térmicos*), one of 100,000 kilowatts, and the other of 200,000. In this field they are also studying the possibility of using extensive layers of peat for sources of energy.

ii

From what we have examined in the previous sections, it can be inferred that Cuba proposes to carry out a process of accelerated development which will mean a significant expansion in an economy that either had stagnated before or was increasing very slowly.

The principal objections, also applicable to many other Latin American countries, which have traditionally been raised to the industrialization of Cuba, and which many people still hold, are that it is possible to obtain better results by taking advantage of the production of raw materials, that the domestic market is very restricted, and that the sources of energy are very limited.

If we examine the first of these objections, it becomes clear that the prospect of an increase in the production of sugar is slight, or nonexistent. In the long run, the role of this sector would hardly be very dynamic, especially with reference to employment. On the other hand, the development of other activities is not competitive with the development of the sugar sector in financial, natural, or human resources.

With regard to the limited market, the objection does not hold, since the Havana market alone, a city of more than a million inhabitants, with a per capita income of around 800 pesos annually, represents an interesting market for many industrial lines. Furthermore, the establishment of industrial enterprises has a multiplying effect and generates a new demand. Havana, it should be added, constitutes one of the largest local markets for industrial products in Latin America.

The third objection is the only valid one. As a matter of fact, if a domestic source of fuel is not developed, the possibility is that the demand for fuel will increase proportionately more rapidly than the total economy. Sources of hydraulic energy are very scarce in Cuba, the extraction of oil is limited, and all there is in this line are peat deposits, the use of which industrially is very much in doubt. Perhaps the solution may lie in nuclear or solar energy, but this is a long-range prospect. It is evident, then, that the problems of energy will constitute the principal limiting factor in industrial development.

Another limiting factor is the balance of payments. As a matter of fact, the development in the Cuban economy shows a definite tendency toward a higher level of self-sufficiency. While it is expected that the total production in the next few years will increase at a rate of around 8 per cent or 9 per cent a year, exports will increase at a much lower rate. Since it will be difficult to reduce the coefficient of imports very much, the orientation of the process will have to be made very carefully, if it is not to provoke dangerous imbalances in payments. This limiting effect of the development would be lessened, or compensated for, if Cuba could count on foreign aid sufficient for the acquisition of capital goods necessary for industrialization. This would be possible from the countries which have a highly centralized economy.

Another aspect to which it is necessary to call attention in order to complete this study is one that is related to the orientation of the process of industrialization that Cuba is carrying out. First, the intention is to attain a higher integration in the whole industrial complex, that is, to make an improvement in industrial relations from the point of view of the possibility of a substitution of imports and the creation of a number of industries oriented toward exportation.

Second, we observe a clear intention of decentralization in the location of factories, which will stimulate the development of regional economies.

Third, there is a tendency toward the development of the industries that can make better use of the natural resources of Cuba. If this is accomplished, a very important part of the industrial program will be attained. At first there was evident a desire to free Cuba from the importation of finished products, overlooking the very real possibilities of making use of the raw materials close at hand, or the need for increasing the number of basic industries.

In short, the prospect for industrial development in Cuba is decidedly promising. An orientation has already been defined in those branches in which the availability of international resources offers advantages. At the same time, organizational readjustments are being made in order to facilitate the tasks of control and the efficient development of the industrial sector. Also, it is evident from the efforts mentioned above that the scarcity of skilled labor is being met through intensive training and by contracting for foreign technicians. Along with all of this, Cuba has understood how important it is to carry out scientific investigations with the purpose of making better use of its natural resources, something which is rare in Latin American countries.

Over against these favorable factors, the problems of organization and supply will probably persist for some time to come. But these problems need not be insoluble.

The above statements are predicated certainly upon whether Cuba is permitted to develop its industrial programs without outside interference. Naturally, if any international tension is prolonged, or if new aggression against Cuba takes shape, the development of the industrial programs will suffer serious setbacks, as happened in 1961 and 1962. In these years the country had to put itself on a war footing several times, with a consequent general mobilization which included industrial workers and produced a reduction in production.

Another important requisite for the accelerated industrialization of Cuba is that financial and technical assistance on the part of the socialist countries shall be increased in the next few years, and that debt service be postponed until the present program is carried out. In this way Cuba, at the end of this decade, can become one of the most industrialized countries in Latin America, and be in a position to improve notably the standard of living of its population.

Part I

Agriculture

Appendix

Comparisons of Crop Production before and after the Revolution

A reliable index of total agricultural output did not exist in Cuba before the Revolution. There was, of course, abundant statistical information on the annual production of the traditional export crops—sugar, tobacco, and coffee—and, in recent years, also on the output of rice. Moreover, fairly reliable estimates were available for the production of some highly commercialized crops, such as potatoes. On the other hand, data were very weak for the output of subsistence crops like *malanga*, corn, and *yuca*, and inadequate in the case of livestock production.[1]

Since an adequate index of the aggregate value of farm output was not constructed during the first years of the new regime, it is not possible to determine *precisely* the changes experienced by total agricultural production after the Revolution.[2] Nevertheless, the limitations imposed by the lack of data are much less important for crop production, and it is possible to estimate rather closely the direction and the approximate magnitude of the change in the total output of crops: 1) between the last years before the Revolution and the end of the first period of agrarian reform; 2) between 1961 and 1962; and 3) between 1962 and the years before the Revolution.[3]

These comparisons are possible because the value of the four crops for which better data are available represents a substantial share of the total value of crop production (see Table 1), and because at least in the first two of the periods compared, the percentage change in the production of the major crops are sufficiently high to largely offset any probable changes in the output of crops for which no statistical information is available.

Comparison of Crop Output before the Revolution and at the End of the First Period of the Agrarian Reform

For the purpose of this comparison "output at the end of the first period of the agrarian reform" is represented in the case of all crops, except rice, by the figures listed for the year 1961 in Tables 4 and 5 of Chapter III. These figures include either harvests started and finished during the first months of the year 1961 (such as sugar cane and tobacco) or harvests which began in the second part of 1960 and ended in the first months of 1961 (like coffee and potatoes). The figures therefore reflect the outcome of work done largely in 1960 and can hence be related to the institutional framework which existed during the first phase of the agrarian reform.

For rice, however, it seems advisable to base comparisons on production during the calendar year 1960, and not 1961. There are several reasons to recommend this procedure. First, it is not clear whether the output indicated for the year 1961 in Table 5, Chapter III, refers to the *calendar* year 1961 or to the *agricultural* year 1961-62.[4] If the latter were the case, the output recorded would correspond to rice which was not only harvested but also sown after the institutional reorganization of 1961: clearly the production indicated by the "1961" figure should then be analyzed with other outputs of the second period of agrarian reform.

In the second place, even if the output included were that of the calendar year 1961, it would be debatable whether the "1961" figure should be used to assess the developments of the first period of the agrarian reform. Figures of rice output during a given calendar year include in Cuba three components. The first corresponds to rice harvested during the first months of the calendar year, which are also the last months of the "spring crop" (*cosecha*

Table 1. Estimated Value of Total Agricultural Output at Producers' Prices in Cuba in 1958

	Value	Proportion of Value of:	
	(Millions of pesos)	Crop or Livestock Output	Agricultural Output
Sugar Cane	266.6	54.1	36.5
Rice	45.5	9.2	6.2
Coffee	32.3	6.5	4.4
Tobacco	45.2	9.2	6.2
Other Crops	104.0	21.0	14.2
Total Crop Production	493.8	100.0	67.5
Beef	112.9	47.6	15.5
Pork	25.9	10.9	3.5
Poultry	13.9	5.9	1.9
Milk	72.0	30.3	9.9
Eggs	12.5	5.3	1.7
Total Livestock Production	237.2	100.0	32.5
Agricultural Production	731.0		100.0

Source: INRA, Production Department.

de primavera) started toward the end of the previous year; a second component includes rice harvested around the middle of the year (*cosecha de frío*); and the third is formed by rice harvested during the first period of the next "spring crop" insofar as it falls within the calendar year considered. Hence figures for rice production during a calendar year are significantly influenced by harvests which take place in its second half. The figure of rice output during calendar 1961 would therefore be misleading as an indication of the institutions prevailing until the end of 1960.

For these reasons, it seems more appropriate to consider the output of calendar 1960 as an estimate of the production of rice at the end of the first period of the agrarian reform, and to use the "1961" figure as an indicator of rice output in the second period.[5]

"Crop output before the Revolution" is taken as the average production of the years 1957 and 1958. It should be noted that crop production during these years was *not* affected by the spreading of the revolutionary war during the second half of 1958. In effect, the consequences of the war are in most cases reflected in the production figures for 1959 and not in those for 1958. This follows from the fact that most crops are harvested in Cuba during the first months of the year, and from the procedure adopted, according to which when the harvests start in the last months of the previous year the output is assigned to the years in which the harvests are finished.[6]

The comparison can now proceed in two steps. It is necessary to estimate in the first place the effect of changes in the output of sugar,[7] rice, tobacco, and coffee on the level of the total production of crops. This is done for each crop by applying the respective weight shown in Table 1 to the percentage change of output with respect to the base period. The results of these operations are shown in Table 2. *By themselves* the changes in the production of the four principal crops would have caused total crop output to be in (early) 1961, 14.1 per cent higher than in the base period.

It is necessary to allow in the second place for the unknown changes in the production of the "other crops" in Table 1. This can be done by making different assumptions about the magnitude of these changes. If, for example, it is assumed that the production of the "other crops" *decreased by 10 per cent*—which of course implies that the output of some crops fell in order to offset the large gains made in potatoes, tomatoes, cotton, and oil-

Table 2. Percentage Changes in the Output of Four Crops Between 1961 and 1957-58 and Effect on Total Crop and Agricultural Output

	Per Cent Change with Respect to 1957-58	Percentage Effect on Crop Output	Percentage Effect on Agricultural Output
Sugar	19.9	10.8	7.3
Rice[a]	26.1	2.4	1.6
Tobacco	13.4	1.2	.83
Coffee	−4.2	−.27	−.18
		+14.13	+9.65

a. Refers to output of year 1960.
Source: Tables 1, 2, and 4 in Chapter II, Tables 4 and 5 in Chapter III, and Table 1 in this Appendix.

bearing crops—then the total output of crops would have risen by 12 per cent over the base period. If, on the other hand, this assumption is reversed and a *10 per cent increase* in the output of the "other crops" is assumed, total crop output would have risen by 16.2 per cent over the average level of 1957-58.

Different hypotheses about the changes in the production of the "other crops" thus determine relatively small variations in the percentage increase of total crop output. Moreover, the analysis shows that even if quite pessimistic assumptions are made about the crops for which production data are not available, total output of crops at the end of the first phase of the agrarian reform would have been about 12 per cent higher than in 1957-58.[8]

Finally, the impact of the growth of crop production on the level of aggregate farm output can be estimated. This can easily be done by a suitable change in the weights, i.e., using those which measure the relative importance of the different crops in the value of aggregate agricultural output rather than in the value of total crop production. If a 10 per cent decrease or a 10 per cent increase in "other crops" output are postulated as before, then percentage increases in total agricultural production would be 8.2 and 11.0 over 1957-58.

As expected, the increase in total agricultural production determined by the growth of crop production is quite high, whatever assumptions are made for the output of "other crops." Moreover, owing to the lower weights of "other crops" in total agricultural production, different assumptions about the growth of production of these crops determine smaller *absolute* differentials for the resulting percentage increase of total farm output.

Comparison of Crop Output in 1961 and 1962

The same procedure can be applied to estimate the change in the output of crops between 1961 and 1962, two years for which the output of the four main crops is also known. For 1962, however, considerably less information is available for the production of the "other crops." Nevertheless, it is known that the output of potatoes declined by 25.9 per cent (see Table 13, Chapter III), and, as explained in the text, there are reasons to believe that the production of *viandas* also fell sharply. Because the value of root crops must still represent a very high proportion of the value of the production of "other crops,"[9] the latter almost certainly declined. In the absence of more information, the (probably optimistic) assumption of an unchanged production of these "other crops" is made.

Table 3 summarizes the results of the computations made to assess the impact on total crop output and on total agricultural production of changes in the output of sugar cane, rice, tobacco, and coffee. It can be seen that the decline with respect to 1961 is substantial, with the fall in sugar output being the principal cause. The sharp reduction in rice output is, on the other hand, more than offset by the steep rise in coffee production.

Table 3. Percentage Changes in the Output of Four Crops Between 1962 and 1961 and Effect on Total Crop and Agricultural Output

	Per cent change with respect to 1961	Percentage Effect on Crop output	Percentage Effect on Agricultural output
Sugar	−29.9	−16.17	−10.91
Rice[a]	−24.4	− 2.24	− 1.51
Tobacco	1.0	.09	.06
Coffee	50.9	3.31	2.23
		−15.01	−10.13

a. Change with respect to 1960 (see text).
Sources: Tables 4, 5, 10, and 13, Chapter III.

Comparison of Crop Output in 1962 and before the Revolution

It is possible finally to compare the output of crops in 1962 and that of the base period. Table 4 summarizes the corresponding information for the four principal crops. It is seen that the combined effects of the large decline in sugar output and the moderate fall in rice production are not fully offset by the increases in the production of coffee and tobacco.

The overall negative result is not changed if we assume that the output of "other crops" increased 5 per cent over the base period (in which case total production of crops would have fallen by 3.75 per cent with respect to 1957-58), nor if we postulate (with optimism[10]) a rise of 10 per cent in the output of the

Table 4. Percentage Changes in the Output of Four Crops Between 1962 and 1957-58 and Effect on Total Crop and Agricultural Output

	Per cent change with respect to 1957-58	Percentage Effect on Crop output	Percentage Effect on Agricultural output
Sugar	−15.9	− 8.60	− 5.80
Rice[a]	− 4.7	− .43	− .29
Tobacco	14.7	1.35	.91
Coffee	44.5	2.90	2.0
		− 4.8	− 3.3

a. Refers to output of calendar year 1961 or of the agricultural year 1961-62 (see text).

Sources: Tables 1, 2, 4, Chapter II; Tables 10 and 13, Chapter III.

"other crops" (in which case the fall of crop output in comparison with the base period would be 2.7 per cent). These same assumptions, plus the hypothesis of unchanged output of livestock products in 1962,[11] would indicate declines of total agricultural output of 2.6 and 1.9 per cent with respect to the base period.

Part II

Education

Appendixes

Appendix A

The Political Content of Cuban Education, 1962

The intention to use the Cuban educational system for political and social purposes has been openly declared. "Without preferential attention to the peoples' education we could not expect the revolutionary purposes to be fulfilled," stated the Minister of Education in 1959. On the same occasion he explained that "The school of the State should be called the National School because it has been created to serve the interests and requirements of the nation."[1] With similar implications, Castro has declared that education is the Revolution's most important task and that books are its strongest weapon. Such declarations are indications of the changes in the philosophy and purposes of Cuban education which have been introduced and extended throughout the system.

Some quotations about the intentions and syllabus of Cuban education are given in what follows. I well recognize that such limited treatment is quite inadequate for a balanced understanding of the real nature, impact, or effectiveness of the political teaching. A page or two from the textbooks is hardly a summary of a comprehensive system and no doubt the teachers, their students, the school organization, and the revolutionary activities are far more influential than the books in use. Yet the books have importance especially when printed in thousands of copies, and they may indicate the general approach. At the least they are examples to add to other information.

Several of the passages are long enough, I hope, to provide some chance to see how well the coherence and rationale of the doctrine fits its Cuban context. Adaptation to surroundings is often a fair test for survival. To see in the following selections only confirmation of the Marxist-Leninism which Castro has already espoused may be to miss more significant questions. No doubt many aspects of the dogma will be as disturbing to many readers as they are to myself. But in order to know whether the doctrine which is now being taught in Cuba will be fully accepted (or even to understand how a doctrine *can* be taught by teachers who mostly received their training before the Revolution),[2] it is necessary to put aside personal viewpoints and ask what sense this sort of teaching will make in the experience of the students and teachers.

Political content must be interpreted in its widest sense. It might better be described as the revolutionary content of Cuban education. As the Revolution has been social, economic, and political, so also has each of these elements been injected in full measure into Cuban education.

The effectiveness of the new teaching should be judged not only as politics on an island of the cold war but as a "package" solution to poverty, inequality, and dependence being "sold" to a Caribbean people. That it is no soft sell is quite evident from the size of the educational effort. But neither is it indoctrination at gunpoint. There is more than a touch of relevance in the message; much of what is emphasized about economic imperialism, land reform, or the privileges of the rich, for example, already finds a ready market in Latin America. (The reader will recall that the Alliance for Progress has recognized the urgency of basic social problems.)

Whenever possible, I have given the numbers of copies of each document printed to indicate coverage. Naturally this is only a rough measure of readership and a far cry from any approximation to impact or acceptance.

A General Statement of the Political Role of Education

The ideology and content of Cuban education is put in some detail in the Official Report by the Cuban government to the UNESCO Conference on Education and Economic and Social Development held in Santiago, Chile, in 1962. After a brief summary of the present educational system, its enrollments and organization, the statement of the Cuban government turns to the political role of education.

"Principal Problems in connection with the content and orientation of education:[3]

"The bourgeois ideology regarded education as a phenomenon isolated from its economic basis. In fact, however, education as an ideological superstructure is closely linked with the means of production—that is to say, with the productive forces and the relationships of production.

"Throughout the whole history of human society education has been a product of the social classes which dominated at each stage. The content and orientation of education are therefore determined by the social classes which are in power.

"In Cuba, those in power are the workers, the peasants, the progressive intellectuals and the middle strata of the population, who are building a democratic society in which group and class privileges are disappearing and in which private ownership of the basic means of production is being eliminated. If anyone wishes to know the aims of our education, they should study the interests of the workers, peasants, intellectuals and the middle strata of the population and they will find their answer. It is these which determine the purpose, the objectives, the orientation, the content and the methods of education in our country.

"It is in the interests of the society of workers, peasants and intellectuals which we are building that education should be heightened, deepened and broadened on a strictly scientific basis. When the people of Cuba embarked on this task, they began from the superficial and corrupt educational system which had existed before the Revolution and radically transformed its ideological aims; an education for competition, for servitude, for subjection to the privileged classes and bondage to foreign imperialism gave way to an education for a workers' and peasants' democracy, for the increase of production through socialist emulation, an education designed to free men from prejudices and to equip them for the defense of their country and of the cause of the workers.

"The aims of education in the New Cuba include those of instilling in our children and young people an unreserved love for their country and a sense of solidarity with the workers and peoples of all lands in their noble struggle for a free and happy life, and of teaching them to abhor imperialist wars of plunder and to strive steadfastly for peace.

"The content of the school syllabus will be directed towards awakening the young people to their duties as citizens of the Socialist Fatherland.

"The teaching programmes must help to develop a love of country and love, for the workers and peasants, for the people as the suppliers of labour and the source of all social wealth. They must teach the meaning of the struggle against exploitation and poverty. They must stress, as a value within socialist society, affection and respect of young people for their families. They must encourage a morality the foundation of which is the struggle against social inequality. They must stress the underlying causes of inequality and its terrible consequences. They must bring out the meaning of peace and the implications of aggressive war, as a basis for encouraging a concern for peace and unity among all peoples. They must promote everything which is favourable to peaceful coexistence between States with differing social systems, and they must encourage the struggle against injustices, corruption and exploitation, both in political systems and among individuals. They must emphasize the value of the struggle against colonialism and imperialism and provide the scientific knowledge required for life in society.

"Everything must be done by persuasion, by reason, by the analysis of facts and by the study of the experience of mankind. The pupils must not be taught in a dogmatic way or according to theoretical schemes, but through the stimulation of their intelligence and their creative imagination.

"They must be trained to understand the value of science in the sphere of nature as well as in the study of society, and its importance for the utilization of historical experience in the quest for freedom.

"They must be taught what freedom is and what democracy really is. The meaning of a workers' and peasants' democracy must be explained as distinct from the democracy of the big land-owners, the industrial and business magnates, and the exploiting and privileged classes. It must be explained why worker-peasants' democracy is the most democratic kind of democracy—if the tautology may be excused

—which is possible in a class society, i.e., in any society organized as a State.

"All this must be done with the help of actual examples and through the encouragement of an interest in objective reality. A key part must be played in the syllabus by compulsory study of the examples of the great men of our Country, of America and of the World, and the roles which they played in their times. The memory of the heroes and martyrs must be constantly alive in the Students' Councils. At the same time, the programme and study outlines must demonstrate and explain how history is created by the people and how the heroes are great because they embody history and the people.

"Stress must also be laid on the importance of education for socialism and on the value of science in economic, social and cultural development. The pupils must be taught to avoid prejudices and to believe in humanity and in its bright future of prosperity, freedom and happiness. They must be led to realize that the future belongs to the people and to those who work, study and seek the happiness of their fellows.

"They must be brought to have a high sense of the duty to work; that is to say, they must be taught to abandon the false notion of work as a punishment and they must be taught the necessity of work.

"An attitude of respect towards communal property must be developed in the pupils.

"They must be taught to take care of everything which belongs to the community and of which they make use as members of the community; desks, slates, gardens, buildings, the city, the parks, the factories and the cultivated fields. Everything belongs to the people; socialism means just this; social ownership and social production.

"They must be taught the value of emulative work and the difference between capitalism and socialism as being based on the difference between competition for private gain and emulation for the sake of increasing the output of the community.

"All this will increase the sense of responsibility of the students and strengthen ties of solidarity. They must also be taught the duty of defending their socialist country and of dying, if necessary, in the defense of national independence and of the achievements of the Revolution.

"They must be taught the revolutionary and moral significance of the national slogans: *"Patria o Muerte"* ("My Country or Death") and *"Venceremos"* ("We shall win").

"Finally, the young people must become accustomed to the tireless struggle for human dignity and to believing firmly in final victory if their acts are guided by the principle: "Everything for man and for the sake of the good man." Thus we are fulfilling the ideal of Martí, whose wish was that, in the first Law of the Republic which he helped to create, the full dignity of man should be exalted.

"At the same time, since another of the aims of education for socialism is that of providing the necessary technical and scientific training to produce workers who are capable of directing and increasing production, and since the means of production are in the hands of the State, it is logical that, for many different ideological, practical and pedagogic reasons, education should be linked with productive labour.

"Our plans and programmes aim at the elimination of verbalism and learning by rote and at making education a living matter, in which theory is identified with practice and linked with social labour.

"Karl Marx pointed out that the factory system shows us "the germ of the education of a future epoch when for all children, from a certain age, productive labour will be combined with education and gymnastics, not only as a means of increasing social production but as the only means capable of producing men developed in every aspect."

"Here we see two basic aims of socialist education: *The linking of education with productive labour* as a means of *developing men in every aspect.* Educating in productive labour, making the students familiar with the details of production through practical experience, enabling them to learn its laws and the organization of its processes; that is, educating them in the very root of all cultural, technical and scientific progress, and giving them an ideological and moral training leading to an all-round education.

"Contact with production, when the children are brought to the factories and farms, has an ideological, or, one might say, moral value; it brings them into relationship with the life and atmosphere of the centers of production. In this way the spirit of companionship is developed in them as well as an understanding of the problems of work and an interest in production.

"The link with useful social labour also has a justification of a didactic nature. It has been demonstrated that, when theory is related to practice, instruction is more effective. The interest awakened in the pupils when they discover the relationship between theory and practice is an incentive which teachers must take into account. This relationship is the most valuable source of motivation in school learning."

Primary Schools

The new orientation has been implemented through changes in textbooks and syllabus, in the training courses for new and old teachers, in new organization within schools and the school system. Old textbooks have been re-evaluated, new ones have been written or translated. One comment in a report I saw appraised an old textbook as racist, imperialist, and pro-Yankee. Many new textbooks have been printed and some imported. One of the new series has been printed in magazine form on the presses of the old *Revista Bohemia.* Detailed syllabuses for each level of primary education have been produced with newspaper format. These outline the program for each subject for every grade of primary school. The summary outline of the social studies program for grades four to six reads as follows:

Social Studies—Essential Content of the Syllabus[4]

1. *THE REVOLUTION IN POWER*

(1) *How we took power*

   (a) The Batista tyranny (10 of March). The dismal consequences for the country.
   Information: in the publications of the period.

   (b) Assault of the Moncada barracks. *"History Will Absolve Me:"* an indictment of the tyranny. 26 of July Movement.

   (c) Antecedents and landing of the "Granma," (the yacht bringing Castro and 82 followers to start guerilla action against Batista). Route followed by the ship from Mexico, until the landing in Bélic, Oriente.
   Study of Oriente province.

   (ch) Incorporation of the peasants, workers and students in the fight against the tyranny. Participation of the Cuban women: Lidia and Clodomira, Emma Rosa Chuy and others.

   (d) Martyrs of this period: Frank País, José A. Echeverría and others.
   Information: biographical synthesis of Echeverría in the pamphlet *"Recollections of the Inauguration of the School Center 13th March."*

   (e) The invasion: Camilo Cienfuegos and Ché Guevara. Comparison with Maceo and Gómez, in 1896. Locate on the map the route of the invasion.
   Study of Las Villas province.

Information: Campaign Diary of Camilo Cienfuegos. Pp. 3 and 4 of *"From Colony to Colony."* Pp. 37-43 of *"Cuba Does not Owe its Independence to the U.S.A."* *"Like This Is My Country"* (a geography), *Núñez Jiménez,* pp. 93 and 109.

Conclusions:

1. The Batista tyranny, as a product and tool of imperialism, served to impose on our people a regime of brutal oppression which guaranteed to the utmost the exploitation of our riches by the American monopolies.
2. *"History Will Absolve Me"* shows the irreconcilable attitude of the people to the tyranny and sketches the foundation of the revolution.
3. The armed revolt unites all Cubans to fight, in mountains and cities, against the tyranny.

2. *THE DEMOCRATIC, ANTI-IMPERIALIST REVOLUTION AND THE NATIONAL LIBERATION*

(a) January First 1959. Yankee manoeuvres. The triumphal march of the Rebel Army.
Information: Publications of the period. Speeches by Fidel on the anniversaries of the 2nd of January (1960, 1961, 1962). Locate and trace on the map the route followed by Rebel Army, from the Sierra Maestra to the city of Havana.

(b) Liquidation of the army and other repressive organs of the tyranny. Conversion of barracks into schools. Locate on the map the places where the barracks were converted into schools.

(c) Establishment of the National Militias. Role they perform in the defense of the Fatherland and national sovereignty.
Information: Report of Fidel on the attacks of Playa Girón, in the Popular University (23-IV-1961). Speeches of Fidel at the graduation of the Militia Corps.

(ch) Promulgation of the Law of Agrarian Reform. Study.
Information: *"The Agrarian Reform"* by Severo Aguirre

Ch. 1 of *"Condena"* (condemn) and Ch. 1 of *"Derechos"* (rights) in the pamphlet *"Words and Ideas of the Declaration of Havana."*
Indicate on the map the regions where large *latifundia* existed.

(d) The reform of education. Education within the reach of everybody. Books and publications serve the people.

Year of Agrarian Reform 1960

(e) Destruction of the *latifundia*. Radical change of our economic and social structure. Collectivization of Agriculture. Cooperatives and people's farms. Favorable achievements. Locate on the map the principal cooperatives and farms of the community or region where school is located.
Information: Pp. 88 to 91 of *"Manual of Civic Responsibility"* MINFAR (Ministry of the Armed Forces).
First National Production Meeting (reports on farms and cooperatives).

(f) Nationalization of the American monopolies. Petroleum and the help of the Soviet Union. Press publications. Use world map and terrestrial globe to show the route followed by the petroleum tankers from the Soviet Union to Cuba. The Cuban archipelago: islands and keys. Cuba, Size, Surrounding seas.
Neighbouring countries and peoples.
Sea currents of the Atlantic Ocean.

(g) The declaration of Havana. Study.

(h) Why Cuba is a socialist country. What it means that the U.S. is a capitalist country. The way socialism manifests itself, in the world. The way capitalism appears in the world. Fundamental basis of socialism.
Locate the socialist countries on the world map and the globe.
Locate the capitalist countries and the dependent colonial countries.
Refer to the way of life in socialist and capitalist countries. Simple information about both economic systems, for students of 4th, 5th and 6th grades.

Locate on the map: Spain, France, England, Holland and Portugal. Capitalist and colonial countries.

(i) The U.S. starts the economic blockade of Cuba. Cuba establishes trade relations with all the countries of the world.
Locate on the map the countries with which Cuba used to trade before (products).
North America. Integrating countries. Their capitals. Seas and oceans. How their people live. Form of government. Principal natural resources.
Locate on map countries with which Cuba trades today (products). The U.S.S.R. Seas and oceans. Principal cities. Exports to Cuba.

(id) Ports which receive our products. Literature. Language, Culture. Form of Government. Agriculture. Industry (heavy and light). Air and sea communications with Cuba.
China. Seas and oceans. Main cities.
India. Climate. Culture. Main cities. Form of Government. Trade with Cuba.
European countries which help Cuba in defeating the imperialist blocade.
The U.S.S.R., Czechoslovakia, Rumania, Bulgaria. Air and sea communications with our fatherland. Cultural, sport, industrial, food, etc., exchanges they have established with us. Language. Culture. Forms of government.

(j) The law of urban reform.

(k) Opportunities for all Cubans, regardless of race, religion, sex, etc.

Year of Education 1961

(l) The people get organized. The Militia. The C.D.R. (The Committees of Defence of the Revolution), the A.J.R. (Association of Young Rebels), the I.N.D.E.R., (National Institute of Sports, Physical Education and Recreation), the F.M.C. (Federation of Cuban Women), the "Revolutionary Pioneers." Information about these bodies in press, television, radio.

(ll) O.R.I., political instrument of the Marxist vanguard directing the Revolution, which will form the United Party of the Revolution.

(m) Proclamation of the socialist character of our Revolution. Playa Girón: first defeat of imperialism in Latin America. Information: speech by Fidel (16-IV-61) at the funeral of the victims of the attack on the Revolutionary Air Force and Ciudad Libertad.

Book: *Playa Girón, Defeat of Imperialism,* first volume, Havana, pp. 401-517.

Locate on map the Zapata Swamp, Larga and Girón Beaches. The insular platform. The coasts. Characteristics of the Cuban coasts.

(n) Financial blow for the revolution: the change of currency.

(ñ) Eradication of illiteracy. Another battle won over imperialism.

Information: speech by Fidel (22-XII-61) (return of the *brigadistas*).

Year of Planning 1962

(o) Planned development of the Cuban economy.

(p) Strengthening of the revolutionary conscience, defense, and economy.

Conclusions:

1. From its beginnings, the Cuban Revolution constitutes the first great defeat of yankee imperialism in America.

2. The Socialist Revolution repairs old injustices, giving land to those who work it in two different ways: one, individual farms (small farmers); and another, collective farms (agricultural societies, farms). Giving to the tenants the houses in which they live; schools, medical care for all Cubans. The Revolution, by nationalizing the firms, has placed in the hands of the people the greatest part of the national wealth.

3. The Socialist Revolution has eradicated illiteracy, preparing the people for the cultural and technical improvements which are indispensable for the construction of socialist society. It has eliminated the public

vices, like gambling. Cuba exercises for the first time her complete sovereignty, in an environment of liberty and justice.

4. The raising of the revolutionary conscience of the masses makes it possible to organize their strength to reach the limits of *"My Country or Death," "We Will Win."*

5. The integration of the different revolutionary sectors provides the basis for the future United Party of the Revolution.

3. WORLD PROJECTION OF OUR SOCIALIST REVOLUTION

(a) The United Nations. *"Cuba is Not Alone."* Speech by Fidel at U.N.

(b) The Organization of American States, tool of imperialism in America. The U.S. Government puts pressure on the governments of Latin America in order to reach a joint action against the Cuban Revolution. The friendly peoples of Latin America. Punta del Este.
Second Declaration of Havana. Locate on map the site of this meeting.
Study of South America. Oceans and seas. Countries. Capitals. How their peoples live. Forms of government. Main natural resources.

(c) Cuba, advance post of the Revolution which will liberate Latin America from the semi-colonialism of the United States.
Locate Latin American countries. Information of press, radio and television.

(ch) Aid of socialist countries to defeat the trade blockade. Solidarity of all the peoples of the world with the Cuban Revolution.
Locate on the map the countries of the world which solidly rise with our Revolution.
European and Asian countries which help Cuba to defeat the blockade. Locate them.

(d) Peaceful coexistence and world peace. Locate countries which constitute the socialist and imperialist camps.

Conclusions:

1. The Cuban Revolution embodies the ideals of the oppressed people of America and the world. Locate these peoples. Locate the peoples who live by oppressing others.
2. Cuba enjoys the sympathy of our brothers of America. Fraternal peoples.
3. The Cuban Revolution shows that we live in the historical period of transition from capitalism into socialism; it shows that imperialism can no longer have its own way, and that a small country, a few miles from the U.S., can, through its decision, face American imperialism victoriously.
4. The Cuban Revolution constitutes a contribution to world peace.

Some examination questions

In 1962 the social studies program in the primary schools was allotted two hours each week in first and second grade and four hours in third grade and above. Political content was not confined to these periods, however, for teachers were encouraged to use aspects of the social studies program in teaching other subjects as reading, writing, language and composition. A French reporter[5] recently listed the following questions used as arithmetic questions:—

"In 1958 there were in Cuba 19,245 primary schools in the country and towns. During the first two years of the Revolution 5,190 more were created. How many schools were there in 1961?"

"Cuba spends each year 25 pesos per inhabitant on education. Denmark spends 25 also, France 15, Latin America 5. What is the difference between expenditure per inhabitant in France and Cuba?"

"During the tyranny each matchbox contained 72 matches. Today each box contains 84. How many additional matches do we get today?"

"In the socialist countries, the annual increase of industrial production is 1/7th of production the preceding year. In the capitalist countries it is a 1/20th. What will be this year's production of tractors in a factory which last year produced 14,000 units, (a) if the factory is *in* a socialist country, (b) if it is *in* a capitalist country?"

"The Ku Klux Klan was founded in the United States in 1886 to maintain by terror the supremacy of the white race. For how many years has this infamous society existed in our neighbour's land?"

"In 1959, in the city of New York, about 6,112 youths were arrested for murder and 4,331 accused of other crimes. How many juvenile delinquents were arrested in New York in 1959?"

Secondary Schools—History

The framework for teaching history

It would be incorrect to imagine that all political comment was inserted in such a crude and simplified manner. Above primary levels, the social studies syllabus included study of the Marxist view of the stages of historical development. A detailed outline was introduced in the middle of 1961, used at first in teacher study groups and later as the program in the basic secondary schools. The outline of the secondary syllabus gave rise to *Trabajo y Lucha* (*Work and Struggle*), the first in a series of introductory history texts. 150,000 copies were printed. Its preface begins:—

The Ministry of Education issues this book with a definite purpose; to assist teachers, students and all the people in the teaching and study of the history of man from a socialist point of view . . . *Trabajo y Lucha* is not presented as a definitive work; it merely aspires to contribute in some way to the education of the Cuban people. It is hoped that this outline will encourage further study and a deepening understanding and practical awareness of the creative science of Marxist-Leninism.

The book proceeds from the beginnings of man and "the origins of the first social system" to "the transitional period" in which discussion of the Mesolithic, the Neolithic, and the Iron Age is set within the three-fold framework of the instruments and techniques of production, the relations of production, and the superstructure of institutions and ideas. From primitive communities the book reaches slave-owning society which is analyzed in five stages: "a) the growing development of the slave system: war, the forces basic to slavery; b) the State, representing the interests of the dominant class; c) culture in the hands of the exploiting class; d) the conditions for maintaining slavery; and e) the stages within the means of slave production.—The States of the Ancient Orient; The States of the Classical Era, Greece, and Rome; and The Establishment of Colonies, Imperial Rome."

Book I ends by describing the transition to Feudal Society. Just before this, at the end of the description of slavery in Classi-

cal Rome, it gives the following description of the origins of
Christianity:—

Christianity[6]

"Christianity is but one of the manifestations of the crisis of slave-
holding society, and in its origins it arose as a protest movement among
the oppressed and exploited majority. Its adherents belonged to the
working classes, who accepted the new religion in the hope of a better
future, not only in the 'other life' but on earth as well.

"The Jewish people suffered under a two-fold exploitation: they
were exploited by the Romans on the one hand and by the indigenous
priestly aristocracy on the other. In their despair they sought consola-
tion in the expectation of a Messiah who would save them from their
plight. The new faith was widely propagated throughout the ancient
world until it reached Rome, where it was converted into a disciplined
organization ruled by bishops who transformed the original revolutionary beliefs into something very different. They were so anxious
to rid the Christian religion of anything in the nature of a protest or
rebellion against the established regime that they preached to the
oppressed the virtues of resignation and meekness and even of scorn
for the wordly goods which they lacked.

"Their aim was naturally to serve the interests of the powerful and
the rich, and in every respect the religion was adjusted to fit the interests of the latter.

"The Church was concerned to bring about and maintain the economic protection of the ruling class, whose supremacy was based on
the subjugation of the majority.

"It is for this reason that, by the Third Century, Christianity was
emerging victorious, without offering any opposition to the slave-
holding Roman State, with the result that the emperors Constantine
and Theodosius gave official protection to Christianity, which had
become a magnificent instrument in the hands of the governing minor-
ities. The slave-holders accepted the Christian doctrine of love for
one's neighbour provided that it was not used to attack their property
or their interests."

The secondary school syllabus for 1962 described how the
study should progress. Twelve lessons are devoted to Slavery, 10
to Feudalism, 25 to Capitalism, and 25 to "How the people live
under Socialism and how they will live under Communism."
Capitalism is discussed in sections describing England, England's
time as the leading capitalist nation, the new bourgeois revolu-

tions (North American, French, Latin American), the working class, monopoly, and imperialism, the division of the world among the capitalist powers, and the contradictions within capitalism. Other history outlines used in the teacher training institutes show more emphasis on Cuban history, starting from the "Pre-Conquest Era" and dealing at length with the "Spanish Colonial Domination." The "struggles for national independence" lead on to a study of "Cuba, the Evolution of the Republic towards the Revolution of Liberation, Anti-imperialist, Patriotic and Socialist." Beginning with "The Treaty of Paris, the North-American Intervention, the Joint Resolution and the 1901 Constitution and the Platt Amendment," the final section of the program deals with the *"Republica Mediatizada"* ("The Puppet Republic"), the struggle for political power (Gómez, Menocal—"The Heyday of Dictatorship," Zayas—"Government according to the Law," "The Tyranny" of Machado and the martyrs Mella and Trejo). From the "betrayal of the 1933 Revolution" the syllabus moves to the Constitution of 1940 and then to *"La Revolución Cubana."* The bibliography for these courses includes the *Manual of Political Economy* by the USSR Academy of Sciences, and books by Marx, Lenin, Engels. Writings dealing specifically with Cuba were also included by Blas Roca, Núñez Jiménez, Carlos Rodríguez, Fidel Castro, Ramiro Guerra, Fernando Portuondo del Prado, Severo Aguirre, Pino Santos, J. Ordoqui, and E. Roig.

Universities—Economics

In the universities, basic courses in dialectical and historical materialism were made part of the curriculum for every first and second year student. All university students will receive "ideological grounding that will permit them to see science, life and political problems with the scientific perspective offered us by Marxism-Leninism," wrote the present head of INRA.[7] In certain subjects the emphasis is greater.

In political economy, the syllabus is clearly Marxist, though dogmatism is far from rigid. Textbooks from the Russian Academy of Sciences are largely used. The program of studies embraces economic theory, history and geography with considerable emphasis on mathematics, statistics and accounting. Some technology of industrial physics, chemistry and agriculture is introduced in the second and third years. Linear programing and the methodology of planning are taught. At one university we visited we were told by an economics professor that capitalist economics was considered in some detail in the fourth year, particularly the work of Keynes, Leontief and Chenery. Criticism of some of the weaknesses and errors in Marxist economics, he said, was treated as a matter of course.

The Literacy Campaign

By far the most influential books in Cuba, judging by the number printed and issued, were the two manuals used in the literacy campaign. Two million copies of *Venceremos* were printed and a million of *Alfabeticemos*. Both were issued free. There were clearly enough copies of *Venceremos* for every family to have had one, although its appeal as reading matter was probably restricted to the barely literate. *Alfabeticemos* was designed for the *brigadistas* and volunteer teachers but this very fact indicates its ability to achieve a wider audience. Although both books were prepared late in 1960, their huge circulation explains the attention given here.

The Primer for Students

Most of the material in *Venceremos* is not specifically political in the sense of containing political statements. It does however contain material with strong associations, for example the title itself, which is part of the main political slogan of the revolution: *"Patria o Muerte—Venceremos"* (My Country or Death—We will win).

Each section in *Venceremos* starts with a picture of some familiar activity (and the lesson is supposed to start with a discussion of this). Facing it there are one or two words or sentences, and these contain messages with more and more content as the book progresses. The first one shows a meeting of the OEA (Organization of American States), without comment. The next lesson starts with a picture of a tractor working a field, with two boys waving to the driver, and the opposite page is headed INRA and goes on: "The agrarian reform was born in the mountains.

The agrarian reform gives land to rural workers. The agrarian reform goes forward." One of the last lessons starts with a picture of a demonstration abroad and the text reads "CUBA IS NOT ALONE. All the peoples are helping us. United we shall overcome aggression. They cannot halt the Revolution. Demands for liberty come from all peoples."

The remainder of each lesson consists of exercises in which students have to read and then write words or short sentences, supply missing words in the same sentences, and then insert capital letters. Here the words are usually common ones, like "river," "woman," etc., though there are also the following first names of political leaders: "Fidel," "Camilo," "Raúl," "Blas," together with common names like "Pepe," "Mario," and "Mercedes" (nearly all the names, incidentally, are those of men). Most sentences are commonplace, like "Drink your coffee," or "The sea is quiet," or "Cuban dances are beautiful"; though there is one striking exception, an exercise built around the phrases: "Young and old united, we swear with Fidel, to defend Cuba together. We shall never be defeated!"

The Handbook for Teachers

The teacher's aide *Alfabeticemos*[8] is much more political. The instructor is told at the outset: "[With the elimination of illiteracy] it is proposed to bring almost one-third of our population to understand the revolutionary process and its rapid development, as well as to raise production through raising their cultural and technical level." The manual starts by giving the teacher some practical tips, such as "Get to know your pupils and encourage them so that they don't lose heart." The teacher is advised to point out the advantages to the country and themselves of literacy, to remember that many pupils may have defects of vision or hearing, that bossiness should be avoided; and he is instructed how to proceed (when to get the pupils themselves to write, how to introduce new letters, etc.).

The bulk of this manual consists, however, of 24 "Themes of revolutionary orientation" which deal with the issues raised in *Venceremos*. (There is a guide showing where to look in *Alfabeticemos* for the issues raised in the learner's manual.) These "Themes" start with quotations from revolutionary leaders

(16 from Fidel Castro, 5 from José Martí, 2 from Núñez Jiménez, 1 from Raúl Castro). The first theme deals with "The Revolution," and starts—"The peoples need revolution to develop and make progress." The second is entitled "Fidel is our leader" and states:

And like all the great leaders known to history, Fidel Castro mobilises the best qualities of his people, and has immense confidence in the wisdom, strength and courage of the people. We Cubans respect and feel affection for the chief who led us in arms against tyranny and foreign domination. We respect the man who guided us in the struggle to make Cuba a free and prosperous country, in which we live educated and happy. And together with the highest leader of the Revolution, we also respect and feel affection for the leaders who share his responsibilities, such as President Dorticós, Raúl Castro, Ché Guevara, Juan Almeida and others (p. 24).

Other themes explain and justify the general lines of government policy in agriculture, housing, health, education, industry, racial discrimination, international trade, foreign affairs, etc. The state of affairs before the Revolution is contrasted with the current situation. For example, the theme of "Popular Recreation" starts as follows:

The National Institute for the Tourist Industry (INIT), is an organization created by the revolutionary government. This organization is engaged in providing the people with healthy and cheap means of recreation. Tourism has always been in Cuba an important source of income. Some people called it "the second crop." Every year a large number of North American tourists came to our shores and left many dollars in the country. But in the past tourism was based on the wrong foundations. Tourists were attracted to our country by gambling, prostitution and vice, and although this brought us a lot of income, it discredited us internationally. The revolutionary government wants to attract tourists to our country on a different basis. On the basis of coming to look at the beauty of our land, the loveliness of our beaches, the unequalled blue of our sky, the happiness and satisfaction which our people feel today. It is clear that tourism here has declined considerably owing to the intense campaign which the United States is waging to discredit us. But no matter. INIT is trying all the time to create new tourist centres, new places of recreation, which will be enjoyed by a people which formerly found itself deprived of healthy diversions, because these were beyond its economic means. . . . Today prospects have been opened for the Cuban people not only of material happiness, but of spiritual happiness too, through the opportunities that INIT offers of enjoying the beauty of our country (pp. 62-63).

Other themes deal with racial and religious discrimination. On racial discrimination:

Racial discrimination has no *raison d'être*. Science has shown that all men are equal, that there are no essential differences between a white man, a negro or a man of yellow race . . . The people of Cuba is formed by various ethnic groups. On the one hand are the whites, descendants of the Spaniards, who in the conquest and colonization of our country almost completely exterminated the primitive indigenous population; on the other hand, the negroes were brought from Africa to be used as slaves. The fact of slavery led the colonizers to consider the slave as an inferior being, almost as a thing. Despite this, the two basic groups of our population were intermingling as the centuries passed, giving rise to the mulatto who can be considered the most characteristic type of our people[9] (p. 41).

On religion:

Our Revolution is democratic and therefore respects all religious sentiments. If religion includes noble and just ideals, if it follows the precepts of Christ on equality, love and work for all, the Revolution, which embodies all these ideals, is therefore the culmination of the doctrine. Revolutionary law has been equally favourable to catholics, protestants and atheists; that is to say, there has been no discrimination in putting its benefits within the reach of all. The Revolution is convinced that the poor, irrespective of their religious ideas, are willing to defend its principles and its laws. However, the Revolution cannot allow evil-minded groups, shielding themselves behind false religious sentiments, to carry out counter-revolutionary acts. As our leader, Fidel Castro, has said: "There cannot be a uniquely just measure in human society, I do not think that there can be one good deed in the civil society of mankind, which cannot be accommodated in a healthy and just religious conscience" (p. 59).

Foreign affairs are the main theme of chapters headed "Friends and Enemies," "Imperialism," "International Trade," "War and Peace," "International Unity," and "The Revolution Wins Every Battle." The text is bitterly and strongly anti-imperialist and frequently identifies imperialism with "the United States," often describing the latter as the "North American monopolists" or "the interests of Yankee imperialism." The following passages appear representative:

Cuba, like all countries which struggle for full independence, has many friends and also powerful enemies. Her friends include those peoples who, like herself, hope to achieve true independence and complete liberty, the peoples of Latin America and certain Afro-Asian peoples who also struggle against the common imperialist enemy. We foster this friendship through direct contacts, since governments do not always respond to the desires of these peoples. We also consider as friends those peoples who have achieved absolute freedom, and who help in an honest and disinterested way countries which are struggling against the colonial yoke imposed by imperialism; in this class are the Soviet Union, The People's Republic of China and the other Socialist countries. Our main enemies are imperialists. They are enemies because they see in our country the example for all oppressed peoples to rise, ready for the struggle and unafraid. They are enemies because they do not know how to resign themselves to losing the sources of juicy profits made at the cost of the life, the sacrifice and the labour of the exploited. They are enemies because they know that even their own people will find in the example of Cuba the road to true liberation. We have, as Fidel Castro would say, honour enough not to be friends of those who attack us, harm us and want to interfere in the future and in the progress of our people. Cubans want the best relations with all the other peoples of the world, including the people of North America. Cubans are not turned into enemies of that people by the injuries we receive at the hands of evil Yankee politicians, representatives of the monopolistic interests of the United States, who harm their own people almost as much as ours (pp. 43-44).

One of the most recent economic aggressions of imperialism was the blockade which they tried to impose on us, by refusing to buy our products or sell us theirs; this measure failed because many other countries such as China, Czechoslovakia, Canada, Japan, the Soviet Union, etc., have increased their commercial links with our country (p. 67).

Such sentiments are not confined to the chapters on foreign relations. Nationalization, industrialization, health, and tourism are discussed in a way which links former troubles to imperialist exploitation. The chapter condemning racial discrimination begins: "Racial discrimination always has an economic foundation. The exploiting countries, in order to justify the hold which they had on other peoples, considered that these peoples belonged to an inferior race with the right neither to freedom nor to the full dignity of man" (p. 41).

No mention is made here of the United States although at the end of the book the Ku Klux Klan is described as a "North American racist organization which persecutes the Negro citizens." Chapter 24, which completes the main section of the book, discusses the First Declaration of Havana and is followed by 6 pages containing the actual text.

The final section in *Alfabeticemos* is a vocabulary of "words which it is useful to clarify." Many are defined in a way that would cause no great surprise if found in any dictionary. Thus the first entry is "Agricultural activities: jobs which are developed in the area of agriculture," and the last "Zumo: juice." However, sometimes a definition has political content. For example: "Associated Press: a North American news agency in the service of the interests of Yankee imperialism"; "Auto-aggression: to attack one's self with the object of having a pretext for attacking others. A tactic used by imperialism"; "China: a country in Asia which has carried out a social revolution, permitting it, in 10 years, to take a leap out of the backwardness in which it lived, and make itself one of the most developed countries in that continent"; "World disarmament: proposition of the Soviet Union with the object of ending the arms race and suppressing armament, thus initiating peaceful coexistence"; "Organization of American States: Organization which groups together American countries, used by Yankee imperialism to impose its policy on Latin American countries"; "Underdeveloped countries: countries which have not achieved their complete economic development because of the exploitation of their riches by a foreign country."

Adult Classes

Topical comment on political matters is often introduced into adult classes through "the mural," a large-sized blackboard to which are pinned headlines and other cuttings from the Revolutionary newspapers. About three-quarters of all *Superación Obrera-Campesina* classes have a mural as have very many of the other adult classes. The Ministry of Education officially encourages their use. The technique in classes I visited was for a student to read some headline or sentence and then to comment on what he had read. Sometimes this would lead to a discussion. The pedagogical value of this method for checking the reading and comprehension of new literates is undoubted. Equally certain is the wider coverage it gives to the political viewpoint of *Revolución*, *El Mundo* and *Hoy*,[10] the three main Cuban newspapers. There may also be some similarities between this sort of personal exposition of official political statements and the "study-circle" discussions of an individual's political views which have been held in China and Russia.

Because professional teachers may also instruct adults, the political program designed for the primary schools may have much wider influence. Ideas introduced into the school curriculum almost certainly will appear within the adult classes. Thus the social studies program for the primary schools may well have affected the political content of many adult courses. In the same way any lack of conviction which a teacher feels towards some parts of the official syllabus on inequality, imperialism, etc., might reduce the effectiveness with which he teaches it.

Publications

Many ministries have put out technical publications relevant to their work: both INRA and the Ministry of Industries are producing books and pamphlets of technical, mainly apolitical, instruction.

In 1962, bookshops still sold and displayed old publications of varying political colour. The main Havana libraries included a wide range of titles. Whether there was any official intention to curtail this selection was uncertain. Nor was it easy to tell how significant was the variety.

Probably of much greater importance are the books running off the presses. Here the general trend is clear but there are exceptions. Some books are not political at all. Many are by Latin American authors. A few are political surprises. The following two lists give the authors and titles of books published in 1961 by the National Press and by the National Council of Culture. In addition to the titles listed, the National Press published the full set of *Obras Revolucionarias*, the major speeches of the Cuban leaders. It is not clear what proportion of total publications the following books represented but it is probably fair to believe that editorial policy of all publications, as well as policy towards all imports of books, is governed by the same principles which Castro once suggested the newspapers should follow.

We should make available to public opinion those questions which help the economy of the country, and help improve its culture and develop the conscience of the people; we must develop the Revolutionary conscience of the people; we must explain the fundamental principles of the Revolution, its reasons and its justice, we must discredit the enemies of the Revolution and the arguments against the Revolution, because they lack reason and ethics. And since all the information media are in the hands of the Revolution, we should place that formidable power in the service of a strong revolutionary conscience of the people.[11]

Books published by the National Press of Cuba during 1961 (10,000 to 150,000 copies of each title were printed)

AUTHOR	TITLE
Fidel Castro	La Historia Me Absolverá
Julius Fucik	Reportaje al Pié de la Horca
Blas Roca	Fundamentos del socialismo en Cuba
Nicolai Ostravski	Asi Se Templó el Acero
Sergei Smirnov	Héroes de la Fortaleza de Brest
Dimitri Fúrmanov	Chapáev
Elmar Grin	El Último Almiar
Jacques Romain	Los Gobernadores del Rocío
Lu-Sin	Novelas Escogidas
Anatole Kuznetzov	Continuación de una Leyenda
Ricardo Güiraldes	Don Segundo Sombra
	Four Czech novels
Karl Marx	El Capital
M. Ilin	Un Paseo por la Casa
Juan Marinello	Guatemala Nuestra
José Martí	Ideario Pedagógico
Academy of Sciences USSR	Psicología
V. P. Rozhin	La Dialéctica Marxista-Leninista
Academy of Sciences USSR	Manual de Economía Política
Academy of Sciences USSR	Fundamentos de la Filosofía Marxista
V. I. Lenin	El Estado y la Revolución
V. I. Lenin	El Imperialismo, Fase Superior del Capitalismo
H. O'Connor	El Imperio del Petróleo
Mao Tse Tung	Sobre el Arte y la Literatura
John Reed	10 Días Que Estremecieron al Mundo

Anna L. Strong	Las Comunas Chinas
Ramiro Cuerra	Azúcar y Población en las Antillas
Voltaire	Cándido o el Optimismo
Carlos Luis Fallas	Manita Yunai
C. Freinet	Escuela Popular Moderna
Leo Huberman	Los Bienes Terrenales del Hombre
V. I. Lenin	Sobre la Juventud
V. I. Lenin	Sobre la Religión
Núñez Jiménez	Así Es Mi País (A Child's Geography of Cuba)
Joaquín Ordoqui	Elementos para la Historia del Movimiento Obrero en Cuba
Anton S. Makarenko	Conferencias sobre Educación Infantil
Aníbal Ponce	Educación y Lucha de Clases
Elvio Romero	Esta Guitarra Dura
Gregoria Ortega	Panamá
Augusto Pila	Los Fundamentos del Beisbol
Ch. D. Kemper and J. H. Soothill	El Imperio del Banano
Rito Esteban	Lucha de Clases y Movimiento Obrero
	Los Más Famosos Cuentos Franceses

Books Published by the National Council of Culture in 1961

AUTHOR	TITLE	NO. OF COPIES
J. A. Portuondo	Bosquejo Histórico de las Letras Cubanas	10,000
R. M. Merchán	Cuba, Justificación de Sus Guerras	n.a.
C. Villaverde	Excursión– a Vuelta Abajo	25,000
J. A. Saco	Papeles sobre Cuba (T.I.)	5,000
F. G. Lorca	Conferencias y Charlas	5,000
F. G. Lorca	Divan de Tamarit	5,000
R. Tagore	Poesías	5,000
Cintio Vitier	Los Poetas Románticos Cubanos	20,000
Carlos Enriquez	Tilín García	5,000
Samuel Feijóo	Mateo Torriente	2,000
M. Pogoloti	El Camino del Arte	15,000
E. García Buchaca	La Teoría de la Superestructura	50,000
Fidel Castro	Palabras a los Intelectuales	100,000
Samuel Feijóo	Dibujos	2,000
R. Tagore	Cuatro Ensayos	5,000
	Revista Nacional de Teatro	10,000
	Revista de Artes Plásticas	5,000
	Revista "Pueblo y Cultura"	15,000
	Nueva Revista Cubana	5,000
	Segunda Declaración de la Habana	20,000

Appendix B

Cost Calculations

The data and assumptions on which are based the very approximate average cost calculations for 1962 given in Table 3, Chapter VIII, and elsewhere are explained below. All 1962 expenditures are budgetary estimates taken from the *"Presupuesto por Actividades de 1962"* of the Ministry of Education. Enrollment totals are as given in the text but often divided into general and scholarship students. Average cost calculations for the 1960-61 school year, also included in Table 3, Chapter VIII, are taken directly from an analysis made by the Statistical Department of the Ministry of Education, Havana.

School Education

Primary education: government expenditure on primary education grew from $61.8 million in 1961 to $84.9 million in 1962. Over half of the increase in 1962 was for schools recently constructed, for 1500 new teachers and for running the newly nationalized schools. In 1962, $5.3 million was for school meals.

Assuming enrollments are 1,350,000 as estimated, average cost per primary school student for 1962 would be $59 or $63 if the cost of meals is included. This may be compared with $54 per student in 1961.

Primary teacher training: the total budget in 1962 for Minas del Frío, Topes de Collantes and central administration of these two schools was $3.5 million. If we divide central administrative expenditure in the ratio of students, Topes de Collantes takes nearly $2 million, and the cost per student would be about $800 in Minas and $1,168 in Topes. If we divide central expenditure according to the ratio of local school expenditure, the average costs are $763 and $1,212. Of course, these figures are on the basis of the budget estimates. As only 191 of the 230 positions budgeted for teaching staff were filled, actual costs may well be reduced by about 5 per cent.

The Makarenko Institute for training adult teachers was allocated $1.4 million in the 1962 budget, which would be $941 for each of the 1500 students enrolled.

The budget for the old teacher training schools was $2.2 million in 1962, which allowed for 367 teachers and 35 assistants. As more than 4,000 students were said to be enrolled, cost per student would be less than $550.

Secondary Education: General Stream. In the basic secondary schools nearly a third of the budget in 1962 went to capital expenditure. In 1961, the average cost per student per year was $139 for urban students and $1,353 for rural secondary students. By 1962 the budgeted cost per urban secondary student had risen to $222 and the budget for scholarship students to $757.

In the pre-university institutes the annual cost per student had risen from $218 in 1961 to $383 in 1962 and about $1,948 per student under the scholarship program.[1] The increase in costs per student in 1962 was almost entirely the result of the decrease in enrollments and an increase in salaries. The latter appears to be a budgetary over-estimate for it allows for 1,359 teaching staff, 698 administrative staff and 32 auxiliaries in the nationalized schools. In fact, not 1,359 but 1,062 teachers were employed in 1962. If the allowance for salaries is reduced in this proportion, cost per student would be $313 per year.

Technological Schools and Institutes: the national budget for 1962 allowed $18.5 million for technological schools and institutes, $6.3 million for the non-boarding schools and $12.2 million for the boarding schools.

If differences in expenses between the technical schools and institutes are ignored, the cost per student according to planned enrollments in the technological stream was $858 per student, which may be compared with $784 per student in 1961.

Schools of Commerce: the budget for 1962 was $2.8 million under the regular program and $1.3 million under the new scholarship program. This would be $182 per day student and $3,611 per scholarship student, of which apparently there were only 368. The former may be compared with an average cost in 1961 of $140.

Adult Education

The literacy campaign: as explained in the text, the budget allocation specifically for the 1961 campaign was only $12.3 million.

But 33,960 of the school teachers of the Ministry of Education worked in the campaign, and their salaries were paid from the normal school budgets. As a first approximation, the cost of the Ministry of Education teachers and staff may be added to the basic campaign costs. Assuming, therefore, that the proportion of teachers employed (33,960 of the total 39,150) also indicates the division of administrative and other staff costs, and taking this fraction $\dfrac{3396}{3915}$ of seven months (7/12) of the 1961 budget for salaries ($77.7 million), gives $39.3 million as the approximate cost of the Ministry staff. Adding this to the central funds allocated directly to the campaign gives $51.6 million as a rough figure for total cost. In terms of budgetary cost this would represent $73.0 per literate taught, $57.6 per illiterate studying.

The choice of seven months is fairly arbitrary, based on a rough calculation of the time which teachers necessarily would have been absent from school teaching, because of the literacy campaign. Note, however, that changing this estimate would change the estimated cost per illiterate.

Seguimiento 1962: in the ordinary *Seguimiento* classes, salary rates were $125 monthly for full-time teachers and for inspectors (roughly one for every 24 schools). The activists, responsible for several classes, received $35 and the part-time non-professional teachers received $25 monthly. These salaries would imply very roughly a budget for a year of ten months of $6.7 million. If this is treated as two-thirds of the total expenditure (the proportion of salaries to total expenses in the original budget allocation), it would mean an annual expenditure on *Seguimiento* of about $10 million, or one million more than what I understood to be the revised estimate. The difference could well be accounted for if fewer teachers were on the payroll in earlier months, if vacation periods were unpaid, or by errors in this rough calculation.[2] The order of magnitude, however, seems right. On the basis of this calculation, the annual cost per student would be about $32 for those attending *Seguimiento* classes and barely more than $2 for those in the family circles.

Continuation courses in the army were allocated $620,000 in the Ministry of Education's budget which, if enrollments were 24,668, would suggest an annual cost per student of about $25.

Night schools: the budget estimate for the traditional night schools, which could use expenditure in previous years as a guide, was $4.3 million or $76 per student enrolled. Salaries and social security accounted for almost all of this. Expenditure on materials and services, only $160,000, was much less in proportion than for other evening classes, possibly because most of the equipment necessary had already been purchased in previous years.

Superación Obrera-Campesina: In *Superación Obrera-Campesina* classes, professional teachers were paid $125 monthly and nonprofessionals $25. If salaries were two-thirds of total expenses, this might mean an annual expenditure in 1962 of about $4,000,-000, or $43 per student. If total expenditure was nearer the $7,000,000 mentioned earlier, annual cost per student would be $75.

Appendix C. Level of Schooling Attained, by Age[a]

AGE	TOTAL	GRADE OR YEAR COMPLETED Primary Schooling								
		None	1	2	3	4	5	6	7	8
Total	4,940,873	1,530,090	292,506	525,021	638,651	573,295	390,033	446,586	90,143	226,069
6- 9 years	564,344	420,258	71,978	48,257	18,331	4,204	1,316	—	—	—
0-14 years	667,865	224,011	69,663	105,959	100,215	73,754	46,144	25,353	9,196	7,698
5-19 years	557,925	133,304	25,217	59,535	77,028	71,216	53,827	53,437	17,877	31,358
0-24 years	521,165	112,673	21,167	52,373	74,032	70,229	50,719	55,278	12,647	31,442
5-29 years	453,568	89,222	17,391	44,346	64,787	63,601	45,844	54,204	10,668	28,689
0-34 years ...:	403,993	82,081	15,277	39,324	58,035	57,366	40,930	50,485	8,797	25,414
5-39 years	383,417	79,610	14,711	38,131	56,214	54,398	38,371	48,588	8,214	24,618
0-44 years	346,743	77,072	13,888	35,361	50,803	48,653	32,388	42,115	6,643	21,122
5-49 years	292,781	68,693	12,102	29,539	41,750	39,837	26,384	35,931	5,563	17,958
0-54 years	210,138	51,366	8,587	20,776	29,229	28,103	18,097	26,277	3,829	13,267
5-59 years	139,328	36,805	5,832	13,500	18,987	18,210	11,394	16,669	2,381	8,462
0-64 years	152,069	46,830	6,597	15,284	20,753	19,085	11,132	16,523	2,061	7,629
5-69 years	105,562	40,271	4,547	10,639	13,294	11,688	6,591	9,703	1,115	4,136
0-74 years ...:	67,034	29,566	2,753	6,122	7,709	6,536	3,525	5,713	634	2,286
5-79 years	35,219	15,452	1,427	2,957	3,835	3,371	1,804	3,952	272	1,095
0-84 years	20,755	10,959	748	1,606	2,092	1,776	928	1,442	147	537
5 years and more	18,967	11,917	621	1,312	1,557	1,268	639	916	99	358

AGE	TOTAL	High School					Vocational				University	
		1	2	3	4	5	1	2	3	4	1 to 4	5 years and more
Total	4,940,873	20,836	17,532	14,102	13,981	22,111	13,833	11,679	15,262	45,679	31,527	21,937
6- 9 years	564,344	—	—	—	—	—	—	—	—	—	—	—
0-14 years	667,865	2,842	1,300	620	—	—	807	303	—	—	—	—
5-19 years	557,925	4,996	4,370	3,731	2,832	2,631	5,952	3,990	2,659	2,368	1,597	—
0-24 years	521,165	2,849	2,554	2,329	2,536	3,935	2,471	2,504	4,498	8,726	6,889	1,314
5-29 years ....'	453,568	2,396	2,241	1,882	1,948	3,728	1,311	1,298	2,795	7,995	5,637	3,585
0-34 years	403,993	1,946	1,696	1,317	1,504	2,820	798	844	1,529	5,516	4,514	3,800
5-39 years	383,417	1,617	1,513	999	1,075	2,082	753	886	1,027	4,558	3,237	2,815
0-44 years	346,743	1,552	1,324	1,039	1,093	1,725	564	603	815	4,401	2,940	2,642
5-49 years	292,781	1,072	965	788	890	1,600	410	481	618	3,309	2,387	2,504
0-54 years	210,138	663	619	560	711	1,226	278	266	423	2,269	1,578	2,014
5-59 years	139,328	325	340	260	438	782	143	147	306	2,094	1,038	1,215
0-64 years	152,069	259	250	225	383	661	170	160	301	2,004	793	969
5-69 years	105,562	152	164	154	233	424	77	92	139	1,220	435	488
0-74 years	67,034	89	110	107	187	281	60	58	78	665	244	311
5-79 years	35,219	40	49	57	90	140	22	25	39	297	137	158
0-84 years	20,755	19	23	26	47	52	10	7	23	171	66	76
5 years and more	18,967	19	14	8	14	24	7	15	12	86	35	46

a. The number in each group does not include those who have completed a higher level of education.
Source: *Censos de Población, Viviendas y Electoral 1953,* Havana, Cuba. Tables 36 and 37, pp. 119 *et seq.*

Part III

Industry

Appendix

Table 1. Physical Volume of Output in Some Industrial Lines

	Unit	1951	1952	1953	1954	1955	1956	1957	
Sugar	Thousand tons	5,759	7,225	5,152	4,890	4,528	4,740	5,672	5
Beer	Thousand HL	1,255	1,437	1,188	1,202	1,179	1,205	1,292	1
Cigars	Millions	364	391	375	316	340	377	409	
Cigarettes	Millions	8,334	8,975	8,740	9,357	9,341	9,539	9,803	10
Textiles and rayon fiber	Thousand tons	10	8	9	10	9	10	10	
Sulphuric acid	Thousand tons	27	24	26	28	28	32	32	
Refined petroleum	Thousand tons	308	338	362	391	435	477	1,819	2
Cement	Thousand tons	382	419	405	420	424	416	656	
Electric power	Thousand KWH	836	918	1,006	1,088	1,200	1,324	1,354	1
Gas	Million cubic meters	52	57	60	60	58	60	59	

Source: Statistical Yearbook, United Nations, 1960.

Table 2. Industries Expropriated by Law No. 890, October 13, 1960.

Types of Industry	Number
Sugar mills	105
Distilleries	18
Manufacture of alcoholic beverages	6
Soap and perfume factories	3
Factories of milk derivatives	5
Chocolate factories	2
Flour mills	1
Packaging and containers	8
Paint factories	4
Chemical products	3
Basic metallurgy	6
Paper mills	7
Lamp manufacture	1
Textiles and clothing	61
Rice	16
Food products	7
Oil and grease	2
Coffee toasting	11
Printing	1
Construction enterprises	19
Electric plants	1
Total	287

Source: Law No. 890 (October 13, 1960).

Table 3. Assets of the Consolidated Enterprises of the Ministry of Industry
(At March 31, 1962)

	Millions of $	Percentage
Fixed assets		
Machinery, equipment, and installations	1,062.4	71.8
Buildings and constructions	337.2	22.8
Furniture and office equipment	25.7	1.8
Land	33.7	2.3
Others	19.1	1.3
Total	1,479.1	100.0
Depreciation	−551.1	
Total fixed assets, net	928.0	
Current assets		
Inventories of finished products	249.4	21.4
Inventories of work-in-progress	36.4	3.2
Inventories of raw materials and other materials	197.3	16.9
Other inventories	63.7	5.4
Amounts collectible	601.4	51.5
Other	18.8	1.6
Total	1,167.0	100.0
Provision against loss	−12.7	
Total current assets	1,154.3	

Source: Ministry of Industry.

Table 4. Breakdown of Employment in Consolidated Enterprises belonging to the Ministry of Industry (In thousands of persons)

	1961				1962			
	Workmen	Technicians	Salaried Personnel	Total	Workmen	Technicians	Salaried Personnel	Total
Heavy Industries	70.1	4.5	14.2	88.8	72.3	5.7	15.3	93.3
Power and metallurgy	10.6	1.2	1.5	13.3	15.1	1.9	2.1	19.1
Electricity and gas	5.1	0.8	0.6	6.5	6.8	1.3	1.0	9.1
Petroleum	1.1	0.1	0.3	1.5	1.4	0.2	0.5	3.8
Metallurgy	1.9	0.2	0.3	2.4	3.1	0.2	0.5	3.8
Mechanical	2.5	0.1	0.3	2.9	3.8	0.2	0.3	4.3
Extractive industries and heavy chemistry	59.5	3.3	12.7	75.5	57.2	3.8	13.2	74.2
Mining	4.7	0.1	0.3	5.1	3.8	0.3	0.3	4.4
Nickel	2.7	0.2	0.9	3.8	3.1	0.3	1.2	4.6
Salt	0.6	–	0.1	0.7	0.6	–	0.1	0.7
Sugar	45.1	2.5	10.3	57.9	42.0	2.5	10.6	55.1
Paper and fiber board	2.1	0.1	0.4	2.6	2.2	0.2	0.4	2.8
Cement and ceramics	2.2	0.1	0.3	2.4	2.3	0.2	0.2	2.7
Heavy chemistry and fertilizers	1.3	0.2	0.3	1.8	2.1	0.2	0.3	2.6
Synthetic fibers	1.0	0.1	0.1	1.2	1.1	0.1	0.1	1.3
Light Industries	51.9	2.2	7.8	61.9	65.8	2.9	7.5	76.2
Food[a]	2.1	0.1	1.0	3.6	4.3	0.1	1.3	5.7
Beverages	4.5	0.1	1.3	5.9	4.2	0.1	1.0	5.3
Tobacco	9.6	0.3	0.5	10.4	13.0	0.4	0.6	14.0
Textiles	8.0	0.4	0.8	9.2	9.0	0.6	0.7	10.3
Clothing[b]	9.5	0.2	0.5	10.2	11.6	0.2	0.8	12.6
Tannery and leather derivatives	5.7	0.2	0.3	6.2	7.3	0.3	0.7	8.3
Light chemistry[c]	6.1	0.5	2.8	9.4	7.6	0.6	1.4	9.6
Light machinery[d]	6.0	0.4	0.6	7.0	8.8	0.6	1.0	10.4
Totals	122.0	6.7	22.0	150.7	138.1	8.6	22.8	169.5

a. Includes only flour. The other industries of this type are under the Department of Industries of INRA.
b. Includes knitted goods.
c. Includes soaps and perfumery, pharmaceutical products, gum, plastics, glass, and phosphorous.
d. Includes metal containers, electrical equipment, paper and cardboard machinery, lumber, recovery of raw materials, and local industries.
Source: Ministry of Industry.

Table 5. Number of Factories of the Ministry of Industry, by Province, 1962

	Total	Pinar del Río	Havana	Matan-zas	Las Villas	Cama-güey	Oriente
Heavy Industries							
Automotive	15	—	15	—	—	—	—
Sugar	188	9	21	31	55	27	45
Cement	4	3	—	—	—	—	1
Ceramics	7	—	6	—	—	1	—
Electricity	80	9	8	1	21	16	25
Fertilizers	23	5	12	3	1	1	1
Gas	2	—	2	—	—	—	—
Synthetic Pulp	5	—	1	1	1	2	—
Mechanical	47	—	33	6	2	3	3
Ferrous metallurgy	9	—	9	—	—	—	—
Non-ferrous metallurgy	19	—	16	1	—	1	1
Mining	23	8	2	1	2	3	7
Nickel	3	—	—	—	—	—	3
Petroleum	3	—	1	—	1	—	1
Paper	7	—	4	1	2	—	—
Heavy chemistry	9	1	4	1	1	1	1
Salt	8	—	—	1	2	2	3
Farm equipment	14	1	8	1	1	2	1
Naval construction	13	1	1	1	3	2	5
Light Industries							
Mineral waters and soft drinks	23	2	11	1	3	1	5
Beer and malt	6	—	4	—	1	—	1
Cigars	10	—	8	—	2	—	—
Paper and cardboard	35	—	31	1	2	—	1
Manufacture of piece goods	179	7	153	—	6	—	13
Leather goods	281	13	137	37	54	4	36
Cans and metal containers	8	—	6	—	1	1	—
Electrical equipment	15	—	15	—	—	—	—
Phosphorous	13	—	10	2	—	1	—
Hard fiber	7	1	3	3	—	—	—
Gum	7	—	5	2	—	—	—
Flour	175	13	5	24	43	18	72
Thread and piece goods	30	—	28	1	—	—	1
Soap and perfumes	11	—	10	1	—	—	—
Liquors and wines	15	—	9	—	3	—	3
Lumber	82	1	62	2	5	5	7
Paint	5	—	5	—	—	—	—
Plastics	16	—	16	—	—	—	—
Pharmaceutical products	52	—	52	—	—	—	—
Scrap metal recovery	8	1	3	1	1	1	1
Twist tobacco	56	2	16	3	21	4	10
Tanneries	29	2	7	3	8	4	5
Knitted goods	54	—	53	—	—	—	1
Glass	5	—	5	—	—	—	—
Specialty textiles	27	—	27	—	—	—	—
Local industries	102	3	69	2	3	7	18
Graphic arts	75	1	60	1	6	2	5

Source: Ministry of Industry, September, 1962.

Table 6. Physical Production, Planned and Provisionally Estimated, of Some Important Products for the Year 1962[a]

Products	Units	Planned	Provisional estimate	Percentage difference
Food and beverages				
Raw sugar	Thousand tons	5,000	4,816	— 3.7
Refined sugar	Thousand tons	650	740	+13.8
Wheat flour	Thousand tons	139	149	7.2
Bread and crackers	Thousand tons	53,100	51,154	— 3.7
Beer	Thousand HL	903	903	—
Cigarettes	Millions	14,400	14,400	—
Textiles and clothing				
Cotton textiles	Tons	15,300	12,900	—15.7
Rayon textiles	Tons	5,600	4,300	—23.2
Leather shoes	Thousand pairs	6,490	4,771	—26.5
Rubber shoes	Thousand pairs	5,623	3,900	—30.8
Intermediate products				
Sulphuric acid	Thousand tons	202	166	—17.8
Fuel oil	Thousand tons	1,438	2,079	44.6
Gas oil	Thousand tons	491	558	13.6
Gasoline	Thousand tons	724	668	— 7.7
Rayon cord	Tons	3,340	2,844	—14.9
Rayon yarn	Tons	1,085	890	—18.0
Superphosphates	Tons	49,600	49,600	—
Detergents	Tons	16,500	16,500	—
Tires	Thousands	448	380	—15.2
Gray cement	Thousand tons	934	890	— 4.7
Sinter of nickel and cobalt	Tons	20,000	16,140	—19.3
Sulphur of nickel and cobalt	Tons	16,700	13,530	—19.0
Copper concentrate	Tons	24,200	18,500	—23.6
Electric power	Thousand KWH	2,390	2,260	— 5.4

a. Not included is the production of new factories that began production in the course of 1962.

Source: Ministry of Industry. (Estimated in August, 1962.)

Table 7. Value of the Production of the Consolidated Enterprises of the Ministry of Industry (January-June, 1962) (In Millions of Pesos)

	Goal	Actual	Actual as Percentage of Goal
Food	464.8	447.8	96
Sugar	429.9	413.7	96
Flour	34.9	34.1	98
Beverages	46.4	46.0	99
Mineral water and soft drinks	10.2	9.8	96
Beer and malt	24.7	24.9	101
Liquors and wines	11.5	11.3	98
Tobacco	53.6	46.8	87
Cigarettes	35.9		89
Twisted tobacco	17.7	14.7	83
Textiles	62.8	51.3	82
Hard fibers	4.2	4.2	100
Knitted goods	10.3	7.0	68
Piece goods	48.3	40.1	83
Clothing and footwear	34.7	20.0	58
Clothing	21.1	9.9	47
Leather goods, shoes	13.6	10.1	74
Wood and cork	9.8	6.3	64
Lumber	6.7	4.2	63
Fiberboard	3.1	2.1	68
Paper and cardboard	96.7	97.5	101
Paper and cardboard	83.1	84.5	102
Synthetic pulp	13.6	13.0	96
Leather and skins	7.1	6.1	86
Leather goods	4.5	3.3	73
Tanneries	2.6	2.8	108
Rubber and derivatives	19.4	12.3	63
Gum	19.4	12.3	63
Chemical products	89.6	65.6	73
Heavy chemistry	14.1	13.0	92
Fertilizers	18.2	14.3	79
Synthetic fibers	5.4	4.8	89
Phosphorous	3.9	3.7	95
Soaps and perfumes	22.9	16.9	74
Pharmaceutical products	18.9	7.3	39
Paint	6.2	5.6	90

Table 7. Continued

	Goal	Actual	Actual as Percentage of Goal
Petroleum derivatives	83.1	84.5	102
Non-metallic minerals	18.8	16.8	89
Cement	10.5	9.5	90
Ceramics	1.9	0.9	47
Glass	6.4	6.4	100
Basic metals	21.4	16.7	78
Ferrous metallurgy	12.1	10.9	90
Non-ferrous metallurgy	9.3	5.8	62
Metallic products	29.0	21.5	74
Machines	13.9	7.9	57
Containers	14.5	12.9	89
Electrical equipment	0.6	0.7	117
Automotive	1.5	1.3	87
Plastics	5.1	2.7	53
Mining	26.3	21.5	82
Mining	4.1	3.0	73
Nickel	21.9	18.2	83
Mineral resources	0.3	0.3	100
Electricity and gas	37.1	38.2	103
Electricity	35.8	36.9	103
Gas	1.3	1.3	100
Totals	1,107.2	1,002.9	91

Source: Ministry of Industry.

Table 8. Programed Industrial Investment in New Plants
(Millions of pesos)

Industries	Total	1961[a]	Periods 1962-65	Periods 1966-70	Due in Operation	Country of Origin of Equipment
Food industries						
Flour mills	4.0		4.0		1962	b
Flour mills	4.0		4.0		1963	b
Yeast, bread	0.4		0.4		1963c	Bulgaria
Salt (ITABO)	0.8	0.5	0.3		1962	One half from USA
Slaughter houses	2.5		2.5		1963	Hungary
Peanut oil extraction	1.3		1.3		1963	Bulgaria
Soya bean oil	0.5		0.5		1963	Bulgaria
Cotton seed oil	1.2		1.2		1963	Bulgaria
Tomato products	0.9	0.3	0.6		1962-63	Yugoslavia
Animal feed	0.1		0.1		1962	Cuba b
Pasteurized milk	2.5		2.5		1962-64c	b
Ice	1.0		1.0		1963	Bulgaria
Chocolate	0.8		0.8		1963-64	b
	20.0	0.8	19.2			
Textile industries						
Thread and piece goods	1.4	1.2	0.2		1962	East Germany
Thread and piece goods	23.3		23.3		1964c	China
Thread and piece goods	12.6		12.6		1963c	East Germany
Kenaf bags	3.6	2.6	1.0		1962	East Germany
Kenaf macerator	1.1	0.5	0.6		1962	East Germany
Kenaf bags	4.5		4.5		1964c	East Germany
Macerator	1.3		1.3		1964c	East Germany
	47.8	4.3	43.5			

					Year	Country
Clothing and footwear						
Footwear	1.6		1.6		1964	East Germany
Footwear	1.6		1.6		1965	East Germany
Clothing	0.1	—	0.1		1962	[b]
	3.3		3.3			
Wood						
Pencils	3.0	0.1	2.9		1963	China
Plywood	0.4	0.1	0.3		1962	[b]
Celotex	1.6		1.6		1964[e]	[b]
	5.0	0.2	4.8			
Leather						
Pigskin	1.5		1.5		1963	[b]
Rubber and derivatives						
Hose and straps	9.0		3.0	6.0	1964[e]	China
Chemical products						
Synthetic fibers	1.0	0.2	0.8		1967[e]	East Germany
Superphosphates	6.5		6.5		1964[e]	East Germany
Ammonia and derivatives	54.0		6.0	48.0	1963-68	USSR
Calcium carbide	0.8		0.8		1964	Hungary
Sodium chloride	10.0		7.0	3.0	1966[e]	China
Citric acid	0.2		0.2		1963	Poland
Essential oils	0.3		0.3		1963	Poland
Butyl acetate	0.8		0.1	0.7	1966[e]	Poland
Alcohol acetate derivatives	15.1		2.3	12.8	1966[e]	[b]
Refining of cane wax	1.4		1.4		1964	[b]
Sulphonated castor oil	0.1		0.1		1963	[b]
Glass wool	0.4		0.4		1963	Hungary
Brewers' yeast	3.0		3.0		1964	France

Table 8. Continued

Industries	Periods				Due in Operation	Country of Origin of Equipment
	Total	1961[a]	1962-65	1966-70		
Brewers' yeast	2.2	0.2	2.0		1966[c]	East Germany
Recovery of yeast	0.3		0.3		1964	East Germany
Caffeine	0.3		0.3		1963	b
Pancreatic insulin	0.2		0.2		1963	b
Antibiotics	2.3	0.5	1.8		1965[c]	b
Serums	0.8		0.8		1965[c]	b
Recovery of raw materials	0.6	0.2	0.4		1963	b
	100.3	0.9	32.1	67.3		
Petroleum derivatives						
Refining	11.0		11.0			USSR
	11.0		11.0			
Non-metallic minerals						
Cement	12.9		12.9		1965[c]	East Germany
Cement	11.5	0.1	1.0	10.5	1967[c]	Rumania
Processing of kaolin	1.8		1.7		1962	East Germany
Processing of silica	0.2		0.2		1962	Bulgaria
Electrical ceramics	1.5		1.5		1964[c]	East Germany
Refectories	2.5		2.5		1965	Poland
Processing of feldspar	0.5		0.5		1964	b
Sheet glass	3.1		3.1		1963	Poland
Conglomerate glass (includes light bulbs)	8.4		8.4			
	42.4	0.1	31.8	10.5		
Basic metals						
Iron and steel plants	150.0		35.0	115.0	1967[c]	East Germany

					Year	Country
Foundry, electric arc	1.1	0.7	0.4		1962	Cuba
Foundry, electric arc	4.0		4.0		1963	Poland
Foundry, gray iron and malleable iron	6.1		6.1		1965	Poland
Cobalt plants	61.5		30.0	31.5	1967c	USSR
Nickel plants	100.0		35.0	65.0	1967c	USSR
Ball bearings	0.3		0.3		1963	b
	323.0	0.7	110.8	211.5		
Metallic products						
Containers	0.8	0.1	0.7		1964	
Pressure washers	0.1		0.1		1962	b
Barbed wire	2.5	0.3	2.2		1963	b
Nuts, screws, washers	1.6	0.8	0.8		1962	Czechoslovakia
Locks and padlocks	0.5	0.3	0.2		1962	Czechoslovakia
Table tops	0.6	0.3	0.3		1962	Czechoslovakia
Picks and shovels	0.9	0.5	0.4		1962	Czechoslovakia
Domestic appliances	12.9	1.1	11.8		1963	b
Files	1.5		1.5		1963	USSR
Soldering electrodes	0.8	0.3	0.5		1963	East Germany
Hand tools	5.3		5.3		1963	Poland
Masons' tools	0.2		0.2		1963	b
Wood screws	1.0		1.0		1963	b
Bobbins, waxing tools	0.5		0.5		1963	b
	29.2	3.7	25.5			
Machinery						
Mechanical plant	8.5		8.5		1963	USSR
Molds and dies	1.6	0.2	1.4		1963	b
Compressors (5 and 10 HP)	0.4		0.4		1965c	Czechoslovakia
Diesel motors and compressors	2.0		2.0		1964	Czechoslovakia

Table 8. Continued

Industries	Total	1961[a]	Periods 1962-65	1966-70	Due in Operation	Country of Origin of Equipment
Shop for manufacture of parts	8.5		8.5		1963	[b]
Gasoline pumps	0.9		0.1	0.8	1964	China
Balances and scales	0.8		0.8		1964	Hungary
	22.7	0.2	21.7	0.8		
Electrical equipment						
Radio and television	1.2	0.1	1.1		1963	Poland
Transformers	4.0		4.0		1964	Czechoslovakia
Motor assembly	0.2		0.2		1964	Czechoslovakia
	5.4	0.1	5.3			
Transport material						
Mariel shipyard	34.3		15.0	19.3	1968	Poland
Casablanca shipyard	15.9		15.9		1964	Czechoslovakia
Bicycles	0.9	0.1	0.8		1963	Czechoslovakia
Spark plugs	1.0		1.0		1963	Czechoslovakia
Automotive assembly	90.0		15.0	75.0	1964	[b]
Automotive assembly	0.9		0.9		1963	[b]
Shock absorbers	1.6		0.2	1.4	1964	China
Piston rings	1.3		0.1	1.2	1964	China
Ignition parts	1.4		0.1	1.3	1964	[b]
	147.3	0.1	49.0	98.2		

Miscellaneous manufactures					1962
Brushes	0.3	0.2	0.1		1963
Plastics	1.3	0.5	0.8		
Orthopedic supports	0.5	—	0.5		
	2.1	0.7	1.4		East Germany [b]
Mining	70.0		70.0		Hungary
Electricity					
Generators	100.9		100.9		USSR
Transmission lines	21.0		21.0		USSR
Distributors	35.0		35.0		USSR
Substations	7.7		7.7		USSR
Others	5.4		5.4		USSR
	170.0		170.0		USSR
Other investments					
Reserves	10.0		10.0		
Auto school	3.0		3.0		
	13.0		13.0		
Totals	1,023.0	11.8	616.9	394.3	

a. Investments already made by December 31, 1961.
b. Not available.
c. Provisional estimates.
Source: Ministry of Industry, investments; and various publications about locations.

Notes

Preface

1. Noyola subsequently died in an airplane crash.
2. He also, rather inconsistently, told me that we would be welcome if we returned six months later.
3. As will be seen later, however, considerable efforts are being made to improve the collection of data.
4. Earlier we had discussed whether it was worthwhile staying in the country to collect material. There were some obvious risks in this, but we were still very interested, and naturally we were reluctant to admit defeat once we had drawn on the Cabot Foundation grant.
5. Curiously enough, under a long-standing agreement, those with a United Kingdom passport have been able to enter Cuba without a visa, at least until recently.

Chapter I

1. Use of primary products does not grow proportionately as fast as income. I have tried to show the various reasons for this in "A Model of Comparative Rates of Growth in the World Economy," *Economic Journal*, LXXII (March, 1962), 45-78.
2. This whole question of the structural causes of inflation is discussed in a forthcoming study, *Inflation and Growth in Latin America* (prepared by the Economic Commission for Latin America).
3. Very small economies have of course only limited prospects of industrialization—unless they widen markets by forming trading areas with their neighbors.
4. The payments crisis has been especially acute in countries which made only

slow progress until recently in developing petroleum resources—e.g., Argentina, Brazil, and Chile.

5. In Brazil and Chile, about one-third of the adult population votes in presidential elections, and in many countries the figure is smaller. Literacy tests, inadequacy of polling stations, complicated registration procedures, and fear of reprisals are among the factors which limit suffrage. In Mexico the proportion is higher, but there has in effect been only one candidate.

6. Julian Alienes y Urosa, *Caracteristicas Fundamentales de la Economía Cubana* (Banco Nacional de Cuba, 1950), p. 52. Earlier figures were obtained by applying a series of global indicators to an estimate of the national income in 1938. (Per-capita income in 1938 was estimated at $105, but by then prices had fallen, activity had considerably slowed down, and the population had grown.) The figures are in Cuban pesos, but the reader will not go far wrong if he treats these as U.S. dollars.

7. During the height of the sugar boom of 1919-20, average Cuban incomes probably exceeded one-half of those in the United States.

8. The world price fell from over 22 cents a pound in May to less than 4 cents in December.

9. See *Anuario Azucarero de Cuba, 1959.*

10. See *Trends and Forces of World Sugar Consumption* (Food and Agriculture Organization). This study was by Viton and Pignalosa. The highest recent figure was 48.2 in 1953.

11. Viton and Pignalosa, *Trends,* p. 41.

12. The participation of the Philippines also rose in this period, however.

13. The 1937 Sugar Act stabilized the quota at 28.6 per cent.

14. U.S. producers continued to get a subsidy of 0.55 cents, and the duty on Cuban sugar was 0.75 cents.

15. The Banco Nacional has often used U.S. wholesale prices to deflate Cuban exports, but the (rather slower moving) index for U.S. exports seems more appropriate, since Cuba undoubtedly benefited from subsidized food sales.

16. There was, for example, production control also in coffee, to help maintain a high internal price.

17. *Memoria, 1956-57* (Banco Nacional), p. 159.

18. The Nicaro plant was completely closed from early 1947 to early 1952, and nickel ore was not extracted in this period.

19. *Memoria, 1956-57.*

20. The serious weaknesses that can be found from 1947 to 1958 are frankly discussed in "Consideraciones sobre el Metodo de Calculo del Ingreso Nacional de Cuba," by Jorge F. Freire Serra of the Banco Nacional, a paper presented to Regional Conference of the International Association for Research in Income and Wealth, Rio de Janeiro, 1959.

21. Alienes, *Caracteristicas.*

22. Estimates of the Banco Nacional (*Memoria*) show a rise of 38 per cent in money income from 1947 to 1957-58. The population rise would have been about 25 per cent, and prices rose somewhat, though not as much in most countries (1947 and 1948 were years of relatively high prices).

23. Between the censuses of 1919 and 1931, the number of foreign citizens in Cuba, mostly Spaniards, rose from 339,000 to 437,000. (In the 1907 census, the corresponding figure had been 229,000.) According to Alienes, *Caracteristicas,* more than a million immigrants entered the country in the period 1902 to 1930.

24. *Symposium de Recursos Naturales de Cuba* (Consejo Nacional de Economía, 1958). The rate of unemployed was 9 per cent during February-April of 1957 but had been 20 per cent in the *tiempo muerto,* idle season, of August-October of 1956. Public works programs were heavy in 1956. (The 1953 census showed a comparable level of unemployment, namely 9 per cent, as the proportion who had been seeking work during the harvesting of the sugar crop; a further 4 per cent had worked fewer than 10 hours during that week.)

25. The census showed that unpaid family workers totaled 4 per cent of the labor force, and in addition over a third of the labor force was in service industries.

26. See Robert F. Smith, *The United States and Cuba: Business and Diplomacy, 1917-1960* (New York: Bookman Associates, 1960), p. 160.

27. Whereas in Latin America as a whole, manufacturing accounted for 20 per cent of the domestic product in 1950 (and higher proportions in Argentina, Brazil, and Mexico), the corresponding figure for Cuba, despite its higher national income, was 18 per cent in 1953 (excluding sugar mills). For other countries, see *Inflation and Growth in Latin America;* for Cuba, see below. A Department of Commerce publication drew attention to the direct effect of the exchange regime on U.S. investment in manufacturing: "A high percentage of U.S. investments in manufacturing in Latin America have resulted from tariff or import restrictions which have made local manufacture or assembly practically unavoidable. Cuba has, with exceptions, followed a tariff policy which permits a considerable freedom of choice between local production and importation. It has also largely avoided non-tariff controls, such as import licensing, quota restrictions and exchange measures" (*Investment in Cuba* [U.S. Department of Commerce, 1956]).

28. It should be noted that United States companies held a large part of the equity in Cuban sugar and that the system was intrinsically precarious, since the sugar quotas were liable to change by the Congress of the United States.

29. One obvious possible step would have been to devalue the peso. But this was hardly possible for a country so heavily dependent, economically and politically, on the United States; apart altogether from political pressures, devaluation must have appeared likely to rule out almost completely the prospect of further private investment by United States firms in the country. One official comment: "It is totally absurd and lacking in all economic logic to make the irresponsible statement that Cuba will depart from traditional principles" (i.e., freedom of exchange, monetary stability and parity with the dollar). (See *The National Program of Economic Action* [Junta Nacional de Economía, 1951]. This was the time when the Cuban peso became legal tender.)

30. Many illustrations of these points can be found in International Bank for Reconstruction and Development, *Report on Cuba* (Johns Hopkins Press, 1951).

31. British, Canadian, and Spanish assets in the sugar industry were almost completely liquidated; so were British railway investments.

32. Large items were petroleum refining capacity and the Moa Bay nickel mining and separation plant.

33. After an understanding was reached on tariffs, the Cuban Telephone Company started in 1957 on a 5-year development program, intended to amount to more than $50,000,000.

34. It may be that some investments, e.g., in petroleum exploration, have been written off and do not appear in Table 4.

35. *Informe al Consejo de Ministros* (Ministry of Finance, 1959).

36. In Venezuela, the only other large country in the region still with an "open" economy in the 1950's, the foreign exchange system came under pressure when (in 1957) the fast expansion of petroleum exports came to an end. Gold reserves ran down, and, despite heavy financial assistance, the bolivar was devalued for many transactions.

37. The effect on employment and incomes in other industries.

38. Harry T. Oshima, in "The New Estimate of the National Income and Product of Cuba in 1953," estimates this figure at "not less than $430" for that year, which was a relatively bad one (*Food Research Institute Studies*, II [November, 1961], pp. 213-27).

39. Assuming the peso was slightly undervalued.

40. "The most serious social problem of the sugar industry is its tendency to create a small upper class of unenterprising entrepreneurs caught in a sterile

routine, together with a large class of unskilled plantation laborers who have no chance to improve their social and economic condition" (Henry C. Wallich, *Monetary Problems of an Export Economy* [Harvard University Press, 1950], p. 11).

41. Consejo Nacional de Economía, *Boletín Informativo* (February, 1958).

42. The acceleration in population growth, as elsewhere in Latin America, was apparently due to the decline in the death rate, which particularly affects those needing employment (including many of those past what would normally be retirement age).

43. Citing similar calculations by the Banco Nacional, the U.S. Department of Commerce report stated that "it is abundantly clear that nonsugar activities will have to be depended on far more in the future than in the past" (*Investment in Cuba*, p. 7).

44. Imports of brandy, wine, whisky, etc., exceeded rum exports.

45. *Investment in Cuba.* The range was quite big, however.

46. Oshima, "National Income and Product." Comparable figures are quoted from the Labor Ministry ($1,500 for employees in manufacturing, mining, and utilities, and $1,400 for public employees, often part-time).

47. So was the structure of pensions. There were separate plans for each industry, with widely different scales.

48. Many peasants are included here.

49. The sugar workers pressed for a 4-day week in 1959. It seems that the revolutionary government has relied heavily on the Communist party to maintain industrial discipline.

50. Wyatt MacGaffey and C. Barnett, *Cuba: Its People, Its Society, Its Culture* (Human Relations Area Press, 1962).

51. IBRD, *Report on Cuba*, p. 190.

52. *Ibid.*, p. 459.

53. *Ibid.*, p. 309.

54. MacGaffey and Barnett, *Cuba*, p. xix.

55. "There is an impression that statistics are unimportant and that their collection requires little or no professional knowledge." In consequence, posts in the various statistical services were filled by political appointees, many of whom did not even perform any work at all (IBRD, *Report on Cuba*, p. 504).

56. Cubans are not famous for punctuality or even remembering their appointments.

57. This was also partly true of Eastern Europe.

58. $372,000,000 reserves of Banco Nacional, *plus* $144,000,000 foreign assets—government and bank—*minus* $166,000,000 reported dollar liabilities (International Monetary Fund, *International Financial Statistics* [March, 1962]).

59. Though the rather high living standards in Cuba made it difficult to approach the Soviet Union with an appeal *ad misericordiam!*

60. The only exceptions are North Viet Nam and a small area in China.

61. New doctors have to spend part of their training in country districts.

62. One should perhaps mention that the new "school city" being built in Oriente is intended exclusively for the children of this province.

63. Rents were reduced 50 per cent if they were less than 100 pesos a month (40 per cent if between 100 and 200 pesos, 30 per cent if higher than 200), under the law of March 10, 1959.

64. Many of the hotels at Varadero were in 1962 set aside for the exclusive use of the unions.

65. Racial discrimination has been greatly reduced, if not ended (though it is hard to discover how common it really was before the Revolution).

66. It seems that more than 20,000 dwellings were constructed in the first 4 years of the Revolution, of which 12,000 were in rural areas, according to data difficult to interpret in an article by José Carneado (*Cuba Socialista* [October, 1962]).

67. The national minimum wage was to be raised to $65.

68. The issue between capitalism and socialism in the underdeveloped world may well depend on what form of incentive is most successful in keeping a man sweating away through a hot day on a farm job.

69. I will not mention military needs.

70. See "Labor in Cuba," *The Nation*, CXCV (October 20, 1962), 238-41, in which Zeitlin gives some of his results. His findings are not inconsistent with the general impression we all formed during our stay in Cuba, where we traveled the length of the island and conversed with hundreds of people. (In general, there was clearly little hesitation on their part about speaking their minds.)

71. Though in many cases they draw life pensions as compensations. One hundred and eighteen thousand who formerly owned houses for letting receive a total monthly pension of $6,000,000 (Carneado, *Cuba Socialista*).

72. It would be wrong to conclude, however, that all refugees (even all adult refugees) are strongly hostile to the regime. There is always a flow from poorer areas to richer ones when entrance requirements are lax, as they were for Cubans wanting to enter the United States. (The big migration of Puerto Ricans into the United States in the past two decades does not necessarily imply great political hostility, for instance.)

73. Members of the refugee's family would hardly have increased their expenditures greatly when his bank credits and other assets came into their possession.

74. This is being raised to 40 pesos under the new social security legislation.

75. Data from the Ministry of Labor. The rise in taxes on wages is mainly due to the fact that in 1962 the voluntary contribution to industrialization was converted into a tax.

76. Examples are wrappings left off foodstuffs, inferior finishing of clothing, and more standing on bus journeys.

77. Bread costs 16 cents a pound and refined sugar 7 cents. Biscuits, cakes, and confectionary seem to cost somewhat more than in the United States, for equivalent quality. In August, 1962, bread could be obtained in Havana without much difficulty, though individual shops often did not have it in stock in the afternoon.

78. Ministry of Labor. These figures should be treated with caution.

79. Oshima, "National Income and Product." Actually, the figures shown for 1953 were in each case except beans less than double the 1962 ration, but 1953 was not a good year. The comparison assumes that everyone gets the ration, when in fact some fail to do so, though farmers are doubtless eating much more in cases where they produce the crops concerned.

80. The same source puts the protein supplied by the Havana rations at 43 grams a day (80 for children up to 7).

81. "National Income and Product." The conversion scales used by Oshima are somewhat different, and, using them, the caloric equivalent of the current ration in Havana would probably be a rather smaller figure than indicated above.

82. Fruit and vegetables have become much scarcer.

83. The research officer mentioned earlier writes that "the diet for adults is just sufficient for basic requirements; the one for children below 7 years is quite adequate as for protein, fats, CHO, and calories." (He adds: "As these things might get into newspapers, please keep my name out of it.")

84. The latest official estimate published is that there was a rise of 21 per cent in the real consumption of goods from 1958 to 1960 (*Report of the Cuban UNESCO Commission, Santiago, Chile* [March, 1962]). It is true that any rise in consumption probably occurred in the first two years, but this figure looks too high to be consistent with other evidence.

85. Though if one wanted to measure the actual volume of manpower available, one should also allow for the considerable voluntary work done by a big

fraction of the labor force, not merely in cane-cutting but also in militia service, etc.

86. According to the Ministry of Labor.

87. Banco Nacional data. Both figures are probably underestimations. Oshima, in "National Income and Product," implies that even these items were somewhat underestimated in the Bank's series, and the 1962 budget was probably exceeded because of weak financial control.

88. Since it is unlikely that available supplies increased in 1962, the big rise in expenditure from 1961 to 1962 implied a decline in total consumption for that year, though possibly still leaving it above 1958 levels.

89. *Gaceta Oficial* (December 31, 1961), pp. 646-47. (This was less than 10 per cent of the national product in Anglo-Saxon terms.)

90. Much of this investment is in facilities for raising poultry and pigs, as part of a policy to increase meat supplies rapidly.

91. This does not mean that any rise has been continuous. In the first two years of the Revolution, real consumption almost certainly rose, but this was partly owing to reasons that could not continue, such as the over-slaughtering of livestock and the running down of inventories, and subsequently there must have been a decline at least partially offsetting the earlier rise.

92. I assume here that socialism implies collective farms. Cooperatives are dealt with in Chapter III, pp. 105-10.

93. A few were taken over; these were properties which associates of Batista were judged to have bought out of funds obtained illegally.

94. This achievement should not be credited entirely to the new organization. The crop had been planted, and to some extent nurtured, before the big wave of expropriation.

95. The countries of Eastern Europe are mostly self-sufficient in (beet) sugar.

96. Michael Kalecki of Poland visited Cuba at the end of 1960; a Czech team of planners was there in 1961; and Charles Bettelheim, a French Marxist, made visits in 1961 and 1962. There were also a number of foreign advisers at a lower level, especially from Chile.

97. *Obra Revolucionaria*, No. 30.

98. During the conference on production, however, Guevara was more cautious. In 1961, "only one or two" of the industrial targets were being fulfilled. "Without statistics, planning is simply the expression of good intentions."

99. *Cuba Socialista*, Vol. I, No. 4.

100. I was in Havana in February, 1962, and was assured by JUCEPLAN officials that this would be the worst month. Output would rise, eliminating shortages, during the year.

101. *Obra Revolucionaria*, 1962 series, No. 7.

102. "What has been our principal failing? A great degree of subjectivism. . . . One must not forget that, only a few months ago, we made promises which have not been fulfilled. . . . I for my part, and I say it sincerely, feel ashamed. . . . [We failed] because we did not make objective analyses, because we fell into a series of illusions and commenced to undertake that by such and such a month we would solve certain problems, according to all the data and all the calculations. But the data and the calculations were false" (*ibid.*).

103. To take one example of many (*Hoy*, September 5, 1962), an official of the transport union said that his union had proposed a scale of taxi charges to the Transport Ministry 9 months previously but was still waiting for a reply.

104. The telegraph system was used to transmit communications such as conference plans (and proposals by those attending); individual requests for school or university admittance (and replies); resolutions of all types (including those in support of athletes competing overseas), etc.

105. I was told that some organizations have refused to make further deliveries to those others that would not settle their bills.

106. In mid-1962 a taxi-driver in Havana could make more in a day (as least before allowing for amortization of his vehicle) than an agricultural laborer could in a week. Mechanics working on their own account could also make a great deal. There have been complaints that some factories were attempting to fulfill targets by offering high wages to attract new workers.

107. There seemed no special reason, for example, why the ex-brewery price of beer should be held down, since supply falls far short of demand, and quite high prices are charged by private proprietors of hotels and restaurants (or else beer is sold only if other purchases are made).

108. An estimate of the Ministry of Labor was that the average income of unskilled workers in cane cooperatives was 658 pesos, while in the state farms it was 870 pesos (data presumably refer to the year 1961).

109. Wallich made an interesting forecast of this problem, more than a decade ago. In *Monetary Problems of an Export Economy,* p. 21, he said, "It is clear, however, that eventually the building up of other industries will encroach upon the peak sugar output."

110. New measures were introduced in late 1962 to penalize absenteeism and to remove its causes.

111. *Central Planning in Poland* (Yale University Press, 1962), pp. 3-4. Montias here refers to East European experience as a whole.

112. Although these changes may well prove beneficial in the end, they came on the top of frequent earlier shifts in organization; and, in the short run, they meant further dislocation.

113. The policy is that nobody's wage will be reduced as long as he continues to hold the same job as he held in August, 1962, though new recruits are hired at the salary shown in the standard scale. The worker getting more than the standard rate receives two pay packets, one containing the standard wage for the job, the other a supplement to bring his pay up to the wage he received previously.

114. I owe the full appreciation of this point, as of many others, to my colleagues on this job.

115. According to an article by Francisco García and Juan Noyola, *Cuba Socialista* (September, 1962).

116. Twenty-one per cent a year, on the Bettelheim version of the plan (drawn up in 1961). The targets suggested by Bettelheim in his 1961 visit have, however, now been reduced.

117. The periods of the investment plan and the output plan do not match, but, nevertheless, the implicit coefficient must be lower than 1. This coefficient expresses the anticipated investment as a multiple of the anticipated change in output. The implication here is that the investment would yield so highly that its cost would be exceeded by the value of the rise in output.

118. The Soviet Union is supplying the equipment for each of these major projects except for the vehicle plant, which will come from Czechoslovakia.

119. It should be noted that there was a strong "welfare" element in investment (homes, schools, beach resorts, etc.) up to 1961 which was also contrary to what had happened in other centrally planned economies. This was possible partly because the essential problem at the outset was to make better use of existing resources. The composition of investment has now changed.

120. The population projection implies that emigration will decline but that not many housewives will be attracted into employment (although only about 20 per cent of the women aged fourteen to fifty-four are currently employed). It is not very optimistic to assume that unemployment will still be over 4 per cent of the labor force in 1965.

121. Construction is to be directed mainly to "productive" investment rather than housing and social areas, as heretofore.

122. The *Report of the Cuban UNESCO Commission* (March, 1962) antici-

pates that the urban population will rise much faster than the rural over the same period. There may, however, have been a real change in intentions, because of the growing realization of the severity of agricultural problems.

123. García and Noyola, *Cuba Socialista.* One of the "basic objectives" of the plan is to achieve a commercial balance for 1965.

124. Bulk loading is now being introduced for sugar, which will ease the seasonal labor problem at the docks as well as raise productivity.

125. It will be recalled that no effective political differences emerged in the Soviet Union so long as the country had reason to believe it might be invaded.

126. It is interesting to note that, in his speech on January 2, 1963, Castro announced that 1963 would be "the year of organization."

Chapter II

1. In the preparation of the final version of this part, I have benefited from the helpful comments of Jacques Chonchol and Max Nolff, who read some sections of an earlier draft. Chonchol's excellent "Análisis Crítico de la Reforma Agraria Cubana" (*El Trimestre Económico,* No. 117 [January-March, 1963], 69-143, which appeared early in 1962 in *Panorama Económico* [Santiago, Chile], Nos. 227, 228, and 229) was a most valuable source of information, especially for some of the developments during what is here called the initial phase of agrarian reform. My greatest debt, however, is to Dudley Seers and to Richard Jolly. They not only corrected many errors and made valuable suggestions but also struggled valiantly to improve my English style. Of course, none of them is responsible for whatever errors remain.

2. The decisive factor was the successful uprising of the Negro slaves of Haiti against their French masters in 1789. During the bloody war that followed, the cane plantations and sugar mills of the then leading sugar producer of the world were ruined, and after independence the former jewel of the French colonial empire never recovered her rank in the production of sugar. The opening of the American market after Independence and the relaxation of Spanish-imposed trade restrictions, first under Charles III and later in 1818, also contributed to the increase in demand for Cuban sugar.

3. Mill mechanization began in the 1820's and was largely completed by 1861, when out of a total of 1,442 mills, 949 were operated by steam power.

4. Although the railroad had been introduced in Cuba as early as 1837, its use by the sugar mills became important only at the end of the century, following sharp reductions in the price of steel rails during the 1870's. As will be seen below, the introduction of the railroads was to influence deeply the Cuban system of land ownership during the first quarter of the twentieth century.

5. The Second War of Independence lasted from 1895 to 1898. During this period, sugar output declined to less than one-third the 1891-94 average. It started rising again during the years of American military occupation (1899-1902). By 1903 production was back to pre-war levels.

6. The Reciprocity Treaty of 1903 provided for a 20 per cent reduction in U.S. tariffs on all Cuban exports entering the United States. A similar reduction was made by Cuba on U.S. goods exported to Cuba.

7. By 1925-27, U.S. investments in Cuba were estimated as just under $1,500,000,000, of which about $800,000,000 was in the sugar industry. Prior to the War of Independence, foreign capital in the sugar industry amounted to $50,000,000. See Gustavo Gutiérrez, *El Desarrollo Económico de Cuba* (1952), p. 91, and *Anuario Azucarero de Cuba,* 1959, p. 17.

8. The term *centrales* designates the large-scale sugar mills which were built during the boom and which by its end had completely replaced the small *ingenios*

of the nineteenth century. A *central* thus included not only the mill itself but also surrounding land, railroads, and other installations.

9. See below, pp. 74 ff.

10. Between 1907 and 1919, half a million immigrants entered the country, of which more than 60 per cent were Spaniards. In the same period, the annual rate of population growth was 3.4 per cent, but the labor force must have risen at a much higher rate since the great majority of the immigrants were fourteen-to forty-five-year-old men. See Julián Alienes y Urosa, *Características Fundamentales de la Economía Cubana* (Banco Nacional de Cuba, 1950), pp. 9, 41.

11. Net imports of coffee had averaged 23,000,000 pounds in the twenties; in the following decade the country's net exports averaged 8,000,000 pounds.

12. After falling to 1.7 per cent during the depressed years of 1931-43, the rate of population growth rose to 2.2 per cent in the forties.

13. See *Investment in Cuba* (U.S. Department of Commerce, 1956), Table 28, p. 48.

14. A study prepared by the United Nations Economic Commission for Latin America estimated that livestock production rose at the low annual rate of 1.09 per cent over the period 1949-50 and 1956-57, that is, at less than one half the rate at which population was growing over the same years. See ECLA, *El Desarrollo Económico de Cuba: Proyecto de Investigación para el Período 45-56*, p. 27.

15. The comparison of the changes in the value of food imports and of the gross domestic product (GDP) lends support to the thesis of lagging increases in the production of the agricultural sector which supplied the internal markets. Food imports fell, of course, in 1953 when the gross domestic product dropped by 13.9 per cent, but they fell *also* in 1954 and 1955, when income had started rising again. This provides some evidence that until the middle of the fifties internal production of foodstuffs was meeting the requirements of domestic demand. In 1956 food imports rose at a slower rate than GDP, but in 1957 the situation was reversed, the rate of change of food imports outpacing that of income, and in 1958 the value of imports of food *increased* greatly, *in spite of* a 7.3 per cent *fall* in GDP.

16. It should be noted, however, that the problem raised by economically undersized farms was somewhat reduced in Cuba by the cultivation of tobacco; tobacco farms can be quite profitable even when small.

17. One hectare equals 2.471 acres.

18. See Lowry Nelson, *Rural Cuba* (University of Minnesota Press, 1950), p. 93.

19. Prior to 1914, mill ownership was predominantly Cuban and Spanish, but after 1920 the American-owned mills produced almost two-thirds of the industry's output. This share fell to 55 per cent in 1939, 47.3 per cent in 1950, and just over 40 per cent in 1954-58.

20. Nelson, whose analysis this section follows, sets this period between 1900 and 1933. See Nelson, *Rural Cuba*, pp. 80, 90-98.

21. The methods by which land was acquired from the small cane growers had at times, a somewhat unsavory flavor. Nelson tells that "the sugar companies purchased land from the peasants where the latter would show a title, but where titles were in question—as so many of them were—recourse was had to the courts" and adds that "there can be no doubt that the contest in the courts was a one-sided affair in which the companies had the overwhelming advantage. They could employ the best lawyers who knew the loop-holes in Cuban land laws. They could, if necessary, corrupt the officials, high and low, with bribes." Nelson, *Rural Cuba*, p. 97.

22. Geographically, the sugar mills were strongest in Matanzas, where they controlled 35.69 per cent of the total provincial area, and least influential in Pinar del Río, where they controlled only 5.09 per cent of the land. In Camagüey,

six American firms had control of 20.79 per cent of the province's area. See INRA, *Boletín de Divulgación*, No. 6, pp. 25, 28.

23. The names of the 40 firms and persons and extent of the individual areas owned by each of them are given in *El Imperialismo Norteamericano en la Economía de Cuba*, by Oscar Pino Santos, and reproduced in *Ciclo de Conferencias sobre Planificación Industrial* (Ministry of Industry, 1961), p. 203.

24. Most of the large cattle ranches were concentrated in the eastern half of the island—the provinces of Las Villas, Camagüey, and Oriente.

25. See Chonchol, "Análisis Crítico." These figures imply, of course, that yields per acre were higher in the large rice farms than in the small ones.

26. In this respect the large sugar estate of Cuba was very different from the feudal latifundium which existed in Mexico before the Revolution and which survives today in most of Latin America, and particularly in the Andean countries.

27. This was the classic "triple bond" which, according to Friedlander, tied the *colono* to the mill. To a considerable extent, however, the control of the *centrales* extended also to the *colono* who owned his land, since he too depended upon the mills for grinding and transporting his cane and for loans to finance his crop.

28. As a result of the preferential treatment afforded to the *colonos* in allocating cane quotas, the proportion of cane grown under the administration system fell to about 10 per cent in the early fifties. To an undisclosed degree, this decline was spurious, however, since "numerous mills grew administration cane in the names of the colonos—real or not—who supposedly had contracted for management services of the mills" (International Bank for Reconstruction and Development, *Report on Cuba* [Johns Hopkins Press, 1951], p. 798). Others created "agricultural companies," that is, "corporations separate from the mills themselves but with essentially the same officers, which assume responsibility for managing the cane land previously classed as 'administration' but, under the new operating company, capable of being classified as 'colonia' cane and therefore eligible for assignment of quotas" (Nelson, *Rural Cuba*, p. 121).

29. By 1957-58 the cane field workers had risen to about 400,000 (*Anuario Azucarero*, 1959, p. 160).

30. Thus administrators operated almost one-fourth of the farm area of Camagüey and somewhat less than one-third that of Oriente, the two provinces where most of the large cattle ranches were located. And although the total number of administrators was under one-fifth that of either owners or tenants, there were more of the former than owners or tenants in the farms having between 1,000 and 5,000 hectares and also in those over 5,000.

31. In Pinar del Río, where some of the most famous tobacco districts are located, 59.5 per cent of all farms were cultivated by sharecroppers.

32. More than one-fifth the holdings of Oriente were run by squatters.

33. It was recovered for a short period in 1947-48.

34. This is the fraction shown by the Banco Nacional official figures. Estimates of the Cuban national income in 1953 by Harry T. Oshima reduce the share of sugar to about one-fifth. See his "The New Estimate of the National Income and Product of Cuba in 1953," *Food Research Institute Studies*, II (November, 1961), 213-27.

35. IBRD, *Report on Cuba*, p. 44.

36. The results of the 1953 Population Census support the conclusion that this was the minimum unemployment rate. The census taken during the height of the sugar harvest showed that at that time 8.4 per cent of the labor force was out of work.

37. Although the census was taken in 1946, it still provides the most reliable data for the study of the pattern of land use during the pre-revolutionary period. Later estimates are somewhat contradictory. Thus, José Arteaga, in a study presented to the *Symposium de Recursos Naturales*, estimated the land in farms

in 9,044,000 hectares for 1957-58, that is, a lower figure than that of the 1946 census. On the other hand, the authors of the *Proyecto de Plan Quinquenal* thought that in 1959-60 farm land was up to 10,068,000 hectares. This figure included probably land cleared of *marabú* and other weeds during the first year of the agrarian reform. The Arteaga estimate was published in INRA, *Números* (July 15, 1958), p. 3, and is quoted in Francisco Dorta-Duque, S.J., *Justificando una Reforma Agraria* (Pontificia Universidad Gregoriana, 1959), p. 23.

38. Land in farms represented a high proportion (78.3 per cent) of the territory of the country, a fact no doubt related to the very favorable topographical and soil characteristics of the island, a large proportion of which is formed by fertile, flat, or gently rolling terrain.

39. In addition to the foodstuffs listed in Table 5, Cuba imported cotton and jute at an average annual rate of about $40,000,000 during 1955-58. This brought the value of the imports which domestic agricultural production could replace to an annual average of about $100,000,000 over this period.

40. IBRD, *Report on Cuba*, p. 87. A United Nations study estimated that cultivated land represented 33.4 per cent of the cultivable area. For countries having roughly similar levels of per-capita income but rather different economic structures, the same study listed the following percentages: Argentina, 20.7; Chile, 46.4; Costa Rica, 75.5; Mexico, 16.7; and Venezuela, 40.0. See *Land Reform: Defects in Agrarian Structure as Obstacles to Economic Development* (United Nations, 1951), p. 100.

41. *Ibid.*

42. The farms of 1-5 hectares cultivated 63 per cent of their land. The inverse correlation between size of the holdings and the proportion of land under crops helps to explain why owners and administrators generally cultivated only a very low proportion of their acreage (16.2 and 14.9 per cent, respectively) and why renters, sub-renters, and especially sharecroppers, most of whom managed small farms, cultivated a high proportion (28.3, 36.8, and 40.7, respectively).

43. In theory, the system implied also a cost for the sugar companies, namely the *profits* they could have made by growing other crops or by raising cattle on the land they kept under cane but did not harvest. This, however, was much less than the cost of the system to the economy as a whole. Given the unemployment of the labor force, the social cost amounted to the *full value-added* of the crops which could have been produced on the same area.

44. The percentage is obtained by applying the proportion of the total cultivated land represented by cane (56 per cent) to the average ratio of unharvested cane land during the period 1953-58 (28.7 per cent). This last ratio was somewhat higher than that of the period 1936-40 (24.2 per cent) and considerably higher than those of the years 1941-43 (18.9 per cent), 1944-48 (6.9 per cent), and 1949-51 (1.6 per cent). Percentages have been computed from data of the American Embassy in Havana, quoted in IBRD, *Report on Cuba*.

45. It would also have needed investments in housing, especially in the cattle ranches of the eastern provinces, where few permanent workers were employed.

46. The development of Japanese agriculture during the last quarter of the nineteenth century is perhaps the best example of the successful application of such methods.

47. An increase in domestic saving was also required.

48. I am not arguing here that public ownership of land *would actually have resulted* in larger volumes of output. What is implied is that, when resources are unemployed, decisions based on considerations of *social* costs will lead the production units to seek a higher level of output than the same units would seek if motivated by the desire to maximize private profits. If other things are equal (indeed a tall assumption in this case) social-cost decisions should lead to higher *actual* production than private-cost decisions.

49. Given the peculiar compartmentalization of the world market for sugar, increases in its production were likely to reduce export revenue.

50. Under the 1937 law, workers' wages were linked to the value of a specified amount of sugar, though a minimum wage set a floor to downward adjustments of the wage rate when the price of sugar fell below a certain level. At times, the government froze wages in the sugar industry in relation to sugar prices which were higher than the then-current market prices.

51. IBRD, *Report on Cuba*, p. 72.

52. On the "sugar mentality," see Henry C. Wallich, *Monetary Problems of an Export Economy* (Harvard University Press, 1950), pp. 10-13, and IBRD, *Report on Cuba, passim.*

53. *Investment in Cuba*, pp. 29-30.

54. *Ibid.*

55. IBRD, *Report on Cuba*, p. 197.

56. *Ibid.*, pp. 197-98.

57. The figures of Table 17 probably understate the actual differentials in productivity, since they record yields in terms of area actually harvested. In most countries this closely approximates the area planted. In Cuba, however, the area planted exceeded the area harvested by a substantial proportion throughout 1953-59 (Table 16).

58. In the cattle industry, three types of units performing different functions could be found. There were, first, the small farms, usually with less than 50 head, on overcrowded natural pasture of poor quality. A considerable proportion of the cattle were born on such farms, kept for about a year, and thereafter (due to the shortage of available grassland) sold to a new type of producers (*mejoradores*), who owned farms of intermediate size having better grassland. After maintaining the cattle for one and a half years, the *mejoradores* would sell them to the operators of the big *latifundia*, which possessed grassland of even better quality and most of the artificial pastures. Here the cattle were reared to slaughter weight (which was reached when they were 36 to 40 months old).

59. *Investment in Cuba*, p. 48.

60. *Ibid.*, p. 42. About three-quarters of the area devoted to rice was under irrigation.

61. Chonchol, "Análisis Crítico," p. 72.

62. IBRD, *Report on Cuba*, p. 105.

63. *Ibid.*, p. 90.

64. *Investment in Cuba*, p. 34.

65. IBRD, *Report on Cuba*, p. 118.

66. The lack of adjustment of the system of higher education to the economic needs of the country was also apparent in other figures of the census. In 1952 there were in Cuba not less than 6,560 lawyers and judges, that is, more than 10 times the number of agricultural engineers and technicians combined.

67. *Investment in Cuba*, p. 30.

68. The high percentage of total living units built after 1945 was somewhat deceiving. "It is presumed"—the Department of Commerce reported in 1956—"that a large part of the 45.3 per cent of rural homes built after 1945 were merely palm or wood-thatched units" (*Investment in Cuba*, p. 187).

69. I have not been able to consult the survey (*Por qué Reforma Agraria*) directly, since it was not available in the main libraries of Havana. The data given here are quoted by Dorta-Duque, in *Justificando una Reforma Agraria*, pp. 82-103, and by Chonchol, "Análisis Crítico," pp. 86-88.

70. Providing at least partial evidence that the families interviewed constituted a representative sample.

71. The income figures included an estimate for consumption of self-produced crops.

72. Fourteen per cent went to clothing, services took 7.5, housing 1.7, and other items 7.4.

73. These included manioc (*yuca*), cooking bananas, *malanga*, sweet potatoes (*boniato*), and *calabaza*.

74. The 1953 census had reported a 41.7 per cent rate of illiteracy in the rural areas. This result confirms again the representativeness of the sample.

75. Other institutions mentioned were the trade unions (6.8 per cent), the Masons (4.3 per cent), and the Church (3.0 per cent).

76. The Department of Commerce reported that until 1956 five large estates expropriated in 1947 were the only cases on record of such action and added that the application of Law 7 of 1948, designed to prohibit the rental of rural property to foreigners, "was so complicated by previous legislation that it was never enforced" (*Investment in Cuba*, p. 32).

Chapter III

1. See his *La Historia Me Absolverá* (Imprenta Nacional de Cuba, 1961), p. 65. There is no point here in discussing the evolution of Castro's thought on the *type* of land reform to be implemented since his speech before the court in 1953. Suffice it to say that in practice the emphasis shifted from reliance on individual, owner-operated holdings and cooperatives of the traditional type to more collectivized forms of agricultural organizations.

2. The benefit was conditional upon continued meeting of the yield requirements.

3. Cooperatives organized by INRA were excepted from this limit.

4. The tax valuation was a fraction of the real value of the property. The government requested the American owners to reassess their property for taxes, but they repeated the same low figures; to do otherwise would have been to admit past tax evasion. *The Wall Street Journal* (March 8, 1960), p. 1, and C.B.S. "Report on Cuba," as quoted by Robert F. Smith in *The United States and Cuba: Business and Diplomacy, 1917-1960* (New York: Bookman Associates, 1960), p. 178.

5. Public land included that possessed by the state, the provinces, or the municipalities. Public land and private land being totally or partly cultivated by tenants, sub-tenants, share-croppers, and squatters were to be distributed first.

6. INRA could vary the amount of land according to factors like soil fertility, distance from urban centers, irrigation needs, etc.

7. Tables 6 through 10, Chapter II.

8. As estimated in the *Proyecto de Plan Quinquenal* (10,068,000 hectares).

9. Expropriation procedures were usually informal. INRA officials negotiated directly with the landowners on the land which the latter could retain and seized the rest; cattle were similarly divided, and in many cases buildings, trucks, and farm equipment were also seized. Inventories were rarely taken, receipts not given. Few bonds were actually issued.

10. Of this, only 1,200,000 hectares had been taken under the Law of Agrarian Reform. As mentioned already, the nationalization of the land of the sugar mills contributed 2,200,000 hectares, and the rest came from gifts and voluntary sales to INRA (900,000 hectares) and from the confiscation of the estates of Batista officials and counterrevolutionaries (163,000 hectares.) This last figure, however, is known to be underestimated. See Jacques Chonchol, "Análisis Crítico de la Reforma Agraria Cubana," *El Trimestre Económico*, No. 117 (January-March, 1963), p. 97.

11. The importance ascribed to INRA was highlighted by the appointment of Premier Castro to its presidency.

12. In addition to its agricultural activities, the Institute had a Department of

Industries which in 1960 was running factories worth 350,000,000 pesos. This department became in 1961 the Ministry of Industries, although INRA retained canneries and some other factories concerned with the production of food. At the same time the Ministry of Agriculture was formally abolished and its remaining functions transferred to INRA.

13. I have followed here the account given by Chonchol, who, in his position of United Nations adviser to INRA, had an excellent opportunity to judge. See his "Análisis Crítico," pp. 95-96. I talked with several officials of the Institute in Havana who confirmed this "fear of bureaucracy" during the first years.

14. One zone in Pinar del Río comprised 873 square kilometers, whereas another in Camagüey stretched over 11,400 square kilometers.

15. The lack of accounting records made an economic classification of these expenditures impossible. Over the whole period during which the country was divided into Zones of Agricultural Development, the total net amount spent by the delegates is believed to have been in the neighborhood of 140,000,000 pesos.

16. See, for instance, "Qué Es la Reforma Agraria?" (which includes excerpts of a speech delivered by Castro in Santa Clara on June 21, 1959), *Boletín de Divulgación* (INRA), No. 6, p. 12.

17. Under Article 53 of the Law of Agrarian Reform, INRA was supposed to issue internal regulations for the cooperatives within 60 days of the promulgation of the law. These regulations were never issued.

18. The cooperatives employed also temporary workers, who might expect to receive a daily salary of three pesos.

19. See Marco Antonio Durán, "La Reforma Agraria en Cuba," *El Trimestre Económico*, No. 107 (July-September, 1960), 424. Durán was a member of the FAO Regional Land Reform Team which visited Cuba between July 12 and August 6, 1959.

20. See Fidel Castro, *Discurso a la Plenaria Azucarera* (December 19, 1960), p. 22.

21. These characteristics were a consequence of the type of holdings intervened, which, as noted earlier, were primarily intended for the fattening of cattle.

22. This explains why the area owned by the sugar mills which was expropriated under the nationalization laws of July and October, 1960—about 2,200,000 hectares—greatly exceeded that of the subsequently organized cooperatives—slightly over 800,000 hectares.

23. Administración General de Cooperativas Cañeras, *Cooperativas Cañeras* (1960), p. 42.

24. Severo Aguirre, "El Primer Aniversario de las Cooperativas Cañeras," *Cuba Socialista*, No. 3 (November, 1961), pp. 21-22.

25. Net profit was to be obtained by subtracting from gross revenue the "advances" paid over the year, general administrative expenses, payments to seasonal laborers, depreciation of the cooperative's capital, taxes, and interest and amortization charges for equipment made available to the cooperative by INRA.

26. Besides being linked administratively with the national authorities, each cooperative was attached for the purposes of the harvest to a specific sugar-mill.

27. Economic Commission for Latin America, "La Reforma Agraria Cubana" in *Panorama Económico* (Santiago, Chile), No. 214 (August, 1960), p. 237.

28. Chonchol, "Análisis Crítico," p. 116.

29. For a period after March, 1960, the rule was reversed, and private farmers were allowed to retain *not more* than 14 head per *caballería*. This was clearly a bad decision, since it eliminated the incentive for better farming practices that would permit feeding the same number of animals in a smaller area. (One *caballería* equals 13.42 hectares, or 33.16 acres.)

30. The 1960 rainfall figure is from *Variedades de Caña, Zafra de 1961* (Ministry of Industries, 1962), p. 26. The same publication considers 1960 a "magnificent year" for rainfall (p. 11). The average annual normal is based on data

compiled by the American Embassy, Havana. The "high" is a figure computed by the Asociación Nacional de Hacendados de Cuba (National Association of Cuban Farmers) on the basis of rainfall records over a 23-year period. These two figures are from Table 78 of *Investment in Cuba* (U.S. Department of Commerce, 1956), p. 175.

31. In 1959, 79.6 per cent of the available cane was cut; one year later the proportion rose to 83.1 per cent. See *Anuario Azucarero,* 1959, p. 111, and A. Núñez Jiménez, *Informe al Pueblo* (INRA, 1961), p. 36. (For 1953-58 see Table 16, Chapter II.)

32. This decision was related to the diversification that Castro announced for the cane cooperatives in August, 1960, according to which the cooperatives would increase employment during the "dead season" by diverting (after the 1961 sugar harvest) about 130,000 hectares from cane into other crops and livestock raising. Before this, however, all cane on the land chosen for reallocation was to be cut.

33. There were 1,343,733 hectares planted with cane. Of these, 1,260,808 were actually harvested. See *Variedades de Caña, Zafra de 1961,* pp. 25, 113.

34. The timing of the latter, mid-April, coincided with the height of the sugar harvest.

35. Harry T. Oshima, "The New Estimate of the National Income and Product of Cuba in 1953," *Food Research Institute Studies,* II (November, 1961), 220.

36. In a closed economy (one in which exports or imports are negligible) cattle production is equal to the algebraic sum of supplies for consumption and the net addition to the cattle reserves. In the case of the Cuban cattle industry, the assumptions of a closed economy were met to a reasonable degree, since net imports of beef represented a very small percentage of total consumption. Coleou estimates the imported component of beef consumption at 0.8 per cent for the years before the Revolution; Oshima gives an estimate of less than 2 per cent for 1953. See Julien Coleou, "L'élevage et les Productions Animales à Cuba," in R. Dumond and J. Coleou, *La Réforme Agraire à Cuba* (Presses Universitaires de France, 1962), p. 68, and Oshima, "National Income and Product," p. 218.

37. Shortly after taking power, the new regime slashed public utility rates by decree and raised the wages of low-paid workers; in 1960 the Law of Urban Reform reduced house rents by 35 or 50 per cent, depending upon their previous levels, and in the countryside a similar development had begun even earlier with the abolition of share-cropping and the granting of free "vital minimum" awards to tenants, who were thereby released of the obligation of paying rents, either in kind or in money. Moreover, it is clear that the rise of employment, especially in the rural areas, benefited largely the low-income groups.

38. INRA, *Un Año de Liberación Agraria,* p. 50.

39. Felipe Pazos, "Comentarios a dos Artículos sobre la Revolución Cubana," *El Trimestre Económico,* No. 113 (January-March, 1962), 7. Dr. Pazos, who was head of the Banco Nacional during the first 11 months of the Castro regime, estimates that the real incomes of the workers rose by 25 to 30 per cent during 1959.

40. A. Milián Castro, "Experiencias de la JUCEI en Las Villas," in *Cuba Socialista,* No. 3 (November, 1961), 47.

41. Chonchol, "Análisis Crítico," p. 139.

42. INRA implied this in *Un Año de Liberación Agraria* and went on to state that the "plans for technical improvement of pastures and cattle raising will rapidly transform Cuba into a large exporter of beef" (p. 50). In a lecture delivered in Mexico on January 4, 1961, Juan F. Noyola was more explicit: "In the case of Cuba there has been not a reduction but an *increase* in the cattle stock and a still more considerable increase in the production of beef and milk as a result of a better utilization of the cattle herds." See his "La Revolución Cubana y su Efectos en el Desarrollo Económico," *El Trimestre Económico,* No.

111 (July-September, 1961), 403. For a similar contention, see L. Huberman and P. M. Sweezy, *Cuba: Anatomy of a Revolution* (2nd ed.; Monthly Review Press, 1961), p. 140.

43. For reasons given in the Appendix, it seems appropriate to take the output of rice during the calendar year 1960 as reflecting the outcome of the first phase of the agrarian reform.

44. As Tables 2, Chapter II, and 5, Chapter III, indicate, coffee harvests have fluctuated with absolute regularity since 1956, from bad years to good ones.

45. The rise may have been partly offset (or reinforced) by deterioration (or improvement) in the mix of different types of tobacco. In the absence of information on quality, it is assumed here that changes did not occur or that they were negligible.

46. For a discussion of the assumptions made and the procedure used to estimate these changes, see Appendix for Part I, pp. 339-45.

47. For example, there were increases in the prices of potatoes, peanuts, henequen, and maize. Information on prices was provided by officials of INRA in Havana. In many cases, it contradicts price information given in the final tables of Jiménez, *Informe al Pueblo*, p. 36.

48. INRA, *Un Año de Liberación Agraria*, p. 41.

49. Land planted with cane represented 56 per cent of the total cultivated area in 1945. The comparison with 1945, however, almost certainly overstates the relative increase of cultivated area.

50. Enrique Cabre, "Intervención," *Obra Revolucionaria*, No. 30, p. 78. The figure given by Cabre, an official of the Department of Farm Machinery of INRA, is considerably lower than the estimate of 670,000 hectares included in the Jiménez, *Informe al Pueblo*, issued in May, 1961.

51. Fernando Pérez, "Intervención," *Obra Revolucionaria*, No. 30, p. 68.

52. Using Cabre's figure and subtracting from it the area allocated to artificial pastures, the new land available for cultivation of crops would represent an increase of more than 40 per cent over the area devoted to crops other than cane in 1945. For the reasons mentioned in the text, the *actual* increase in the cultivated area must have been smaller, however. Moreover, the qualification indicated in note 49 also applies in this case.

53. *Primer Estudio Provisional del Balance de Recursos de Trabajo* (Ministry of Labor memorandum, dated May 23, 1962).

54. See INRA, *Un Año de Liberación Agraria*, p. 62. The total given by INRA is 34,884,000. I have subtracted 1,903,000 spent on lubricants and fuels, 750,400 on buildings, and 189,000 on "direct expenditures; accounting machinery" to derive the figure indicated in the text.

55. Jiménez, *Informe al Pueblo*, p. 26.

56. The average has been computed on data given by Table 6.16 of the *Memoria, 1958-59*, of the Banco Nacional.

57. Chonchol, "Análisis Crítico," p. 98.

58. Pazos, "Comentarios a dos Artículos sobre la Revolución Cubana," pp. 8-9 (italics mine).

59. See Castro, "Qué Es la Reforma Agraria?," p. 8.

60. INRA, *Viviendas Campesinas: Suplemento Estadístico*.

61. See R. Dumond, "Des Problèmes Généraux de l'Économie Agraire Cubaine," in Dumond and Coleou, *La Réforme Agraire à Cuba*, p. 11.

62. In contrast to the rapid growth of ANAP, the number of "vital minimum" awards hardly rose during 1961. Between February and December of that year, only 203 new titles were granted, and the total area distributed rose by only 2,832 hectares during the same period and did not change at all in Pinar del Río, Matanzas, and Camagüey. Moreover, I was told at the Legal Department of INRA that few additional titles had been granted up to August, 1962.

63. See Chonchol, "Análisis Crítico," pp. 119-21.

64. This rule was being revised in mid-1962.

65. "Informe a la Primera Reunión Nacional de Producción," *Obra Revolucionaria*, No. 30 (August, 1961), p. 24.

66. In some cases, various units were 70 kilometers apart. See speech of Carlos R. Rodríguez to the Congress of Cane Cooperatives in *Hoy*, August 18, 1962, p. 7.

67. This land, especially that of the cattle ranches, was controlled by INRA-managed farms during the first phase of the agrarian reform.

68. See Castro, *Discurso a la Plenaria Azucarera* (December 19, 1960), p. 23.

69. Political elements are found in many other provisions of the statutes. Thus ANAP will work to raise the revolutionary conscience of farmers in general (Art. 4 [g]) and will defend national sovereignty and independence (Art. 4 [h]) and also "peace, peaceful coexistence, and friendship among the peoples [of the world]" (Art. 4 [c]). ANAP is also pledged to defend Cuba's "Patriotic, Democratic and Socialist Revolution," and to work for full implementation of a program which has as one of its goals the elimination of man's exploitation by man (Art. 4 [j]).

70. At the proposal of the association's national directorate which, in turn, is elected by the delegates to the national assembly.

71. The report presented to the second meeting of ANAP in May, 1962, does not give a national figure but indicates that in Pinar del Río there were 109 associations with 6,642 members (an approximate average of 60 members per association). The national average must be lower, however, owing to the lower population density in the eastern provinces.

72. Pepe Ramírez, *Informe a la Plenaria Nacional de la ANAP* (May 17, 1962), p. 15.

73. This form of communal production is found most frequently among tobacco growers in Pinar del Río and Las Villas, where the majority of the 550-odd credit and service cooperatives are located.

74. In fact, ANAP provided more than half the land held by agricultural societies in May, 1962 (see Ramírez, *Informe*, p. 22). Nevertheless, this policy was the result of circumstances and is not to be followed in the future (*ibid.*, p. 19).

75. *Ibid.*, p. 22. There were, in addition, an unspecified number of societies in the Escambray Plan with about 7,500 hectares.

76. *Departamento de Fincas Administradas de la ANAP.* The department has national, financial, and regional administrative levels and appoints the managers of the farms. It expanded rapidly in 1962 and enjoys considerable autonomy within ANAP.

77. These new state-owned units are also favored by the housing and general distribution policies of ANAP.

78. Of these, about 40,000 were small cane producers, 3,000 to 4,000 cultivated primarily potatoes, 20,000 were tobacco growers, and about the same number cultivated coffee.

79. This figure may be somewhat overestimated, since it implies that virtually all small farmers with fewer than 5 *caballerías* had joined the association. But because of the advantages of membership it is not unreasonable to think that most of them did actually belong to ANAP.

80. According to the 1946 census, there were close to 2,200,000 hectares, or 24 per cent of all agricultural land, in farms of less than 67.1 hectares each. Assuming that the same percentage of the land was in farms of that size in 1959-60, such farms would have encompassed about 2,400,000 hectares. Thus, even if all small farmers had joined ANAP, the figure given by INRA in 1961 would seem exaggerated.

81. Obtained by adding to the 2,400,000 hectares estimated in the preceding footnote the almost 150,000 hectares controlled by the new ANAP-administered

farms and adjusting downward the assumption of 100-per-cent membership of small farmers in ANAP.

82. According to figures quoted at the production meeting in August, 1961.

83. The proportion was somewhat higher in Camagüey, where most of the large livestock ranges had been "intervened" in the second half of 1959. From a total of 1,593,532 head, the people's farms owned 372,110 and the cane cooperatives 55,672 head. Felipe Torre, "Algunas Cuestiones sobre el Desarrollo de la Ganadería en Camagüey" in *Cuba Socialista*, No. 8 (April, 1962), p. 43.

84. See Santos Ríos, "Informe a la Primera Reunión," p. 32.

85. Castro, *Discurso a la Plenaria Azucarera*, p. 16.

86. *Ibid.*, p. 32.

87. *Ibid.*, p. 23.

88. *Ibid.*, p. 24.

89. See Dumond, "Des Problèmes Généraux," p. 18. Dumond qualified the *règle d'or* by bringing in technical or economic impossibilities and by pointing to the danger of exaggerating the number of new crops grown in farms run by administrators with scant technical knowledge.

90. *Discurso a la Plenaria Azucarera*, p. 28.

91. *Ibid.*

92. Aguirre, "El Primer Aniversario," p. 24.

93. "Informe de la Administración General de Cooperativas Cañeras" *Obra Revolucionaria*, No. 30 (August 1961), p. 52.

94. Aguirre, "El Primer Aniversario," p. 24.

95. "It is inconceivable that, when cane was uprooted, the cane that was yielding 40,000 or 50,000 *arrobas* was demolished, and the cane that was yielding 20,000 or 25,000 *arrobas* was left standing, yet cane was demolished with that lack of care. It is inconceivable that, when cane was uprooted, the land next to the *central* was chosen for this destruction . . . and, on the other hand, that land be left untouched that was at great distance from the sugar mill." Carlos R. Rodríguez, "Speech to the sugar workers" on July 18, 1962, as quoted in *Panorama Económico Latinoamericano*, Vol. V, No. 56, p. 13. Several INRA officials also told me about these mistakes.

96. Informe de la Administración General de Cooperativas Cañeras," p. 52.

97. Alfredo Menéndez Cruz, "La Transformación de las Cooperativas Cañeras en Granjas Cañeras," *Cuba Socialista*, No. 14 (October, 1962), p. 39.

98. *Ibid.*, p. 40.

99. Rodríguez, "Speech to the sugar workers," p. 12. See also speech by Guevara in *Hoy*, May 5, 1962, p. 3.

100. Coleou gives these figures in his "L'élevage et les Productions," p. 68. Oshima's estimate for 1953 is 66.1 pounds ("National Income and Product," p. 219).

101. On the other hand, the statistical average is now much more meaningful than before because of the more even distribution of income.

102. Net imports of beef were negligible before 1959.

103. INRA, *Un Año de Liberación Agraria*, p. 51. Coleou's estimate for production in the years preceding the Revolution is 1,250,000 chickens per month "L'élevage et les Productions," p. 66.

104. A production of 1,000,000 chickens per month was quoted by INRA's Production Chief Eduardo Santos Ríos at the National Production Meeting in August, 1961, and it was said to represent 50 per cent of "consumption" at that time. Another report at the meeting quoted the same output figure but estimated "normal monthly consumption" at about 2,500,000 chickens. (As in other reports of Cuban officials, "consumption" refers really to the "quantity demanded at the current price.") See Santos Ríos, "Informe a la Primera Reunión," and Julio Serrate, "Intervención," *Obra Revolucionaria*, No. 30 (August, 1961), 26, 42.

105. One half of the eggs incubated used to come from the United States and imports of baby chicks were also very high. See *Investment in Cuba*, p. 50.

106. Serrate, "Intervención," p. 42.

107. Eduardo Santos Ríos, "Tecnificar Nuestra Agricultura Es Hacerla Más Productiva," *Cuba Socialista*, No. 9 (May, 1962), p. 63.

108. The rationing allowed a *monthly* per-capita consumption of two pounds in Havana; the national *yearly* average before the Revolution was 4.5 pounds according to Coleou, "L'élevage et les Productions," p. 68, and 4.62 according to Oshima, "National Income and Product," p. 219. The comparison probably overstates the growth of production, however. Consumption in Havana must have been much higher than the average before 1959; thus according to INRA (*Un Año de Liberación*, p. 51) 82.9 per cent of all chickens were produced in Havana province, and a high proportion of these were probably also consumed in the capital (as much as 80 per cent of all broilers were marketed alive, thus reducing the possibilities of large sales to the other provinces). In addition, rations were apparently not being fully met in mid-1962 (Rodríguez, "Speech to the sugar workers," p. 20).

109. Coleou, "L'élevage et les Productions," p. 68.

110. Again, the average would now be more meaningful than before.

111. During the period 1950-59, imports of eggs represented between 45 per cent and 60 per cent of supply. (*Investment in Cuba*, p. 50). This proportion seems to have declined later, however. Coleou estimates it at 26 per cent for the years preceding the Revolution ("L'élevage et les Productions," p. 68).

112. It is not clear whether the production of rice indicated corresponds to calendar 1961 or to the agricultural year 1961-62. For the reasons given in the Appendix, it should be analyzed with the developments of the second period of agrarian reform *even if* it relates to calendar 1961. There is no doubt, however, that rice production fell sharply in 1961-62. Santos Ríos wrote in May, 1962, that "during 1961 national production [of rice] declined perceptibly" (*Cuba Socialista* No. 9 [May, 1962], 57), although the context of the article suggests that he was really referring to production in the agricultural year 1961-62. Officials at the Rice Administration of INRA also told me that production had decreased significantly in this period but for what they frankly acknowledged to be political reasons did not give the precise magnitude of the decline.

113. Root crops or *viandas* include cooking bananas, *malanga,* sweet potatoes (*boniato*), and manioc (*yuca*).

114. Santos Ríos, "Informe a la Primera Reunión," p. 30.

115. *Ibid.* I have translated literally the Spanish *abastecimiento,* although it is obvious from the context of Santos Ríos' remarks that he is thinking of the "quantity demanded at the current price."

116. Eduardo Santos Ríos, "Tecnificar Nuestra Agricultura Es Hacerla Más Productiva," *Cuba Socialista*, No. 9 (May, 1962), p. 65.

117. The exact average would be 201.24 pounds and is computed assuming that children under seven represent 18.5 per cent of the total population. This ratio has been estimated on the basis of data of the Economic Commission for Latin America, according to which 13.3 per cent of the total population was in the 0-4 year group, and 22.7 in the 5-14 year one. See ECLA, *Economic Bulletin for Latin America*, V, Statistical Supplement, Table 5.

118. Oshima, "National Income and Product," p. 218. This figure includes 50.8 pounds of potatoes, which are considered as *viandas* in the rationing scheme.

119. As indicated in Table 13, production of potatoes also declined in 1961-62.

120. The fact that Santos Ríos called the *viandas* "the principal failure" in the same article in which he acknowledged that production of rice had "declined perceptibly" and that losses had been suffered in the cultivation of cotton also

suggests a rather large fall in the output of root crops. See his "Tecnificar," pp. 57, 58, 65.

121. Eighteen per cent according to the 1946 agricultural census and over 28 per cent according to Oshima. Oshima believes that the census seriously underestimated the production of subsistence crops ("National Income and Product," pp. 213, 220).

122. At times not even this was done in the discussions of the plan at the provincial and local levels. INRA officials freely admitted that in the feverish atmosphere of the production meetings some farm administrators accepted targets which implied the cultivation of more land than they had.

123. See Alfredo Menéndez Cruz, "Problemas de la Industria Azucarera," *Cuba Socialista*, No. 12 (August, 1962), p. 4, and Rodríguez, "Speech to the sugar workers," p. 13.

124. Severo Aguirre, "Ante el Tercer Aniversario de la Reforma Agraria," *Cuba Socialista*, No. 9 (May, 1962), 45.

125. Carlos R. Rodríguez, "Entrevista," in *F. Castro, O. Dorticós, Guevara, Rodríguez Hablan*, p. 15. Rodríguez calls this an "instructive mistake."

126. Santos Ríos, "Informe a la Primera Reunión," p. 35.

127. Vergelino Soldívar, "Intervención," *Obra Revolucionaria*, No. 30 (August, 1961), p. 96.

128. This was the mistake most frequently mentioned to me during the visits to the farms. This shortcoming of import policy was particularly costly because by 1961 American-made equipment was deteriorating owing to the difficulties of importing spare parts.

129. See, for instance, Administración General de Cooperativas Cañeras, "Informe," *Obra Revolucionaria*, No. 30 (August, 1961), p. 53.

130. Rodríguez, "Entrevista," in *F. Castro, O. Dorticós*, p. 75.

131. The establishment of a supplies department in ANAP—originally unintended but hastily organized under pressure to continue supplying private farms with fertilizers, insecticides, cement, wire, and other inputs—is a convincing example of the serious disruption of the distribution system in 1961. See Pepe Ramírez' candid remarks on this unplanned addition to ANAP in his *Informe*, pp. 32-36.

132. ". . . in the distribution of fertilizers, we have very many deficiencies. . . . we do not have the adequate transport for this violent shipment of fertilizer" . . . "fertilizer is sent many times without complete formulas and the *compañeros* have complained that, when passing by [people's] farms and [cane] cooperatives, the people have had to have the fertilizer analyzed in order to know of what formula it was." See Eduardo Santo Ríos, "Informe," *Obra Revolucionaria*, No. 30 (August, 1961), 25.

133. Santos Ríos, "Tecnificar," p. 57. What I was told in the visits to the provinces supports the view of a serious bottleneck in the distribution system in 1961. One of the provincial offices had ordered fertilizers in January; it received them in August. Some of the state farms I visited had received too much fertilizer, and faced therefore the problem of storing it; others had not obtained enough. INRA officials did say, however, that the problem of distribution had diminished considerably in 1962.

134. It will be recalled that in May of 1961, the average size of the people's farms was about 9,000 hectares (see Table 8). There is some evidence that in the following year the *granjas* were enlarged still further. In effect, according to an article published in *Trabajo*, there would have been in August, 1962, 277 state farms with a total area of 2751 thousand hectares. This last figure should be treated cautiously, however. See *Trabajo*, No. 14 (August, 1962), 12.

135. The magnitude of the task faced by a manager will perhaps be understood better from the characteristics of some of the big farms in Camagüey. The Jose Martí farm stretches over more than forty thousand hectares, has sixteen

modern rural towns, eleven people's stores, 10.5 thousand head of cattle, 104 irrigation turbines, and six dairies. Six thousand people live on it, and the labor force of permanent and seasonal workers reaches 2.8 thousand. (*Diario de la Tarde* [August 15, 1962], p. 6). The Roberto Reyes farm (which I visited) is about the same size, has 22 thousand head of cattle, 75 thousand chickens, and more than 1.2 thousand workers. The area of the farm is divided into 18 separate units.

136. See Rodríguez, "Entrevista" in *F. Castro, O. Dorticós*, pp. 68, 72. I was told the same thing during the visits to the farms.

137. "In selecting the soil we have frequently chosen the worst topography, the most eroded land, or that of the worst physical conditions." Santos Ríos, "Tecnificar," p. 55.

138. I was told in Camagüey that some peasants refused to use fertilizer until they saw its effects on yields. This provides, of course, the possibility of turning a disadvantage into an advantage within a short period.

139. This occurred especially in the cultivation of rice and cotton.

140. Rodríguez, "Entrevista," in *F. Castro, O. Dorticós*, p. 73.

141. Pepe Ramírez' report to the second meeting of ANAP in May, 1962, recognized that "farmers of more than 5 *caballerías* have been facing serious difficulties in obtaining credit through the agencies of the Banco Nacional in recent times." *Informe*, p. 28.

142. In his speech on rationing in March, 1962, Dr. Castro stated, "The principal effort of the Revolution, of the people, of the Integrated Revolutionary Organizations, is at this moment agriculture" (*Obra Revolucionaria*, No. 7, p. 17). The opening paragraph of Santos Ríos' critical article in the May issue of *Cuba Socialista* repeated this (p. 50).

143. As noted already, imports represented a large proportion of the total consumption of eggs, and the poultry industry was also heavily dependent on imports of baby chicks and of eggs for hatching.

144. Before 1959, virtually all the consumption of lard was met by imports. See Coleou, "L'élevage et les Productions," p. 68, and Department of Commerce, *Investment in Cuba*, p. 29.

145. See Declaración Final de la Reunión Nacional de la Producción, *Obra Revolucionaria*, No. 30, p. 246.

146. See, for example, the statement by the Minister of the Economy, Regino Boti, in *Obra Revolucionaria*, No. 30, especially pp. 17-19.

147. See *ibid.*, No. 7 (1962), p. 13.

148. *Ibid.*, p. 15.

149. *Ibid.*, pp. 13-14.

150. *Ibid.*, p. 13.

151. Severo Aguirre, "Ante el Tercer Aniversario de la Reforma Agraria," pp. 39-49, and Eduardo Santos Ríos, "Tecnificar Nuestra Agricultura Es Hacerla Más Productiva," *Cuba Socialista*, No. 9 (May, 1962), 50-66.

152. Santos Ríos, "Tecnificar," p. 64.

153. Aguirre, "Ante el Tercer Aniversario de la Reforma Agraria," *Cuba Socialista*, No. 9 (May, 1962), 49.

154. Summarized in the November-December, 1959, issue of the *Revista del Banco Nacional*, p. 1209.

155. See "*Un Año de Liberación Agraria*," p. 41.

156. See Regino Boti, "Informe a Reunión Nacional de la Producción," in *Obra Revolucionaria*, No. 30, p. 18.

157. Per capita consumption outside Havana would have had to be about 110 eggs, to fulfill the 1962 national average contemplated in the plan.

158. Santos Ríos, "Informe," *Obra Revolucionaria*, No. 30, p. 29.

159. Santos Ríos, "Tecnificar," p. 63.

160. Santos Ríos, "Informe," *Obra Revolucionaria*, No. 30, p. 32.

161. Aguirre, "Ante el Tercer Aniversario de la Reforma Agraria," p. 44.

162. Santos Ríos, "Informe," in *Obra Revolucionaria*, No. 30, p. 35 (italics added).

163. Santos Ríos, "Tecnificar," p. 66.

164. *Ibid.* The same fault is emphasized by Ramírez' report to ANAP in May, 1962. (See his *Informe*, p. 41.)

165. See Alfredo Núñez Pascual, "Ordenamiento de la Producción Agrícola," *Revolución* (August 28, 1962).

166. Although already in May, 1960, Professor Dumond had strongly recommended the adoption of a set of statistical forms prepared by Chonchol, which would have kept account of the costs and output of each production unit, hence providing valuable quantitative information for planning.

167. Partly because the forms which should have been used since January 1, 1962, arrived at the provincial offices a few months later, and also because of initial resistance or inability of the peasants in some state farms to fill them in, when they arrived.

168. See *Hoy*, August 23, 1962, p. 7.

169. Rodríguez acknowledged in 1962 that the importance of sugar as a source of foreign exchange had been underestimated. See *F. Castro, O. Dorticós*, p. 67.

170. See Rodríguez' speech to the Congress of Cane Cooperatives in *Hoy*, August 18, 1962, p. 6.

171. See Carlos R. Rodríguez' speech to the sugar workers on July 18, 1962, in *Panorama Económico Latinoamericano*, Vol. V, No. 56, p. 13. According to Rodríguez when he became president of INRA in February, 1962, at the height of the sugar harvest, nobody in the Institute was held responsible for the cutting of the cane on the land of the cooperatives, which meant that the units dependent on the Ministry of Industries had also to organize the agricultural phase of sugar production (*ibid.*, pp. 13-14).

172. The vote registered 1,381 delegates in favor of the transformation and 3 against it.

173. See Premier Castro's speech in the final meeting of the Congress of Cane Cooperatives, and Alfredo Menéndez Cruz, "La Transformación de las Cooperativas Cañeras en Granjas Cañeras" in *Cuba Socialista*, No. 14 (October, 1962), p. 39.

174. On the other hand, the higher wages paid in public works may continue to attract workers to the urban areas. However, as explained in the first chapter of this book, measures aimed at preventing undesired shifts of manpower between sectors, were being taken in the second half of 1962.

175. Other measures to raise average cane yields, and the allocation of cane plantations in the neighborhood of the sugar mills, remained an essential part of INRA's policy but, as Alfredo Menéndez Cruz correctly assessed, these are intermediate and long-run tasks. See his "Problemas de la Industria Azucarera," *Cuba Socialista*, No. 12 (August, 1962), p. 12.

176. The initial target, set at the beginning of June, was 209.1 thousand hectares but by the end of August it had been raised to 222.5 thousand hectares. See *Hoy*, June 29, 1962, and Comisión Nacional Azucarera, "Informes rendidos por las Comisiones provinciales azucareras sobre trabajos efectuados hasta Agosto 31, 1962."

177. Dumond, "Des Problèmes Généraux," p. 27.

178. Rodríguez, "Intervención," *Obra Revolucionaria*, No. 30, p. 206.

179. See "Carta de Carlos R. Rodríguez al Consejo Nacional de la CTC," *Revolución* (September 7, 1962), p. 5.

180. Aguirre, "Ante el Tercer Aniversario de la Reforma Agraria," p. 46.

181. Carlos R. Rodríguez in speech to Congress of Cane Cooperatives, *Hoy*, August 18, 1962, p. 6.

182. Carlos R. Rodríguez in speech to the sugar workers on July 18, 1962, reprinted in *Panorama Económico Latinoamericano,* Vol. V, No. 56, p. 20.

183. Rodríguez, "Entrevista," in *F. Castro, O. Dorticós,* p. 72.

184. A level of output high enough to meet the ration requirements was expected "much earlier than 1965-66."

185. See Chapter X on industry, Table 3.

186. *Hoy,* July 21, 1962, p. 7. These represent increases of about 30 and 90 per cent, respectively, over the average production of the years 1960-61 and 1961-62.

187. Aguirre mentions an annual income of 800 million pesos (higher than the income generated by the sugar industry at the present) as the 1970 target set by Premier Castro for the cattle industry. See his "Ante el Tercer Aniversario de la Reforma Agraria," p. 49.

188. Labor shortages appeared for the first time during the sugar harvest of 1961, and became more acute one year later when large numbers of urban voluntary workers were needed to harvest the cane, in spite of the small volume of the 1962 crop; they reappeared toward the end of 1962, when it was necessary to rely heavily on students and volunteer workers to pick the coffee harvest in Oriente.

189. See Chapter I, Table 17.

190. See Chapter I, Table 12.

191. Of course, by this time some of the Soviet machinery imported during the early 1960's will also need to be replaced.

192. In the sugar industry, however, the mechanization of the havest has become indispensable owing to nearly full employment in agriculture. The quality of the performance of the 1,000 harvesting machines which are being introduced is crucial. Plans called for 15 per cent of the cane to be harvested by the new machines, and considerable savings in labor were expected. If these are realized, the seasonal pressure on the farm labor supply would be considerably diminished, and the numerous problems of mobilizing a large number of workers during the harvest would be reduced.

193. The scarcity results in part from the relative neglect of agricultural training before the Revolution (see pp. 93-95), and in part from the emigration of a higher number of professionals and administrators in the years following the victory of the new regime.

194. In 1962 there were 683 students registered in the schools of agronomy of the Universities of Havana and Santa Clara, and 185 studying veterinary at the same universities. This meant that in 1962 there were more than twice as many students of agronomy as agronomic engineers in the whole country in 1952; the number of 1962 veterinary students was just under one-half that of all veterinarians in 1952. Although in the case of agronomy students, the comparison may be affected by differences in definition, it is clear that the government is making serious efforts to increase the supply of high level agricultural experts. This is also apparent from the fact that well over half of the agronomy and veterinary students at the University of Havana were in the first year. (See Table 14, Chapter VII, and further details in Part II.)

195. Two thousand young peasants from the cane cooperatives and state farms were supposed to go to the Soviet Union in 1962 to study farm administration, and plans called for the training of about 3,500 others in the management schools of Rancho Boyeros and Santa María del Rosario.

196. INRA has organized crash programs in fields such as tractor mechanics, artificial insemination, poultry breeding, coffee and cacao cultivation, and apparently a large number of young peasants have been sent to the socialist countries to study agricultural techniques. For example, 948 peasants returned in July, 1962, from the Soviet Union after completing one year of training in agricultural techniques. Moreover, in 1963, INRA planned to start programs of *Mínimo*

Técnico with the eventual aim of increasing the skills of about half of all agricultural workers.

197. See Rodríguez, "Entrevista," *F. Castro, O. Dorticós,* pp. 67-68.

198. For example, the high proportion of first-year students in the schools of agronomy and veterinary implies that the stock of agronomists and veterinarians will rise substantially only after 1966; the reallocation of land between former cane cooperatives and people's farms is only expected to be realized after careful studies have been made; it is also questionable how much young peasants with little previous educational training can learn in one year of studies in the Soviet Union.

199. That is, those having between five and fifty *caballerías* (67.1 to 671 hectares). These farmers have been promised compensation when their land is expropriated. See Rodríguez, "Entrevista," in *F. Castro, O. Dorticós,* p. 70.

200. Thus, in his report to the annual meeting of ANAP in May, 1962, Pepe Ramírez, after acknowledging that the larger farmers had faced serious difficulties in obtaining credit in the recent past, indicated that "it was necessary to grant promptly production credits to the peasants having more than five *caballerías,* given that their production is needed to meet the consumption of the people." (See his *Informe,* p. 28.)   Rodríguez expressed similar ideas with respect to the large producers of cane in July, 1962. See *Panorama Económico Latinoamericano,* Vol. 50, No. 56, p. 14.

201. In August, 1962, many INRA officials appeared to be quite unaware of a change of policy with respect to the *rich farmers.*

202. A cyclical downturn in coffee production was also expected. See Rodríguez, "Entrevista," *F. Castro, O. Dorticós,* p. 75. In June, 1963, Rodríguez explicitly acknowledged that in 1963 total farm output had been lower than in the previous year. See *Comercio Exterior,* Mexico (June, 1963), 441.

Chapter IV

1. Although, as stated earlier, I have few doubts that the Ministry of Education obtains as accurate and representative data as possible for their own use in planning, I exclude from this generalization some of the broader target figures published in documents designed for readers overseas such as *Cuba y la Conferencia de Educación, Desarrollo Económico y Social,* the Cuban report of the UNESCO conference in Chile, March, 1962. A number of 1962 predictions have clearly not worked out, and sometimes impressions given by historical series depend on a definition which can make them misleading.

Yet in support of my general view on reliability, it may be appropriate to quote the offer of the Cuban government, made at the UNESCO conference in 1962, "to place at the disposal of organizations convening the Conference as well as to technical and educational groups, student federations and university centres of Latin America the sources of information necessary" to verify its educational claims.

A number of economists have kindly read and made comments on all or some of the educational chapters of this study. I would particularly thank Gary Becker, Edward Dommen, Michael Farrell, and Shane Hunt. David Braybrooke suggested some improvements for Appendix A, and Ian Wright suggested some improvements in style. The detailed criticism of Dudley Seers and Andrés Bianchi has been invaluable. But, inevitably, the last word must be the author's. While I am therefore indebted for all the assistance friends have given me, they cannot be held responsible for whatever errors remain.

2. Although Table 2 refers to persons in *employment* and includes non-Cubans, it also shows the result of the past shortage and imbalance of technical education in Cuba described later in this section.

3. Excepting the lack of balance among them—one nurse for every three doctors, for instance.

4. Not, of course, without some assumptions, but these are seen to be quite reasonable in Cuba back to the 1920's. They are: 1) That immigration and emigration have not been large enough to disturb the pattern. If net immigration had been significant or the more educated had been more likely to emigrate or the less literate to immigrate, the overall effect would be to bias the present viewpoint by making the historical picture look worse than in fact it was. 2) If the better educated tend to live longer, this will improve the apparent record of the past.

Effects 1 and 2, acting in opposite directions, may to a degree be self-canceling.

To the extent that replies to the 1953 census questionnaire were based strictly on years of schooling during adolescence, the above two assumptions are sufficient to allow the census data to be treated as an accurate indication of the past. It is possible, however, that some replies were biased upwards by including adult and informal education and biased downwards, in literacy tables for instance, by the respondent having lost a skill he once possessed. Since adult education in Cuba was never of great overall effect, the procedure used seems reasonable.

The ages for primary school are assumed to lie between six and fourteen, and the ages for advanced schooling to be above fourteen. This gives as column 2, Table 1, the school years to which the primary school figures of each age-line correspond.

Note that because each column of Table 1 only contains the number of students who stopped at that level of schooling, it underestimates the historical size of that level of school enrollments by the numbers who studied further and are counted in subsequent columns which refer to higher education.

5. An investigation which seems worth pursuing in its own right as a means of testing the relationship between education and life expectancy.

6. Ramiro Guerra Sánchez, Superintendent of Cuban Schools. *"Adelantos en el Año Escolar Próximo Pasado,"* Boletín No. 10, Republica de Cuba, Secretaría de Instrucción Pública y Bellas Artes (Havana, 1927), pp. 5-6.

7. UNESCO, "Proyecto Principal de Educación," *Boletín Trimestral* (No. 14, Especial, Abril-Junio, 1962). Table 4, p. 146.

8. Fifteen through nineteen years old for secondary students, twenty through twenty-four for university students.

9. Fulgencio Batista, *Piedras y Leyes* (Mexico, 1961), p. 95. "Sergeant-teachers" were rural schoolmasters with the rank of an army-sergeant, part of Batista's program of using the military to extend education in rural areas.

10. National income figures are taken from the Banco Nacional, but increased by 30 per cent according to the estimates of Harry T. Oshima, "The New Estimate of National Income and Product of Cuba in 1953," *Food Research Institute Studies,* II (November, 1961).

11. International Bank for Reconstruction and Development *Report on Cuba* (Johns Hopkins Press, 1951), pp. 405 and 434.

12. *Ibid.,* p. 425. Readers should bear in mind that politicians are given to exaggeration about opponents. There seems little doubt, however, that reaction against the state of affairs the World Bank Report described has been a stimulus to present educational reform.

13. *Ibid.,* p. 404.

14. An "officialized" university was one that could grant degrees accepted as valid in Cuba but which did not receive financial support from the Cuban government.

15. Batista, *Piedras y Leyes,* pp. 99, 103.

16. According to figures given in *La Situación Educativa en América Latina,* UNESCO, p. 255.

17. Argentina 27 per cent, Uruguay 24 per cent, Panama 23 per cent, Chile 19

per cent, Costa Rica, 16 per cent, Cuba 12 per cent. The Latin American average was 10 per cent.

18. Argentina, Costa Rica, Ecuador, Haiti, Mexico, Panama, Paraguay, Venezuela managed with 5 per cent or less. Only the Dominican Republic, with 32 per cent, spent more.

19. U.S. Department of Commerce, 1956, *Investment in Cuba,* basic information for U.S. businessmen, p. 182.

20. Enrollments in 1958-59 had slipped back again. If the peak enrollment of 669,286 in 1956-57 is used, the rate of growth is 1.9 per cent for the 7 years from 1950.

21. UNESCO, *International Directory of Adult Education,* p. 117.

Chapter V

1. There are a number of statements of government leaders to suggest that it was quite literally the educational tables of the 1953 census which summarized to them the educational challenge they faced.

2. Fidel Castro, *La Historia Me Absolverá* (3rd ed.; Havana), pp. 41-42.

3. Ministry of Education, *Message of the Minister of Education to the People of Cuba* (November 30, 1959), Ch. X.

4. U.N. General Assembly official records A/PV872, p. 126, para. 135.

5. "Ser culto para ser libre," chosen as the slogan of the Year of Education. For its political implications, see Appendix A, Part II.

6. This figure is no more than a personal estimate. The only number I was told was the total of 6,000 teachers who had left Cuba. But clearly most professional and technical persons have suffered a decline in material standards of living since the Revolution, and their conditions of work may have changed considerably. They may more easily afford the tickets to leave. Whether these reasons are sufficient to assume that 6 per cent of all those who left were from a group which numbered only 4 per cent of the *labor force* and less than 1.5 per cent of total population is left to the reader to judge. Emigrants usually include a higher than average proportion of the active labor force, although the circumstances of Cuba may make it an exception.

White collar workers and professional people comprised 69 per cent of the 30,000 or more refugees in Miami by December, 1960. Wyatt MacGaffey and C. Barnett, *Cuba: Its People, Its Society, Its Culture* (Human Relations Area Press, 1962), p. 273.

7. The category does not include managers, administrators, and directors (who numbered 94,000) nor skilled workmen.

8. It is not within my purpose to discuss when, from whom, or amongst whom the Marxist elements within Cuban education arose. It is sufficient to note, as here and in the Appendix, the importance and character of this influence within the philosophy and form of Cuban education today.

9. Budgetary figures for 1962, wherever used within this study, are taken from the *"Presupuesto por Actividades de 1962,"* Ministry of Education, Havana, which is in current use within the Ministry of Education. Revised figures (Resolution 924) were copied from a government circular which I was shown but do not possess.

10. In the $27.6 million shifted to JUCEPLAN, I have no information as to whether a cut was intended or made.

11. National income in 1952, 1955 and 1956, according to the Banco Nacional, was $2,030m., $1,865m. and $2,034m. For 1959 it was estimated to be $2,500m. I have accepted H. T. Oshima's conclusion that Cuban national income has been consistently underestimated and have increased each of the original figures by 30

per cent to $2.6 b., $2.4 b., and $3.3 b. The effect of this procedure is to lower the percentages of national income apparently devoted to education by nearly a quarter. It is these reduced percentages that are used here.

12. All figures from UNESCO, *Basic Facts and Figures* (1961), pp. 72-79, referring to various years between 1957-58 and 1960.

13. Report of the Ministry to the International Conference on Public Education, Geneva, Switzerland, July 2-13, 1962, p. 2.

14. In economic jargon, the "opportunity cost," defined as the value of the economic alternatives foregone by using existing resources as one does.

15. Of course the teachers are usually better qualified and older and their time is worth more. But this is seldom sufficient to offset the numerical bias. T. W. Schultz estimated that 59 per cent of the cost of graduate or professional school education in America is income foregone; at secondary level it is about the same. The same is true *a fortiori* for full-time adult education. T. W. Schultz, "Capital Formation by Education," *Journal of Political Economy*, LXVIII (December, 1960), 571-83. Data refer to 1956.

16. Opportunity cost calculations value only those who would have been employed. Unemployment and a host of other details need careful consideration if the calculation is to be more than an illustration.

Chapter VI

1. The Revolutionary Organizations included:

MNR	—Milicias Nacionales Revolucionarias
AJR	—Asociación de Jóvenes Rebeldes
PSP	—Partido Socialista Popular
CTC	—Confederación de Trabajadores de Cuba
FNCP	—Federación Nacional de Colegios Privados
CNP	—Colegio Nacional de Periodistas
FNTA	—Federación Nacional de Trabajadores Azucareros
FMC	—Federación de Mujeres Cubanas
MINFAR	—Ministerio de las Fuerzas Armadas Revolucionarias
DR-13M	—Directorio Revolucionario 13 de Marzo
FAC	—Federación de Asociación Campesina
M-26J	—Movimiento 26 de Julio
CNP	—Colegio Nacional de Pedagogos
FIEL	—Frente Independiente de Emisoras Libres
CESEC	—Confederación de Estudiantes de Segunda Enseñanza de Cuba
INRA	—Instituto Nacional de Reforma Agraria
FEU	—Federación Estudiantil Universitaria

Later many of these organizations were incorporated within ORI, the integrated party of the revolutionary organizations.

2. For details of this and all subsequent calculations of average cost, see Appendix B, Part II.

3. John K. Galbraith, *Economic Development and Perspective*, U.S. Information Service (1962), p. 15.

4. Selections from both books are included in Appendix A for Part II.

5. *Trabajo*, December, 1961, p. 67.

6. Lowry Nelson, in *Rural Cuba* (University of Minnesota Press, 1950), noted that Cuban farmers, if provided with reliable and informative reading matter, could easily be led to do much more reading than they do. "They are possessed of real intellectual curiosity . . . which might well be exploited . . . in a programme of adult education" (p. 216).

7. 174,000 being 21.2 per cent of 800,000, a rough estimate of the population twenty years old or more of sixth grade or above.

8. Published for the Second National Congress of Education in September, 1961, and on display in the Educational Exhibition at the Third National Congress of Education one year later.

9. Dorita Smith and Richard Cortright, both of the Laubach Literacy Fund, kindly made a thorough analysis of the basic primer, including a word count and a detailed analysis of a sample lesson. As they point out, the best test of a book is its effectiveness in use. But they rated *Venceremos* high for its spacing, layout, the variety of its exercises and repetitions, and for the teaching tips offered in its accompanying manual. The weak points lay in the absence of any visual aid to assist the students' memory, "which raises the question as to how early in the primer the student can actually begin to read; that is, how soon he can master the recognition of the written symbols." The book is also weakened by a lack of systematic progression from the known to the unknown, by if anything too much variety (two-thirds of the 630 different words are repeated less than 3 times), and by a lack of orderly approach to the teaching of writing. Of particular consequence is the end achieved by new readers upon completion of the primer. The two pages used as the final exam would require from a reader but a low level of literacy. Both pages contain 3 sentences of 5 to 8 words each. Standard simple syntax is used. Thus their conclusions regarding the book are very similar to my conclusions regarding the campaign. It is easily possible for any adult to have successfully completed the book within the time and circumstances of the campaign. The real test of success must be whether the illiterate continues with further practice and begins to read regularly and easily.

10. In August, 1961, Cuba had two national television networks in operation, covering the six provinces and over 80 per cent of the territory. There were, according to estimates of the Cuban government, 400,000 sets in use, permitting a maximum audience of two to three million Cubans. Republic of Cuba, Ministry of Foreign Affairs, *Cultural Bulletin*, I, No. 3 (August, 1961).

11. Lost to the national economy; leisure and home activities would, of course, be reduced.

12. At least in the early stages, classes were for those who already had some basic education.

13. The Cuban National Census, Table 36, gave the number of persons aged fifteen or more (in 1953) with less than a third-grade education as 1,407,700. Of these, 522,000 had completed first or second grade. As the literacy campaign embraced most of the remainder, the number not in the literacy campaign but enrolled in *Seguimiento* appeared to be about half of those eligible.

14. See page 239.

15. As the number of adult classes is clearly less than the number of available schoolrooms, one wonders if it is part of deliberate policy to use informal buildings because of their central and conspicuous location or, just possibly, as a way of avoiding any unfortunate association with childish study.

16. It is not always clear just in what sense the term "grade" is used for adult classes. For instance, the Ministry's basic handbook on *Superación Obrera-Campesina* says: "However, the sense of the term grade is not the same which has been used now, since there are great differences between adult and child instruction." But the same paragraph continues in a way which suggests it is in content and style rather than standard that the instruction may differ: "A worker, a peasant or any adult already has the culture which life provides; this is the very experience that his work, his home, his union, his revolutionary organization and such have given him." Ministry of Education, *La Superación Obrera-Campesina* (March, 1962), p. 8.

17. From the Report of the Ministry to the International Conference on Public Education in Geneva, 1962. The style of description must undoubtedly be read

in the perspective of classes for adults with a bare minimum of previous formal education and largely taught by untrained teachers.

18. For political importance of murals, see Appendix A of Part II.

Chapter VII

1. Here, as elsewhere, "primary schools" include both pre-school classes and the first six grades of primary school. They do not include grades seven and eight which before 1959 were "superior" primary classes and included within primary school statistics.

2. Unfortunately, the assessments made by the evaluation section of the Ministry of Education have not yet been released. I understood that the assessments which had been made were tentative and incomplete. The informal estimate given here should accordingly be treated with great caution.

3. Even before nationalization, private schools, many of them under the administration of the Catholic Church, were subject to curriculum and other decisions by a board of technical advisors and to classroom visits by government monitors—usually militia women—just as were public schools. Government regulations did not prohibit religious training, which is a right guaranteed in the Fundamental Law. But in his May Day Speech, 1961, Castro said about religious instruction, "The churches can remain open; religion can be taught there." Wyatt MacGaffey and C. Barnett, *Cuba: Its People, Its Society, Its Culture* (Human Relations Area Press, 1962), contains further information.

4. Note that the figures for 1956-57 given in Table 3, Chapter IV, omit private schools and include 26,389 superior primary enrollments in grades 7 and 8.

5. This is an "unadjusted school enrollment ratio" which shows total primary school enrollments (of any age) as a percentage of estimated population aged seven through fourteen. Because primary enrollments can include many persons outside the seven through fourteen age group, the ratio can quite easily be in excess of 100 per cent, especially when catching up on a backlog of under-enrollments.

6. Percentages for other Latin American countries have been taken from UNESCO, *Boletín Trimestral* (No. 14, Especial Abril-Junio, 1962), p. 191. The figures are taken from questionnaires completed by the countries concerned. The same source gives the estimated primary enrollments for Cuba as 1,573,000, which far exceeds the figures I was given in Cuba. I have accordingly relied on the smaller figures for constructing Tables 3 and 4. My estimate of 101 per cent is based on Table 4 and the population estimate given in the UNESCO report.

7. Calculated from the figures in Table 3.

8. UNESCO, *Basic Facts and Figures* (1961), Table 4.

9. For the content of this program, see Appendix B, Part II.

10. In the late 1940's the state actually owned only 452 school buildings (280 urban, 172 rural), rented 1,370 (1,177 urban, 193 rural), and borrowed, rent-free, 4,426 (1,242 urban, 3,184 rural). International Bank for Reconstruction and Development, *Report on Cuba* (Johns Hopkins Press, 1951), p. 432.

11. I refer to the buildings themselves, not to teaching equipment

12. Armando Hart, "La Revolución y los Problemas de la Educación," *Cuba Socialista* (December, 1961), 46. Note that the estimates given by Hart for 1962 and future years differ from those obtained by dividing enrollments by the number of teachers shown in Table 3.

13. Why this differs from the 15,613 given in the plan of Table 11 I do not know. It may be that the other is purely a planning figure, in which case present under-enrollment reflects upon the probability that other targets will be realized. It may be that coverage is different. It may also indicate the reliability of the

statistics, particularly as neither the totals for staff or enrollments obtained directly from the Ministry agree with the totals of Tables 10 and 11 obtained from a different source. A later figure—obtained from an article by the Minister of Education—gave enrollments as 18,122 for both technological schools and institutes in 1962.

14. According to figures in *"Cuba y la Conferencia de Educación, Desarrollo Económico y Social"* (1962), p. 69, which are, at least for these two schools, somewhat overstated.

15. The 1961 target specified 2,000.

16. 5 Poles, 1 Argentinian, 2 Cubans.

17. The Spanish machinery, I was told, belonged to the workshops of the Belén School. The Chinese and Bulgarian equipment, much the most numerous, was recently imported.

18. It seemed to me that pressures on time might make it preferable to buy fewer machines and more textbooks.

19. Formerly, it was a private Catholic school.

20. The enrollment, according to *"Cuba y la Conferencia de Educación, Desarrollo Económico y Social,"* was 600 with 60 teachers in February, 1962. The drop-out among students had been 94, or 16.6 per cent over seven months. The drop-out rate in 1961 for all technological schools was 17 per cent.

21. Pp. 163-66.

22. Figures from UNESCO, *"Basic Facts and Figures"* (1961), Tables 23, 24, and 25.

23. The reforms are outlined in detail in *La Reforma de la Enseñanza Superior en Cuba*, Consejo Superior de Universidades (Havana, 1962).

24. The former Catholic University of St. Thomas of Villanueva in Havana, which in the early 1950's had about 500 students and 83 faculty, has now become the Makarenko Institute for adult teachers.

25. In Oriente: 3 Mexicans, 2 Argentinians, 1 Kenyan, and 5 Spaniards.

26. These salaries can be stretched for visitors from overseas, although there are restrictions on the proportion of salaries which can be converted into foreign exchange.

27. Carlos Rafael Rodríguez wrote, "Now the humanities can flourish in our universities" and "studies will be given their proper importance." A new department of philosophy, he added, was not yet created because of lack of time to prepare teachers and textbooks with a Marxist interpretation. "La Reforma Universitaria," *Cuba Socialista* (February, 1962), 35.

28. In, for instance, *La Reforma de la Enseñanza Superior en Cuba*, p. 13, and *"Cuba y la Conferencia de Educación, Desarrollo Económico y Social,"* p. 99.

Chapter VIII

1. D. C. McClelland, *The Achieving Society* (Van Nostrand, 1961), provides some interesting evidence on how incentives and the desire to succeed have been stimulated by education with clear tangible economic results.

2. For instance, in the preface to *La Reforma de la Enseñanza Superior en Cuba*, Consejo Superior de Universidades (Havana, 1962), and José Altshuler, "La Enseñanza Tecnológica Universitaria y Nuestro Desarrollo Económico," *Cuba Socialista* (April, 1962), 13-24.

3. John K. Galbraith, *Economic Development in Perspective*, U.S. Information Service (1962), p. 40.

4. The fact that many of the eligible adults who are not teaching or studying do take their extra time as they prefer is probably a point against this.

Chapter IX

1. I am therefore grateful to the Ministry and to its directors. Additionally, I wish to extend especial thanks to the Economic Commission for Latin America and its director, Dr. Raúl Prebisch, and to the Central Coordinating and Planning Office of Venezuela and its chairman, Dr. Manuel Pérez Guerrero, for permitting me to interrupt my regular duties and carry out this study of Cuba.

Thanks are also due to my friends, Jorge Ahumada, Darío Pavez, and Eduardo Valenzuela, whose wise counsel contributed greatly to this analysis.

2. The population of Cuba increased from 1.6 million to 2.9 million from 1900 to 1919, at a rate higher than 3 per cent annually.

3. In 1959 there was one automobile for every 27 persons in Venezuela; one for 51 in Argentina; one for 83 in Mexico; one for 130 in Brazil. Society of Motor Manufacturers and Traders, *National Institute Economic Review*, No. 17 (September, 1961).

4. In seven Latin American countries there were assembly plants and factories making parts and replacements. In Cuba there were only two factories of tubes and tires, and these imported raw materials. Even so, the production there was less than that for Uruguay and Chile, which had fewer automobiles.

5. Resolution No. 94 (November 21, 1959). Comandante Ernesto Guevara was the first head of the department.

6. Law No. 851 (July 6, 1960); and Resolution No. 1 (August 6, 1960).

7. These investments are calculated at book value and may be broken down into millions of U.S. dollars, as follows: sugar companies, 330; Electric Bond and Share, 300; Cuban Telephone Company, 80; and oil companies, 90, which comes to a total of 800. These figures are based upon "U.S. Investments in Latin American Economy," Department of Commerce of the United States, and on official estimates of the Cuban government.

8. Law No. 890 (October 13, 1960).

9. See details in Appendix, Part III, Table 2.

10. Law No. 891 (October 13, 1960). The Royal Bank of Canada and the Bank of Nova Scotia were not included in the nationalization.

11. Arrangements for payment were generally 10 per cent in cash, and the rest in 120 monthly payments.

12. Fidel Castro defined the socialist character of the Revolution in a speech delivered on April 16, 1961, several days after having repulsed the invasion of the Bay of Pigs.

13. Law No. 932 (February 23, 1961).

14. All with less than 10 factories each.

15. All with more than 80 establishments: sugar has more than 175; leather goods, 281; textiles, 179; and flour, 176.

16. Study Time Table of the School for Administrators

Subjects	Classes	Individual study	Circles	Others	Total
Organization and management	190	190	50	—	470
Technical and general	100	100	40	—	240
Political economy	220	220	110	—	550
Accounting	95	—	60	—	155
Mathematics	145	165	60	—	350
Statistics	105	45	20	—	170
Style and spelling	75	—	—	—	75
Visits to factories	—	—	—	100	100
Physical culture and voluntary work	—	—	—	210	210

Subjects	Classes	Individual study	Circles	Others	Total
Assemblies and talks	—	—	—	135	135
Elective	—	125	—	—	125
Specialization	—	—	—	275	275
Totals	930	845	380	720	2,855

Source: School of Administration.

17. *Boletín* No. 154 (January-February, 1962), University of Havana.

18. We must add a 4 per cent tax on wages and salaries. At first this tax was voluntary and refundable but now it is compulsory. It is estimated that it now amounts to 40 million pesos.

19. We were told by an official of the revolutionary government, who had an active part in the credit operation with Cuba, that it was hard to believe the conditions offered by China. When the date for amortization was brought up, the decision was left to Cuba, but was finally fixed for 1966, five years after the delivery of the machinery and when this machinery would be in full production. Furthermore, payment could be made in goods produced by this same machinery. If Cuba could not begin to service the debt on the date specified, there would be no trouble about postponement.

20. Definition of the Ministry of Labor, Comandante Augusto Martínez Sánchez, made at the Twenty-Sixth National Congress of Workers of Revolutionary Cuba, September 3, 1962.

21. "Lenin indicated as fundamental principles of the organization of socialist emulation: publicity, the possibility of comparing the results of emulation and the successes attained by isolated collectives, the practical application of the experience of the workers of the vanguard, and information about these experiences transmitted to all the participants in social production." Quoted by Martínez Sánchez on the occasion mentioned above.

22. Resolution No. 5798 of the Ministry of Labor, August 27, 1962.

23. The Eleventh National Congress of CTCR, article by Carlos Fernández, published in *Cuba Socialista,* No. 2 (1962).

24. A reduction in the number of unionized agricultural workers is due to the fact that some 123,000 of them became members of agricultural cooperatives, and consequently were no longer members of a union.

25. Resolution No. 16782 of the Ministry of Labor (August, 1960).

26. Resolution No. 5797 of the Ministry of Labor (August 27, 1962).

27. Law No. 1022, April 27, 1962, modified the functions of these commissions.

28. Up to September, 1962, this card had only been delivered to those who were unemployed, though delivery to others had begun.

29. In Havana alone there were 70,000 students holding scholarships in 1962.

30. According to Professor Bettelheim, agricultural and industrial wages rose 19 per cent between 1958 and 1961, while production rose only 5 per cent in agriculture and 8 per cent in industry. Wages in construction rose 39 per cent; and production, only 25 per cent.

31. At a price 30 per cent higher than the price in the United States. We were told by one of the administrators that the Canadian firm was a subsidiary of one in the United States.

32. *Report on Industrial Improvement in Cuba,* made by Comandante Guevara, Minister of Industry, at a session of the Universidad Popular, *Obra Revolucionaria,* No. 17, on March 15, 1961. Guevara made the same point in later speeches.

33. According to the Mexican economist Juan Noyola, Adviser of JUCEPLAN, in a lecture delivered at the National University of Mexico early in 1961. This was printed in *El Trimestre Económico,* No. 111 of that year.

34. The new program planned for 1962 will give employment to 13,000 workmen, with a total investment of 150 million pesos.

Chapter X

1. The mission was headed by Juan Noyola. The other members were Jacques Chonchol (Chile), O. Fernández Balmaceda (Argentina), Sigmund Slavinsky (Poland), Thomas Vietorisz (United States), and Ricardo Rodas (Honduras). Jorge Ahumada, Supervisor of the Mission, had a significant role in it. Carlos Matus (Chile) worked with it part of the time.

2. Hypothetical Sketch of the Five Year Plan, December, 1960.

3. The Five Year Agricultural Plan was prepared by Jacques Chonchol of the FAO.

4. These programs were based upon studies made by groups of experts from the United Nations.

5. Sketch of the 1962-65 Plan for Cuban Economy (September, 1961).

6. Regino Boti, Minister of Economy, in the First National Meeting on Production, Havana, August, 1961, *Obra Revolucionaria* (Havana: Imprenta Nacional, 1961).

7. Ernesto Guevara, *Report on Industrial Improvement* (March 15, 1961).

Part I, Appendix

1. For a discussion of the limitations of data before 1959 see Harry T. Oshima, "The New Estimate of the National Income and Product of Cuba in 1953," *Food Research Institute Studies*, II (November, 1961), 220.

2. On the other hand, on the basis of the estimates of the changes in the production of crops made in this Appendix, and of data on the consumption of livestock products, it is possible to determine the *direction* in which total farm output moved.

3. The two last comparisons are, however, less precise than the first.

4. The figure has been taken from the published version of the interview given by the President of INRA, Carlos R. Rodríguez, to the Chilean *Instituto Popular* on June 30, 1962. In it Rodríguez stated that "production of rice will increase [in this period] from 230,000 to 690,000 tons." Although the end year of the period is stated—1965—the base year is not explicitly defined. From the context, however, it is clear that the base year Rodríguez had in mind is either calendar 1961 or (more likely) the agricultural year 1961-62. See Carlos R. Rodríguez, "Entrevista" in *F. Castro, O. Dorticós*, p. 72.

5. This procedure seems moreover justified because it is likely that the "spring harvest" of 1960-61 was high, whereas that of 1961-62 was low. The former must in effect have been favored by the abundant rainfall in 1960. The high estimate for rice production in 1961 included in Chonchol's article also provides indirect evidence in this direction. Chonchol wrote his report in July of 1961, when the results of the "spring harvest" of 1960-61 were already known. The fact that actual production in 1961 was sharply below this estimate points to failures in the harvest in the middle and the second half of the year. This interpretation is, moreover, consistent with the figure quoted by Rodríguez (which probably refers to the agricultural year 1961-62) and with the low levels allowed by the rationing in March, 1962.

6. For example, the very low output of coffee indicated for 1959 corresponds really to the harvest period which extends from September, 1958, to May, 1959, and is therefore partly explained by the impact of the war in Oriente, where most of the coffee is grown.

7. In the absence of relevant data, output of sugar is taken as an indicator of the production of sugar-cane throughout these comparisons.

8. The comparison with 1957-58 is somewhat misleading to the extent that it could be understood to imply that the increase occurred over a three-to-four year period. In fact, the percentage rises would be nearly the same if only 1958 were taken as the base period and also if changes were related to the output levels of 1959. In most cases the increase of crop production took place in the agricultural years of 1959-60 and 1960-61.

9. The ratio was over 40 per cent in 1953. See Oshima, "The National Income and Product of Cuba in 1953," Table 3.

10. Given the probably large fall in the output of root crops.

11. This obviously over-optimistic assumption is made with the sole purpose of isolating the effects of changes in the production of crops on total agricultural output.

Part II, Appendix A

1. Armando Hart, "*Message of the Minister of Education to the Cuban People,*" Ministry of Education, Havana (November 30, 1959), pp. 9, 30.

2. The length of service of school teachers in Cuba today has bearing on their loyalty and dedication to the new teaching. As the figures from the 1962 budget show, two-thirds of the primary teachers received their basic training and were teaching before the Revolution.

Length of Service	*Number of Primary Teachers*
Ten years or more	10,849
Five years or more	4,475
Other pre-Revolutionary	5,511
Total pre-Revolutionary	20,835
Post-Revolutionary	10,453
TOTAL	31,288

In addition to these national teachers are 1,298 INRA volunteers trained after the Revolution and 5,919 teachers of recently nationalized schools, almost all of whom would have been trained before 1959.

3. Extract from "*Cuba y la Conferencia de Educación, Desarrollo Económico y Social,*" sect. d, pp. 24-27.

4. Repetitions within the syllabus of references to other documents are not repeated in this translation.

5. Serge Lafauve, "Castro peut-il tenir," *L'Express* (September 20, 1962), 20. I saw similar examples in some of the schools I visited.

6. *Trabajo y Lucha,* I, 113-14.

7. Carlos R. Rodríguez, "La Reforma Universitaria," *Cuba Socialista* (February, 1962), 34.

8. The English translation of the title would be: "Let us make people literate."

9. In the 1953 census, 73 per cent of the population were recorded as white, 12 per cent as Negro, 15 per cent as "*mestiza*" (mulatto), and 0.3 per cent as "*amarilla*" (literally, of yellow race).

10. Present daily circulation of *Hoy,* the official Communist organ, is 250,000. Circulation in 1950 was 25,000. I do not have figures for the other papers.

11. Fidel Castro, "*The Press has the Great Task of Orienting the People*" (March, 1961). Text of a speech in honor of the editor of *Revolución*.

Part II, Appendix B

1. The scholarship cost per student is remarkably high. This may be a budgetary over-estimate, particularly as it apparently refers mainly to current expenditure.

2. Or, of course, a miscalculation of the revised budgetary estimate.

Index